WJEC GCSE HISTORY

Changes in
Health and Medicine
c.1340 to the present day

Changes in
Crime and Punishment
c.1500 to the present day

R. Paul Evans
Alf Wilkinson

DYNAMIC LEARNING

HODDER EDUCATION
AN HACHETTE UK COMPANY

Every effort has been made to trace all copyright holders, but if any have been inadvertently overlooked, the Publishers will be pleased to make the necessary arrangements at the first opportunity.

Although every effort has been made to ensure that website addresses are correct at time of going to press, Hodder Education cannot be held responsible for the content of any website mentioned in this book. It is sometimes possible to find a relocated web page by typing in the address of the home page for a website in the URL window of your browser.

Hachette UK's policy is to use papers that are natural, renewable and recyclable products and made from wood grown in sustainable forests. The logging and manufacturing processes are expected to conform to the environmental regulations of the country of origin.

Orders: please contact Bookpoint Ltd, 130 Milton Park, Abingdon, Oxon OX14 4SE. Telephone: +44 (0)1235 827720. Fax: +44 (0)1235 400454. Email education@bookpoint.co.uk Lines are open from 9 a.m. to 5 p.m., Monday to Saturday, with a 24-hour message answering service. You can also order through our website: www. hoddereducation.co.uk

ISBN: 978 1 5104 03192

© R. Paul Evans, Alf Wilkinson 2018

First published in 2018 by
Hodder Education,
An Hachette UK Company
Carmelite House
50 Victoria Embankment
London EC4Y 0DZ

www.hoddereducation.co.uk

Impression number 10 9 8 7 6 5 4 3 2 1

Year   2021 2020 2019 2018

Cover photo © Trinity Mirror/Mirrorprix/Alamy Stock Photo; © Topfoto.co.uk

Illustrations by Aptara, Inc.

Typeset by Aptara, Inc.

Printed in Italy

A catalogue record for this title is available from the British Library.

CONTENTS

Introduction

Changes in health and medicine, c.1340 to the present day

Changes in crime and punishment, c.1500 to the present day

Introduction

About the course

During this course you must study four units, each contributing a different weighting to the GCSE qualification:

- **Unit 1** Studies in depth (Wales and the wider perspective) – weighting of 25 per cent of the GCSE qualification.
- **Unit 2** Studies in depth (History with a European/World focus) – weighting of 25 per cent of the GCSE qualification.
- **Unit 3** Thematic study, which includes the study of a historical site – weighting of 30 per cent of the GCSE qualification.
- **Unit 4** Working as a historian – non-examination assessment – weighting of 20 per cent of the GCSE qualification.

These studies will be assessed through three examination papers and a non-examination unit.

Units 1 and 2 each consist of a one-hour examination made up of a series of compulsory questions. These will focus upon the analysis and evaluation of historical sources and interpretations, as well as testing second order historical concepts.

Unit 3 consists of a one-hour-and-15-minute examination made up a series of compulsory questions. These will focus upon second order historical concepts, such as continuity, change, cause, consequence, significance, and similarity and difference.

Unit 4 will consist of a non-examination assessment. It will involve the completion of two tasks, one focusing on source evaluation and one on the formation of different historical interpretations of history.

About the book

This book covers two options for the Unit 3 Thematic study – *Changes in health and medicine in Britain, c.1340 to the present day*, and *Changes in crime and punishment, c.1500 to the present day*. You will only need to study **one** of these options.

How this book will help you with WJEC History

It will help you to learn the content

Is your main worry when you prepare for an exam that you won't know enough to answer the questions? Many people feel that way – particularly when a course covers over 500 years of history! And it is true; you will need good knowledge of the main events and the detail to do well in this thematic study. This book will help you acquire both the overview and the detail.

The text explains the key content clearly. It helps you understand each period and each topic, and the themes that connect the topics. Diagrams also help you to visualise and remember topics. Drawing your own diagrams is an even better way to learn!

This book is full of sources. The course deals with some big issues and sources help pin those issues down. History is at its best when you can see what real people said, did, wrote, sang, watched, laughed about or cried over. Sources can help you understand the story better and remember it because they help you to see the big concepts and ideas in terms of what they meant to people at the time.

Think questions direct you to the things you should be noticing or thinking about in the sources and text. They also help you practise the kind of analytical skills that you need to improve in history.

The **topic summary** at the end of every chapter condenses all the content into a few points, which should help you to get your bearings in even the most complicated content. You could read that summary before you even start the topic to know where you are heading.

It will help you to apply what you learn

The second big aim of this book is to help you apply what you learn, which means to help you think deeply about the content, develop your own judgements about the themes, and make sure you can support those judgements with evidence and relevant knowledge. This is not an easy task. You will not suddenly develop this skill. You need to practise studying an issue, deciding what you think and then selecting from all that you know the points that are really relevant to your argument. One of the most important skills in history is the ability to select, organise and deploy (use) knowledge to answer a particular question.

The main way we help you with this is through the **focus tasks**. These are the big tasks that appear at the beginning of each chapter so that you can build your big picture of the story over time. We then ask you to revisit the focus task at the end of the chapter to help you think through the big issues.

It will help you prepare for your examination

If you read all the text and tackle all the **focus tasks** in this book you should be well prepared for the challenges of the exam, but to help you more specifically:

Practice questions at the end of each chapter provide exam-style questions.

Examination guidance at the end of the unit (pages 118–128 for *Changes in health and medicine in Britain, c.1340 to the present day* and pages 251–261 for *Changes in crime and punishment, c.1500 to the present day*) contain a model exam paper as well as step-by-step guidance, model answers and advice on how to answer particular question types in the thematic paper.

Changes in health and medicine in Britain, c.1340 to the present day

The Big Story: changes in health and medicine in Britain, c.1340 to the present day

This thematic unit covers a vast period of time – over 650 years – and includes a lot of detail. Each chapter covers the continuing story of the development of health and medicine in Britain. You will need to keep on connecting these little stories to the big story. That is what this section helps you with. It gives you an overview of the themes you will be studying and some activities to help you see the patterns over time. Good luck!

Feeling poorly

What happens today when you feel unwell? Where do you go to get help? Perhaps you self-diagnose. You go either to the supermarket or the pharmacy and buy medicine, or perhaps ask the pharmacist's advice. How do you know the medicine you buy is safe to use? How do you know it will work? You've probably seen the adverts on the television or in the newspaper, but how do you really know it is safe to take and to use? Who controls the development and marketing of medicines today? Who do you think did it in medieval times? Did they even have medicine in medieval times?

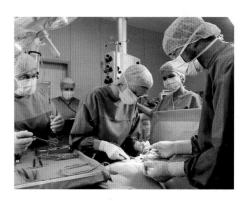

You might visit an 'alternative medicine' provider. Some people prefer 'natural healing', using herbs and traditional methods, such as Chinese acupuncture, **homeopathy** or **osteopathy**. More and more people are convinced the best way to diagnose illness and then cure it is through natural remedies.

If it is an emergency you might go straight to the accident and emergency (A&E) department of your local hospital, or call an ambulance to take you there. You might have a bit of a wait but there is emergency treatment available 24/7, with nursing staff and hospital consultants on call to deal with any kind of emergency.

Most likely you will make an appointment with your GP (general practitioner). It is usually possible to get an appointment within a day or so. Once there you might see the doctor, a nurse-practitioner or even the practice nurse. Whoever you see will try to decide what is wrong with you using a variety of techniques. They might take your temperature: when was the thermometer invented? How did they take your temperature before thermometers? They might listen to your breathing using a stethoscope. How did they do that before stethoscopes were invented? They might ask for a urine sample; this is widely used to test for some illnesses. Or take a blood test. Perhaps they might just look at you, or listen to what you have to say. If they can decide what is wrong with you they might issue a prescription for medicine and send you on your way.

But what if they cannot decide? What happens then? In all probability you will be referred to a specialist, and there will be yet more tests. Eye tests, MRI scans, physio tests; specialists have a huge array of tests to probe and try to discover the cause of your ill health. It might be a quick process, but sometimes it takes a long time to finally discover the *cause* of your illness.

Thinking about health and medicine

EVENT A: TREATMENTS – PENICILLIN, THE FIRST ANTIBIOTIC

'We had an enormous number of wounded with infections, terrible burn cases among the crews of armoured cars. The usual medicines had absolutely no effect. The last thing I tried was penicillin. The first man was a young man called Newton. He had been in bed for six months with fractures of both legs. His sheets were soaked with pus. Normally he would have died in a short time. I gave three injections of penicillin a day and studied the effects under a microscope. The thing seemed like a miracle. In ten days' time the leg was cured and in a month's time the young fellow was back on his feet. I had enough penicillin for ten cases. Nine were complete cures.'

EVENT B: TREATMENTS – HERBAL MEDICINE

'Medicine for dimness of the eyes: take the juice of the celandine plant, mix with bumblebees' honey, put in a brass container then warm until it is cooked and apply to the eyes.'

EVENT C: EXPLAINING DISEASE – THE FOUR HUMOURS

Hippocrates wrote: 'Man's body contains Four Humours – blood, phlegm, yellow bile and melancholy (black) bile. When all these humours are truly balanced, he feels the most perfect health. Illness occurs when there is too much or too little of one of these humours or one is entirely thrown out of the body.'

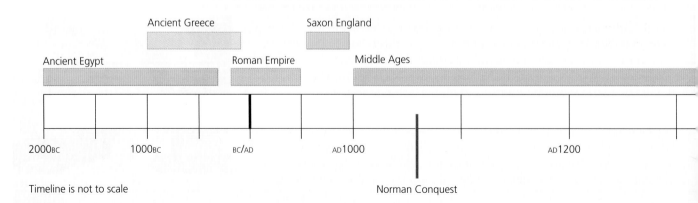

Ancient Greece

Saxon England

Ancient Egypt

Roman Empire

Middle Ages

2000BC   1000BC   BC/AD   AD1000   AD1200

Timeline is not to scale

Norman Conquest

EVENT D: EXPLAINING DISEASE – GOD SENDS DISEASE

'Terrible is God towards men. He sends plagues of disease and uses them to terrify and torment men and drive out their sins. That is why the realm of England is struck by plagues – because of the sins of the people.'

EVENT E: PUBLIC HEALTH – THE NHS BEGINS

'On the first day of free treatment on the NHS, Mother went and got tested for new glasses. Then she went further down the road to the **chiropodist** and had her feet done. Then she went back to the doctor's because she'd been having trouble with her ears and the doctor said he would fix her up with a hearing aid.'

EVENT F: EXPLAINING DISEASE – PASTEUR AND GERM THEORY

Louis Pasteur, a French scientist, published his 'germ theory' suggesting that bacteria or 'germs' were the true causes of diseases. His germ theory replaced all previous ideas about the causes of disease.

EVENT G: TREATMENTS – THE BLACK CAT REMEDY

'The stye on my right eyelid was still swollen and inflamed very much. It is commonly said that rubbing the eyelid with the tail of a black cat will do it much good so, having a black cat, a little before dinner I tried it and very soon after dinner the swelling on my eyelid was much reduced and almost free of pain.'

EVENT H: TREATMENTS – WASH, EXERCISE, DIET

'Every day wash face and eyes with the purest water and clean the teeth using fine peppermint powder. Begin the day with a walk. Long walks between meals clear out the body, prepare it for receiving food and give it more power for digesting.'

EVENT I: SURGERY – WITHOUT ANAESTHETICS

Robert Liston, a famous London surgeon, once amputated a man's leg in two and a half minutes but worked so fast he accidentally cut off his patient's testicles as well. During another high-speed operation Liston amputated the fingers of his assistant and slashed the coat of a spectator who, fearing he had been stabbed, dropped dead with fright. Both the assistant and the patient then died of infection caught during the operation or on the hospital ward. Liston worked really fast because there were no **anaesthetics**.

EVENT J: PUBLIC HEALTH – FRESH WATER, BATHS AND SEWERS

Sextus Julius Frontinus wrote: 'There was a great increase in the number of reservoirs, fountains and water-basins. As a result the air is purer. Water is now carried through the city to **latrines,** baths and houses.'

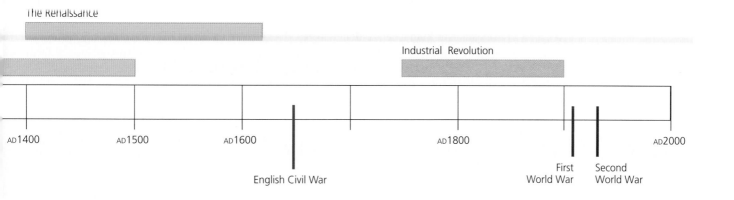

Treating the sick

Deciding what is wrong with you is only half the battle, however. How do you put it right? What *cure* should the doctor use to put right any illness? There are plenty of potential cures to choose from. Whole industries have grown up producing medicines, tablets and technology to treat patients, and to make money out of it. How is the doctor or specialist to decide which is the best treatment to use? What works for one person might not work for another. And how do they decide the right level of dose in each particular case? In other words, how do they get the 'cure' right?

Feeling poorly in the seventeenth century

In early 1685 Charles II felt poorly. He called in his doctors. According to some accounts there were 14 of them, who were often arguing over cause and potential cure. These were, of course, supposed to be the best doctors in the country! On 2 February Charles fainted, so the doctors had to decide what to do with him. First of all they bled him, taking over 400 ml of blood from his right arm. He did not respond, so they took another 200 ml of blood, and gave him an emetic, to make him vomit. This was a mixture of antimony, sacred bitters, rock salt, mallow leaves, violet, beetroot, camomile flowers, fennel seed, linseed, cinnamon, cardamom seed, saffron, cochineal and aloes. This would in theory clear any impurities out of his system. The next day they took more blood (300 ml this time), and gave him a mixture of barley water and syrup to gargle. He was also given more laxatives to clear out his bowels. His treatment seemed to consist of continuous bloodletting, laxatives and emetics. Not surprisingly he became weaker and weaker. He did not respond to the treatments and on the morning of 6 February Charles II died.

Recent research suggests that King Charles II died of kidney failure, probably linked to gout. Gout was a common disease among the upper classes at the time. The very worst treatment for kidney failure is to bleed a patient, so it appears that King Charles' doctors played a large part in killing him! So why did they bleed him? What were they trying to do? Were doctors in the seventeenth century so ignorant that they did not know the cause of the illnesses they were being asked to treat? Is the situation any different today? Today's doctors still find it hard to pinpoint the cause of some illnesses, and to effectively treat them.

ACTIVITY: MEDICINE MINI-DICTIONARY

As you work your way through this book you will come across various herbs, medicines, diseases or operations that you may not have heard of before. When you do, carry out your own research to find out all about them. Write your own definition of each one, with notes, and create your own mini-dictionary of medicine through time.

THINK

1 Do you think King Charles' doctors knew the *cause* of his illness? Do you think they had a clear idea of how to *cure* the illness?

2 How similar, and how different, are the ways in which Charles' doctors and doctors today approach someone who is poorly?

3 In your opinion, has the way sickness is treated improved, or got worse, between 1685 and today? Explain your answer.

Answers to the activity from pages 8–9:

A 1943 B 900s C 450BC D 1348 E 1948 F 1860 G 1788 H 390BC I 1830s J 100

But people are healthier now, right?

You would think that people are healthier in today's world. People eat better, more regular meals, have higher incomes, there is much more food available, everyone is well-housed and warm, people are educated into making healthy choices. Surely that means they are healthier today. But it seems not everyone agrees.

Human Teeth Healthier in the Stone Age Than Today

(*Health Magazine*, 19 February 2013)

Medieval diets were far more healthy. If they managed to survive plague and pestilence, medieval humans may have enjoyed healthier lifestyles than their descendants today.

(BBC News website, 18 December 2007)

The UK is among the worst in western Europe for levels of overweight and obese people. In the UK, 67% of men and 57% of women are either overweight or obese. More than a quarter of children are also overweight or obese – 26% of boys and 29% of girls.

(*Guardian*, 29 May 2014)

The stories above cast doubt on the idea of people being healthier today than ever before. The story from *Health Magazine* is based on archaeological examination of teeth. They found evidence of fewer cavities, less oral disease and less bone disorder than today. The BBC News website story is based on research into medieval records carried out by a Shropshire GP. The *Guardian* news story is taken from NHS England statistics. Can it really be the case that people today are less healthy than in medieval times? How can we investigate this idea further? How might you measure if people are healthier now than in previous periods of history?

One measure might be how long people live – if people live longer today then surely that means they are healthier?

The evidence is pretty clear from this data. Men, on average, now live twice as long as they did in Anglo-Saxon times. Surely that tells us that men, at least, are healthier today than 1000 years ago? But do our ideas change if we use another set of statistical data?

THINK ?

1 What are the strengths of figures such as those showing the average age of death?

2 What are the limitations of these kinds of figures? Remember, until recently infant mortality was so high (often 33 per cent of children failed to reach the age of seven) that *average* figures for life expectancy are lowered.

3 According to the data in the table, when were British men healthiest? How can you tell?

4 According to this data, when were British men unhealthiest? How can you tell?

5 How tall do you think, on average, British men will be in:
   a) 2100
   b) 2200
   c) 2500?

Period	Average male height
Anglo Saxons	5 feet 6 inches (168 cm)
Normans	5 feet 8 inches (173 cm)
Medieval	5 feet 8 inches (173 cm)
C17th	5 feet 5 inches (165 cm)
Victorians	5 feet 5 inches (165 cm)
C20th	5 feet 8 inches (168 cm)
Today	5 feet 10 inches (178 cm)

▲ Table: Average height of British males, compiled from various sources, but mostly skeletal data

Anglo-Saxon — Died aged 40

Medieval — Died aged 35

Seventeenth century — Died aged 36

Victorians — Died aged 46

1930s — Died aged 60

1950s — Died aged 65

Today — Died aged 80

▲ **Source A:** A healthy living pyramid from the Australian government showing the proportions of different food groups in a healthy diet

Making sense of all this data

People are living longer, and growing taller, at least according to the data shown here. Does that mean we are healthier? The figures on the previous page refer solely to men, and are averages. These figures therefore are only part of the picture. (There is much less skeletal data for women, for example, hence there is not enough reliable information to compile a 'height' list for women covering the period we are studying.) Leaving aside the limitations of the data, we are faced with a series of conflicting evidence; some suggesting people are now healthier, but equally some suggesting people may live longer but are not necessarily healthier. How can we reconcile this conundrum, and begin to reach a conclusion?

It is very easy to get data for today, or from the last two centuries. Since Victorian times the government has collected masses of data about every aspect of people's lives. But how do you find meaningful data from the seventeenth century, or the thirteenth century? Would it perhaps be more helpful if we looked at child mortality, or deaths in childbirth, both of which have been major killers throughout much of history? What other aspects of peoples' lives might we consider?

Nowadays people are bombarded with advice on how to live a more healthy life: drink less alcohol, give up smoking, take more exercise, eat less sugar and fats, and so on. Nearly every week it seems new advice appears to help people deal with their unhealthy lifestyle choices. New diets are continually proposed. One of the latest is the 'Stone Age diet', where you eat and exercise like Stone-Age hunter-gatherers.

THINK ?

1 Can you think of any other measures we might use to decide whether or not people are healthier today than in previous centuries?

2 Find out what you would eat if you were to follow the 'Stone Age Diet'.

3 Why, if people are healthier than ever before, do they need all this advice?

4 Why are modern people so obese?

5 What are the foods we eat that are bad for us? And who decides what is good and bad?

ACTIVITIES ?

1 On your own version of the table below, keep your own 'food diary' for a week. Make a note of what you eat and when.

	Monday	Tuesday	Wednesday	Thursday	Friday	Saturday	Sunday
Breakfast food							
Breakfast drinks							
Lunch food							
Lunch drinks							
Dinner food							
Dinner drinks							
Snacks							

2 Study the 'healthy living pyramid' from Source A. Use a different colour for each section of the pyramid, and then highlight your food diary to show how much food you are eating from each of the different groups.

3 Now use the pyramid to decide whether or not you are eating healthily.

4 If you are eating unhealthily, make a list of how you could change your diet to make it healthier.

Keeping clean

You have already discovered, from your timeline activity (see pags 8–9) that the Ancient Greeks clearly knew of the link between cleanliness and healthiness. So why was it so difficult to keep clean throughout most of history?

The answer is much the same as the reason most people drank ale or 'small beer' instead of water – not because they were addicted to alcohol but that water was both expensive and very dirty! It was quite common for waste to be discharged into a river before drinking water was taken out of the same river. There were few laws and health regulations. Local corporations (councils) and mayors were reluctant to take action to provide clean water because it would cost money, and, as most people were relatively poor, it would be the small number of richer people who would have to foot the bill. People had to collect their water from wherever they could. And that often meant the local river or stream. What is surprising is the lengths people went to in order to try to keep themselves and their houses clean. Some towns had public baths from the early 1500s and, of course, if you were rich you could have your own private water supply brought direct to your house.

Everyone today gets treated the same, don't they?

If you are ill then under the National Health Service (NHS) everyone has equal access to care, at least in theory. Whether you are rich or poor, live in the town or the countryside, are young or old you get treated by the NHS. However, consider this newspaper headline, from January 2015, highlighting the inequalities in cancer care. Apparently in deprived areas patients sometimes get poorer treatment than in richer areas.

> **National Audit Report highlights gap between rich and poor which could prevent 20,000 deaths per year**
>
> (*Daily Mirror*, 15 January 2015)

Was this the case in the past? Did everyone get the appropriate treatment whether they could pay for it or not? We have already seen that King Charles II was treated very differently to any patient today, and he presumably had plenty of money to pay for medical attention.

How successful might your treatment be?

Most doctors today would be very surprised if their 'cures' for various illnesses did not work. It might take a while to find the correct dose, or the right medicine, but usually, in most cases, patients recover. Some illnesses are more deadly than others. Some cancer recovery rates are still very low, for example. But other illnesses that were fatal in times gone by, like measles, have all but been eradicated.

Source B: Killer diseases of late twentieth-century Britain

- Cancer
- Heart disease
- Respiratory disease (for example, flu)
- Liver disease
- Dementia/Alzheimer's disease
- Accidents

THINK ?

1 Why was it so difficult for most people to keep clean throughout most of history?

2 Do you agree that people are healthier today than they were in other periods of history?

3 Study Source B.
   a) Which of these diseases do you think of as 'old people's' diseases?
   b) Which of these diseases do you think of as 'young people's' diseases?
   c) Which do you think of as 'lifestyle' or 'affluence' diseases?
   d) Which do you think were killer diseases in earlier times?

1 Causes of illness and disease

This chapter focuses on the key question: What have been the causes of illness and disease over time?

Not surprisingly, medieval people did not really understand the causes of most diseases. Famine and war were perhaps the main killers of this period. A bad harvest caused by drought or flood, too hot or too cold weather, meant malnourishment for many. And malnourished people catch disease more easily. Dysentery, typhoid, smallpox and measles were all widespread. Some historians estimate that perhaps 10 per cent of England's population in the early fourteenth century died of these diseases. Childbirth was a dangerous time for women, and it is likely that 30 per cent of children died before the age of seven. Poverty was, perhaps, the biggest killer though. This chapter explores how the causes of disease change throughout the period, but also to a surprising extent remain the same.

FOCUS TASK

As you work through this chapter make a 'Cause of illness and disease' card for each cause you come across. On it, make bullet points that show the impact this had. You will need these cards in subsequent chapters. The first one has been done for you.

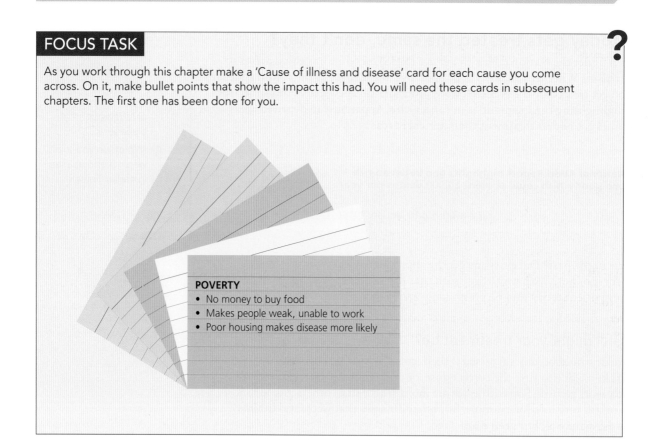

POVERTY
- No money to buy food
- Makes people weak, unable to work
- Poor housing makes disease more likely

Problems in the medieval era – poverty, famine and warfare

Poverty

Most people in medieval England depended on their fields for food. A bad harvest meant hunger or starvation; a good harvest meant plenty to eat and often some to sell to those living in the towns. By 1300 the population of England was around 4.75 million, probably the largest it had ever been. There had been 30 years of good harvests. Most people lived in the countryside and worked in agriculture. Perhaps 25 per cent of rural families had enough land to support themselves, but many did not. Many had no land at all. It is estimated that 40 per cent of rural families had to buy some or all of their food. Often farm work had to be supplemented by wage labour in order to make enough money to survive. As landowners were enclosing more and more land for sheep – much of the country's wealth came from the wool trade – paid work was often hard to come by.

Most people therefore lived on or near the poverty line, eating bread and pottage, a kind of stew made from beans, peas and oats, with herbs or a little meat or fish if available. Rabbit, chicken and fish were sometimes eaten, but the penalties for poaching were severe. A bad harvest meant difficult times for many people. Many animals would be slaughtered in the autumn because of a lack of winter fodder. Child mortality was high and malnutrition common for many, even in a good year.

Famine

Famine was a regular occurrence, although sometimes more fatal than others. Severe winters and rainy and cold summers could ruin planting and harvesting, leaving many people starving. The worst incidence of famine took place in England and Wales from 1315–17, when it is estimated that up ten per cent of the population died. There are (unconfirmed) reports of cannibalism, and many children were abandoned by parents unable to feed them. During a famine in Chester in the years 1437–49, it was recorded that peasants resorted to making bread from peas. When crops failed many people were weak from malnutrition and had no energy to work the land. During times of famine, people resorted to killing their horses and farm animals for food as well as eating seed grain, which were all needed for a harvest to make up the previous shortfall. Therefore, even when the weather improved the effects of the famine could rumble on for a number of years.

> THINK
> 1 What were the major effects of famine?
> 2 Why were the poor so susceptible to famine?

Medieval warfare

Archaeological excavations of medieval sites show bodies with unhealed wounds inflicted by sword or axe, often gangrenous. At the start of the medieval period armies were relatively small, and therefore deaths in battle few. Later in the period, armies were much bigger. At the Battle of Townton, in 1461, an estimated 22,000 to 28,000 soldiers were killed fighting. Wars were also dangerous if you were in a besieged town, city or castle. If you held out too long or refused calls to surrender, once the attacking army broke in, inhabitants were often killed or driven off with nothing. Finally, most medieval armies tried to provision themselves as they travelled across the country. Enormous quantities of fodder, grain and food were required. Medieval monarchs could seize whatever they wanted – usually promising to pay later, but many did not – and thus frequently villages, farms, towns were left short of food for themselves. The passage of an army through your neighbourhood could lead to having your house burnt down, your livestock stolen or your crops taken. Medieval soldiers were paid infrequently so were not averse to helping themselves to food!

Accidental death

Accidents were common and often fatal as, for example, the case of Maud Fras, who was killed by a large stone accidentally dropped on her head at Montgomery Castle in Wales in 1288. At Aston, Warwickshire in October 1387, Richard Dousyng fell when a branch of the tree he had climbed broke. He landed on the ground, breaking his back, and died shortly after. Or the case of Johanna Appulton who in August 1389 in Coventry was drawing water when she fell into the well. The incident was witnessed by a servant who ran to her aid and while helping her fell in also. This was overheard by a third person who also went to their aid – he too fell in – and all three subsequently drowned.

Storing crops over winter brought their own problems too. 'Saint Anthony's Disease', for example, was caused by a fungus growing on stored rye in damp conditions. Once the rye was ground into flour and baked into bread those who ate it developed painful rashes and in some cases, even died.

▲ Source A: Medieval illuminated letter showing someone being hanged

> ### THINK ?
>
> 1 Why do you think young people were so at risk of dying from ill-health in medieval times?
> 2 Which of the medieval killer diseases are still dangerous today?
> 3 Was the passage of a medieval army more dangerous for the soldiers, or for the villagers whose land they passed through?
> 4 Study Source A. Why might an illuminated prayer book show someone being hanged?

What did medieval people think made them ill?

During this period people had a wide range of beliefs about the causes of illness.

God

Religion played a huge part in most people's lives so it is not surprising that people thought God had a part to play in the spread of diseases. Christian Anglo-Saxons often blamed illness and disease on God, saying he was reminding people of the need to live a decent life. If someone was living a sinful life, then a difficult illness was God's way of punishing them for their sins. And if society as a whole was being sinful, or moving away from the true path of faith and the directions of the pope, then an epidemic or plague was a just reward, sent by God, to remind people of their duties to the church.

Bad smells

Some people began to notice the link between disease and bad air, or bad smells. Mortality was higher in the towns and cities than in the countryside. People lived closer together, alongside their animals and their filth. Travellers often said you could smell a town long before you could see it. So it is hardly surprising that many people thought disease was spread by bad smells infecting neighbours and friends.

Everyday life

Most people believed illness and early death was inevitable. So many children died before the age of seven that in many ways it seemed quite natural. Also childbirth was a very dangerous time for women, and it was expected that if his wife died a man would need to remarry to provide his children with a new mother. Warfare and famine were frequent. Everyday life was an uncertain business.

The supernatural

Mystery and magic and the supernatural world were used by some to explain unexpected happenings. Viking sagas suggest many believed disease was caused by magic, or even elves and spirits. Witchcraft was feared and many believed the world was full of demons trying to cause mischief and death. Any sudden diseases or misfortunes could easily be blamed on the supernatural, especially as the church painted a picture of a life where 'good' fought 'evil'.

The four humours

By far the widest-held belief was that people were ill because their **four humours** were out of balance. Every doctor agreed with Hippocrates and Galen that illness was caused by losing their equilibrium. Every doctor had a chart showing which illnesses were caused by which humour that they would use alongside a zodiac chart showing when was the best time to treat illnesses, plan an operation or even pick the herbs needed for medicine. (See Chapter 4 for more on the four humours and zodiac chart.)

ACTIVITIES

1 Which do you think are the best explanations of the causes of illness outlined on this page? Rank them in order along a line like this one:

Best explanation   Worst explanation

2 Repeat the activity, this time showing which explanations you think medieval people would find most convincing. Can you explain any differences?

Lack of hygiene in the medieval and early modern eras

ACTIVITY

Look carefully at this picture of London in 1347. Some of the things making life unhealthy are highlighted with a text box. Others are not. Make a list of all that you can find.

This pestilence is caused by stinking air so I will use an even more terrible smell to ward off the bad air carrying the pestilence. Twice a day I will put my head in a bucket full of PRIVY waste and breathe the fumes for half an hour. That will keep the pestilence away.

I treated arrow wounds with the King's army. A blacksmith made me a tool to take the arrow out. Then honey on the wound to help it heal. That'll teach you to walk behind the target at archery practice.

Your humours are out of balance. Go to a surgeon who'll bleed you and go again in six months.

People used streams as toilets.

There were public toilets but one was over the Thames which supplied some of the city's water.

Wells for drinking water were often close to cesspools for dumping sewage.

A certain cure for the pestilence? A holy remedy made from the finest herb and dust from the true Holy Cross on which Christ was crucified. Only one silver penny!

What made towns so unhealthy?

In the Middle Ages towns were much smaller, and fewer in number, than today, yet they were still very unhealthy places. There was little regulation or restriction on what you could or could not build. Houses were crowded together and sanitation very limited. Improvements depended on the corporation that ran the town and most wanted to keep costs as low as possible.

▲ Source B: A medieval town, from *Look and Learn* magazine in 1976

Life in a town or city was fraught with danger. You might get killed by a **cut-purse**, or run over by a horse and cart. You might get caught up in a fire. Fires spread rapidly as most houses were made of wood and thatch.

Homes were unhealthy too. Floors were covered in straw or rushes which were rarely changed. This was the perfect breeding ground for rats, mice, lice and fleas - ideal for spreading diseases and infection. There were few windows, and usually smoke from the fire - essential for cooking - would have to make its way out via a hole in the roof. Only rich people had glass windows and chimneys, so homes were dark and smoky; not very healthy!

Towns were unhealthy because so many people lived so close together. There were few regulations about building or waste disposal. Clean water was in short supply, often taken from rivers and streams that were contaminated with waste. Butchers brought their animals into the town or city alive and slaughtered them – they were then faced with the problem of how to get rid of the waste. Industries like tanning were carried on nearby, creating smells and waste. There was no 'zoning' in towns – industry and houses were mixed together higgledy-piggledy. There were no dustbins or dustbin men to collect the rubbish – it just accumulated in the streets until the rain washed it away. Cesspits might be dug next to wells, allowing one to contaminate the other – or the cess pit was emptied infrequently – you had to pay people to take the waste away.

Everywhere there were animals – horses for transport, creating tons of dung every week; or domestic pigs roaming around eating scraps before being slaughtered. There were no sewers, so household waste was chucked out into the street and left to rot. If you were unlucky the overnight piss-pot might be chucked out of an upstairs window as you were passing below. Keeping food fresh was difficult, so you had to shop for food every day, and shopkeepers would try to sell food that was going off rather than throw it away. Water for washing – either clothes or people – was hard to come by, so people were not perhaps as clean as they might be. Water for drinking was also rare, hence most people would drink 'small-beer' rather than risk the water. What was permissible in the countryside or in a small village became deadly in towns. Disease spread quickly. No wonder medical people thought disease was spread by bad smells!

THINK

1 Why, in your opinion, were towns so unhealthy in medieval times?

2 How did this cause illness and disease?

3 Look at Source B. Identify all the health hazards shown in this image. Can you find at least six?

4 To what extent does Source B agree with the text on this page? Which offers the better interpretation of medieval towns – Source B or the text? Why?

A case study of the Black Death: what does this disease tell us about the causes of disease in medieval times?

In 1348 a ship docked at Melcombe in Dorset, bringing with it the Black Death. People must have known it was coming as it had spread across the known world from Asia. Its impact was devastating. In some places whole villages were wiped out. Historians disagree over just how many people were killed by the epidemic of 1348–49, but estimates vary from 50 to 66 per cent of the British population.

What did people think caused the Black Death?

The truth is that people at the time did not really know much at all about the causes of ill-health, but they had plenty of theories! Here are just some of the suggested causes of the Black Death in England.

Bad smells, from an overflowing privy or rotting food, corrupt the air.

Invisible fumes are spreading across the country.

The four humours are out of balance in each victim.

The planets can explain it. Saturn is in conjunction with Mars and Jupiter and that always means something bad happens.

God is angry with us – not enough people have been going to church or behaving properly.

People have been wearing fancy new clothes, and showing off their wealth. This has made God very angry and therefore he has sent a plague, like he did in biblical times, to teach us to behave better.

There was a huge earthquake in China in 1347. China is where the Black Death started in 1347.

The Jews have poisoned the wells and springs.

It is important to remember that historians today still debate the exact causes of the Black Death. The prevailing argument is that it was bubonic plague spread by rats. However, others suggest that it was spread by close contact between humans. Archaeologists have not found lots of rat bones, suggesting the plague wasn't spread by rats, and the fact that mortality rose in winter suggests the Black Death may have been something other than bubonic plague all together. If we find it difficult to understand what caused the disease, what chance did people in the Middle Ages have of understanding the cause of, and then effectively curing, such a rampant disease?

> **THINK** ?
>
> Do you find any of these causes surprising? If so, why?

21

The impact of the Black Death upon Wales

By 1349, the Black Death had reached Wales and, starting in the south-west, it quickly spread across the country. Historians believe that over a third of the population of Wales (around 100,000 people) died as a result of the plague and, in some instances, the result was the complete abandonment of some settlements. The spread of the disease was rapid across Wales:

- It is believed that the coastal trading port of Haverfordwest in Pembrokeshire, which had trading links with Bristol, was the first town to experience the outbreak of the plague. Over half of the town's population died, causing a severe reduction in trade and leaving large parts of the town abandoned.

- The neighbouring towns of Pembroke and Carmarthen, which also had maritime links with Bristol, were soon afterwards affected. In the case of Carmarthen, the trade in the town was seriously disrupted, with fairs cancelled and the taxation collected from mills, fisheries and market tolls being virtually wiped out.

- In the south-east, the town of Caldicot, which also had close links with Bristol, was badly affected.

- Within a few months the plague had struck settlements in North Wales; at Deganwy in Caernarvonshire all the **bondmen** died, while at Nantconwy there were 147 bondmen before the plague struck but only 47 afterwards. Wherever it struck the disease took a heavy toll (see Source C).

- The market towns of Ruthin and Denbigh in the north-east were particularly badly hit (see Figure 1.1).

- The lead mining communities around Holywell in Flintshire were badly afflicted and the financial records for the Chamberlain of Chester record a sharp fall in revenue due to the Earl of Chester from taxes. Before 1348 the lordship of Englefield generated an income of over 100 shillings from taxes but after 1349 just 4 shillings was collected, the records stating that this was because 'the miners there have for the most part died, and the survivors refuse to work there'.

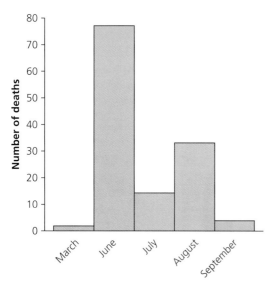

▲ **Figure 1.1:** Graph showing the number of deaths from the plague in Ruthin town during 1349

Source C: An extract from a fifteenth century poem by Llywelyn Fychan called 'Haint y Nodau/The Pestilence'

'Haint y Nodau'

Nid oes drugaredd, gwedd gwiw,
gan y nod, gwenwyn ydiw.

Y nod a ddug eneidiau
y dillynion mwynion mau.

Trist y'm gwnaeth, trwy arfaeth trais,
ac unig, neur fawr gwynais.

Dwyn Ieuan wiwlan ei wedd
ymlaen y lleill naw mlynedd;
ac weithian fu'r twrn gwaethaf,
oera' swydd yn aros haf,
dihir fy nghol a'm gofeg:

dwyn Morfudd, dwyn Dafydd deg,
dwyn Ieuan, llond degan lu,
dwyn â didawddgwyn Dyddgu,
a'm gadaw, frad oerfraw fryd,
yn freiddfyw mewn afrwyddfyd.

'The Pestilence'

The plague has no mercy,
fine aspect, it is poison.

The plague took the lives
of my gentle darlings.

Its wilful violence made me sad
and lonely, I lamented greatly.
Handsome Ieuan was taken
nine years before the others:

and now the worst turn of all has happened,
grimmest job awaiting summer,

the memory and thought of it is painful:
Morfudd was taken, fair Dafydd was taken,
Ieuan, everyone's cheery favourite, was taken,
with an unceasing lament Dyddgu was taken,
and I was left, feeling betrayed and stunned,
barely alive in a harsh world.

Case study: The deserted medieval village of Cosmeston

The small medieval village of Cosmeston near Penarth in the Vale of Glamorgan was a typical example of a Norman manor. Centred upon a fortified manor house constructed in the twelfth century by the Norman De Costentin family, the village consisted of a number of small stone houses with thatched roofs, accommodating a population of around 100 people. Many of the peasant homes were one-roomed buildings in which the whole family would have cooked, eaten and slept, all in the same room. Some of the outlying farms consisted of longhouses where the farmer and his family shared the house with their animals. Each property would have a garden in which vegetables such as leeks, onions, garlic, peas, beans and herbs were grown. The village also had a kiln house which contained a kiln for drying the grains from the harvest and an oven for bread baking.

It is thought that the majority of the villagers died during the Black Death of 1348–49 or during one its later outbreaks, leaving Cosmeston a deserted medieval village.

▲ **Source D:** Following an archaeological dig in the 1970s the deserted medieval village of Cosmeston has been re-created as it would have appeared in 1350

THINK

1 What factors can you identify to explain:
   a) how the Black Death arrived in Wales in 1349
   b) how it spread across Wales during 1349?

2 How useful is Source D to a historian studying the impact of the Black Death?

3 Use Figure 1.1 and your own knowledge to describe how Wales was affected by the arrival of the Black Death.

4 Through the work of archaeologists and historians the medieval village of Cosmeston has been re-created as it might have looked in 1350. Working in pairs, think of some of the arguments that can be put forward to justify the reconstruction of such sites.

Being ill in the seventeenth century

The biggest killer diseases in the seventeenth century were: 'fever, consumption, teeth, griping in the guts, and convulsions'. Just the very descriptions tell us how little physicians and surgeons understood about the causes of disease, let alone cures. These diseases are not so very different from the killer diseases of the sixteenth or fifteenth centuries, or, for that matter, earlier times.

THINK

1 Look carefully at the bill of mortality for London, February 1664 (Source E). Which are
   a) the diseases that kill the most people
   b) the diseases that kill the least people?

2 How has this list changed since medieval times?

3 What has happened to the population of London in the week 21–28 February 1664? What does that tell us about how healthy life in London was?

4 Why does the bill of mortality refer to 'the plague'? What was the impact of the plague in that week?

▲ Source E: Weekly mortality bill, London, 21–28 February 1664

The content of the mortality bill reads:

The Diseases and Casualties this Week.

Abortive	2
Aged	32
Bleeding	1
Childbed	5
Chrisoms	9
Collick	1
Consumption	65
Convulsion	41
Cough	5
Dropsie	43
Drowned at S Kathar. Tower	1
Feaver	47
Flox and Small-pox	15
Flux	3
Found dead in the Street at Stepney	1
Griping in the Guts	15
Imposthume	1
Infants	7
Kingsevill	1
Mouldfallen	1
Kild accidentally with a Carbine, at St. Michael Wood-street	1
Overlaid	1
Rickets	9
Rising of the Lights	2
Rupture	2
Scalded in a Brewers Mash, at St. Giles Cripplegate	1
Scurvy	4
Spotted Feaver	2
Stilborn	13
Stopping of the Stomach	11
Suddenly	1
Surfeit	7
Teeth	27
Tissick	12
Ulcer	1
Vomiting	1
Winde	1
Wormes	1

Christned { Males — 121, Females — 111, In all — 232 }

Buried { Males — 195, Females — 198, In all — 393 } Plague 0

Decreased in the Burials this Week — 69

Parishes clear of the Plague — 130   Parishes Infected — 0

The Assize of Bread set forth by Order of the Lord Maier and Court of Aldermen, A penny Wheaten Loaf to contain Eleven Ounces, and three half-penny White Loaves the like weight.

A case study of London in 1665: what does the Plague tell us about changes in the way people thought disease was caused?

Plague came often to major towns and cities. In 1604, 30 per cent of the population of York died in an outbreak of the plague. In 1665 around 100,000 people died of the plague in London. That was nearly 25 per cent of the population. Other towns and cities were affected too, for example Eyam in Derbyshire. Most doctors fled, fearing for their lives. Wealthy people fled the city for their country houses until the plague left, but in many cases that just spread the plague to new places. Studying the plague, and what people thought caused it, gives us a great opportunity to decide how much had changed between the Black Death in 1348–49 and the Plague in 1665.

What did people at the time think caused the plague?

The truth is that people in the early modern period did not really know much at all about the causes of the plague, but they had plenty of theories. Below is a picture of a plague doctor wearing the protective outfit designed by Charles de Lorme in Italy in 1619.

Stick

Nose cone full of sweet-smelling herbs

Pink-tinted glass in the face mask

Mask

Stout hat with wide brim

Very thick waxed gown

Stout boots

Thick gloves

Amulet (jewellery to ward off evil spirits) hidden under sleeve of coat

◄ Figure 1.2: A plague doctor wearing a protective outfit designed by Charles de Lorme in Italy in 1619

THINK

1 Look closely at the plague doctor's clothes and equipment in Figure 1.2. What do they tell you about what people at the time thought caused the Plague?

2 Look back at page 21 on what people in medieval Britain thought caused the Black Death in 1348.

3 From your work in this chapter, which of these causes do you think people in 1665 still believed caused the Plague?

THINK

1 Study Source F. Try to imagine what it would be like living in one of these houses. How do you keep clean and tidy? Where do you get your water from? Where do you go to the toilet? How likely is your washing to dry or to stay clean? What would happen if your neighbour fell ill?

2 To what extent does Doré's engraving agree with the other evidence we have from Victorian times about living in the new towns?

3 What were the 'killer diseases' of the nineteenth century?

4 How did industrial jobs bring new causes of illness and disease?

5 How similar, and how different, were the causes of illness and disease in medieval towns and the new industrial towns?

The effects of industrialisation and the incidence of cholera and typhoid in the nineteenth century

Were the new industrial towns really that bad to live in?

The Victorians were exceptional at collecting data, and this is a great help in trying to discover what life was like in industrial towns. For example, we know that in Bethnal Green, in East London, in 1842 richer people lived on average to the age of 45, whereas labourers lived until they were just 16. In Manchester at the same time 57 per cent of all children died before they reached their fifth birthday. Social surveys from the time show that often a whole family lived in one room, or in a cellar liable to flooding; many children shared a bed, and toilets and water supplies were shared by many families. There are plenty of other statistics we could use but these examples tell us that yes, indeed, the new industrial towns were grim to live in.

Contagious diseases, such as typhoid, typhus, diarrhoea, smallpox, tuberculosis, scarlet fever, whooping cough, measles and chicken pox, all spread rapidly in such poor and overcrowded conditions. No wonder 57 per cent of children died before they reached the age of five. Perhaps the best indicator of how bad conditions were is the prevalence of rickets, known in the nineteenth century as 'the English Disease'. This is a crippling bone disease common in infants caused by calcium deficiency and lack of fresh air and sunlight, and is a clear indicator of malnutrition.

New hazards in industrial life

Added to the overcrowding were the new industrial diseases. Young boys forced to climb up chimneys came into contact with soot and gases. Percivall Pott, an English surgeon, identified scrotal cancer in many of these chimney boys. Young girls making matches at factories across London developed 'phossy-jaw' caused by the fumes from the phosphorous used to make the match heads. Parts of the jaw would be eaten away, or glow greenish-white in the dark. It also caused brain damage. Coal miners developed pneumoconiosis, a disease of the lungs, caused by inhaling dust below ground. Machines in the new textile factories rarely had guards, and hands and arms were often caught in the machines. There were few regulations controlling working conditions and accidents were common, with no compensation and little prospect of further work.

▲ **Source F:** Engraving by Gustave Doré of part of London in 1872

Here comes cholera

Perhaps the biggest concern at this time were the cholera epidemics of 1831–32, 1848, 1854 and 1866. Cholera is a bacterial infection caused by consuming contaminated food or water. It originated in Bengal, in India, and slowly spread across the trade routes, much like the Black Death in 1347. People knew it was coming, but hoped it would not arrive. At the time no one knew what caused cholera, or how to cure it.

> **Source G:** UK deaths from cholera
>
> | | |
> |---|---|
> | 1831–32: | 50,000 |
> | 1848: | 60,000 |
> | 1854: | 20,000 |

BOARD OF WORKS
FOR THE LIMEHOUSE DISTRICT.
COMPRISING LIMEHOUSE, RATCLIFF, SHADWELL & WAPPING.

In consequence of the appearance of **CHOLERA** within this District, the Board have appointed the under-mentioned Medical Gentlemen who will give ADVICE, MEDICINE, AND ASSISTANCE, FREE OF ANY CHARGE, AND UPON APPLICATION, AT ANY HOUR OF THE DAY OR NIGHT.

The Inhabitants are earnestly requested not to neglect the first symptoms of the appearance of Disease, (which in its early stage is easy to cure), but to apply, WITHOUT DELAY, to one of the Medical Gentlemen appointed.

The Board have opened an Establishment for the reception of Patients, in a building at Green Bank, near Wapping Church, (formerly used as Wapping Workhouse), where all cases of Cholera and Diarrhœa will be received and placed under the care of a competent Resident Medical Practitioner, and proper Attendants.

THE FOLLOWING ARE THE MEDICAL GENTLEMEN TO BE APPLIED TO:--

Mr. ORTON,
56, White Horse Street.

Dr. NIGHTINGALL,
4, Commercial Terrace, Commercial Road, (near Limehouse Church.)

Mr. SCHROEDER,
53, Three Colt Street, Limehouse.

Mr. HARRIS,
5, York Terrace, Commercial Road, (opposite Stepney Railway Station.)

Mr. CAMBELL,
At Mr. GRAY's, Chemist, Old Road, opposite "The World's End."

Mr. LYNCH,
St. James's Terrace, Back Road, Shadwell.

Mr. HECKFORD,
At the Dispensary, Wapping Workhouse.

BY ORDER,

BOARD OFFICES, WHITE HORSE STREET,
26th July, 1866.

THOS. W. RATCLIFF,
Clerk to the Board.

▲ Source H: Notice issued in Limehouse in 1866 giving advice for dealing with cholera

Typhoid

Typhoid is a bacterial infection, passed from human to human through contaminated food and water or faeces. It is caused by poor sanitation and lack of cleanliness, especially washing of hands and clothes. It had killed people since the times of the Ancient Greeks, and was especially noticeable in armies. The new industrial cities, where it was very difficult to keep clean and maintain a clean water supply, were fertile places for typhoid, and it was endemic – present virtually all the time. It was no respecter of rank. Prince Albert, husband of Queen Victoria, died in 1861 from typhoid caught from the drains at Windsor Castle.

In 1897–98 in Maidstone, Kent, an outbreak of typhoid occurred. Over 1800 people, out of a population of 34,000, caught the disease and 132 died. It was the largest single epidemic of the disease in Britain to date. There were over 200 reported cases in just the first eight days. Local medical services were overwhelmed; doctors and nurses were drafted in from across the country to deal with the disease. The cause of the disease was eventually traced to a nearby reservoir – Borming Reservoir – supplying part of the town. Once this was closed down the outbreak was brought under control.

▲ Source I: Medal awarded to nurses who worked in Maidstone 1897–98

> **THINK**
>
> 1 Study Source H. What advice does it give to people who think they have cholera?
>
> 2 How does this advice compare with contemporary ideas about the spread of disease?
>
> 3 Look at Source I. Why do you think nurses treating typhoid in Maidstone were issued with a medal?
>
> 4 What does that tell us about the way people at the time thought about:
> a) nurses and
> b) typhoid?

Cholera epidemics in Wales

During the summer months of 1832, 1849, 1854 and 1866, Wales was severely affected by outbreaks of cholera, which caused hundreds of deaths. During the 1832 outbreak, the industrialised town of Merthyr Tydfil was worst affected, recording 160 deaths, closely followed by Swansea with 152 deaths. In the north-east the market town of Denbigh recorded 47 deaths and the industrial town of Holywell 49 deaths. However, it was the outbreak of 1849 that had the most dramatic impact.

Cholera appears in Cardiff, 1849

The long, hot summer of 1849, proved to be the ideal breeding ground for cholera. The drought conditions caused many normal supplies of fresh water to dry up and this forced people to use less safe sources of water, such as contaminated rivers and canals.

The first recorded case of the 1848–49 cholera epidemic in Wales appeared in Cardiff on 13 May 1849. By early June, the outbreak was widespread, with 14 deaths from cholera being recorded on 7 June. A peak was reached in August with 91 deaths, and by the time the disease died away in November over 396 people had died from contracting cholera (see Source J). For more on outbreaks of cholera in Cardiff in the nineteenth century see Chapter 7.

Cholera appears in Merthyr Tydfil, 1849

During the summer months of 1849, cholera quickly spread outside Cardiff into the South Wales valleys. The heavily industrialised town of Merthyr Tydfil was severely hit, experiencing one of the highest death tolls in England and Wales, with over 1682 individuals having died from the disease by November of that year.

The first outbreak in the town was recorded on 21 May at Heol-y-Giller when a child of four was infected. The **Board of Guardians** introduced measures for cleansing the town but their efforts had little impact. As was the case in Cardiff, the infection reached its height in August, and it did not finally disappear until November (see Source J).

While there were no hospital facilities in Merthyr at this time, the ironmaster Josiah John Guest opened a refuge for the healthy and a night dispensary for cholera cases where free medicines could be obtained.

Source J: The monthly death rates from cholera recorded for the districts of Cardiff and Merthyr Tydfil between May and November 1849

	May	June	July	August	September	October	November
Cardiff	39	135	69	91	55	3	1
Merthyr Tydfil	16	349	539	548	190	37	3

Source K: An extract from the journal of Lady Charlotte Guest, taken from an entry dated 31 July 1849

I am sorry to say that the accounts of the cholera at Dowlais (an area of Merthyr) are fearfully bad. They are beyond anything I could have imagined, sometimes upwards of twenty people dying in one day, and eight men constantly employed in making coffins. Poor Miss Diddams, one of our infant School-Mistresses, is dead. One of the medical assistants sent down from London is dying, and the whole place seems in a most lamentable state. I am greatly grieved at the conditions of my poor home.

Cholera spreads to other parts of Wales

As Source L illustrates, the cholera outbreak of 1849 was not just confined to Cardiff and Merthyr Tydfil. Other South Wales towns such as Carmarthen, Llanelli, Neath and Swansea were badly affected. While the north did not experience such severity of deaths, the port of Holyhead recorded 42 deaths and the industrial towns of Holywell and Flint recorded 46 and 35 deaths respectively.

Source L: Cholera deaths recorded in towns across Wales during 1849

Newport	209	Ystradgynlais	107
Pontypool	61	Llanelly District	45
Tredegar	203	Swansea	262
Aberystwyth	223	Carmarthen	102
Crickhowell	95	Welshpool	34
Cardiff	396	Newtown	6
Neath	245	Holywell	46
Margam	241	Flint	35
Maesteg	33	Caernarvon	16
Bridgend	50	Holyhead	42
Merthyr district	1,682	Amlwch	22

THINK ?

1 What factors can you identify to help explain why a cholera epidemic broke out in Cardiff and Merthyr Tydfil in 1849?

2 Use the information in Sources J, K and L, as well as your own knowledge, to describe the impact of the cholera epidemic upon Cardiff and Merthyr Tydfil in 1849.

3 Why do you think people living in Victorian times feared cholera so much?

▲ **Source M:** Gravestones of cholera victims in Wales

The spread of bacterial and viral diseases in the twentieth century

In the twentieth century both bacterial and viral diseases continued to spread. The outbreak of flu after the First World War and the recent occurrence of AIDS are two examples of this. (You can find out more about how bacteria cause disease on page 44.)

Case study: a visit by 'The Spanish Lady' in 1918–19. More devastating than the Black Death?

In 1918 a flu **pandemic** spread around a war-weary world. An estimated 20–40 million people worldwide died as a result. It was a particularly devastating strain, evolved from bird flu and thought to originate in China. It is said to have infected 20 per cent of the world's population, and proved most deadly for 20–40-year olds. Initially it was thought to be a result of German biological warfare, or an effect of prolonged trench warfare and the use of mustard gas. What is clear is that mass troop movements in 1918 after the end of the First World War helped rapidly transmit the disease across the globe. Homecoming troops then spread the disease to the civilian population.

In the UK the government imposed censorship about the spread of the infection in a bid to prevent panic, but newspapers were allowed to report the seven million deaths in Spain, hence the name given to the disease: Spanish Flu, or 'The Spanish Lady'. A visit from 'the Lady' could be deadly: apparently healthy people at breakfast time could be dead by tea time. In a post-war weary and weakened population it spread rapidly, but no one knew why. Symptoms were quite general at first: headaches, sore throat and loss of appetite. Those who recovered seemed to recover quickly, so the outbreak was originally known as 'Three-Day Fever'. Hospitals could not cope. In a few months in the UK around 280,000 people died, mostly young men and women. Up to 20 per cent of those infected died. Australian troops were stationed at Sutton Veny in Wiltshire from 1915 to 1919, and there was a military hospital there. Part of the cemetery is now a Commonwealth War Graves Commission site. Many Australian victims of the flu epidemic are buried there.

> **Source N: A children's skipping song, 1918–19**
> *I had a little bird,*
> *it's name was Enza.*
> *I opened a window*
> *and in-flu-enza*

THINK ?

1 Is it accurate to compare the 1918–19 flu pandemic with the Black Death (see page 21)?

2 What can we learn about the causes of illness and disease in the twentieth century from the flu pandemic?

Source O: Headstones marking the graves of Canadian soldiers who fell victim to the flu epidemic, St Margarets, Church, Bodelwyddan in Denbighshire

Case study: the fight against AIDS

AIDS, or acquired immune deficiency syndrome, was first identified in 1981 in the USA where doctors noticed that large numbers of homosexuals were dying from causes that could not easily be identified. It took until 1983 for scientists to discover that a viral infection was attacking the immune system that protects the body from disease. Since then AIDS has become, according to some authorities, a pandemic, spreading across the world like the Black Death or cholera. By 2014 it was estimated that 40 million people around the world had died from AIDS, and that another 40 million are living with the disease. In the UK there are over 100,000 people, mostly young, living with AIDS and it is thought that 25 per cent of them have no idea that they have the disease.

It is thought that AIDS originated among primates in central Africa and spread to humans there around the turn of the twentieth century. People do not die of AIDS, but often from catching very simple infections, like common colds, because the weakened immune system cannot fight off infection. AIDS is usually caused by: having unprotected sex with a male or a female who has the disease; by sharing hypodermic needles; by contaminated blood transfusions; and from mother to child during pregnancy or breast-feeding. Freddie Mercury, lead singer of the rock band Queen, is just one of many high-profile people who have died from having the disease.

As you can tell, AIDS is very much a disease of a modern lifestyle. Sex and drugs play a large part, but not the only part, in spreading AIDS both within the UK and around the world. Countries where sexual behaviour is more strictly controlled seem to have fewer cases of AIDS. More isolated communities also seem to have fewer people with AIDS.

THINK ?

1 What message is Source P trying to put across?

2 How is this message similar to, and different from, messages put out about the Black Death (page 21)?

◄ Source P: An AIDS poster from the 1980s

Reactions to AIDS

The speech bubbles below illustrate some of the ways in which people have reacted to the spread of AIDS.

If we repent our sins we will be cured.

AIDS is God's punishment to us for our sinful lifestyles.

People suffering from AIDS should be isolated from the community so that they are unable to harm others.

AIDS can be caught by touching others.

Other people have shown compassion and have set up charities both to treat victims and to try to find a cure. Governments and international organisations, such as the **World Health Organization**, have spent millions of pounds on awareness campaigns in attempts to slow the spread of the disease. Given this range of responses, have our attitudes to disease changed all that much over the last 1000 years?

AIDS is seen as a modern-day equivalent of the Black Death, cholera or Spanish Flu, spreading remorselessly across the globe, leaving millions dead in its wake. But is that really the case? What could you do to stop catching the Black Death, or cholera, or the Spanish Flu? Not a lot. These epidemics were no respecter of age, class or sex. AIDS is *different*. It is spread in a clearly identifiable way which can be avoided. Some people argue that there is no *need* for anyone to catch AIDS. If you like, it is a 'lifestyle choice' to behave in a way that makes catching the infection more likely. Also, we know how to stop AIDS spreading. In 1918, 1831–32 or 1348 no one had the faintest idea how to stop those epidemics from spreading.

Some people see the story of AIDS as a pessimistic one. New diseases and epidemics are always going to break out, and science and technology are not always going to be able to control them. Some people paint an 'apocalyptic' picture of the end of the world where society is wiped out by epidemics.

Others see AIDS in a more optimistic light. Yes, it is an epidemic that has killed millions but governments and international organisations are working hard together to control the spread of the disease and will find a cure.

ACTIVITIES

1 Make two lists: one listing all the similarities between AIDS and the other epidemics you have studied and the other listing all the differences between AIDS and the other epidemics.
2 Compare the two lists. What conclusions can you draw?

FOCUS TASK REVISITED

1 Your focus task was to make a 'cause of illness and disease' card for every cause you came across as you worked through this chapter.

2 Take your 'cause of illness and disease ' cards and sort them into categories – which are, in your opinion, the *most important* causes, and which are the least important?

3 Re-sort your 'cause of illness and disease' cards according to the time they were most important – for example, the plague might be most important in medieval times but not today.

4 What *patterns* can you discover in the causes of illness and disease?

5 Look back at the 'killer diseases of late twentieth-century Britain '(Source B, page 13), in the Big Story chapter of this book. Make 'cause of illness and disease' cards for each of those diseases too.

6 How have the causes of illness and disease changed from medieval times to today?

ACTIVITIES

Throughout history, poverty has been the main cause of illness and disease. Do you agree?

1 In pairs, prepare notes for a class debate about the causes of illness and disease. One of you can make notes agreeing that poverty was the main cause, the other can prepare notes suggesting other reasons.

2 When you have your notes, join with others who have the same view as you, and produce an agreed set of notes. Split your arguments into 'major' and 'minor', then choose two speakers to present your ideas to the rest of the class.

3 After the debate the whole class can then decide if poverty was the main cause of illness and disease.

TOPIC SUMMARY

- For much of this period many of the causes of disease were not clearly known or understood.
- Poverty and poor living conditions helped cause illness and disease throughout the period.
- Accidents remain a major cause of illness, disease and death.
- Towns were often unhealthier than the countryside.
- Epidemics continue to be a major cause of illness and disease.
- Childhood was an especially dangerous time.
- It was very difficult for people to keep clean even if they tried to.
- Warfare and famine were major causes of disease throughout the period.
- The growth of industry introduced new diseases into towns and cities.

Practice questions

1 Complete the sentences below with an accurate term.
The Black Death swept through Europe during the .... century.
The outbreak of plague in 1665 badly affected the city of ....
In 1918 many people died from a major flu ....
During the 1980s a new disease emerged called ....
(*For guidance, see page 119.*)

2 Describe the main causes of disease in the new industrial towns of the nineteenth century. (*For guidance, see page 122.*)

3 To what extent were poor living conditions the most important cause of illness and disease over time? (*For guidance, see page 126–128.*)

This chapter focuses on the key question: How effective were attempts to prevent illness and disease over time?

It is very difficult to effectively prevent illness and disease when you do not really know the causes. For much of this period people could treat the symptoms of a disease, rather than the disease itself. Nevertheless, even the Ancient Greeks advocated healthy living as a means of keeping well and since then, as people increasingly identified causes of illness, as we have seen already in Chapter 1, preventative measures have become increasingly important – so much so that today as much effort is put into preventing disease as in treating it. This chapter explores attempts throughout the period of trying to prevent illness and disease.

FOCUS TASK

As you work through this chapter we would like you to build up a 'mind map' of attempts to prevent illness and disease. This will help you decide if there are any links between the different sections of this chapter, and to see if later attempts at prevention build on earlier ones. It is important that you use your 'mind map' to try to build up a 'Big Picture' of disease prevention across the whole period studied.

? Early methods of prevention of disease with reference to the Black Death

The Ancient Greeks had some understanding of the prevention of disease. Hippocrates was born in Kos, in Greece, in 460BC. He is regarded by many as the father of modern medicine and was perhaps the first physician to regard and treat the body as a whole, rather than as individual parts. Hippocrates based his thinking and writing around the theory of the **four humours**. In order to prevent illness and disease all you had to do was to keep the four humours of blood, phlegm, yellow bile and black bile in balance. Hippocrates also believed diet, exercise and rest had a huge part to play in prevention of disease. The Arabs believed in the importance of cleanliness and fresh air and the Romans built huge aqueducts to bring fresh water to their towns, with most Roman villas having a bath and toilet with running water. However, much of this was lost when the Romans left Britain around AD410. Most medieval physicians continued to be trained in, and believed in, the theory of the four humours. (We will be exploring the theory of the four humours in more detail in Chapter 4.)

The role of the church

The church was very influential in medieval times, and it argued that physical illness was a manifestation of spiritual illness. In other words, people became ill because they were either living in an unchristian way or they were not praying hard enough. To stop the Black Death the church ordered people to take part in processions through towns and villages to the local church, and pray for forgiveness. Some people took this further: they made life-size candles and burned those in church, asking to be spared. Others took to walking around the streets whipping themselves in order to purify themselves in God's eyes, and thus hope to be spared from the Black Death.

▲ Source A: Monks with the plague being blessed by a priest from a fourteenth-century manuscript

Other attempts to prevent catching the Black Death

Many other suggestions were made if you wanted to avoid the Black Death. Some argued you should not eat too much, or you should not bathe. Having a bath opened the pores of the skin and allowed disease into the body. Some said washing would keep you clean and keep the Black Death away! Others suggested avoiding sex, as having sex weakened the body's defences against illness, or drinking vinegar and/or wine; drinking urine once a day; bathing in urine three times a day; bleeding to let out the evil spirits that might cause disease; killing all the cats and dogs as they spread disease; even carrying a posy of sweet-smelling herbs with you as this would stop the bad smell that some thought caused the disease. Putting coins in vinegar when paying for your shopping was also thought to prevent passing on the disease.

Some people came closer to effective prevention, without really knowing why. King Edward III ordered the streets of London cleaned of all the filth, arguing that the smell spread the Black Death. Other more practical advice was to avoid coming into contact with people who had the disease. House doors of those with the Black Death were often boarded up and a big red cross painted on them, warning people to keep away. Many people attempted to avoid the Black Death by fleeing – but unwittingly all this did was to help spread the Black Death even further.

As you can see from the proposed preventative measures, and as you already learned in Chapter 1, no one really knew what to do to stop the Black Death spreading, or to keep people safe from it.

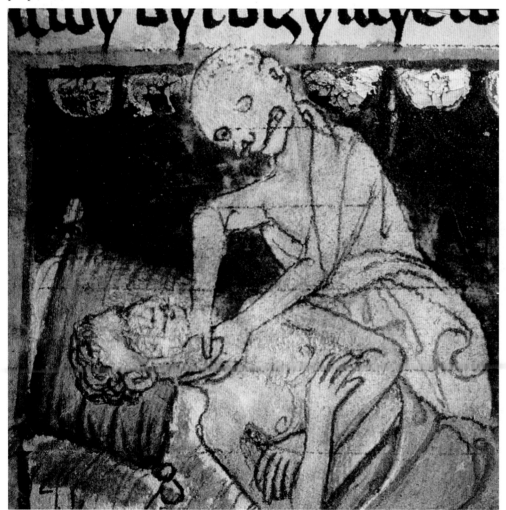

▲ Source B: Death strangling a victim of the Black Death, painted by Werner Forman in 1376

THINK

1 Which of the preventative measures suggested do you think might have helped people avoid the Black Death? Why?

2 What do all these suggestions tell us about medieval attempts to prevent illness and disease?

3 Look at Source A. How can you tell these monks have the Black Death? Why is the priest blessing them?

4 Look at Source B. It is from a fourteenth-century prayer book and was painted in 1376. What do images like this tell us about attempts to prevent catching the Black Death?

5 What do Sources A and B tell us about medieval attitudes to the prevention of illness and disease?

Alchemy, soothsayers and medieval doctors

Alchemy

THINK **?**

1 To what extent did alchemy help the prevention of illnesses and disease?

2 Look at Source C. How has the artist chosen to portray the alchemist?

3 How useful is Source C to understanding of the part played by alchemy in preventing disease?

There was often very little difference between scientists and alchemists in medieval and early modern times. Some of the most eminent scientists – Roger Bacon in the thirteenth century, Isaac Newton in the seventeenth century, for example – delved into alchemy. Most of their experiments were attempts to turn 'base' metals such as lead into gold, but many scientific discoveries were made by these experiments, although no one managed to create gold from another substance. These scientific discoveries became important later, and helped others, such as William Harvey, in their work (see page 64).

Alchemists by their nature tended to be secretive about their experiments, and so all kinds of stories grew about them, about what they were doing, and what they had achieved. Many were searching for the 'Elixir of Life', which was supposed to keep you young forever. One alchemist claimed to be 1000 years old but when pushed for evidence could give no proof. Obviously if you could discover this Elixir of Life you could make a fortune and ensure everyone could be free from illness and old age. This new medicine, or 'quintessence' as it was known, often made by repeatedly distilling vinegar, was meant to remove all impurities from the body. Sometimes strong medicines containing poisons, such antimony or mercury, would be used to make a patient violently sick, thus being seen to prevent disease.

Gullible people were prepared to advance large sums of money to alchemists in exchange for turning lead into gold or for providing longer life. John Dee (1527–1608/9) was an adviser to Queen Elizabeth I and a famous mathematician. He was also a famous astronomer. From 1580 onwards he spent much of his time investigating the world of magic, trying to discover how to communicate with angels, in order to find out more about the Creation of the Earth by God. He did not see a distinction between his mathematical investigations and his study of magic and demons or his search for the secret of long life. Gerard of York, Archbishop of York until his death in 1108, was reported to be a student of the 'dark arts', magic and medicine although this may have been more a result of his attempts to reform the church against the wishes of his clergy than his own interests.

▲ **Source C:** *The Alchemist*, by David Teniers the Younger, seventeenth century

Soothsayers

There were very few qualified doctors in medieval England. Most people would depend on the local 'wise woman'. These would build up knowledge of sickness and disease over several generations, and each would have their own favourite methods. Some of them might even work! Soothsayers were also supposed to have powers of prophesy – to be able to see the future, and were often consulted by local people for a variety of purposes. They would collect plants and herbs, special stones, anything that might help, and carry this about with them in a willow basket. They would, for a price, put together special charms to be worn as protection against evil. Remember, the church strongly argued that most illness and disease was caused by evil, or by not living a Christian enough life.

Case study: can we believe most of what was written about Mother Shipton?

Mother Shipton became famous as a fifteenth-century soothsayer. She was born in a cave near Knaresborough, in Yorkshire, around the year 1488 and died around 1561. You can still visit the cave today. It is one of Yorkshire's top tourist attractions. Next to the cave is a petrifying well – the only one in England – where the water has a high mineral content. Drinking it, or bathing in it, was said to keep you fit and healthy. From the sixteenth century people have visited the well for that purpose.

Mother Shipton is said to have been extremely ugly, but she gained quite a reputation for prophesying events. Local people came to her, then people from across the whole of Yorkshire and, eventually, from the whole of England. Her prophesies were first published in 1641, where this illustration of her is thought to have come from. Each subsequent edition of her prophesies included more and more predictions for the future, including that the world would end in 1881, or 1891, or 1981, depending on which version you believed!

She is perhaps a famous – or should that be infamous - example of many local soothsayers that we know nothing about, but who played an important part in helping medieval people avoid illness and disease.

Medieval doctors

As we have seen already, doctors were few and far between in medieval England. There were monks before Henry VIII abolished the monasteries in 1536 who would provide simple medical care; there were **apothecaries** who made up their own herbal remedies; there were **barber-surgeons** who might pull out a bad tooth or set a broken arm (see page 48); and there were physicians, probably trained at one of the new universities in Italy or Paris. Unfortunately, very few of them knew much about prevention of disease, because so little was known about causes of disease.

THE FAMOUS MOTHER SHIPTON.

▲ **Source D:** A seventeenth-century engraving said to be of Mother Shipton

> **THINK** ?
>
> 1 How accurate a depiction of Mother Shipton do you think this is?
>
> 2 How useful is Source D in finding out about Mother Shipton?
>
> 3 Does Source D prove that Mother Shipton existed? Explain your decision.
>
> 4 In what way does Source D help us understand how Mother Shipton, and soothsayers, helped prevent disease?
>
> 5 Which, in your opinion, were the most successful methods of preventing disease in medieval times?
>
> 6 How effective were medieval attempts to prevent disease?

The application of science to the prevention of disease in the late eighteenth and early nineteenth centuries

'Prevention is better than cure!'

During the eighteenth century this saying began to be heard more and more, as people rediscovered the Classical World, and the Ancient Greek's belief in fresh air, exercise and diet. John Bellers produced a book in 1714, his *Essay towards the Improvement of Physick* in which he argued that 100,000 people died each year 'for want of timely advice and suitable medicine'. It was a time of fads. Vegetarianism became fashionable, as did teetotalism. Both would keep you healthy and prevent disease. Regular bloodletting would prevent an imbalance of the four humours building up. Fresh air and exercise were all the rage – at least for those with the time and money to indulge it.

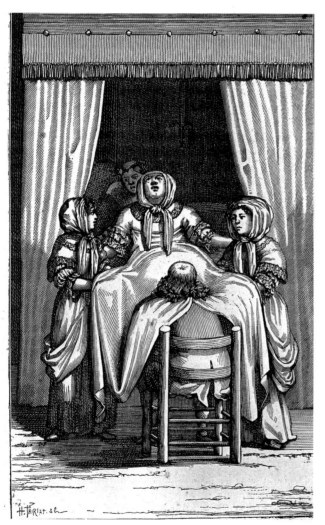

▲ **Source E:** An engraving depicting childbirth in the eighteenth century

The cold water treatment

'Taking the cure' at a spa became part of the season. It was widely believed that the waters of places such as Llandrindod and Builth Wells were beneficial to health and were preventative measures as well as cures. Visiting the seaside, places such as Rhyl, Llandudno and Aberystwyth, and swimming in the ocean was recommended to keep you healthy. It became fashionable to have your own 'plunge pool' of cold fresh water in the garden – as near to a source of fresh water as possible – and this was the perfect end to a brisk walk around the estate. Later in the period, the water would be piped inside the house and cold water bathing indoors became the trend. Eating 'cooling' foods was regarded as an essential part of the therapy. Drinking at least a litre of cold water every morning was supposed to clear out the impurities from the bowels that caused illness and disease. Many wealthier people in the eighteenth and nineteenth centuries adopted such measures in a bid to remain healthy.

Child-bed fever

As we have seen, childbirth was a very dangerous time for women. Alexander Gordon was a naval surgeon who worked in London for several years before returning to his native Aberdeen. While there he studied an outbreak of child-bed fever and worked out what caused these deaths. He noticed that women in outlying villages who were treated by the village wise woman or midwife rarely caught the fever, whereas those treated by doctors or midwives moving from patient to patient were much more likely to die. He realised that he himself was responsible for some of the deaths. His proposed cure was simple: medical practitioners ought to wash their clothes frequently, and wash their hands in chlorinated water to try to limit the spread of disease. When he published his results in 1795 he was derided by the whole of the medical profession and it was many years before his ideas were implemented.

> **THINK** **?**
>
> 1 How effective, in your opinion, are these 'fads' and 'cures' at preventing disease?
>
> 2 Study Source E. Can you identify any factors likely to cause either harm or death to the mother or newborn child? Do you think the midwife is familiar with the ideas of Alexander Gordon? How can you tell?

The rise of the scientific method

A series of inventions helped people keep healthy. The microscope (for seeing infections), the stethoscope (for listening to a patient's breathing) and the kymograph (for measuring blood pressure) all became part of a doctor's armoury in the early nineteenth century, allowing better investigation of health. Many scientific papers were published. James Lind, for example, identified the cause of scurvy in 1753. He insisted that sailors be given doses of lime juice and/or fresh fruit every day to keep them healthy (hence English sailors' nickname as 'Limeys'). During the eighteenth century many texts were written as a result of extensive scientific investigation of illnesses. These papers were published in order to bring about better treatment and prevention.

John Snow and cholera

Perhaps the greatest example of the application of science to disease prevention in the nineteenth century was the work of John Snow in London in 1854, during the cholera epidemic. Cholera, as we saw in Chapter 1 (page 27) was one of the killer diseases of the nineteenth century. John Snow, a London physician, carefully plotted on a street plan each and every cholera case in the area around his surgery (Figure 2.1). Within a few weeks over 500 deaths occurred in the neighbourhood of Broad Street.

He noticed that in a nearby area, where there was a brewery, the brewery workers didn't catch cholera, because they drank beer rather than water. He used statistics to illustrate the link between the quality of the water from different sources and cholera deaths. He thus showed that the Southwark and Vauxhall Waterworks Company was taking water from sewage-polluted sections of the Thames and delivering the water to homes with an increased incidence of cholera. He came to the conclusion – without being able to decisively prove why – that the source of the local infection was one particular water pump in Broad Street. When he took the handle off the pump – forcing residents to obtain their water elsewhere – the disease declined.

CHOLERA!

Published by order of the Sanatory Committee, under the sanction of the Medical Counsel.

BE TEMPERATE IN EATING & DRINKING!
Avoid Raw Vegetables and Unripe Fruit!.
Abstain from COLD WATER, when heated, and above all from *Ardent Spirits*, and if habit have rendered them indispensable, take much less than usual.

SLEEP AND CLOTHE WARM!
☞ **DO NOT SLEEP OR SIT IN A DRAUGHT OF AIR,**
Avoid getting Wet!
Attend immediately to all disorders of the Bowels.
TAKE NO MEDICINE WITHOUT ADVICE.

Medicine and Medical Advice can be had by the poor, at all hours of the day and night, by applying at the Station House in each Ward.

CALEB S. WOODHULL, *Mayor.*
JAMES KELLY, *Chairman of Sanatory Committee.*

▲ Source F: Poster issued in 1854 telling people how to prevent being infected by cholera

THINK

1 According to Source F, how do you avoid getting cholera?

2 Do what extent does this agree with the ideas of John Snow?

3 What does Source F tell us about ideas of preventing disease in the nineteenth century?

4 Are they any different to earlier times?

5 What impact do you think the scientific method had on prevention of illness and disease in the eighteenth and nineteenth centuries?

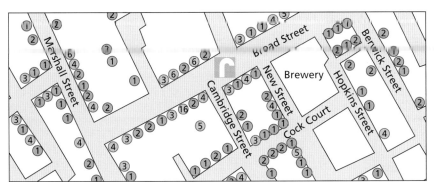

Pump
1 or 2 deaths from cholera
3 or more deaths from cholera

◀ Figure 2.1: A copy of part of Snow's map detailing deaths in the Broad Street area

The work of Edward Jenner and vaccination

The story of Dr Jenner is inspirational – an inspired guess, based on experiment and scientific method, produced a vaccine that protected people from one of the most deadly infectious diseases of the period. And yet Jenner was ridiculed as a country doctor and **vaccination** questioned as an effective method of controlling smallpox – an argument still reflected today in the debate about the utility of vaccination in preventing disease.

Smallpox

Smallpox is an acute contagious disease caused by the variola virus. It was one of the world's most devastating diseases. It was declared eradicated in 1980 following a global vaccination campaign led by the World Health Organization. But in earlier times it was an absolute killer. Between 30 and 60 per cent of those who caught smallpox died. Survivors carried the legacies of smallpox for life. Some were left blind; virtually all were disfigured by scars. Smallpox had long been endemic in Britain, and had been a feared killer since the seventeenth century. Major epidemics had killed at least 35,000 in 1796, and 42,000 between 1837 and 1840. The disease was no respecter of rank – Queen Mary died of smallpox in 1694. People thought it was caused by miasma, or 'bad air'.

Vaccination is not new – it dates from the eighteenth century. And **inoculation** has been used long before that, being widely used in the Far East for many centuries. Lady Mary Montagu came across it in Istanbul and introduced it to England in 1721. Her husband had been Ambassador to the **Ottoman Empire** and she had seen it used there. She had personally survived a smallpox outbreak that killed her brother and left her scarred. Basically, a mild form of smallpox was introduced into a scratch made between finger and thumb. The person being inoculated then developed a mild form of the disease, but became immune to the stronger version of smallpox. When smallpox broke out in England Lady Montagu had her children inoculated. And it worked.

A country doctor changes everything ...

Edward Jenner, a country doctor in Gloucestershire who had studied in London, heard the local gossips say that milkmaids who caught cowpox never seemed to catch smallpox. He reasoned that having cowpox must give them immunity from smallpox, but how could he prove it? He experimented on local people. He chose a nine-year-old boy, James Phipps, who had had neither cowpox nor smallpox. He injected him with pus from the sores of a milkmaid with cowpox. James developed cowpox. Later, when he had recovered, Jenner gave him a dose of smallpox. James was immune. Jenner had proved that an injection of cowpox stopped people catching smallpox. He knew it worked, but didn't know how! He submitted a paper to the **Royal Society** in 1797 but was told he needed more proof. So he carried out more experiments, including on his own 11-month-old son, all the time keeping detailed notes and records.

Finally, in 1798, Jenner published *An Inquiry into the Causes and Effects of the Variolæ Vaccinæ, or Cow-Pox*. He continued to work on vaccination and in 1802 was awarded £10,000 by the government for his work, and a further £20,000 in 1807 after the Royal College of Physicians confirmed how effective vaccination was.

What impact did vaccination have on smallpox?

Reaction to Jenner and his work was mixed. Those who charged up to £20 a time to inoculate patients saw that their livelihoods were threatened, and poured scorn on the whole idea of change. Many people felt it was wrong to inject cowpox into humans. Some argued that smallpox was God's punishment for living a sinful life and so we should not interfere, or limit the spread of the disease. Others thought it should be up to parents to decide whether their children should be treated or not. Yet others – some actually in favour of vaccination, others opposed to it – felt strongly it was not the government's job to interfere in such things. In 1840, partly as a result of the dreadful epidemic of 1837–40, vaccination was made free to all infants, and in 1852 it was made compulsory, but not strictly enforced. It seems strange that a **laissez-faire** government, which was reluctant to interfere in most aspects of life, would make vaccination compulsory. This, surely, tells us a lot about the fear of smallpox as a killer disease. There was an anti-vaccine league set up in England in 1866, to oppose the idea of compulsory vaccination (see Source H on page 42). It was not until 1871 that the government became much stricter – parents could be fined for not having their children vaccinated. Once the death rate fell dramatically the government in 1887 introduced the right for parents to refuse vaccination.

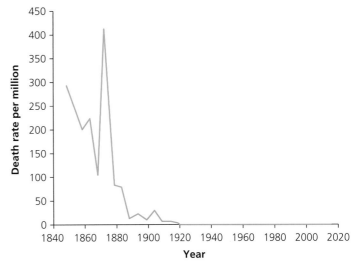

▲ Figure 2.2: Graph showing deaths from smallpox, 1848–1920

THINK

1 Why was smallpox so deadly?

2 What is the difference between inoculation and vaccination?

3 Is Source G pro-Jenner or anti-Jenner? How can you tell?

4 What part did chance, government, science and technology or the role of the individual play in the discovery of a cure for smallpox?

5 How does the work of Jenner help us understand the world of medicine in early modern Britain?

6 Is vaccination a 'success story'?

7 Why do you think the government made vaccination compulsory?

▼ Source G: Edward Jenner vaccinating patients against smallpox

The Cow-Pock — or — the Wonderful Effects of the New Inoculation!

The influence and spread of inoculation since 1700

In the twentieth century, what were once endemic diseases and childhood killers, such as polio, measles, diphtheria and whooping cough, had almost been eliminated through vaccination programmes. The World Health Organization has led the campaign to eliminate these diseases throughout the world. The last known case of smallpox was in Somalia in 1977 – quite a success story and all stemming from on the work of Edward Jenner in a small country town in Gloucestershire.

In England more and more vaccines have been introduced since the Second World War. Polio vaccine was introduced in 1955, measles in 1963, MMR (measles, mumps and rubella) in 1988 and Hepatitis B in 1994. If we are travelling abroad it is now common to receive anti-malaria and anti-yellow fever vaccinations. There are vaccinations for babies, for children, for young adults and for pregnant women. All these have had a profound impact on what were once killer diseases. The **infant mortality** rate has fallen dramatically – in 1800 it averaged over 150 per thousand, by 1900 this had risen to around 170 per thousand, whereas today it is between 4 and 5 deaths per thousand live births (see Figure 2.3). Much, but not all, of this fall is down to the effects of immunisation.

Yet the very success of immunisation has led to debate about whether or not government has the right to impose vaccinations on us.

MEN AND WOMEN OF THE TOWER HAMLETS,

And all who value Parental Liberty!
....
MR. THOMAS ERNEST WISE

Of 31 Clayhill Road, Bow

HAS BEEN IMPRISONED

for 10 days at the behest of the

VILE, FILTHY, VACCINATION LAW.
....
HE WILL BE

LIBERATED ON SATURDAY, SEPT. 27th.

Mr. WISE has been fighting a battle for freedom on behalf of
Thousands of parents.

****
It is intended to give Mr. WISE a warm welcome on his return home,
and to show him that We honour

Our First Vaccination Martyr.

▲ Source H: A poster from the 1870s

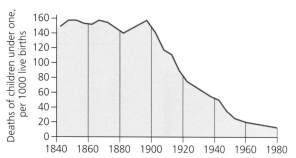

▲ Figure 2.3: The rate of infant mortaility (the death rate of children under one years old), 1840–1980

THINK

1 What does Figure 2.3 tell us about the following:
   ☐ infant mortality
   ☐ inoculation
   ☐ health
   ☐ prevention of disease?

2 Look at Source H.
   ☐ What did some Victorians think about vaccination?
   ☐ Why were they opposed to vaccination law?

3 Look at Source I (on page 43).
   ☐ Why is this author in favour of vaccination?
   ☐ How similar and how different are the ideas used in each of these sources?

The MMR debate

In 1998 Dr Wakefield published a paper in the *Lancet*, a medical journal in Britain, suggesting there was a clear link between the MMR routinely given to all young children and autism. It claimed that evidence from his small study showed that being vaccinated with the MMR vaccine led, in some cases, to the development of autism. Even though they were only preliminary results, unverified by any other researcher, the press made a huge story out of it, and the proportion of parents having their children vaccinated plummeted. To be successful 95 per cent of the target population must be vaccinated, otherwise there is a chance of someone with the disease passing it on to others, and an epidemic can break out.

Since then a fierce debate about vaccination has raged, both here in the UK and around the world.

> **Source I: Extract from the *Guardian*, 3 February 2015**
>
> *To the anti-vaxxers: please don't give measles to my tiny, helpless future baby.*
>
> *Herd immunity isn't about my individual hypothetical baby, or yours – it's about public health, investing in a collective. It's a testament to the idea that we can care about human life independent of self-interest. That empathy extends beyond our own children ...*

In effect, the argument is about choice – do I have the choice, as a parent, not to have my baby vaccinated? There is plenty of evidence that for some, about one per cent of children, vaccines produce a reaction. These are not usually very serious – the UK Vaccine Payment Fund, set up to pay compensation to those badly affected by vaccination, has paid out 20 times in the last ten years – but reactions can be serious. But if you put that against the decline, and in some cases, disappearance, of highly infectious diseases then most people think vaccination a good thing. Except, of course, if you think vaccination is wrong, or that vaccines are poison, or that they are used by big business to generate vast profits from unnecessary medicines. What is noticeable is that the UK had its first major outbreak of measles in 2012–13. Vaccination rates in the UK remain around 93 per cent – not enough to ensure immunity.

Dr Wakefield's study has since been repudiated by the medical world, and shown to be bad science. But the uncertainty it has caused led to many people distrusting all vaccines and the re-emergence of some diseases the World Health Organization had declared eliminated.

> **THINK** ?
> 1 What was Dr Wakefield arguing?
> 2 How carefully researched was his report?
> 3 What impact did his study have?
> 4 Do you think that the debate on inoculation is because the policy has been so successful that we no longer remember how deadly these diseases are?

The discovery of antibodies and developments in the field of bacteriology

As we have seen, both Edward Jenner and John Snow made massive strides in preventing disease without really being able to prove scientifically why their methods worked. All this changed with the work of Louis Pasteur and Robert Koch in the late nineteenth century.

Louis Pasteur, Robert Koch and germ theory

Louis Pasteur was a French scientist working in Paris. He discovered germ theory, and this changed medicine for ever. He proved that tiny organisms called bacteria caused many diseases and so to prevent disease all you had to do was kill the bacteria. Robert Koch, a German, took this work a step further as he began to identify the specific bacteria that caused specific diseases, thus making the science of bacteriology possible. Koch also realised that antibodies – a natural defence mechanism of the body against germs – could help to destroy bacteria and build up an immunity against the disease, thus keeping the body free from illness and disease. The discovery that each antibody worked specifically on only one bacteria was crucial to an understanding of how the body fought off disease. If you could introduce a weakened form of the disease into the body, as Jenner did with cowpox, then, when the deadly version of the disease attacked, the body would be able to resist. You can find out more about the work of Pasteur, Koch and his student Ehrlich in Chapter 4 (page 65).

▲ Source J: Louis Pasteur

▲ Source K: Robert Koch

THINK

1 How important is science in improving disease prevention?

2 Who played the bigger part in advancing preventative medicine, Pasteur or Koch?

FOCUS TASK REVISITED

1 As you worked through this chapter you will have built up a 'mind map' of attempts to prevent illness and disease. This should now help you decide if there are any links between the different sections of this chapter, and see if later attempts at prevention build on earlier ones. It is important that you use your 'mind map' to try to build up a 'Big Picture' of disease prevention across the whole period studied.

2 Use your mind map to work out *how effective* preventive efforts have been. When were they most effective? Least effective?

3 Finally, try to find links between your ideas about prevention of illness and disease and the 'causes of disease' cards you made for Chapter 1. Are there any obvious links you can make, or are they really two separate topics?

ACTIVITIES

1 Draw an annotated timeline, from AD500 to today, across the middle of a page, showing the attempts to prevent illness you have investigated in this chapter.

2 Place any attempts to prevent illness and disease that you think were successful *above* your timeline; and attempts to prevent illness and disease that you think were particularly unsuccessful *below* your timeline.

3 When, in your opinion, were attempts to prevent disease and illness *most* successful? Why?

TOPIC SUMMARY

- In the medieval period there were lots of suggestions on how to prevent illness and disease, but no one really knew how to do so.
- Living a decent Christian life was thought to be very important, as important as exercise and diet.
- As science developed, so scientific method came closer to identifying the best ways to prevent disease.
- Jenner and Snow came up with effective preventative measures, but were unsure why they worked.
- Pasteur and Koch made the real scientific breakthrough – all work since then has been based on their discoveries.
- Alchemists spent many hours searching for the key to eternal life, without finding it.
- King Edward III ordered the streets of London cleaned, thus making a link between dirt and disease.
- People could produce and sell anything, without restriction, claiming to be able to prevent disease.
- Some people still argue today about the effectiveness of vaccination.

Practice questions

1 Complete the sentences below with an accurate term:
   Apothecaries were medical ....
   Cholera was mainly spread by contaminated ....
   Vaccination against smallpox was pioneered by Edward ....
   The name commonly given to the vaccine against measles, mumps and rubella is ....
   (*For guidance, see page 119.*)

2 Study Source C (page 36), Source F (page 39) and Source G (page 41). Use these sources to identify one similarity and one difference in the prevention of illness and disease over time. (*For guidance, see page 120–121.*)

3 Describe the methods used by people during the medieval period to prevent catching a disease. (*For guidance, see page 123.*)

4 How effective was the development of vaccination in the prevention of illness and disease in the nineteenth and twentieth centuries? (*For guidance, see page 125.*)

3 Attempts to treat and cure illness and disease

This chapter focuses on the key question: How have attempts to treat illness and disease changed over time?

Throughout history, people have fallen ill, and doctors of various types and specialisms have attempted to cure them, perhaps not always successfully. Increasingly a scientific approach, based on observation, experimentation and measuring has led to new discoveries, medicines and techniques that have improved the chances of a successful cure, although some people today seem to prefer natural or alternative cures. This chapter looks at these changing attempts to treat and cure illness.

FOCUS TASK

As you work through this chapter, carefully make a note of each cure for an illness you come across and add it to your copy of the table opposite. The first one has been done for you. That way you will build up a detailed list of the different ways of treating illness mentioned. You will need the final two columns when you revisit the focus task at the end of this chapter.

Illness or disease	Cure		
Headache	Drink camomile tea and lie down		

Traditional treatments and remedies common in the medieval era

Herbal medicines

Herbs were widely used as remedies for a variety of ailments in the medieval period. Herbal medicines often contained ingredients such as honey and a mixture of other plants that we now know do help cure infections. Sometimes herbal treatments were written down in books called 'herbals' with pictures of the ingredients and explanations of the exact quantities of each ingredient and how to mix the potion. They included prayers to say while collecting the herbs to increase the effectiveness of the remedy. There were also guides as to when to pick the herbs – some recipes would only work if the ingredients were picked on the night of a full moon, or when the moon was waning, or similar. If picked at the wrong time this would mean the herbal remedy would not work. Herbal remedies were also often closely guarded family secrets, handed down through generations from mother to daughter.

Source A: A cure for headache, from an early fourteenth-century book from Venice

Drink warm camomile tea and then lie down on rosemary and lavender-scented pillows for fifteen minutes.

Source B: Advice from Rycharde Banckes, a late medieval herbalist

Gather leaves of rosemary and boyle them in fayre water and drinke that water for it is much worthe against all manner of evils in the body.

Source C: Instructions to prepare an ointment, from *The Knight With the Lion* by Helen Lynch, based on medieval French stories of King Arthur

Take equal amounts of radish, bishopwort, garlic, wormwood, helenium, cropleek and hollowleek. Pound them up, and boil them in butter with celandine and red nettle. Keep the mixture in a brass pot until it is a dark red colour. Strain it through a cloth and smear on the forehead or aching joints.

Source D: Bald's *Leechbook*, an Anglo-Saxon (nine or tenth century) cure for a stye in the eye

Take equal amounts of onion/leek and garlic, and pound them well together. Take equal amounts of wine and bull's gall and mix them with the onion and garlic. Put the mixture in a brass bowl and let it stand for nine nights, then strain it through a cloth. Then, about night-time, apply it to the eye with a feather.

Source E: A Welsh thirteenth-century cure for toothache

Take a candle of sheep' suet, some eringo (sea holly [Eryngium maritimum]) seed being mixed therewith, and burn it as near the tooth as possible, some cold water being held under the candle. The worms (destroying the tooth) will drop into the water, in order to escape from the heat of the candle.

Other common medieval remedies

Bleeding

The most favoured way to fight illness, and restore the balance of the four humours, was by bleeding. This was done either by 'cupping' (see Source F) or by using leeches (see page 48). Monastery records show some monks were bled up to eight times a year. Illness was said to be caused by the body creating too much blood so it was obvious that bleeding patients would restore their vitality. Purging was also used to rid the body of excess liquid and impurities.

Urine in diagnosis and prescription

Doctors had one other indispensable tool for diagnosing sickness and putting it right. Urine was a vital diagnostic tool. The physician would look carefully at the colour and compare it to a chart (see Source G). He might smell it and, in some circumstances, taste it to help him decide what was wrong with the patient. The remedy prescribed would then depend on the diagnosis. Again, many patients today still have to submit a urine sample as part of the process of deciding what is wrong with them.

Zodiac chart

Finally, no self-respecting physician would visit a patient without his most important tool of all – a zodiac chart (see Source H). Charts like this would tell a physician which parts of the body were linked to which **astrological** sign, and thus dictate what he might do to cure a patient – some things might work for an Aries, for example, but not for a Pisces. It might also tell him when was the best time to carry out his treatment, and even when to pick the herbs used in medicines – herbs picked at the wrong time of the moon's cycle, for example, might do more harm than good. It was a complicated business for physicians to decide what was causing an illness and how it might best be treated.

Other treatments

And of course there were still plenty of 'quacks' or unlicensed traders who roamed around the country, visiting out-of-the-way places and appearing at markets and fairs, offering all kinds of treatment and cures – some better than others.

▲ **Source F:** Bloodletting, from an illuminated medieval manuscript

▲ **Source G:** A urine chart used by physicians in the medieval period

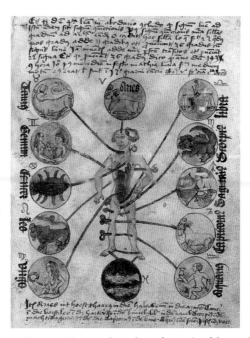

▲ **Source H:** A zodiac chart from the fifteenth century

> ### THINK ❓
>
> 1 Look at Sources A–E. Do you think any of these cures were effective? Rank them in order of how well you think they work. Explain the order you have chosen.
>
> 2 Would they do any harm?
>
> 3 How would medieval people learn about such cures?

THINK

1 The barber surgeon in Source I is cutting hair and his assistant is washing hair. How can you tell from the image that he is a surgeon too?

2 Do you think Source J is an accurate image of a patient using leeches? How can you tell?

3 The *Régime du corps*, written by Aldobrandino of Siena (probably in 1285),was the first French published medical text book. Does that make it a reliable source for us?

Barber-surgeons and the use of leeches

In the medieval period surgeons were mostly barber-surgeons, with little training or medical knowledge, save that gained by an apprenticeship and experience. You would find barber-surgeons in most towns. They would pull teeth, mend broken limbs, carry out bloodletting as well as cut your hair (see Source I). They would also carry out simple surgery. Sometimes they might combine their trade with that of apothecary, producing herbal medicines of various degrees of effectiveness. They might be the only medical professional available to many people, certainly to those who could not afford a physician.

The use of leeches

Leeches have been used in medicine for over 2500 years. They slowly suck blood, in a natural form of bloodletting. Their saliva contains a natural anti-coagulant that also anaesthetises the wound area, reducing pain from the bite of the leech. It was thought in medieval times that leeches only removed 'impure' blood from the body, leaving 'good' blood behind (see Source J). The use of leeches continued well beyond the medieval period. Indeed, demand for leeches in the nineteenth century was so high that they very nearly became extinct in the wild. They were used as an alternative to cupping and are still used in some procedures today.

▲ Source I: Engraving of a barber-surgeon by Jost Amman, 1568

▲ Source J: Patient being treated with leeches, from the French medical treatise *Régime du corps*, published in 1256

Common treatments in medieval Wales

The 'mediciner' in the laws of Hywel Dda

In the laws of Hywel Dda, the 'mediciner' (physician or healer) occupied an important place in the household of any medieval Welsh prince or lord. Through their herbal remedies they were expected to be experts who could treat the sick, repair broken bones and provide potions to alleviate illnesses. The laws even included a list of payments to be charged for particular treatments.

Dynion Hysbys (wise men)

Found in many parts of Wales during the medieval period, the Dyn Hysbys (wise man) fulfilled a special role in society. He was said to possess the power to break spells and undo the evil spread by witches to heal and safeguard people and animals. He used charms that consisted of a prayer or blessing together with a spell or magic word, and a reference to the signs of the zodiac. Written on a piece of paper, the charm was placed in a jar that was sealed and hidden in the building housing the sick animal. The owner was instructed not to remove the cork, for it was believed that the evil spirit troubling the animals would remain trapped in the jar for ever.

The physicians of Myddfai

Throughout the medieval period most illnesses were treated with herbal potions obtained from physicians. One family of such physicians lived in the village of Myddfai in Carmarthenshire, and are thought to have operated there from the thirteenth century through to the eighteenth century.

Rhiwallon Feddyg (Rhiwallon the Doctor) and his three sons, Cadwgan, Gruffudd and Einion lived in the parish of Myddfai in the thirteenth century. They were the court doctors to Rhys Gryg, the Lord of Dinefwr. They wrote down their cures and remedies which are today preserved in the ancient manuscript *Llyfr Coch Hergest* (*Red Book of Hergest*). Their entries gave instructions for diagnosis and prognosis of illnesses, as well as treatment by surgery, by herbal medicines, by bloodletting and by cauterising. Their medicines were made from herbs, animals and minerals collected from the fields and hedgerows around Myddfai. They would grind the herbs using a pestle and mortar, then add boiling water to make herbal drinks or mix them with plant oil to make ointments.

The Myddfai physicians used the stars to help prevent illness. They believed the movement of the planets dictated what patients should eat and drink each month of the year. In August, for example, patients were advised to eat plenty of broth (cawl) and vegetables, and to put white pepper in their broth. They were also advised to avoid drinking beer or mead during that month.

> **Source K:** A remedy for an infected wound taken from an account written by the physicians of Myddfai and recorded in the *Red Book of Hergest*, written in the mid-fourteenth century
>
> Take a black toad which is only able to crawl and beat it with a stick until it becomes angry and so that it swells until it dies. Then take it and put it in an earthenware cooking pot and close the lid on it so that the smoke cannot escape nor the air get into it. Burn the toad in the pot until it is ashes and put the ashes on the gangrene.

> **THINK** ?
> 1 Why do you think the Dyn Hysbys (wise man) occupied an important position in Welsh society during the medieval period?
> 2 Study Source K. How useful is the *Red Book of Hergest* to a historian studying how illness and disease was treated in Wales during medieval times?

The influence of curative wells in Wales

Since pagan times wells have been associated with supposed healing qualities. They were alleged to cure nearly all ills which afflicted the human body, from eye complaints to rheumatism, skin disorders, warts, lameness, fractures and sprains.

During the early Christian era many wells became associated with saints, such as Saint Teilo, Saint Dewi, Saint Beuno, Saint Gybi and Saint Mary, and across the principality over 200 chapels and churches were built at or near holy wells (see Table 3.1). Many wells became the focus of pilgrimages, the most famous being that of Ffynnon Gwenfrewi at Holywell in Flintshire (see focus box on the right).

For complaints to do with the eyes, bathing the infected eye with water from the well was considered to be effective, while for ailments such as rheumatism and skin disorders, immersion into the well itself was considered necessary. At most wells, offerings were made to the saint and this usually involved throwing bent pins, buckles or coins into the water. A common ritual across North Wales for getting rid of warts involved finding a piece of sheep's wool on the way to the well, pricking the wart with a pin and then rubbing the wart with the wool. The pin then had to be bent and thrown into the well. The wool had to be placed on the first whitethorn tree the visitor saw on their way home. It was believed that the wind would disintegrate the wool on the tree, causing the warts to break up and vanish.

Anglesey	9
Caernarvonshire	22
Denbighshire	15
Flintshire	10
Montgomeryshire	8
Merionethshire	14
Breckonshire	8
Radnorshire	4
Cardiganshire	14
Pembrokeshire	33
Carmarthenshire	14
Glamorganshire	24
Monmouthshire	7

▲ **Table 3.1:** The number of chapels and churches built at or near holy wells across Wales during the early Christian period

> **THINK** **?**
>
> 1 What does Table 3.1 and Source L suggest about the importance of wells in the treatment of illness and disease during medieval times?
>
> 2 Why did the well at Holywell develop into such an important place of pilgrimage?

THE LEGEND OF SAINT WINEFRIDE, HOLYWELL

It is believed that Winefride lived in Holywell during the 620s. Around that time she was visited by a prince named Caradoc who came from Penarlag (Hawarden) and he tried to seduce her. She resisted his advances and fled towards the nearby church of Saint Beuno where a service was being held. In anger, Caradoc drew his sword and cut off Winefride's head. At this moment the priest Beuno came out of the church and went to Winefride's aid. While praying he replaced her head on her body and restored her to life. On that spot a great spring erupted (the site of the present well). The ground then opened and swallowed up Caradoc. Winefride lived out the rest of her life as a nun, eventually moving to Gwytherin where she became abbess and it was there that she died around 660.

Over the coming centuries, a chapel was built over the well and it became a major centre of pilgrimage. Pilgrims flocked to the holy waters in the belief that it would cure them of their ills, which caused the well to become one of the Seven Wonders of Wales (see Source L).

▲ **Source L:** Ffynnon Gwenfrewi, the well of Saint Winefride at Holywell

Treatments in the early modern period

A lot of traditional treatments and remedies from the medieval era continued to be used in the early modern period but there were also some new developments.

'Ladies of the manor', such as Lady Johanna St John, played a role in healing in this period. As well as running a large household they would compile recipe books of cures (see Source M for one of her recipes).

> **Source M: Lady Johanna St John's cure for a bleeding nose**
> *A sheet of white paper, wett it in vinegar and dry it in an oven – when it is dry, wett it again and dry it as before, so doing 3 times, then make it into a powder and snuff up some of it into the nose, often, as well, when it does, and when it bleeds.*

During the early modern period some physicians wrote in English rather than Latin, in an attempt to help more people. Herbs were also used in a more coherent way than was previously the case by incorporating the doctrine of signatures (the idea that if a plant looked like a part of the body it could be used to treat that part of the body when it was ill) as well as astronomy.

New ingredients were also appearing from around the world. Rhubarb was hailed as a wonder-drug when it was first introduced from Asia. Tobacco was brought from North America by Walter Raleigh and, despite James I writing a famous book about the evils of tobacco, it quickly found many uses in herbal remedies. In fact there is a record of some schoolboys at Eton being beaten for refusing to smoke tobacco. Apparently smoking a pipe was regarded as an excellent way to keep the plague at bay!

The scientific approach to medicine, which involved observation, experiment and recording results, brought not just new ingredients for herbal medicines but new ideas on how to deal with disease too. New studies of mental illness, often referred to as 'melancholy', and other disciplines such as midwifery were also conducted during this period. Some individuals began to identify lifestyle issues such as taking fresh air and improving your diet as ways of preventing illness, rather than relying on doctors to cure them once they became ill.

> **THINK** ?
> 1 When would you rather have been ill – the medieval or early modern period?
> 2 Which treatments do you think were more effective, those of the medieval or early modern period? Why?

James Simpson and the development of anaesthetics

Surgery was accompanied by pain. Many surgeons believed patients *should* experience pain, as it helped them appreciate the efforts being made on their behalf. Copious amounts of alcohol or opium was often used to try to subdue a patient and thus make an operation easier to perform, although getting the right dose was very tricky. Sir Humphrey Davy was one of the first to use nitrous oxide, or laughing gas as we know it (see Source L). He invited his friends to inhale the gas from oiled silk bags. Quickly the gas was used as an anaesthetic to relieve pain during operations, but it was difficult to control the dose. In 1846 Robert Liston successfully amputated a leg using ether as an anaesthetic, copying his ideas from an American dentist, although one drawback of this was that sometimes the patient woke up in the middle of the operation!

In 1847 the Scottish scientist James Simpson (1811–70) used chloroform, after experimenting on himself and his friends, to reduce pain in childbirth. Chloroform induces dizziness, sleepiness and unconsciousness in patients, and needs to be carefully administered. Not surprisingly there was opposition in many quarters to the use of these painkillers, but this was partly overcome in 1853 when Queen Victoria used chloroform while having a baby. If it was good enough for the queen then it was good enough for anybody. All these painkillers had to be inhaled as a general anaesthetic in order to work. Finally, in the 1850s, coca leaves from South America were used to produce cocaine that could be used as a local anaesthetic – on the first occasion as drops in the eye. The use of cocaine rapidly spread, especially once it could be produced chemically after 1891. By the end of the century operations no longer had to be painful.

Anaesthetics did not necessarily make operations safer. As we have already seen, it was difficult to get the dose right with early painkillers. Also, surgeons tried more difficult operations because they could take longer to operate. But unfortunately, there was still no control over infection. Some surgeons had higher mortality rates using anaesthetics than before, so in the 1870s some stopped using chloroform altogether.

THINK ?

1 Why was pain seen to be a 'good thing' by surgeons?

2 To what extent does Source N show that anaesthetics did not necessarily make operations safer?

3 What part did science play in developing effective anaesthetics?

4 Why was it so difficult to get the dose right in early anaesthetics?

5 Humphrey Davy used nitrous oxide as a 'recreational drug', so why did the government recently (May 2016) ban the sale of nitrous oxide?

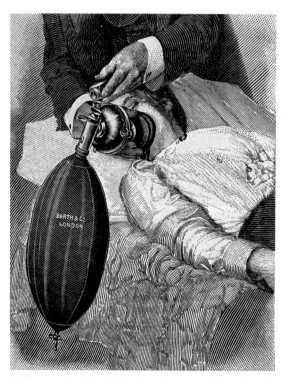

▲ **Source N:** Administering nitrous oxide and ether in the 1840s, as shown in a 1922 book on advances in medicine

▲ James Simpson, photograph by Brigham

Joseph Lister and the use of antiseptics in the later nineteenth century

If we cut or graze ourselves today the first thing we do is wash the cut, then apply some antiseptic cream or a plaster. The idea is to prevent dirt getting into the wound, and to prevent infection. It is widely known that dirt and infection can kill. But all this is relatively recent. The biggest killer after surgery was sepsis, otherwise known as hospital **gangrene**, an infection caught during or after an operation. Surgeons completely opposed the idea that they themselves spread infection, through dirty clothes and **unsterile** equipment.

Ignaz Semmelweis was the pioneer in antiseptics in 1847. He was in charge of the maternity ward at Vienna General Hospital in Austria. He dramatically reduced the death rate on his maternity ward from around 35 per cent to less than 1 per cent by insisting that doctors wash their hands in calcium chloride solution before treating their patients. Despite publishing his results, very few other hospitals introduced the procedure.

Joseph Lister

Joseph Lister (1827–1912) was an English surgeon who, perhaps more than anybody, improved the chances of surviving surgery. After Pasteur published his germ theory (see page 65) Joseph Lister used an operating room sterilised with carbolic acid. He based his ideas on experiments he carried out on frogs. Frogs, as cold-blooded amphibians, whose blood flowed more slowly, could be observed more clearly. Lister could see the impact of the changes he was introducing. His surgical instruments were sterilised with carbolic acid too. He also soaked the wound from time to time with carbolic acid, and used dressings sterilised in exactly the same way. Doing this he managed to reduce the mortality rate in his operations from 46 per cent to 15 per cent in only three years. In 1871 he invented a machine that sprayed carbolic acid over the entire room, surgeon, patient, assistants, everything. Others copied his methods and Lister became known as the 'Father of Antiseptic Surgery'.

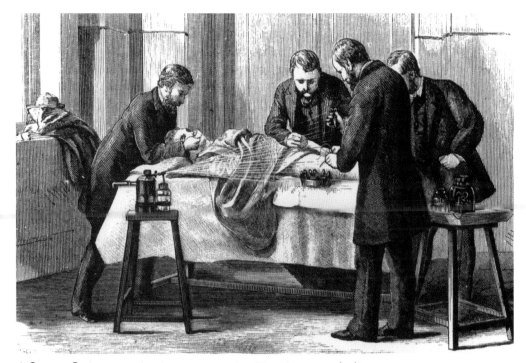

▲ Source O: An operation in progress using Lister's new carbolic spray

> **THINK ?**
>
> 1 Look at Source O. What would it be like for (a) the patient, and (b) the medical staff, using this equipment?
>
> 2 In what ways is this an improvement on what went on before Lister and antiseptic surgery?

Aseptic surgery: a real change at last?

Further improvements were made later in the century with the development of aseptic surgery. This followed on from the work of Robert Koch who discovered in 1878 that most disease was spread not by air but by contact with an infected surface. This led on to attempts to create a germ-free environment in which to carry out operations as a way of avoiding spreading infection.

In 1881 Charles Chamberland, a French biologist, invented a steam steriliser for medical instruments. He discovered that heating them in water at 140°C for 20 minutes completely sterilised them, making surgery much safer. This was the start of developing much simpler, less ornate and easier ways to sterilise tools for operations. As you might expect, few surgeons initially adopted this. The next step was by Gustav Neuber, a German surgeon in Kiel, who is recognised as having the first sterile operating theatre. He insisted on thorough scrubbing before staff entered the theatre; even the air in the room was sterilised. He published a paper on the process and his results in 1886 and this quickly set the standard for others to follow.

Surgical clothing

The final part of the battle against infection was the very gradual adoption of protective clothing – William Halsted in America started his team wearing surgical gloves because one of the nurses developed an allergic reaction on her hand to the carbolic spray they were using. He asked the Goodyear Rubber Company to make special thin rubber gloves for her to use. Berkeley Moyniham, a respected British surgeon working in Leeds, became the first in Britain to wear gloves for an operation, and later made a point of always changing his clothes for surgical gowns before entering an operating theatre. He was regarded by most surgeons as an oddity for doing so. In fact on one occasion his wife was presented with a bouquet made out of old rubber gloves.

Source P: Berkeley Moyniham recalls his days as a student in Leeds in the 1880s

The surgeon arrived and threw off his jacket to avoid getting blood or pus on it. He rolled up his shirt sleeves and, in the corridor to the operation room, took an ancient frock from a cupboard; it bore signs of a chequered past, and was utterly stiff with old blood. One of these coats was worn with special pride, indeed joy, as it had belonged to a retired member of staff. The cuffs were rolled up to only just above the wrists, and the hands were washed in a sink. Once clean they were rinsed in carbolic-acid solution.

THINK

1 What is the difference between antiseptic surgery and aseptic surgery?

2 Which in your opinion had the greater impact?

3 How had these new methods altered the approach of the surgeon training students at Leeds in the 1880s?

4 Consider Source P.
   a) What impact has the move to antiseptic and aseptic surgery had on this surgeon?
   b) What example is he setting his students?
   c) This source was written down many years after the events it describes – does that affect its utility?

Twentieth-century developments

Marie Curie and the development of radiation

Marie Curie has been described as the most famous female scientist of all time (see Source Q). She won the Nobel Prize in 1903 *and* in 1911. She is the only person to have won a Nobel Prize in both physics and chemistry, and was the first woman to win a Nobel Prize for science.

Marie Curie was born in Poland, and began work as a governess, as her father could not afford to pay for university. She was subsequently invited to live with her sister in Paris and was thus able eventually to attended university. She and her husband were the first to discover and isolate radium and polonium. These radioactive elements played a key role in destroying tissue, and thus opened up a way of treating cancer. Despite her husband being killed in a road accident in 1906, Marie continued to work – her 1911 Nobel Prize was for discovering a means to measure radiation. She also played a leading role in developing mobile X-ray units during the First World War, which could be used nearer the front line and thus making diagnosis and treatment of injured soldiers quicker and easier. She died in 1934, aged 67, from diseases brought on by excessive exposure to radiation.

> **Source Q: Extract from an obituary for Marie Curie, *New York Times*, 1934**
>
> *Few persons contributed more to the general welfare of mankind and to the advancement of science than the modest, self-effacing woman whom the world knew as Mme. Curie. Her epoch-making discoveries of polonium and radium, the subsequent honors that were bestowed upon her – she was the only person to receive two Nobel prizes – and the fortunes that could have been hers had she wanted them did not change her mode of life. She remained a worker in the cause of science, preferring her laboratory to a great social place in the sun.*

▲ Source R: Marie Curie in her laboratory

> **THINK** ❓
>
> 1 How useful is Source Q in helping us understand Marie Curie's role in improving treatments of disease?
>
> 2 Look at Source R. What impression of Marie Curie and her work do you get from this image? Do you think it was posed? How useful is it to us in studying her work?

The roles of Fleming, Florey and Chain regarding antibiotics

Penicillin had been discovered in the nineteenth century. Indeed, Lister had used it once to treat infection in a wound, but had not published his notes. During the First World War Alexander Fleming observed that antiseptics seemed unable to prevent infection, especially in deep wounds. He decided to try to find something that would kill the microbes that caused infection. One of the most dangerous was staphylococci, which caused **septicaemia**. In 1928, on returning from holiday, he noticed a mould – penicillin – that had grown on one of his Petri dishes. He also noticed that the staphylococci bacteria around the mould had been killed off. That was the start of the story of penicillin. He called it an antibiotic, meaning 'destructive of life'. Fleming published his results in 1929, but could not raise enough funds to develop the drug.

In 1937 Howard Florey and Ernst Chain, working at Oxford University, began to research penicillin after reading an article by Fleming. They overcame the difficulties of producing enough of the drug. They experimented first on mice, in 1940, and then on humans, in 1941. Their first trial, a policeman badly infected after being scratched by a rose bush, died after five days when their stock of the drug ran out, but the trial proved how effective penicillin was.

The Second World War provided a huge incentive to the development of the drug and in 1943 it was used for the first time on Allied troops in North Africa, with great success. America and Britain jointly produced huge quantities of penicillin and without doubt it saved many lives in 1944 and 1945. After the war it was widely used to treat many illnesses such as bronchitis, impetigo, pneumonia, tonsillitis, syphilis, meningitis, boils, abscesses and many other kinds of wounds. Fleming, Chain and Florey received the Nobel Prize for Medicine in 1945. Other antibiotics followed, such as streptomycin in 1944; tetracycline in 1953; and mitomycin in 1956.

ALEXANDER FLEMING, 1881–1955

- Trained as a doctor and served in the Army Medical Corps during the First World War.
- He became professor of his medical school in 1928 and published many papers on bacteriology, immunology and chemotherapy.
- He was knighted for his work in 1944.
- He was jointly awarded the Nobel Prize in 1945 for his work on penicillin.

THINK **?**

1 What part did chance play in the discovery of penicillin?

2 What part did war play in the development of penicillin?

3 Who, in your opinion, deserves the title, 'Father of Penicillin'? Why?

4 What does Source S tell us about the chances of wounded soldiers recovering (a) during the Second World War, and (b) during the First World War?

▲ Source S: An advert for penicillin, 1945

Dr Christian Barnard and transplant surgery

The earlier part of this chapter will have shown you that there have been huge changes in the way surgery is carried out, and in its success rates. There have also been major changes in the *types* of surgery undertaken. The year 1952 saw the first kidney transplant. In 1961 the first British implanted heart pacemaker – an electrical device that keeps the heart pumping blood around the body – was developed, along with heart bypass surgery. In 1967 the world's first heart transplant operation was undertaken in Cape Town, South Africa, by Dr Christian Barnard. His patient lived for 18 days. There were two main problems – the availability of replacement organs (still a major problem today) and rejection of the transplant. This has been largely solved by the development of immunosupressive drugs, such as cyclosporine, which help the body accept the replacement organ. Now, transplants are routine with 181 heart transplants having taken place in England in 2014 alone.

Hip replacements (replacing worn-out joints with new artificial ones) were introduced in 1972, bringing mobility to many who previously had found walking difficult. Out of date? Keyhole surgery is now commonplace, reducing the intrusiveness of operating on someone. There are even robotic operation systems licensed in the USA. Mortality rates from operations are carefully monitored and there are even 'league tables' for hospitals and surgeons so patients can choose the 'best' place for their treatment.

Modern advances in cancer treatment and surgery

Following on from the pioneering work of Marie Curie, throughout much of the twentieth century radiation therapy has been used to treat cancerous cells, becoming more and more refined and easier to target as technology has improved the technique. This has been supplemented by chemotherapy, the use of powerful drugs to kill cancerous cells. This has become more widespread since the Second World War and is often used for cancerous cells that are out of reach of surgery. Encouraging results have followed from a combination of surgery or radiation therapy and chemotherapy. Cancer is still a major killer, but more and more types of cancer are either being cured or controlled by these treatments. The key to success is often early diagnosis.

Finally, surgery is also used to remove cancerous growths. Mastectomy (removal of a woman's breast) or lung transplants are perhaps the most common forms of surgery used today to fight cancer. Surgery is always viewed as something of a gamble, as it is quite common for the cancer to return even after successful surgery to remove the infected tissue. In earlier times surgery was often required to find out if a patient had cancer. Now, with scanning techniques and fibre-optic micro cameras, it is possible to 'see' inside a patient's body without major surgery, thus reducing the impact of diagnosis.

ACTIVITY

Working with a partner, prepare a debate to argue which of the advances in surgery in the twentieth century mentioned on this page had the biggest impact on illness and disease.

THINK

1 Why was it so difficult at first to successfully transplant organs?
2 How have these difficulties been overcome?
3 It is ethical to use the body parts of one person to keep another person alive?

Alternative treatments: what if you could not afford to see the doctor?

We have seen throughout this book that many people either *chose not* to visit a medical professional, or *could not* afford to. They relied on family remedies, or the local 'wise woman' to treat them. This hadn't changed for the first half of the twentieth century at least, as Source T shows.

A growing belief in alternative medicine

Controversies like the thalidomide case, where a medicine prescribed for morning sickness and nausea in pregnant women caused babies to be born with missing limbs, made some people distrust orthodox medicine, and there has been a huge increase in interest in what became known as alternative or holistic medicine. Treatments such as hydrotherapy, aromatherapy, hypnotherapy and acupuncture became popular in some quarters. Many of them were based on old, traditional treatments using herbs and 'pure' treatments designed to work in harmony with the body, rather than as a chemical barrage against illness. Nearly every high street now includes a health food shop where a wide range of alternative herbal remedies are freely available to buy. Acupuncture, for example, is a traditional Chinese method of treating illness by sticking needles into various parts of the body and tapping into the natural flows of energy around the body. Prince Charles has long been a supporter of homeopathy, claiming, in a speech to the World Health Organization in Geneva in 2006, that it is 'rooted in ancient traditions that intuitively understood the need to maintain balance and harmony with our minds, bodies and the natural world'.

Not everyone agrees. The British Medical Association has described homeopathy as 'witchcraft' and the government's chief scientific adviser dismissed it as 'nonsense'. The evidence appears conflicting, but nevertheless alternative medicine has a strong hold on many people who dislike the idea of filling one's body with chemicals.

> **Source T:** From an interview with Kathleen Davys, who lived in Birmingham. She was one of 13 children. The local doctor charged sixpence a visit – and that was before paying for any treatment or medicine
>
> *Headaches, we had vinegar and brown paper, for whooping cough we had camphorated oil rubbed on our chests, or goose fat. For mumps we had stockings round our throats and for measles we had tea stewed in the teapot by the fire – all different kinds of home cures. They thought they were better than going to the doctor's. Well, they couldn't afford the doctor because sixpence in those days was like looking at a £5 note today.*

ACTIVITY ?

Discuss with an older relative about home cures, or do some research into home remedies to find out what people did in the recent past.

THINK ?

1 You might remember the nursery rhyme 'Jack and Jill'. Jack went to bed to mend his head with vinegar and brown paper. Does this mean nursery rhymes can be a useful source of evidence for knowledge about medicine?

2 What are the similarities between Figure 3.1 and the Ancient Greek theory of the four humours?

Holistic Medicine – Healing the Total Person

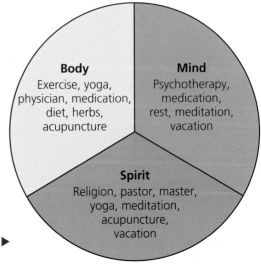

Figure 3.1: How one organisation promotes ▶ holistic medicine

FOCUS TASK REVISITED

1 Having worked through this chapter carefully you should now have a note of each cure for an illness you have come across, in your copy of the table below.

Illness or disease	Cure	Effectiveness at the time	Effectiveness today
Headache	Drink camomile tea and lie down	5	5

2 Fill in the final two columns, giving the cure a rating for effectiveness (1 = low, 5 = high), both for how people at the time thought of it as a cure, and how you, today, rank it as a cure.

3 What can you deduce about attempts to treat and cure illness and disease from your completed table?

4 Now you have explored causes of illness, attempts at prevention and attempts to cure illness, when do you think was the best time to be ill? Why?

ACTIVITIES

1 Draw a spider diagram showing attempts to treat and cure illness. You have your table from the focus task, which should now list all the illnesses and cures you have come across in this chapter.

2 How do they link together? Is there a direct link between medieval herbalists and alternative medicine today? Or between the more scientific approach of the early modern period and the twentieth century? And how are you going to show these links? Your diagram might look something like this:

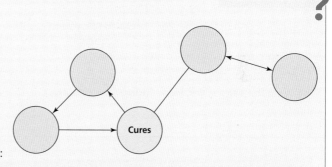

TOPIC SUMMARY

- Some early herbal treatments were surprisingly effective.
- The scientific approach, based on observation, experimentation and measuring, ushered in great changes to the treatment of disease.
- The effective use of anaesthetics and antiseptic made surviving surgery much more likely.
- Technology and discoveries have transformed treatment of disease in the twentieth century.
- Some people prefer to rely on non-invasive 'natural' medicine to treat illnesses.
- Apothecaries and barber-surgeons were surprisingly effective at treating some illnesses and diseases.
- Great efforts were made to make surgery and surgeons cleaner – although not all surgeons appreciated this.
- Transplants are now increasingly common, and very successful ways to treat disease.
- However, many changes only helped people if they could afford to visit the doctor.
- Some diseases have been conquered, but others remain a problem for society.

Practice questions

1 Complete the sentences below with an accurate term:

A famous family of Welsh doctors during the medieval period were the physicians of ....

Medieval doctors often based their diagnosis on the chart of the ....

The development of radiation was pioneered by Marie ....

Dr Christian Barnard is best remembered for .... surgery.

(*For guidance, see page 119.*)

2 Study Source F (page *47*), Source I (page *48*) and Source O (page *53*). Use these sources to identify one similarity and one difference in the treatment of illness and disease over time. (*For guidance, see page 120–121.*)

3 Describe the development and use of antiseptics in the nineteenth century. (*For guidance, see page 123.*)

4 Explain why the development of antibiotics was important in the cure of illness and disease in the twentieth century. (*For guidance, see page 124.*)

4 Advances in medical knowledge

This chapter focuses on the key question: How much progress has been made in medical knowledge over time?

It is easy to assume that medical knowledge in medieval times was limited, yet there is plenty of evidence of successful medical treatment, if you had access to a doctor, even from the Stone Age. It was perhaps the Renaissance, and the later arrival of scientific method, that really changed our understanding of illness and made significant advances in medical knowledge, something that continues apace today. This chapter explores many of the 'turning points' in the growth of medical knowledge.

FOCUS TASK

For each section of this chapter, we would like you to decide what progress has been made in medical knowledge, and then to try to measure 'how much'. Each section will have a card like this:

Complete the card as you work through the section.

Breakthrough:	To what extent [1–5]
Galen	....
....	....
....	....

Common medical ideas in the medieval period

Where did medieval ideas about health come from? People have always known how to look after themselves. There is clear evidence of successful operations carried out with flint tools in the Stone Age. Archaeological evidence showed that some of these patients survived. The Indus Valley civilisation was well aware of the importance of clean running water and sewers. There is even a structure identified as a huge Public Bath house in Mohen Daro, dating from around 2500BC. Pharaohs in Ancient Egypt had their court physicians, and we know about some of their medical practices from papyrus records recovered from tombs. The Greeks had asclepions, or places of healing, that were temples to Asclepius, the god of healing. The Romans went to great lengths to bring fresh water to their towns and cities. Their bath-houses and underfloor heating can be found in most Roman towns, for example, Isca in Caerleon. Bald's *Leechbook* is an Anglo-Saxon medical text full of remedies and medicines, some of which modern medical research has shown worked.

Yet much of this medical knowledge seems to have been 'lost' during the so-called 'Dark Ages,' after the Romans left. Muslim writers, such as Ibn Sīnā, played a very important role in saving much of this lost knowledge, translating the works of Ancient Greece and Rome into Arabic, that eventually passed on to Western Europe. At this time there is no doubt that Arabic medicine was much in advance of that in Western Europe.

THINK ?

What, according to Source A, were the main differences between Muslim and European medicine?

Source A: An account written by a Muslim doctor Usama ibn Munqidh, c.1175

*They brought to me a knight with a sore on his leg; and a woman who was feeble-minded. To the knight I applied a small **poultice**; and the woman I put on diet to turn her humour wet. Then a French doctor came and said, 'This man knows nothing about treating them.' He then said, 'Bring me a sharp axe.' Then the doctor laid the leg of the knight on a block of wood and told a man to cut off the leg with the axe, upon which the marrow flowed out and the patient died on the spot. He then examined the woman and said, 'There is a devil in her head.' He therefore took a razor, made a deep cross-shaped cut on her head, peeled away the skin until the bone of the skull was exposed, and rubbed it with salt. The woman also died instantly.*

Hippocrates, Galen and the four humours

Perhaps two men, more than any others, contributed to the Western view of medicine at this time. These were Hippocrates and Galen. We have already come across Hippocrates, 'the father of modern medicine', in Chapter 2. New doctors around the world still take the Hippocratic Oath when they start to practise. Altogether there are around 60 texts remaining that are attributed to Hippocrates, although many may have been written by his followers.

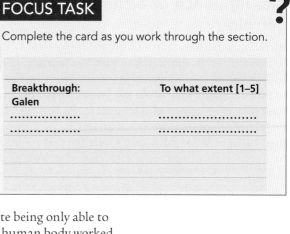

Galen was born in what is now Turkey in AD130. He studied medicine in Egypt before moving to Rome. He followed the ideas of Hippocrates, but was able to take them further. Although prevented from practising on people, he believed dissection was the best way to discover the secret workings of the human body. Despite being only able to dissect animals, he developed a better practical knowledge of how the human body worked. Three years working as a doctor in a gladiator school gave him plenty of opportunity to further improve his knowledge and techniques. Galen also placed great emphasis on listening to a patient's pulse as a diagnostic tool – a technique still widely used today.

Galen's work arrived in Europe via Islamic texts and beliefs. Greek translations were made in Salerno, in Italy (the first medical university dating from around AD900), and rapidly became accepted as university medical texts. Church leaders looked carefully at Galen's works and decided that they fitted with Christian ideas because throughout he referred to 'the Creator'. Doctors believed his ideas were correct and that it was nearly impossible to improve his work. As Salerno was a common stopping-off point en route to the Holy Land, Galen's ideas rapidly spread throughout Europe and became accepted as medical orthodoxy.

The four humours

Key to both Hippocrates and Galen's medical knowledge was the theory of the **four humours**. Hippocrates wrote:

> The human body contains blood, phlegm, yellow bile and black bile. These are the things that make up its constitution and cause its pains and health. Health is primarily that state in which these constituent substances are in the correct proportion to each other, both in strength and quantity, and are well mixed. Pain occurs when one of the substances presents either a deficiency or an excess, or is separated in the body and not mixed with others.

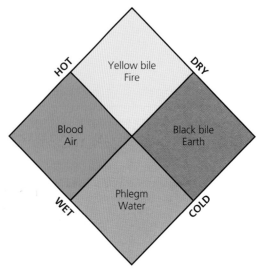

▲ Figure 4.1: The four humours

So to remain healthy a body needed to keep the four humours in balance. As you can see from Figure 4.1, some humours are 'hot' and therefore create sweating illnesses; and some humours are 'cold', creating illnesses such as melancholia.

Different foods and different seasons could affect the humours, so it was important to do all things in moderation to keep the body in balance. During the medieval period much of the medical knowledge was based on the idea of the four humours and keeping them in balance. It was only later, during the Renaissance, that people began to challenge the work of Galen, and develop new medical knowledge.

The influence of alchemy and astrology

Alchemy, as we have seen in Chapter 2, was closely linked to science, and to the search to turn base metals such as lead into gold. Alchemists also searched for the 'Elixir of Life' so that people could live forever. Many of them were monks or priests who were often the best educated people. Much of their work had an impact on science and medical knowledge. Alchemists were the first to produce hydrochloric acid and nitric acid; they identified new elements such as antimony and arsenic, and paved the way for the new science of chemistry. Some of the equipment they developed is still in use today.

Doctors believed that the movement of the stars influenced the personalities of people and the inner workings of the human body. Hence, to be successful, you needed to study the stars. By the end of the 1500s, physicians in many countries of Europe were required by law to calculate the position of the moon before carrying out complicated medical procedures, such as surgery or bleeding. Each part of the body was associated with an astrological sign. Medicines could only be effective if the plants were collected at the right cycle of the moon. Medicines and surgery were only safe at the correct time of the month (see Source B).

> **Source B: An extract from the work of Henri de Mondeville, a thirteenth-century French surgeon, quoted in Nathan Belofsky, *Strange Medicine***
>
> *The humours are agitated at that time [a full moon]. The brain waxes in the skull as the water raises in the river ... thus the membranes of the skull rise up and consequently come nearer to the skull, so that they could be more easily damaged by surgical instruments.*

▲ Source C: From a medieval manuscript showing two monks in their laboratory

The role of the church in developing medical knowledge

The church was central to most peoples' lives in medieval times, so its attitude to medicine would have a profound influence on medical progress and developments. Most importantly, the church encouraged people to pray for deliverance from illness, for forgiveness of their sins, and to prepare for the afterlife. (Remember, most surgery was extremely dangerous.) As well as prayer, offerings could buy **indulgences**, and going on a pilgrimage to a holy shrine might bring about a cure. Pilgrims would often leave a miniature copy of the infected body part at the shrine, and hope that prayer and belief would indeed bring about a cure.

The church set up university schools of medicine throughout Europe where physicians could be trained using the texts of Hippocrates and Galen. It might take ten years to train as a physician. In fact it was often through these university schools and in monasteries that the old texts were hand copied by monks and thus survived. Many of them arrived in the West in Arabic translation (see page 60). Most studies of dissection were still based on Galen's writings and his work on dissection was based on working on animals. Therefore the church's insistence on using Galen and his works widely limited progress in understanding the workings of the human body. Scientists who tried to insist on scientific method and observation often ran into difficulty. Roger Bacon, a Franciscan monk and lecturer at Oxford University, was arrested around 1277 for spreading anti-church views.

> **THINK** ?
> 1 Do you think astrology and alchemy helped or hindered advances in medical knowledge at the time?
> 2 Why were science and alchemy so closely linked in medieval times?
> 3 How did the church help advances in medical knowledge?
> 4 Look at Source C. What do you think these monks might be doing? Do you think the artist has been into a laboratory? How can you tell?
> 5 How useful is Source C in helping us understand the part played by (a) alchemy and (b) the church in advances in medical knowledge?

The influence of the medical work of Vesalius, Paré and Harvey in the sixteenth and seventeenth centuries

The Renaissance and Galen

Initially, the **Renaissance** led to a revival of all things ancient. Many of Galen's works were re-translated from Arabic into Greek and Latin. Texts were compared and efforts made to get back to the original meaning. By 1525 his complete works had been published in Greek and translations into Latin soon followed. Galen was regarded as the font of all medical knowledge, to be slavishly copied.

Galen's position was soon to be challenged. The very essence of the Renaissance was to question things. And the more artists and surgeons studied anatomy, and the more humans they dissected, the more they began to notice discrepancies between what Galen said and what they were discovering for themselves. The initial reaction was that Galen was right and the current anatomists were wrong. But gradually enough opinion grew to successfully challenge Galen and cast doubts on his observations. Once challenged on anatomy, other challenges followed. The medical world seemed to be split into two, depending on how strongly you supported Galen. It also seemed to split into two between physicians, who mostly learned from texts and lectures and thus largely supported Galen's ideas; and surgeons, who were exploring the human body on a daily basis and were learning by experimenting and experience. Scientific discovery played a part in this as new tools, like the microscope, allowed both scientists and medical men to look at things in ever more detail. But so too did William Caxton and his printing press, which allowed the much more rapid spread of ideas from 1476 onwards.

Vesalius and anatomy

Andreas Vesalius (1514–64) was born in Brussels but studied medicine in Paris and Padua in Italy. He was appointed professor of surgery and anatomy in Padua. Perhaps most importantly he carried out his own dissections and firmly believed anatomy was the key to understanding how the human body worked. In 1543 he published *De humani corporis fabrica libri septem*, which completely changed attitudes to medicine. Vesalius challenged Galen's works on human anatomy, and developed much more accurate views of the inside of the human body by, unlike Galen, looking at and dissecting humans rather than animals. His work was very influential for early modern medicine both because it gave doctors more detailed knowledge of human anatomy and because it encouraged them to investigate critically the claims of ancient medical authorities.

FOCUS TASK ?

Complete the card as you work through the section.

Breakthrough: Vesalius	To what extent [1–5]
....	....
....	....

Paré and treating wounds

Ambroise Paré (1510–90) began his medical work as an apprentice to his elder brother, a barber-surgeon. He is perhaps the most famous example from the sixteenth century of someone who adopted the new scientific ways of treating disease. He trained at the Hotel du Dieu hospital in Paris before becoming a surgeon in the French army for 30 years. At the siege of Milan in 1536 he ran out of hot oil for cauterising wounds. He made up a mixture of egg yolk, turpentine and oil of roses to dress raw wounds – much less painful and, as he discovered the next morning, much more effective at encouraging healing. He also used **ligatures** to tie-off wounds after amputation – again instead of cauterisation – and found that wounds healed better. Later he helped develop artificial limbs for those who had lost a hand or a leg due to their wounds. His time as an army surgeon allowed Paré to observe his patients and treat them more effectively. He published his experiences in a book, *Les oeuvres* in 1575, and became famous across Europe. He is considered one of the fathers of modern surgery.

THINK ?

1 What changes did the Renaissance bring to medical knowledge?

2 Who do you think had the greater impact – Vesalius or Paré?

3 What do you think helped bring about change more – war or science and technology?

WILLIAM HARVEY

- Born in Kent in 1578 and educated at Cambridge University.
- Studied medicine at the University of Padua in Italy.
- Returned to England in 1602 and set himself up as a physician. His career benefited from his marriage to the daughter of Elizabeth I's physician.
- Accepted a post at St Bartholomew's Hospital in 1609 and worked there for the rest of his life. Appointed physician to both James I and Charles I.

William Harvey and the circulation of blood

Harvey's most famous work, *On the Motion of the Heart*, was published in 1628. It, more than any other book at the time, challenged the work of Galen and the Ancients, and changed medicine for ever.

While studying in Padua, Harvey was taught that the veins in the human body had valves, and blood pumped only one way. But no one understood how or why. Later in his career Harvey experimented on animals, and it was during this experimentation that he discovered blood was pumped around the body in a circular motion. This led to his famous discovery of the circulation of the blood.

His discovery was made partly as a result of theoretical work – he was unable to see the tiny capillaries which are the smallest blood vessels – but also as a result of experiment and observation. His work on cold-blooded amphibians, whose blood circulates much more slowly, allowed him to see blood pumping around the body and his most famous experiment, described in his book, showed blood moving in a patient's forearm. With this experiment he was able to show convincingly that the heart worked as a pump, and that blood flowed in a 'one-way system' around the human body.

He was also able to show that Galen's belief that the liver, not the heart, was the centre of the human body, was completely wrong. Galen also believed that the liver made new blood to replace that lost around the body. Harvey's work on the circulation of blood around the body proved that this was wrong, and also challenged the idea of 'bleeding' as a cure – if Harvey was right then it was impossible for the body to have too much blood.

How was Harvey's work greeted by contemporaries?

As you might imagine, those who supported Galen totally rejected Harvey's work. They argued that Harvey could not see capillaries and therefore could not prove their existence – it was another 60 years before capillaries were observed in action. Some refused to accept the role of experiments in challenging the ancient texts. Many were very conservative and resistant to change. In fact Harvey himself told a friend that he lost many patients after 1628 because of his 'crack-pot ideas'.

THINK ?

1 How was William Harvey able to prove that blood circulated around the human body?

2 Why did people oppose his work?

3 What does the story of William Harvey tell us about medical knowledge in the seventeenth century?

4 Is it fair to say that William Harvey's work changed medicine for ever?

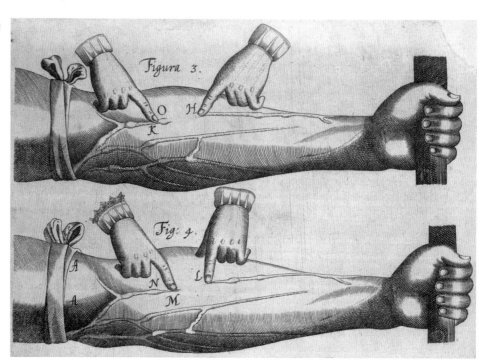

▲ **Source D:** From *Exercitatio anatomica de motu cordis et sanguinis in animalibus*, by William Harvey, 1628, showing how blood circulates through the veins

Nineteenth century advances in medical knowledge: improved knowledge of the germ theory

Pasteur and Koch

At the beginning of the nineteenth century most people still believed ill-health was caused by bad air, the 'spontaneous combustion' of disease or an imbalance of the four humours. Germ theory changed all that. As we have seen in Chapter 2 (page 44), by the 1880s and 1890s huge steps had been taken in identifying the cause of disease, thus enabling techniques to be developed to effectively treat illnesses.

Three people played a major part in this breakthrough: Pasteur, Koch and Ehrlich. They were not the only ones, but they led the way in experimental science. Louis Pasteur was the first person to establish the link between germs and disease. He argued that micro-organisms were responsible for disease, and that if only we could discover these micro-organisms then a vaccine could be developed to specifically target the disease. This allowed him to develop effective vaccines to target specific diseases. His first work was on chicken cholera and this led in 1880 to an effective vaccine against rabies.

Robert Koch took this work further. In the laboratory he was able to link particular germs to particular diseases, in effect developing the new science of bacteriology. In 1882 he identified the specific bacillus that caused tuberculosis and in 1883 and 1884 those responsible for cholera, thus confirming the work of John Snow in Britain in 1854 (see Chapter 2, page 39). Following this, he and his students rapidly isolated the causes of many diseases including diphtheria, typhoid, pneumonia, plague, tetanus and whooping cough, all of which were major killer diseases in Britain. He and his team also developed a technique for using dyes to stain bacteria to make it easier to see and study them under a microscope. His work was regarded as so important he was awarded a Nobel Prize in 1905.

Paul Ehrlich

Paul Ehrlich, a German physician and scientist, was one of Koch's students. He epitomises the scientific approach to identifying and treating diseases. He is perhaps best known for Salvarsan 606, developed in 1910, the first effective treatment for syphilis, a sexually transmitted disease (STD), which at the time was widespread. It was called '606' because it was literally the 606th drug he and his colleagues had used to try to kill the germs causing syphilis. Salvarsan 606 was the first of what became known as 'magic bullets', carefully designed drugs targeting the specific germs causing that illness and having little or no effect on any other part of the human body. No wonder people were so excited about the power of science to eradicate disease.

J.W. Power and courses on bacteriology

As a result of the work of Pasteur, Koch and Ehrlich the science of bacteriology was born and new drugs were developed to fight killer diseases. However, as bacteriology was a new field of study and was little known outside of university laboratories, one individual, Dr J.W. Power, the Medical Officer of Health for Ebbw Vale, began a campaign to have courses in bacteriology set up to train Medical Officers of Health in this new science. As a result of his efforts the first courses were established at King's College, London, in 1886. In 1898, a public health laboratory was established in Cardiff to further the study of bacteriology, funded jointly by Glamorgan County Council and the City of Cardiff as part of a drive to improve public health in south-east Wales.

The impact of germ theory

Germ theory completely changed medical knowledge about the causes of diseases and how to treat them. It came about through careful scientific observation and experiment, and established once and for all the link between bacteria and disease.

FOCUS TASK ?

Complete the card as you work through this section.

Breakthrough: Pasteur	To what extent [1–5]
....	....
....	....

THINK ?

1 In what ways did germ theory change medical knowledge?
2 Did Koch deserve a Nobel Prize?
3 Describe the role played by Dr J. W. Power in the history of bacteriology.

The bonesetters of Wales and the foundations of orthopaedics

During the second half of the nineteenth century and the early twentieth century, several pioneer Welsh 'bonesetters' helped to bring about major advances in the treatment of orthopaedic injuries.

Thomas Rocyn Jones (1822–77)

The son of a Pembrokeshire farmer, Thomas Rocyn Jones learned much from his father's skilful treatment of animal diseases. As his experience in his father's veterinary practice grew Jones began to apply the knowledge he had acquired working with animals to the treatment of human injuries.

Following a move to Rhymney in Monmouthshire he quickly built up an extensive practice and established a reputation as a bonesetter of note. He became skilful in the treatment of fractures, dislocations and muscle injuries, devising new methods to set bones. He developed curved wooden splints with a foot piece and experimented with new types of splints for the treatment of severe tendon injuries. He also added wedges to the inner sides of shoes to help off-set foot strain.

These were pioneering methods which Jones was using on a daily basis at least 50 years before they were adopted as standard practice for the treatment of orthopaedic injuries.

The Thomas family of Anglesey

Several generations of the Thomas family of Anglesey established reputations as bonesetters. In 1830, Evan Thomas (1804–84) moved from Anglesey to Liverpool where he set up a practice specialising in the treatment of bone and joint diseases. Evan Thomas had five sons, all who qualified as doctors. The eldest son was Hugh Owen Thomas (1834–91) who, following in his father's footsteps, set up a medical practice in Nelson Street, Liverpool, in 1859. As well as being a doctor he liked to experiment in the design and manufacture of his own splints.

Thomas designed splints to ensure the rest and immobility of injured bones and today he is best remembered for the development of the 'Thomas splint'.

The Thomas splint

The Thomas splint was designed to stabilise the fracture of the femur (thigh bone), putting the leg lengthways to stop the bones grinding against each other. This greatly reduced blood loss, helping to reduce the risk of infection and resulted in a reduction in the number of amputations required.

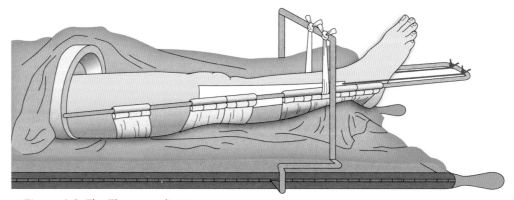

▲ **Figure 4.2:** The Thomas splint in use

Sir Robert Jones (1857–1933), the father of orthopaedics

Born in Rhyl in Flintshire in 1857, Robert Jones was the nephew of Hugh Owen Thomas and from a young age he came under the influence of his uncle's ideas and methods of treating broken bones. After qualifying as a doctor in 1878, he became professional assistant to his uncle before advancing in his medical career. In 1909, he was appointed the first lecturer in orthopaedic surgery at Liverpool University.

During the First World War, Robert Jones was appointed Inspector of Military Orthopaedics and during 1915 and 1916 he made sure that the Thomas splint was available for the treatment of wounded soldiers in the trenches. His insistence in its use had a dramatic impact, causing the death rate from fractures of the femur to fall from 80 to 20 per cent. He wrote manuals on military orthopaedics which had widespread influence on the treatment of injuries at the front. He ended his career by being elected as the first President of the International Society of Orthopaedic Surgery and was knighted for his contributions.

Through such pioneering methods several generations of Welsh bonesetters helped lay the foundations of modern orthopaedic surgery.

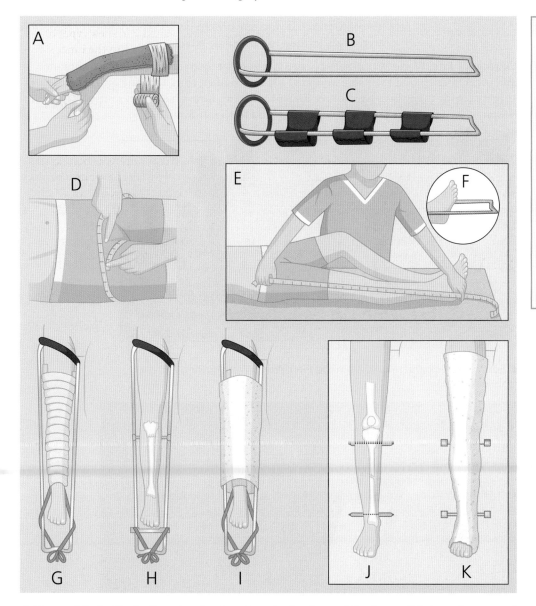

THINK

1 Explain the contribution made by each of the following individuals in the development of orthopaedics:
   a) Thomas Rocyn Jones
   b) Hugh Owen Thomas

2 With reference to Figures 4.2 and 4.3, as well as your own knowledge, explain why Robert Jones has been labelled the 'father of orthopaedics'.

▲ Figure 4.3: An illustration showing how to set a fracture of the femur. It is based on one of the orthopaedic manuals written by Robert Jones

The development of scanning techniques in the twentieth century: X-rays, ultrasound and MRI scans

FOCUS TASK

Complete the card as you work through the section.

Breakthrough: X-rays	To what extent [1–5]
....	....
....	....

The development of scanning techniques has revolutionised medical knowledge, especially in the last 30 years or so. Safe, non-invasive technology allows medical staff to identify disease earlier; understand better how diseases affect and spread through the body; and improve medical care.

X-rays

X-rays were discovered by Wilhelm Röntgen, a German scientist, in 1895, building on work by other scientists. He found that radiation would pass through the body at different rates, depending on whether it encountered bones or flesh. He realised he could photograph bones and his discovery rapidly led to the use of X-rays to investigate broken bones. Initial doses of radiation were high, leading to severe side-effects.

During the First World War mobile X-ray units were set up to check for bullets, shrapnel and other 'foreign bodies' inside wounded soldiers' bodies, thus allowing quicker and safer surgery, saving many lives (see Source E). Since the war, X-rays have been routinely used in hospitals to investigate problems with bones and teeth (see Source F).

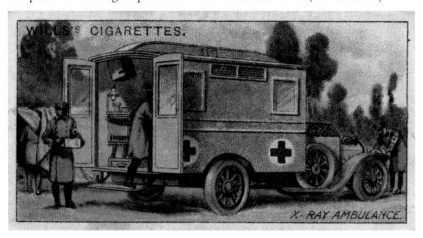

▲ Source E: A cigarette card from the First World War showing a French mobile X-ray van

THINK

1 Why was the development of X-ray technology so helpful in advancing medical knowledge?

2 Which is more useful to us in understanding the impact of X-rays, Source E or Source F? Why?

▲ Source F: A doctor examining a patient using X-ray equipment

Ultrasound

During the Second World War sound waves were used to detect German submarines. The British called this system ASDIC while the Americans referred to it as Sonar. It was after the war that it was realised you could use sound to 'see' inside the human body, by using high frequency sound waves. This avoided the need to use radiation, as in X-rays. It also produced 3D images. Ultrasound is used for images of organs in the body, such as the heart, liver and muscles, rather than bones, thus complementing X-rays. It is also, since the 1970s, routinely used to check the progress of unborn babies, to see if they are growing normally.

MRI

MRI (magnetic resonance imaging) scanning uses radio waves to build up a detailed picture of organs and tissues within the body. It uses powerful magnets to give a high resolution image allowing doctors to see clearly any areas of disease. It is also often used to check how effective previous medical treatment has been. Since the 1980s this has become an increasingly useful tool for doctors investigating the workings of the human body. A group of doctors surveyed in the USA in 2010 said MRI scans were the most useful weapon in their armoury in fighting disease.

PET scans and CT Scans

Positron emission tomography (PET) injects a slightly radioactive tracer into the bloodstream, allowing 3D colour images of tissues and bones to be seen, and is often used to investigate cancers and heart problems. Computed tomography (CT) uses many X-ray images taken at slightly different angles to produce a cross-sectional image of the area of the body, which can be used to diagnose illness or to find the location of, for example, cancerous cells. These procedures are expensive, often costing £1000 a time, and are usually used after the other scanning techniques have raised issues or complications.

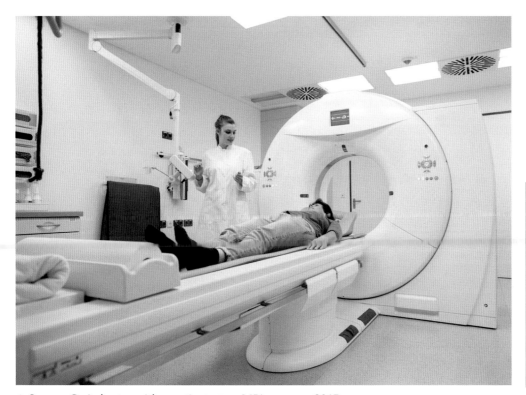

▲ Source G: A doctor with a patient at an MRI scanner, 2015

THINK

1 How have these developments in scanning techniques contributed to the advance of medical knowledge over the twentieth century?

2 Which *one* development would you say has been most significant? Why?

The discovery of DNA and genetic research in the later twentieth century

FOCUS TASK

Complete the card as you work through the section.

Breakthrough: DNA	To what extent [1–5]
....	....
....	....

THINK

1 What are the arguments in favour of three-parent babies?

2 What are the arguments against three-parent babies?

3 What does the issue tell us about the development of medical knowledge?

4 How has recent research into stem cells pushed forward medical knowledge?

In 1953 Crick, Watson and Franklin published a paper about DNA (deoxyribonucleic acid) which carries genetic information about hereditary materials in human beings. Nearly every cell contains identical information. It is how humans reproduce themselves. In 1990 the Human Genome Project set out to build up a complete genetic blueprint of human beings; a task completed in 2003. Understanding DNA has huge implications for medical research and medical knowledge. In 1996 by copying cells (cloning) researchers were able to clone Dolly the sheep in an attempt to 'grow' medicines for humans in sheep's milk. By modifying DNA it has become possible to eliminate genetic diseases. Already genetic engineering has reversed mutations that cause blindness, stopped cancer cells from multiplying and made some cells impervious to AIDS. DNA can be used to screen people for inherited diseases, and ensure babies are born without life-threatening diseases (see Figure 4.4).

Martin Evans and stem cell research

In 2007, Martin Evans, Professor of Mammalian Genetics at Cardiff University, was awarded the Nobel Prize for medicine for his research work on stem cells. Through his research Evans had shown how cells that form all the tissues in a mouse's body (known as embryonic stem cells) could be removed and grown separately in the laboratory. He also helped to create a method to alter genes in mice, placing altered stem cells in the wombs of female mice so they would give birth to genetically modified offspring. This breakthrough, known as gene targeting, has helped the drive to develop new treatments for human illnesses and today genetically modified mice are considered vital for medical research.

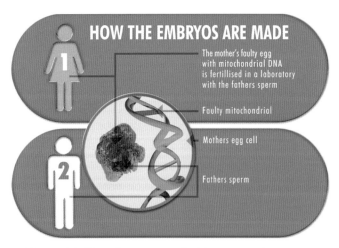

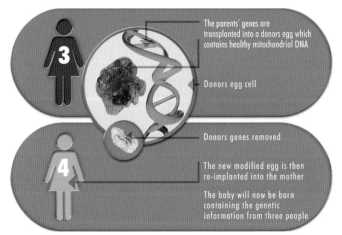

▲ Figure 4.4: How three-parent babies are made

FOCUS TASK REVISITED

1 The focus task asked you to complete various cards to help you decide what progress has been made in medical knowledge.

2 Collect all your focus task cards and plot the information onto your personal copy of this graph:

Massive change

Little change

| Medieval | C16th and C17th | C19th | C20th |

3 Now decide which period had, in your opinion, the *most* progress in medical knowledge, and why.

4 In groups, discuss your answer to Question 3 – do you all agree or are some answers different? (How do you define 'medical progress'?)

ACTIVITY

Use your focus task cards to hold a balloon debate. Take it in turns to present the argument for each bit of medical progress on the focus task cards. At the end of each round take a vote to decide which of the bits of medical progress will be ejected from the balloon. Keep going until you have the 'best' bit of medical progress remaining.

TOPIC SUMMARY

- Medieval people did have some medical knowledge.
- Alchemists and scientists tried hard to find the 'Elixir of Life' but failed, although they did much to improve scientific techniques.
- The Renaissance was when people started to question the 'wisdom' of the Ancient World.
- People like Vesalius, Paré and Harvey radically changed the way illness was understood.
- Germ theory fundamentally altered the way people thought of disease.
- In the twentieth century techniques to 'see' inside the body revolutionised the way doctors identify illness.
- Throughout the twentieth and twenty-first centuries scientists have discovered more and more how the human body works.
- DNA and genetic engineering have introduced further advances in our understanding of illness.
- Some people think we now have too much medical knowledge.

Practice questions

1 Complete the sentences below with an accurate term:
The father of modern medicine is said to be an Ancient Greek called ....
The four humours were said to be made up of blood, phlegm, yellow bile and ....
Vesalius helped to push forward knowledge of human ....
The drug Salvarsan 606 is often referred to as a magic ....
(*For guidance, see page 119*)

2 Study Source C (page 62), Source D (page 64) and Source G (page 69). Use these sources to identify one similarity and one difference in the advancement of medical knowledge over time. (*For guidance, see page 120–121.*)

3 Explain why the work of Vesalius, Paré and Harvey was important in advancing medical knowledge in the sixteenth and seventeenth centuries. (*For guidance, see page 124.*)

4 To what extent was the development of scanning techniques in the twentieth century the most effective advance in medical knowledge over time? (*For guidance, see page 126–128.*)

5 Developments in patient care

This chapter focuses on the key question: How has the care of patients improved over time?

In the UK today if you are sick and in need of medical treatment you either visit your local doctor or, for more serious illnesses, injuries or for an operation, you visit a hospital. All these services are provided under a state-run National Health Service (NHS). However, this has not always been the case. The development of these care facilities has been a very long process. During the medieval period the church dominated provision but from the mid-sixteenth century onwards voluntary and charity institutions began to take an the responsibility for nursing and patient care. During the twentieth century the government began to take an active role in looking after the welfare of its citizens and since 1948 the NHS has been in operation, treating people 'from the cradle to the grave'.

FOCUS TASK

As you work through this chapter gather together information to enable you to complete this time chart. In each section make bullet points to spell out the key features of hospitals, nursing and patient care during that period. At the end of the chapter you will be able to use this information to make a judgement upon the degree of change in patient care that has taken place.

Time period	Types of hospital available	Responsibility for running the hospital	Standard of nursing and patient care
Medieval period			
Sixteenth and seventeenth centuries			
Eighteenth century			
Nineteenth century			
Twentieth and twenty-first centuries			

The role of the church and monasteries from the medieval period up to the mid-sixteenth century

During the medieval period hospitals were essentially religious institutions whose role and functions were very different from what we expect from modern hospitals today. The principal concern of medieval hospitals was the health of the soul over the health of the body. As we have already seen, the emphasis was on care and religion rather than treatment and cure.

Almost all medieval hospitals were run by the church and the building of the monasteries during the twelfth century onwards led to an explosion in the number of hospitals set up between the twelfth and fourteenth centuries. Most monasteries included an infirmary in its layout, such as that of Tintern Abbey on the Welsh border (see Figure 5.1). In most **Cistercian** monasteries a second cloister housed the infirmary. It was intended for the sick and aged members of the community who could no longer manage the hardship of everyday life and was located in the most secluded part of the monastery complex. Wales had a number of Cistercian monasteries spread across the country, with Valle Crucis, Basingwerk and Aberconwy situated in the north, Strata Florida and Cwmhir in mid-Wales and Whitland, Neath, Margam, Llantarnam and Tintern monasteries serving the south. These institutions provided hospitable care for the members of the community and to travellers.

While Cistercian monasteries were located in isolated areas a new religious order emerged in the thirteenth century which based themselves in villages and towns. This was the Franciscan order and their priories provided infirmaries to treat the sick and infirm. Carmarthen friary, founded in 1282, quickly grew to become one of the wealthiest Franciscan houses in Britain; other friaries were set up at Bangor, Brecon, Cardiff, Denbigh, Haverfordwest, Llanfaes, Newport and Rhuddlan. They became centres of primary care for the sick and infirm.

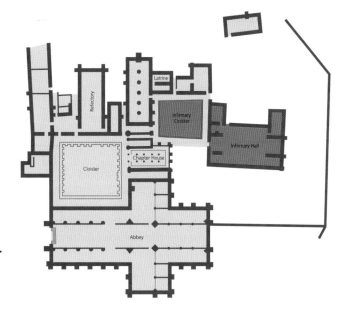

Figure 5.1: A plan of Tintern Abbey which was constructed ▶ in stages between the late twelfth and late thirteenth century. The infirmary (red) was an important part of the monastery

Different types of hospitals in medieval times

The medieval period witnessed a growth in hospitals but only about 10 per cent of them actually cared for the sick (see Figure 5.2). They were called hospitals because they provided 'hospitality', a place of rest and recuperation but not a place to be cured. Some specialised in looking after certain types of people, such as lepers, while others such as St Bartholomew's in London looked after destitute women who were pregnant and supported the infants of mothers who had died during childbirth.

In 1190, the Knights of Saint John of the Order of Hospitallers set up a hospital at Ysbyty Ifan in the hills above Pentrefoelas to care for pilgrims who travelled along the pilgrim route from Bangor Is Coed to Holyhead. It also served as a hostel for travellers; the name Ysbyty Ifan means 'hospital of Saint John'. It was closed down in 1540 during the dissolution of the monasteries.

Leper hospitals

A common incurable and contagious disease during the medieval period was leprosy and a great leprosy epidemic during the twelfth and thirteenth centuries brought about a growth of specific leprosy hospitals. Leprosy inflicted horrible deformities on its victims and they were forced to wear special clothes and ring a warning bell as they walked, and they were not allowed to marry. Many people feared lepers and thought that those with the disease were being punished by God. Leper hospitals were built on the outskirts of towns to limit the mixing with the rest of the population. They provided lodging and food but no treatment.

Almshouses

Almshouses were the medieval equivalent of the modern care home and they were a response to an aging population. Almshouses offered sheltered accommodation and basic nursing, but no medical treatment.

Most were very small, sometimes just a priest and up to a dozen inmates. Most occupants were elderly needing long-term care, but they also contained widows with young children or single pregnant women. Almshouses also gave shelter to travellers and the poor, who would be given a few nights accommodation.

Source A: A local law enforced in the town of Berwick-upon-Tweed in an attempt to stop the spread of leprosy

No leper shall come within the gates of the borough and if one gets in by chance, the serjeant shall put him out at once. If one wilfully forces his way in, his clothes shall be taken off him and burnt and he shall be turned out naked.

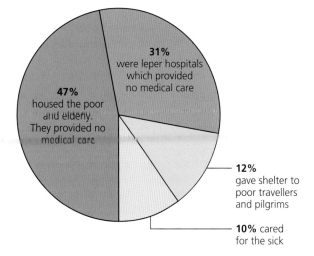

▲ Figure 5.2: Pie-chart showing the type of patient care provided during the medieval period

Christian hospitals

Christian hospitals were set up, paid for and run by the church and they looked after the poor as well as the sick. They did not treat sickness but aimed to make the patients as comfortable as they could. People who were seriously ill and in need of constant care were often not allowed in as they would stop people concentrating on the main purpose of the hospital which was to pray and attend religious services.

Hospitals provided basic nursing, clean and quiet conditions, regular meals and warmth, and sometimes surgery and medicine. The staff were brothers and sisters in religious orders. They cared for the sick and tried to save their souls, but they did not attempt to cure them. There were few, if any, doctors. The staff at St Leonard's in York consisted of several chaplains but no doctors. St Bartholomew's, which had been founded in London in 1123, did not appoint its first doctor until the sixteenth century.

Hospitals were religious institutions and were often referred to as 'Houses of God'. When Walter Suffield, the Bishop of Norwich, left money in his will of 1257 for the construction of the 'Great Hospital' he did so because he believed it was his Christian duty to help the sick, homeless and poor (see Figure 5.3). He also wanted to cleanse himself of his sins to ensure he entered heaven when he died.

Patients were expected to spend much of their day praying and confessing their sins. It was believed that they were poor and sick because they had sinned and they now needed to rid themselves of their sins. This was the function of the hospital. If they prayed, showed that they repented their sins and said prayers for the people who had donated money to the hospital, they would be helped into heaven after death.

The hospital consisted of a hall full of beds, at the end of which were small chapels where monks said mass. Nuns and helpers attended the patients.

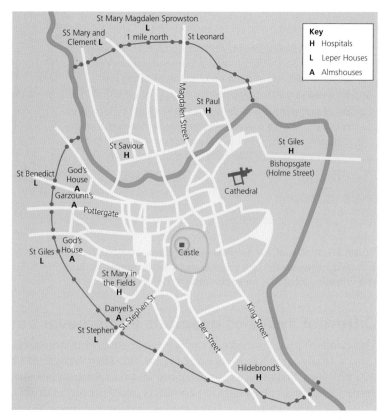

▲ Figure 5.3: A map of medieval Norwich showing leper houses, almshouses and hospitals

> **Source B: An extract from the rules of the hospital of St John in Bridgwater, Somerset, in 1219**
>
> *No lepers, lunatics, or persons having the falling sickness or other contagious disease, and no pregnant women, or sucking infants, and no intolerable persons, even though they be poor and infirm, are to be admitted in the hospital; and if any such be admitted by mistake, they are to be expelled as soon as possible. And when the other poor and infirm persons have recovered they are to be let out without delay.*

THINK ?

1 Use the information in this section to think about the role and function of the hospital during the medieval period, making use of the information in Sources A (page 73) and B and Figure 5.3 to complete the following table.

	What does this source tell you about the types of medical care on offer during the medieval period?	What does this source tell us about the role and function of this type of hospital?	What does this source tell us about attitudes towards the care of the sick?
Source A			
Source B			
Figure 5.3			

2 'The Christian church was concerned with the care rather than the cure of the sick.' How far do you agree with this statement?

The roles of voluntary charities in patient care after the mid-sixteenth century

The mid-sixteenth century onwards witnessed a decline in the role of the church in administering patient care and the growth of voluntary charities taking on that role, especially after the closure of the monasteries.

The impact of the closure of the monasteries

When Henry VIII ordered the dissolution of the monasteries in the 1530s it resulted in the closure of many hospitals and this had a dramatic impact upon patient care. The church now ceased to be a supporter of hospitals and that role now had to be taken on by voluntary charities.

In some areas town or city councils stepped in to take over the running of almshouses that looked after the elderly poor and the hospital, which took care of the poor in general. In London the authorities petitioned the crown to provide funds to endow hospitals such as St Bartholomew's, St Thomas' and St Mary's to enable them to continue to provide services of patient care for their communities. In providing royal funds, it proved to be the first occasion when **secular** support was provided for medical institutions.

The creation of 'royal hospitals' in London

Across London a total of five major hospitals were endowed with royal funds during the mid-sixteenth century to enable them to continue to administer care for the sick and poor of the capital. The endowment usually took the form of the granting of land, which could then be rented out to provide the institution with a steady, though often insufficient, income.

St Bartholomew's Hospital

The dissolution of the monasteries left St Barts in a difficult position as it took away its income. In a bid to keep the hospital open, the city authorities petitioned the king and in December 1546 the institution was granted to the Corporation of the City of London by royal charter of Henry VIII and endowed with properties, land and other income entitlements. The hospital served the poor of the area of West Smithfield.

St Mary Bethlehem (including Bethlem)

St Mary Bethlehem, which included Bethlem Hospital, was dissolved in the late 1530s. In 1546 the Lord Mayor of London, Sir John Gresham, petitioned the crown to grant both institutions to the city. A royal charter was granted in 1547. The Bethlem site concentrated upon looking after the mentally insane.

St Thomas' Hospital

St Thomas' hospital, which had originally been founded c.1100 by a mixed order of Augustinian monks and nuns, provided shelter and treatment for the poor, sick and homeless in the area of Southwark. The monastery was dissolved in 1539 and its hospital closed. With nothing to take its place, the city of London authorities petitioned the crown and in 1551 King Edward VI granted the site by royal charter and the hospital re-opened that year. It quickly re-established itself as a hospital for the sick poor, but also took on the responsibility for treating patients suffering from venereal disease.

Christ's Hospital

Christ's Hospital was founded in 1553 by Edward VI, in the old Grey Friars' buildings in Newgate, London, in response to calls from the bishop of London to provide for the poor. It offered shelter, clothing and food to fatherless children, alongside rudimental education.

Bridewell hospital

The fifth 'royal hospital' was that of Bridewell hospital and prison. Located on the banks of the Fleet river, it received its royal charter in 1553 and had two purposes, the housing of homeless children and the punishment of the disorderly poor.

Endowed voluntary hospitals outside London

The creation of voluntary hospitals did not just take place in London. In towns across the country it was left to the local councils to organise endowments to keep their hospitals open. In Norwich, for example, when Henry VIII ordered the closure of the monastery of St Giles and, with it, its hospital, the town council petitioned the crown.

The hospital was re-founded by a royal charter granted in 1547, which handed control of the hospital to the town corporation. The charter stated that four women were to be employed to 'make the beddes, washe and attend upon the seid poore persons'. During the following century the hospital was transformed from a religious institution into a hospital which, for the first time in its history, began to employ medical staff. By the 1570s the medical staff consisted of a barber (who let blood), a surgeon and a bonesetter. Medical care was now being focused upon its patients.

> **THINK** ?
>
> 1 How did the responsibility of care for the sick and the poor change after the dissolution of the monasteries in the 1530s?
>
> 2 'Hospitals in London during the late sixteenth century began to specialise in the care of particular types of patients.' What evidence can you find to support this statement?

Science and the development of endowed hospitals in the eighteenth century

During the eighteenth century new hospitals were opened, paid for by private individuals, charities or town councils. A number of factors influenced the growth in the provision of hospital care during this century.

The development of scientific enquiry

This period witnessed a growth in scientific enquiry which in turn resulted in a growing interest in medical issues. The founding of the Royal Society in London in 1662 and various medical societies, such as the one established in Edinburgh in 1732, did much to encourage new scientific discoveries. These new societies provided opportunities to discuss ideas about medicine and to analyse and evaluate the results of experiments or trials in new surgical processes. The desire to investigate, experiment and report led to the growth of the Enlightenment, an age of scientific advancement and enquiry, a period which saw the advancement in medical knowledge.

The impact of the Industrial Revolution

Industrial development resulted in several consequences, one of which was a sharp rise in population levels. As the new industrial towns expanded so there was a corresponding demand for increased hospital provision. Part of that demand was met through financial donations from new wealthy industrialists. They wished to use their new wealth to fund the establishment of hospitals, believing that God had given them the responsibility to improve the lives of the poor and sick. One of these early philanthropists was Thomas Guy, a wealthy printer and bookseller who financed the establishment of Guy's Hospital in 1724. He held the Christian belief that the rich should help the poor, and through receiving such help, the poor would be provided with the opportunity to live cleaner and more disciplined lives.

The setting up of endowed hospitals

During the first half of the eighteenth century many new voluntary hospitals were opened, paid for by private individuals like Guy, local charities or town councils who provided the new institutions with endowments to fund their upkeep. Eleven new hospitals were founded in London during this period and a further 46 across the country in the growing industrial towns and cities (see Table 5.1).

Date	Hospital	Location	Endowed by
1719	Westminster Hospital	London	Funded by a private bank, C. Hoare & Co
1724	Guy's Hospital	London	Bequest of a wealthy businessman, Thomas Guy
1729	Royal Infirmary Hospital	Edinburgh	Wealthy patrons of Edinburgh donated funds
1735	Royal Infirmary Hospital	Bristol	Funded by Paul Fisher, a wealthy city merchant
1739	The Foundling Hospital	Bloomsbury, London	Founded by Thomas Coram, a sea captain. He wished the hospital to look after deserted young children
1752	Royal Infirmary Hospital	Manchester	Funded by Charles White, a physician, and Joseph Bancroft, a wealthy industrialist
1766	Addenbrooke's Hospital	Cambridge	Dr John Addenbrooke left £4500 in his will to set up a hospital
1779	The General Hospital	Birmingham	Donations from wealthy landowners and industrialists, including Matthew Boulton

▲ Table 5.1: Examples of some of the endowed hospitals set up during the eighteenth century

◀ **Source C:** An engraving from the 1820s showing Guy's Hospital in London. This was one of the first voluntary endowed hospitals to be established in 1724

> **Source D:** The rules of Guy's Hospital, issued after its foundation in 1724
>
> *The sick must acknowledge the goodness of God in providing so comfortable a situation, care, medicine and skill, while under the afflicting hand of God. They must behave soberly and religiously as Christians.*

The role and function of endowed hospitals

The establishment of endowed hospitals marked a turning point in the development of the hospital. They now evolved from a place to provide basic care of the sick to a centre in which to treat illness and conditions that required surgery. Some of them became centres for the education and training of doctors and surgeons.

Within these institutions the primary role was to look after the poor sick, as people with money normally paid for a doctor and nurse to treat them privately at home. The patients were looked after by nursing helpers who undertook the manual work and ensured that the patients were washed, kept warm and fed regularly. Nursing sisters were able to treat ill patients with herbal remedies. Simple surgery such as the removal of bladder stones and the setting of broken bones was carried out by physicians. Treatment was normally free.

Another function of the hospital was the issue of medicines. During the 1770s a number of dispensaries were set up – the Public Dispensary of Edinburgh in 1776, the Metropolitan Dispensary and Charitable Fund in 1779 and the Finsbury Dispensary in 1780, both in central London.

> **THINK**
>
> 1 What do Sources C and D tell us about hospitals in the eighteenth century?
>
> 2 The growth in the provision of hospital care during the eighteenth century was influenced by developments such as:
>
> - scientific enquiry
> - industrial development
> - funding by private individuals.
>
> Arrange these developments in order of their significance in influencing the growth in hospital provision. Explain your choices.

The establishment of voluntary hospitals across Wales

In Wales, as in England, the treatment of sick patients in hospitals was undertaken in voluntary institutions. A major trigger for the establishment of such institutions was the Industrial Revolution, which produced urbanisation and it was in the new, rapidly expanding industrial towns that some of the first voluntary hospitals in Wales were established. Swansea established an infirmary as early as 1817 and in 1837 the Glamorgan and Monmouth Infirmary and Dispensary was opened in Cardiff, which was renamed the Cardiff Infirmary in 1895. Newport set up a dispensary in 1839, which was later converted into a hospital in 1867. Other South Wales towns established voluntary hospitals slightly later: Aberdare in 1881, Merthyr in 1887 and Bridgend in 1895.

The founding of the Denbigh General Dispensary and Asylum for the Recovery of Health in 1807 resulted in the first institution of its kind in North Wales, providing accommodation for sick people to stay and regain their health under the watchful eye of qualified medical staff. Between 1821 and 1822, the number of patients who passed through its doors totalled 862 and by 1823 it had treated 9,041 people with the opening of an extension wing in 1823. The growing mining town of Wrexham established a dispensary in 1833 followed by an infirmary in 1838. The infirmary reflected the values of the time and would only treat those who could not afford to pay (see Source E). Such institutions were only made possible through the continual voluntary donations received from wealthy philanthropists, which in Denbigh's case was Dr George Cumming, the hospital's first physician.

> **Source E: A section from the rules of Wrexham Infirmary dating from 1838**
>
> Patients to consist of such persons as are too poor to defray the expenses of medical attendance.

Alongside these general infirmaries a number of specialist hospitals were established during the late nineteenth century, including several that served the nation's maritime community.

Stanley Sailors' Hospital, Holyhead

The Stanley Sailors' Hospital was established on Salt Island, Holyhead, in November 1861. Its construction was paid for by a local philanthropist, William Owen Stanley of Penrhos, and initially only treated sailors. Dame Jane Henrietta Adeane (1842–1926), the neice of W.O. Stanley, played a prominent role in the running of the hospital from 1881 onwards, raising funds and helping with the administration. When the hospital was taken over by the military during the First World War she assumed the title of 'commandant' and continued to play an active role. The hospital eventually became a general hospital and was taken over by the NHS in 1948.

Royal Hamadryad Hospital, Cardiff

The brainchild of Dr Henry Paine, Medical Officer of Health for Cardiff from 1853 to 1889, the Hamadryad was a seamen's hospital based in the docklands area of the town. Dr Paine had been concerned that sailors might bring infectious diseases such as cholera, smallpox and typhoid into the town. In 1866, he organised the purchase of a 43-year-old frigate, HMS *Hamadryad*, to be towed from Dartmouth to Cardiff and fitted out as a hospital ship at a cost of £2,791. The hospital ship opened in November 1866 and during its first year admitted 400 patients. The free treatment was funded by a levy of two shillings per 100 tons of shipping at Cardiff docks. By the turn of the century, over 10,000 seamen were being treated each year. In 1905, the wooden ship was replaced by a permanent seamen's hospital built on land close by. It had 54 beds, electric lighting and X-ray facilities. It remained a seamen's hospital until 1948.

▲ Source F: HMS *Hamadryad*, berthed in Cardiff East Dock, opened as a seamen's hospital in 1866

THINK

1 Using examples, explain why philanthropists were so important in the establishment of voluntary hospitals across Wales.
2 What arguments were put forward to ensure that the Hamadryad hospital was built in the docklands of Cardiff rather in the town itself?

Changes in the nineteenth century

Two important developments in patient care occurred during the nineteenth century. One was the emergence of nursing as a profession and the other was the planned design of hospitals. Both of these developments were heavily influenced by one individual – Florence Nightingale.

Growth in the number of hospitals

As the country's population continued to grow throughout the nineteenth century the pressure to provide medical care resulted in the establishment of general hospitals in cities across the country. In 1800 there were approximately 3000 patients in hospitals across England and Wales and by 1851 this figure had risen to 7619. Specialist hospitals had also begun to appear, dealing with such areas as maternity care, orthopaedics, and eyes, nose and throat (see Table 5.2). By the 1860s the cottage hospital movement had resulted in the setting up of small hospitals in rural areas run by general practitioners.

Date of foundation	Developments in specific medical care
1800	Royal College of Surgeons opened
1814	London Chest Hospital
1828	Royal 'Free' Hospital founded by William Marsden
1834	Westminster Medical School
1851	Royal 'Marsden' Cancer Hospital
1852	Great Ormond Street Children's Hospital
1860	Nightingale School of Nursing

▲ Table 5.2: Major hospitals and specialist training institutions established between 1800 and 1900

Conditions within these new hospitals

While there was a growth in the number of hospitals, conditions for the patients within them were generally poor. Cramped, stuffy wards helped infections to spread quickly, and the fact that the wards were seldom cleaned meant that the death rate from infection was high. The quality of nursing was poor, with untrained nurses securing reputations for being dirty, ignorant and often drunk. They received little, if any, training and were often ignorant of the most basic standards of hygiene. The most common complaints waged against nurses were that they were too often dirty and drunk (see Source G). Many thought nursing was a job only for uneducated women who could do nothing else. Nursing was not looked upon as a respected profession and was certainly not seen as a career for a respectable young woman like Florence Nightingale.

> **Source G: A description of nursing at St Bartholomew's hospital in London in 1877. It was written in 1902 by a nurse who had been a sister in the hospital in the 1870s**
>
> *Drunkenness was very common among the staff nurses, who chiefly were of charwoman type, frequently of bad character, with little education. Nursing, as you understand it now, was unknown. Patients were not nursed, they were attended to, more or less. The work was hard – lockers and tables to scrub every day. We did not scrub the floors. The patients had their beds made once a day, and you thought nothing of changing fourteen or fifteen poultices two or three times a day. The nurses never used a thermometer, the dressers and clerks took the temperatures.*

> **THINK**
>
> 'The first half of the nineteenth century saw the opening of many new hospitals but these hospitals did not bring about any improvement in patient care.' What evidence can you find in this section to support this statement?

Florence Nightingale and the professionalisation of nursing

As we have seen, during the first half of the nineteenth century standards of nursing were very poor. What changed nursing were the actions of a number of females – Florence Nightingale, Mary Seacole and Betsi Cadwaladr – all of whom took part in the nursing of British soldiers during the Crimean War (1853–6).

The impact of the Crimean War

The Crimean War was the first war in which reporters sent back reports to newspapers in Britain using the new telegraph system and the public soon began reading about the awful conditions experienced by sick and wounded British soldiers fighting in the Crimea. What got Florence Nightingale interested in the war were the reports she read in *The Times*.

Born into a wealthy family, Nightingale believed God had wanted her to be a nurse and despite opposition from her parents she had trained as a nurse in Germany and in Paris during the early 1850s. After returning to England she worked in several hospitals before the outbreak of the Crimean War in 1853.

> **Source H:** Shortly after her arrival in Scutari, Florence Nightingale wrote to Sydney Herbert, describing the conditions in which wounded and sick soldiers were treated. Her letter is dated 25 November 1854
>
> *It appears that in these hospitals the washing of linen and of the men are considered a minor detail. No washing has been performed for the men or the bed – except by ourselves. When we came here, there was neither basin, towel, nor soap in the Wards. The consequences of this are Fever, Cholera, Gangrene, Lice, Bugs, Fleas.*

▲ **Source I:** Conditions in the military hospital at Scutari in 1854 before the arrival of Florence Nightingale

Florence Nightingale goes to the Crimea

Having secured government funding, Nightingale took 38 of the best nurses she could find and travelled to the British military hospital at Scutari on the Black Sea coast of Turkey. Upon their arrival at Scutari on 4 November 1854 they were appalled by what they saw. There were 1700 wounded and sick soldiers in the field hospital, many of whom were suffering from cholera and typhoid, housed in filthy wards. There were not enough beds or medical supplies. Added to this problem was the fact that the army doctors resented Nightingale's presence and opposed her interference.

However, Nightingale had the support of both Sydney Herbert, Minister of War Supplies, and Dr Andrew Smith, head of the Army Medical Department. Dr Smith ensured that she obtained sufficient supplies of the medical items she needed, and she also had financial backing from *The Times*, which reported upon her improvements.

One of Nightingale's first tasks was to clean the wards. Patients were given a regular wash, clean clothes and had their bedding changed regularly. To help prevent the spread of disease, patients were separated according to their illness, plenty of space was put between each bed and fresh air circulated from open windows. These measures had dramatic results. After just six months only 100 of the 1700 patients were still confined to bed, and the death rate in the hospital had fallen from 42 in every 100 patients to 2 in every 100. Through these reforms Nightingale had laid down new standards of patient care.

> **THINK** ?
> 1 What do Sources H and I tell you about conditions for sick and wounded soldiers in army hospitals at the start of the Crimean War in 1853?
> 2 Describe the changes made by Florence Nightingale to the care of sick and wounded soldiers in the army hospital at Scutari.

▲ **Source J:** A hospital ward at Scutari in 1856 showing the changes to patient care introduced by Florence Nightingale

▲ Source K: Florence Nightingale

Florence Nightingale and the birth of modern nursing

Upon her return to Britain in 1856 Nightingale set up a public fund and was successful in raising nearly £50,000. Much of this was used to set up the Nightingale School of Nursing in a wing of St Thomas' Hospital in London.

In 1859 she published *Notes on Nursing*, which set out the training nurses should receive. The training was very practical and ward based. Training in the school was very strict:

- Nurses were only allowed to go out in pairs.
- They had to live in at the hospital.
- They had to keep a diary of their work, which was inspected every month.

They were taught to be as clean as possible, to change dressings and to be proper assistants to doctors and surgeons. Instead of being minders and cleaners as they had been in the past, nurses were now to be seen as an essential part of patient care and treatment. By 1900 nursing schools had opened around the country using Nightingale's ideas.

Florence Nightingale influences the design of new hospitals

In 1863 Nightingale published *Notes on Hospitals*, which introduced new ideas about the design of hospitals. She believed that new hospitals should consider the importance of 'the proper use of fresh air, light, warmth, cleanliness, quiet and the proper selection and administration of diets'. When St Thomas' Hospital was rebuilt in 1868 it became one of the first hospitals to adopt the 'pavilion principle' devised by Nightingale. This consisted of six separate wards at right angles to a long, linked corridor which encouraged good circulation of air.

The importance of Florence Nightingale

In 1850 there had been no trained nurses in Britain, yet by 1901 there were 68,000. In 1899 the International Council of Nurses was set up in London. Nursing had finally been recognised as a profession, in large part due to the efforts of Florence Nightingale. Hospital design had also undergone radical change. By the end of the nineteenth century many towns and cities had built new hospitals and in their design they embodied many of the recommendations put forward by Florence Nightingale.

Problems in 1850	Solutions found by 1900
Untrained nurses	Trained nurses
Lack of respect for nurses	Nursing recognised as a profession
Cramped, stuffy wards	Spacious, light and well-ventilated wards
Poor sanitation, toilet facilities and sewage disposal	Good sanitation, connected to main drains and piped water supplies
Lack of cleanliness	Clean wards
Unhygienic surgery and dressings	Aseptic surgery and dressings

▲ Table 5.3: Changes in nursing and hospitals between 1850 and 1900

THINK ❓

1 Explain **two** changes introduced by Florence Nightingale which improved the quality of nursing.

2 What key features did Florence Nightingale consider to be essential in the design of new hospitals? Explain why.

The contribution of Mary Seacole (1805–81)

Another nurse who made her mark in the Crimean War was Mary Seacole. The daughter of a Scottish sailor, Seacole was born in Kingston, Jamaica, where her mother ran a medical centre for British soldiers and sailors on the island, and Seacole soon developed a keen interest in nursing. She travelled to Britain in 1854 and volunteered her services to the army in the Crimea.

In 1855 she opened the 'British Hospital' between Balaclava and Sebastopol to treat wounded and sick soldiers. She dealt with jaundice, diarrhoea, dysentery and frostbite, and was often seen going into the thick of the battle with her medicine bag. When the war ended she returned to Britain and in 1857 published an autobiography, *The Wonderful Adventures of Mrs Seacole in Many Lands*, which helped to raise awareness of the contribution of nursing during the Crimean War.

The contribution of Betsi Cadwaladr (1789–1860)

Like Seacole, Elizabeth 'Betsi' Cadwaladr helped with the nursing of soldiers in the Crimea. Born in Bala in north Wales in 1789, Cadwaladr was one of 16 children. At the age of 14 she ran away from home, travelled to Liverpool and then to London where she became interested in nursing. Between 1815 and 1820 she served as a maid to a ship's captain, which enabled her to travel to South America, Africa and Australia. Upon her return to London she trained as a nurse and in 1854, aged 65, she went to the Crimea to help nurse the wounded soldiers.

She did not get on well with Florence Nightingale and there was a clear clash of personalities between them. They were from different traditions – Nightingale respecting rules, regulations and bureaucracy and Betsi responding instinctively to the needs of injured soldiers as they arose, regardless of regulations. Betsi believed that the bureaucracy deprived the wounded soldiers of food, clothing and bandages. Feeling frustrated with Florence's methods of running the hospital at Scutari, Betsi left for the hospital at Balaclava on the Black Sea where she worked tirelessly to improve the quality of patient care. She cleaned wounds and changed bandages, working from 6 a.m. to 11 p.m. However, the war took its toll on her health and she caught cholera and dysentery. She had to leave the Crimea in 1855 and died in 1860. The Betsi Cadwaladr NHS Trust in North Wales commemorates her.

> **THINK ?**
> 1 To what extent were Mary Seacole and Betsi Cadwaladr important in the history of nursing?
> 2 Why did Betsi Cadwaladr not get along well with Florence Nightingale?

▲ **Source L:** Mary Seacole

▲ **Source M:** Betsi Cadwaladr

The impact of the early twentieth century Liberal reforms

The early decades of the twentieth century witnessed the beginnings of the creation of the **Welfare State** when the government began to take some responsibility for managing the care and treatment of the sick and those in need.

Changes in government attitude

During the nineteenth century governments had traditionally followed a policy of laissez-faire, believing it was not their job to interfere with people's lives unless they really had to. During the early twentieth century, however, attitudes began to change and the Liberal governments of 1906–14 broke with the past and introduced a series of welfare reforms designed to help people who fell into difficulty through sickness, old age or unemployment. The reforms tackled such areas as the provision of education, the medical inspection of school pupils, workers, compensation rights and the provision of old-age pensions (see Table 5.4).

Year	Act passed	Effect of legislation
1906	Workmen's Compensation Act	Granted compensation for injury at work
	Education (Provision of Meals) Act	Introduced free school meals
1907	Education (Administrative Provisions) Act	Created school medical inspections
	Matrimonial Causes Act	Maintenance payments to be paid to divorced women
1908	Children and Young Person's Act (Children's Charter)	Made it illegal to sell alcohol, tobacco or fireworks to children
	Old-Age Pensions Act	Over 70s received 5 shillings a week (25p), 7 shillings and 6 pence for a married couple
1909	Labour Exchanges Act	Helped get people back into a job
	Housing and Town Planning Act	Made it illegal to build back-to-back houses
1911	National Insurance Act	Sick and unemployment pay introduced if you paid contributions into the scheme

▲ Table 5.4: Early twentieth-century Liberal reforms

THINK ❓

Study Source N.

● What happens to children's weight in term time?

● What happens to children's weight in holiday time?

● Does this source suggest providing free school meals for 'necessitous children' worked?

● Does this source prove that the Liberal welfare reforms worked?

Case study: School meals in Bradford

Manchester and Bradford local authorities had introduced school meals for 'necessitous children' and led the campaign for the introduction of school meals nationally. One of the first things the Liberal government did in 1906 was to introduce free school meals, but it was not compulsory for local authorities to provide them until 1914, when 14 million were served over the course of the year. Parents could be asked to make a contribution towards the cost if they could afford it, and the rest of the money had to come from local rates.

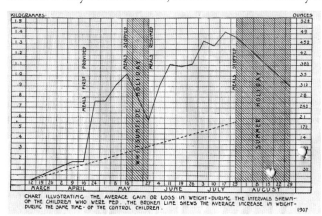

◀ **Source N:** Extract from a report by the City of Bradford medical officer on the effects of school meals, 1907

What were the achievements of the Liberal government of 1906–14?

In introducing the 1909 Budget, Lloyd George stated: 'This is a war budget ... to wage implacable warfare against poverty and squalidness.' But did these measures have as much impact as he stated they would? Medical inspections were introduced in 1907, but poor families could not afford to pay for necessary treatment. Pensions were introduced for over 70s (the average age of death was around 50), but only if you had worked all your life and could prove you were not a drunkard. The National Insurance scheme only applied if you paid regular contributions, but part of the cause of poverty was irregular employment. The 1909 Budget was thrown out in the House of Lords by the Conservative peers, who were opposed to paying for these reforms. It caused a constitutional crisis. Even some Liberals thought they were too expensive. And others, like those in the newly formed Labour Party, felt they did not go far enough.

The National Insurance Act 1911

Among the most significant was the introduction of the National Insurance Act 1911, which laid down the first steps towards the creation of a welfare state. The minister responsible for this Act was David Lloyd George, the Chancellor of the Exchequer. Lloyd George proposed an insurance scheme which involved workers and their employers making weekly contributions into a central fund which was used to give workers sickness benefit and free medical care from a panel doctor if they became ill. Those workers contributing into the scheme would be entitled to receive free medical attention and a payment of 10 shillings (50p) per week for 26 weeks if absent from work due to illness, after which a disability pension of 5 shillings (25p) paid weekly would be available. Many doctors, however, opposed the scheme but Lloyd George got over the opposition by paying each doctor more money for each patient they saw.

A second National Insurance Act was passed in 1913 which extended the scheme to include unemployment insurance. This allowed workers who became unemployed to claim unemployment benefit of 7 shillings per week up to a maximum of 15 weeks.

While this was a major step forward in providing welfare care it also had its limitations. The scheme was restricted to certain trades and occupations and it did not cover families (wives and children), only the insured husbands. Neither did it cover the unemployed, the elderly, the mentally ill or the chronically ill.

Welfare care during the 1920s and 1930s

After the First World War Lloyd George, who was now Prime Minister, promised 'a land fit for heroes' and he initiated a building programme for over 200,000 new houses to be built by 1922 to replace slum housing. He also extended National Insurance to cover a greater proportion of the workforce, allowing insured persons to claim both sickness and unemployment benefit. The payments came to be known as the dole.

During the economic depression of the 1930s it became harder to get good medical care and the government even reduced its contributions to health insurance. Many of the unemployed failed to keep up with their contributions into the scheme and by 1934 there were 4 million insurance policies on which people owed payments. As people had little money they were forced to rely on cheap, easy-to-obtain remedies which had been handed down through the generations.

THINK ?

1 Why were the Liberal reforms so divisive?

2 Which of the reforms do you think might be most successful? Why?

3 What can you learn from Source O about the National Insurance Act 1911?

4 To what extent does the National Insurance Act 1911 mark a change in government attitudes towards the welfare of its citizens?

◀ Source O: A government leaflet issued in 1911 to explain how the new National Insurance Scheme would work

The Beveridge Report

Lloyd George and the Liberal governments of 1906–14 had set up a free health service for insured workers but their wives and children had to pay for any treatment they needed. Visits to and from the doctor, medicine, spectacles and dental treatment all had to be paid for. During the Second World War questions began to be asked about how medical care should be best organised once the war was over.

▲ **Source P:** William Beveridge, in 1942, economist and social reformer

The Beveridge Report, 1942

In June 1941 the wartime government set up a committee to look into welfare provision and it was chaired by William Beveridge, a man who had helped formulate the Liberal welfare reforms of 1906–14. The Beveridge Report was published in December 1942 and it became a best seller with over 600,000 copies sold. It identified 'five evil giants' that needed to be tackled by government action and these were 'Want, Disease, Ignorance, Squalor and Idleness'. While Churchill, the wartime Conservative Prime Minister, was reluctant to act upon the suggestions of the report, the Labour Party, under its leader Clement Attlee, promised to put the proposals into action if it was elected after the war.

Tackling the 'five evil giants'

When the Labour Party was elected into office after a landslide victory in July 1945 it immediately set about implementing the recommendations of the Beveridge Report. It passed a number of Acts which together helped establish the 'Welfare State'.

Battle against want

- National Insurance Act 1946 provided benefits for the unemployed and pregnant women, pensions for the retired, allowances for the sick, widowed and mothers and children

Battle against squalor

- 1946 and 1949 Housing Acts provided financial aid to local authorities to rebuild towns and cities and provided for the building of council houses
- 1946 New Towns Act allowed for the construction of 14 new towns
- 1949 Access to the Countryside Act

Battle against idleness and ignorance

- 1944 Education Act provided free primary and secondary education
- 1947 School leaving age raised to 15
- 1948 Employment and Training Act attempted to establish a skilled workforce

Battle against disease

- 1946 National Health Service Act proposed the setting up of a free health service for all

> THINK
>
> How did the Labour government of 1945–51 deal with the 'five evil giants' identified by Beveridge?

Aneurin Bevan and the origins of the NHS

Aneurin Bevan was born in 1897 in Tredegar, a coalmining town in the South Wales valleys. He was one of ten children, only six of who lived into adulthood. His father was a miner and active trade unionist who died young from pneumoconiosis, the choking black dust disease which was so common among miners. When he turned 13 in 1910, Bevan went to work down the mine with his father. He did not enjoy the work or the long hours, and quickly became involved in the trade union movement, campaigning to improve conditions for miners and their families. In 1919, he won a scholarship to the Central Labour College in London, but upon returning to Wales he struggled to find employment. Eventually he secured a job as a union official and in 1922 was elected member of Tredegar Town Council.

In 1929, Bevan was elected as Labour Member of Parliament for Ebbw Vale and in 1945, following the election of a Labour Government under Clement Attlee, he was appointed Minister for Health and Housing. Bevan's roots in the South Wales coalfields provided him with a firm knowledge and understanding of the hardships facing British society in the mid-twentieth century (see Source Q). As councillor he had served on the hospital committee of the Tredegar Workingmen's Medical Aid Society. For a small weekly subscription, membership of the society provided free medical aid and hospital treatment to workers. In funding their own doctors, hospitals and convalescent homes, such friendly societies served as important providers of medical care. They operated as a miniature national health service and it was this model which Bevan used in 1946 to draft his proposals for the creation of a national health service across the whole country (see Source S).

Source Q: In a speech in the House of Commons during the reading of the National Health Service Bill on 30 April 1946, Aneurin Bevan, the Minister of Health, spelled out some of the weaknesses of the current system of medical care

Voluntary hospitals ... are badly distributed throughout the country. It is unfortunate that often endowments are left to finance hospitals in those parts of the country where the well-to-do live while in very many other of our industrial and rural districts there is inadequate hospital accommodation. Many of these voluntary hospitals are far too small ... furthermore, I believe it is disgusting in a civilised community that hospitals have to rely upon private charity.

Source S: A statement made in 1951 by Aneurin Bevan, the founder of the NHS

Illness is neither an indulgence for which people have to pay, nor an offence for which they should be penalised, but a misfortune, the cost of which should be shared by the community.

▲ Source R: Aneurin Bevan, Minister of Health, delivering a speech in 1947 in which he argued for the need to create a national health service

THINK ❓

1 Study Sources Q and S. What arguments does Bevan put forward for the creation of a national health service?

2 How did Bevan's background and upbringing in South Wales help to influence his desire to create a national health service?

Provision under the NHS after 1946

The National Health Service Act 1946 is considered to be the foundation stone in the creation of the Welfare State. The aim of the Act was to set up a health service that was to be 'free of charge' and available to everyone. The main features of the Act were:

- for the first time every British citizen could have free medical treatment – hospitals, doctors, nurses, pharmacists, opticians and dentists were brought together under one umbrella organisation
- all hospitals were to be brought under state control (**nationalisation**) under the control of the Ministry of Health
- consultants in hospitals received salaries and all treatment to patients in hospitals was to be free
- a national system of general practitioners (GPs) was to be set up and they, along with dentists and opticians, were to receive fees according to the numbers of patients on their registers, not according to the treatment given. All treatment was to be free to the patient
- health centres were to be set up – local authorities were paid to provide vaccinations, maternity care, district nurses, health visitors and ambulances
- the aim was to provide support 'from the cradle to the grave', financed out of taxation through the payment of National Insurance contributions.

These changes, announced in 1946, took two years to complete. A major reason for this was because the Minster for Health, Aneurin Bevan, faced considerable opposition to his proposals, especially from the British Medical Association (BMA) and from many Conservative MPs.

- The BMA opposed the changes – a survey of its members in January 1948 showed that 90 per cent of its members would refuse to cooperate with the NHS.
- Many local authorities and voluntary bodies opposed the nationalisation of all hospitals, fearing they would lose control over them.
- Arguments raged over the enormous costs involved.

However, Bevan was able to win the arguments by agreeing to a compromise which allowed doctors to take on fee-paying patients as long as they treated NHS patients as well. By the spring of 1948 opposition had crumbled and by the time the NHS was officially launched on 5 July 1948 over 90 per cent of doctors had enrolled on the new scheme.

THINK ?

1 Explain why the BMA was initially opposed to the setting up of an NHS.

2 Study Source T. What arguments does Aneurin Bevan put forward to support his idea of creating a national health service?

Source T: An extract from a speech made by Aneurin Bevan, Minister for Health, in 1946

Medical treatment should be made available to rich and poor alike in accordance with medical need and no other criteria. Worry about money in a time of sickness is a serious hindrance to recovery apart from its unnecessary cruelty. The records show that it is the mother in the average family who suffers most from the absence of a full health service. In trying to balance her budget she puts her own needs last. No society can call itself civilised if a sick person is denied medical aid because of lack of [money]. The essence of a satisfactory health service is that the rich and the poor are treated alike, that poverty is not a disability, and wealth is not advantaged.

Source U: An extract from the *British Medical Journal*, 18 January 1946

If the Bill is passed no patient or doctor will feel safe from interference by some ministerial edict or regulation. The Minister's spies will be everywhere, and intrigue will rule.

Hill meets mountain!

◀ Source V: A cartoon published in the *Daily Mirror* in 1946, suggesting that Bevan's proposals to create a NHS were popular

Source W: An account which appeared in the *Daily Mail* on 5 July 1948, the day the NHS officially came into being

On Monday morning you will wake in a New Britain, a state which takes over its citizens six months before they are born, providing care and free services from their birth, their schooling, sickness, workless days, widowhood and retirement. Finally, it helps [pay] the costs of their departure. All this, with free doctoring, dentistry and medicine – free bath chairs, too, if needed – for 4s. 11d [25p] of your weekly pay packet.

In October 1949 Bevan quoted figures to show what use had been made of the NHS since its launch the previous July:

■ 187 million prescriptions had been written out
■ 5.2 million pairs of glasses had been issued
■ 8.5 million people had received free dental treatment

By 1951 only 1.5 per cent of the population remained outside the NHS and when the Conservative government took office that year it agreed to keep the NHS.

Development of the NHS since 1948

The NHS is a very costly service to run and during its 68-year history there have been attempts to introduce changes. Demand for healthcare was huge, much greater than expected. In 1950 the NHS budget was under pressure and in 1952 charges for spectacles were introduced, prescriptions cost 1 shilling (5p) and dental treatment £1. It was the end of a completely free NHS.

Other changes occurred over the following decades:

■ In the early 1960s a new building programme was begun to replace out-of-date hospitals.
■ The Thatcher governments (1979–90) tried to cut the cost of the NHS and encouraged people to pay for private medical care.
■ During the 1990s hospitals were allowed to become trusts and GPs were allowed to become fund holders, buying services from hospitals and other providers.
■ In 1998 NHS Direct was launched, providing 24-hour health advice over the phone.
■ In 2002 primary care trusts were launched to allow for the administration and delivery of healthcare at the local level.
■ In 2004 foundation trusts were launched, run by local managers, staff and members of the public.

THINK

1 Use Source W and your own knowledge to describe the key features of the NHS when it was launched in 1948.

2 How has the NHS changed since 1948 to reflect the demands made upon a modern health service?

FOCUS TASK REVISITED

As you have worked through this chapter you have completed a time chart which has outlined the key developments in hospital, nursing and patient care. This will have provided you with an overview of the key changes, when they occurred, why they occurred and the impact they had. It is important that you use this fact file to build up a picture of the developments in patient care across time.

Use your time chart to identify:

1 which periods witnessed the most dramatic change in the functions and layout of hospitals

2 which periods witnessed the most dramatic change in the standards of nursing and patient care

3 the reasons why these changes occurred when they did.

ACTIVITY

What evidence can you find to support the view that since the beginning of the twentieth century the government has increasingly replaced voluntary organisations as the most important body responsible for providing care for patients?

TOPIC SUMMARY

- In medieval times the church played the principal role in providing hospital facilities and administering patient care.

- Patients entered medieval hospitals not to be cured of their illness but to receive God's protection and to pray and attend religious services.

- The dissolution of the monasteries in the mid-sixteenth century had a major impact upon the care of patients as the church no longer played such an active role.

- During the sixteenth and seventeenth centuries voluntary organisations began to take on the role of setting up and funding hospitals and patient care.

- These tended to be established in large towns and cities, and some came to specialise in the care of particular types of patients.

- During the eighteenth century there was a big expansion in the number of hospitals being built, financed through endowments by wealthy individuals.

- While new hospitals were built, the quality of nursing remained poor, as did the conditions for patients.

- The Crimean War helped change nursing care and this was largely the result of the actions of one woman, Florence Nightingale.

- Nightingale established new standards in nursing and patient care; she turned nursing into a respected profession.

- During the early twentieth century the government began to take on responsibility for the welfare of its people, setting up a National Insurance scheme to provide free medical treatment to those who paid into the scheme.

- The key turning point for national state care was the Beveridge Report of 1942 which recommended the government take action to establish a national system of free medical care.

- The result was the creation of the National Health Service in 1948 which offered free medical care to all from 'the cradle to the grave'.

Practice questions

1 Complete the sentences below with an accurate term:
Most medieval hospitals were closed down following Henry VIII's dissolution of the ....
One of the nurses who treated soldiers during the Crimean War was Betsi ....
The National Insurance Act of 1911 was the work of the Chancellor, David Lloyd ....
The NHS came into being in the year .... (*For guidance, see page 119.*)

2 Study Source C (page 77), Source F (page 79) and Source J (page 81). Use these three sources to identify one similarity and one difference in the care of patients in hospital over time. (*For guidance, see pages 120–1.*)

3 Describe the growth of endowed voluntary hospitals during the eighteenth century. (*For guidance, see page 123.*)

4 Explain why developments in nursing in the nineteenth and twentieth centuries were important in the development of patient care. (*For guidance, see page 124.*)

5 To what extent has the creation of the NHS been the most effective development in patient care over time? (*For guidance, see pages 126–8.*)

6 Developments in public health and welfare

This chapter focuses on the key question: How effective were attempts to improve public health and welfare over time?

Throughout history people have tried to keep themselves clean and healthy, not always successfully. There have also always been attempts by town councils and governments to pass laws to clean up nuisances, keep drinking water clean, and so on. But how successful have they been? Were medieval people, for example, dirtier than Victorian people? And if the measures used to improve public health *have* been successful, why do so many people still live in unhealthy conditions? This chapter explores the developments in public health and welfare over the last 1000 years or so.

FOCUS TASK

1 In the nineteenth century people wanting to reform public health became known as the 'Clean Party', whereas those opposed to it were called the 'Dirty Party'. As you work through *each* section of this chapter make a list, like the one below, of actions that might have been, or were, proposed by the Clean Party, that is, those wanting change; and why they were proposed. The first one has been done for you as an example.

The Clean Party	
Action	Reason
1388 Act of Parliament	To clear away nuisances in the streets

2 Similarly, compile a list of actions that were, or might have been, proposed by the Dirty Party.

The Dirty Party	
Action	Reason

You will need these lists when you have finished studying the chapter.

Public health and hygiene in medieval society

In the medieval period it was said you could smell a town long before you could see it. In Exeter, for example, you entered the town by a bridge crossing a river known locally as 'Shitebrook', where the night-soil men dumped their waste into the river. Mortality was higher in the towns and cities than in the countryside. People lived closer together, alongside their animals and their filth. We have already seen in Chapter 1 how unhealthy towns and cities were to live in. But were all towns and cities the same?

THINK

Look at Source A. Identify all the health hazards you can find in this picture of a medieval town.

▲ **Source A:** A medieval town drawn by the modern artist Norman Meredith, 1969

A case study of Coventry: were all medieval towns dirty and unhealthy places to live?

Surprisingly, the answer to this question is 'no'. Historian Dolly Jorgensen, in a recent academic paper 'What to do with waste', argues convincingly that Coventry council made a concerted and consistent effort to clean up the city.

In 1421 the mayor's proclamation required that every man clean the street in front of his house every Saturday or pay a 12 penny fine, with no exceptions being made. Waste collection services are recorded in 1420, when the council gave William Oteley the right to collect 1 penny from every resident and shop, on a quarterly basis, for his weekly street cleansing and waste removal services. The waste was to be sold to nearby farmers.

The council also specified designated waste disposal locations. Dunghills and waste pits naturally sprang up around the perimeter of the town. The council authorised the use of specific sites for particular types of waste. By 1427, five designated waste-disposal locations are mentioned for Coventry (Dolly Jorgenson only specifically lists four):

- a dunghill outside of the city limit beyond Greyfriar Gate
- a pit in the Little Park Street Gate
- a muckhill near the cross situated beyond New Gate, at Derne Gate
- a pit at Poodycroft.

In total, Coventry's council banned waste disposal in the River Sherbourne nine times between 1421 and 1475. There are, of course, two ways of looking at this. That the council took action, and it was widely ignored. Or, perhaps, the actions worked and when one or two individuals went back to the old ways then residents complained to the council who then took action.

In 1421 all **latrines** over the Red Ditch, a local stream, were ordered to be removed, to allow free flowing of the water, and to prevent flooding. Attempts were made to stop local stables and butchers throwing waste into the River Sherbourne, again to prevent flooding. All this evidence shows active intervention by the mayor and corporation of Coventry when faced with complaints by residents about the state of the town.

THINK ?

1 Does Dolly Jorgenson's paper on Coventry (she uses York as an example too) prove that towns were cleaner than we think?

2 What other actions could Coventry have taken to clean itself up?

3 How significant is the case of Coventry in understanding how clean British towns were at this time?

4 Which source best reflects Coventry as described by Dolly Jorgenson, Source A or Source B? Which source do you think is more realistic? Why?

▲ Source B: Some towns, such as Shrewsbury shown here, made efforts to become clean and orderly

Public health and hygiene in the sixteenth and seventeenth centuries

Look back at the weekly 'bill of mortality' for London for the week 21–28 February 1664 (Source E, page 24). How healthy was London as a place to live in 1664? There were outbreaks of the plague in 1563 (when 17,000 people were said to have died in London), 1575, 1584, 1589, 1603, 1636, 1647 and of course the biggest outbreak of all in 1665. In Aberdeen in 1647 the corporation passed regulations to control the plague including 'poysonne laid for destroying mice and rattons'. Towns and cities were still incredibly dirty and unhealthy places to live.

Yet there had been some attempts to improve public health. Henry VII recognised the menace to health from slaughterhouses and passed a law forbidding them within cities or towns, 'leste it might engendre sicknes, unto the destruction of the people'. In 1532 Henry VIII passed an act of parliament giving towns and cities the power to impose a tax in order to build sewers. Few places did. In 1547 people were forbidden to go to the toilet in the courtyards of the Royal Palaces – they had to find somewhere else to relieve themselves. Elizabeth I is said to have had a bath once every month of her life. Samuel Pepys states in his diary, in 1666, that his wife Elizabeth refused to allow him into the marriage bed until he had washed and had a bath. People were clearly making the link between dirt and disease. Yet towns and cities, and especially London, were growing so fast it was impossible to keep them clean.

After the Great Fire of London in 1666 an act of parliament was passed. 'An Act for the rebuilding of London ... and for the better regulation, uniformity and gracefulness of such new buildings as shall be erected for habitations', was designed to limit fire destruction by making streets wider, by insisting houses were built of stone with tile or slate roofs. Some historians argue that the rebuilding of London after the fire made it a healthier place, yet in 1690 we get yet another act of parliament requiring the paving and cleaning of the streets in London and surrounding areas, followed by further acts over the next few years requiring the removal of dung and the cleansing of common stairways, and prohibiting the keeping of pigs in dwelling houses.

> **THINK** ?
>
> 1 'Medieval towns were relatively clean compared to the sixteenth and seventeenth centuries'. How far do you agree with this statement?
>
> 2 How similar were attempts to clean up medieval Coventry and those of the sixteenth and seventeenth century?
>
> 3 In what way does Source C reinforce the view that London was an unhealthy place in which to live?

◀ **Source C:** Etching by Wenceslaus Hollar, a Czech artist living and working in London, c.1653. It shows part of London before the Great Fire of London

The impact of industrialisation on public health in the nineteenth century

In the nineteenth century many people moved to the cities to live (see Table 6.1). This is where the jobs were. Manchester made cotton, Birmingham made metal goods, Bradford spun and wove woollen cloth, Stoke on Trent made pottery, all in the new workshops and factories. By 1851 more people lived in towns than in the country, and Britain was known as the 'Workshop of the World'. Britain became rich making things and exporting them to the rest of the world.

People had to live close to where they worked, and there were very few building regulations. The supply of water, gas, and later electricity was all left to private companies who needed to make a profit, so areas where there were better-off people might have good supplies, whereas areas of poor people were not well served. As we have already seen in Chapter 5, the government believed in the philosophy of laissez-faire or 'leave it alone' meaning it was not the government's job to regulate things like working conditions, houses, transport and the like – it was up to individuals to do that for themselves. As a result working-class housing in the industrial cities could be very poor (see Sources D and E). In 1842 the average age of death for a member of a labourer's family in rural Rutland was 38; in Manchester, it was 17. And we have already seen in Chapter 1 that in Bethnal Green, in London, it was 16.

THINK

1 Look at Table 6.1 What problems might such rapid growth of towns and cities cause for public health and welfare?

2 Look at Source E. What might it have been like to live in one of these houses?

How might you keep yourself and your family clean, warm and dry?

3 To what extent does the interpretation of towns in Source D reflect both Table 6.1 and Source E in its portrayal of Victorian cities?

4 What evidence do you think Chesney has used to make his interpretation? Do you know any evidence he might have used that might have changed his interpretation to give a better view of Victorian cities?

Town	1801	1851	1901
London	957,000	2,362,000	4,536,000
Birmingham	71,000	233,000	523,000
Manchester	70,409	303,000	645,000
Liverpool	82,000	376,000	704,000
Bradford	13,000	104,000	280,000
Cardiff	2,000	18,000	164,000

▲ Table 6.1: Town growth, 1801–1901

Source D: From '*The Victorian Underworld*', **Kellow Chesney**

Hideous slums, some of them acres wide, some no more than crannies of obscure misery, make up a substantial part of the metropolis [London] ... In big, once handsome houses, thirty or more people of all ages may inhabit a single room.

Source E: A Glasgow slum, ▶ 1868

Investigations into public health in Merthyr Tydfil

In 1844, the Royal Commission on the Health of Towns investigated the state of public health in the rapidly expanding industrial town of Merthyr Tydfil. From a population of 7,705 in 1801, Merthyr had grown to 46,378 by 1851, making it the largest town in Wales. To supply the demand for housing, houses were built as quickly and cheaply as possible. There were no planning regulations and houses were crammed around the industrial sites they served.

In 1845, Sir Henry de la Beche reported on the drainage and sanitation of the town in which he painted a picture of unhygienic, disease ridden and unsanitary conditions across much of Merthyr Tydfil (see Source F).

Source F: Extract written by Sir Henry de la Beche from the *Second Report of the Commissioners for Enquiring into the State of Large Towns and Populous Districts* 1845

In these respects the town [Merthyr Tydfil] is in a sad state of neglect; with the exception of some little care in the main streets and regulations about removing ashes before the doors in Dowlais [a region of Merthyr Tydfil], all else is in a miserable condition. From the poorer inhabitants, who make up the mass of the population, throwing all slops and refuse into the nearest open gutter before their houses, from the impeded course of such channels and the scarcity of privies, some parts of the town are complete networks of filth, emitting noxious exhalations. Fortunately the fall of the ground is commonly so good that heavy rains carry away some of this filth. There is no Local Act for drainage and cleansing. During the rapid increase of this town no attention seems to have been paid to its drainage and the streets and houses have been built at random, as it suited the views of those who speculated in them.

Sir Henry de la Beche noted the scarcity of privies and in some parts of Merthyr up to 50 people had to share one toilet. He found that pumps and wells were often fed by surface water, which was contaminated by house refuse. He concluded that due to poor sanitation, a lack of clean and regular water supply, and filthy conditions, the town of Merthyr was a prime target for outbreaks of cholera and typhoid, epidemics which swept through the town during the first half of the nineteenth century. While little was done to address the problems identified by de la Beche, his work did stimulate further enquiry and in May 1849, T.W. Rammell, a Superintending Inspector, published his *Report to the General Board of Health on a Preliminary Inquiry into the Sewerage, Drainage ... of the town of Merthyr Tydfil 1850*, which reinforced the grim findings of de la Beche.

THINK ?

Use the evidence in Source F and your own knowledge to explain why the town of Merthyr Tydfil experienced frequent outbreaks of disease.

The work of Edwin Chadwick leading to Victorian improvements in public health

In 1854 a letter to *The Times* newspaper stated, 'We prefer to take our chance with cholera rather than be bullied into health.' This epitomises the great struggle that took place in the nineteenth century to persuade the government to act over living and working conditions. Edwin Chadwick was a member of the Poor Law Commission, set up as a consequence of the Poor Law Reform Act 1834. He became convinced that most people were poor because of ill-health rather than idleness, and spent the rest of his life advocating improvements in public health. He published his influential 'Report on the Sanitary Conditions of the Labouring Population' in 1842. Chadwick was instrumental in setting up the Health of Towns Association in 1844, which led to the first Public Health Act in 1848. This was the first time that the government had legislated on health issues.

Chadwick was an influential member of what became known as the 'Clean Party'. The Clean Party were those pushing for government action to improve conditions in towns. The 'Dirty Party', as they became known, were those MPs and others opposed to any such action. Their opposition was largely based on the monumental costs involved. Ratepayers, the wealthier people in a town, were keen to keep their rates (local taxes used to pay for local government) as low as possible so they favoured inaction. It was a member of the Dirty Party that wrote the 1854 letter to *The Times*.

> **THINK** ?
>
> 1 What part did Chadwick play in improving public health in the nineteenth century?
>
> 2 Why was the debate over reform referred to as the 'Clean Party versus the Dirty Party'?

▲ Edwin Chadwick, *c.*1854, physician and social reformer

The government acts at last: the great clean-up

It was the cholera epidemic of 1848, which killed over 52,000 people in England, rather than the Health of Towns Association that finally forced the government to act. They passed the Public Health Act 1848. This allowed local councils to improve conditions in their own town *if* they wished, and if they were prepared to pay for it. They could force towns with a particularly high death rate to take action over water supply and sewage, and to appoint a medical officer of health. The Central Board of Health was created and although it was abolished ten years later, the Act also encouraged local boards of health to be set up to appoint a medical officer, provide sewers, inspect lodging houses and check food which was offered for sale.

It was a start, but by 1872 only 50 councils had a medical officer of health. Some towns, like Leeds, took steps to improve their facilities, but many did not. Other acts followed, such as the Sanitary Act 1866, the Artisans Dwellings Act 1875 and finally the Public Health Act 1875, which was the real breakthrough. This Act had more power. It brought together a range of acts covering sewerage and drains, water supply, housing and disease. Local councils were *forced* to provide clean water, and appoint medical officers of health and sanitary inspectors who were to look after slaughterhouses and prevent contaminated food being sold. Local authorities were ordered to cover sewers, keep them in good condition, supply fresh water to their citizens, collect rubbish and provide street lighting. The Food and Drugs Act 1875 even regulated food and medicines. *Laissez-faire* seemed banished, as government began to take responsibility for public health.

London started building new sewers in 1858, and without doubt new sewers improved living conditions and public health. But there were other contributing factors. The Housing Act 1875 allowed councils to knock down poor housing and replace it. Flush toilets became more widely used in better-off homes and new products, like Pear's soap, became available and were cheap, making it easier for people and clothes to stay clean.

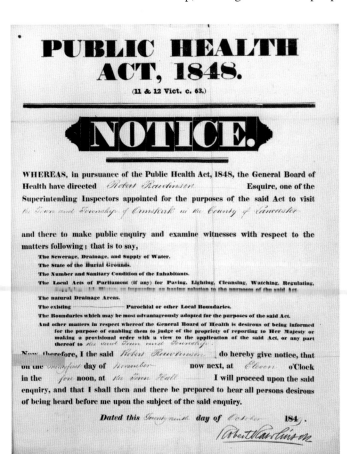

▲ Source G: A poster that appeared in the town of Ormskirk in Lancashire in October 1848. It was signed by the inspector appointed for Ormskirk

> **THINK** ?
>
> 1 What does Source G announce? What is going to happen in November 1848? On whose authority?
>
> 2 What does the poster tell us about the Public Health Act 1848?
>
> 3 Does this poster prove that the Public Health Act 1848 was effective at improving public health in Ormskirk? In Lancashire? In Britain? Explain your answer.

Case study: Sir Titus Salt – an individual acts to improve public health

Titus Salt was born near Leeds and moved to Bradford to work with his father as a woolstapler (wool dealer). He used Donskoi wool from Russia, alpaca fleece from South America and Mohair from angora goats in Turkey to make fine quality worsted cloths. By 1850 he owned and ran five separate spinning and weaving mills in Bradford and was the biggest employer in the area. His firm exhibited at the **Great Exhibition** in 1851, and sent cloth throughout the world. Queen Victoria was a customer for his alpaca cloth. Bradford had grown very rapidly, from 13,000 in 1803 to 43,000 in 1833 and over 100,000 in 1851. Conditions were very poor. One visitor in 1846, a German named George Weerth, wrote home, 'every other town in England is a paradise compared to this hole'. There were over 200 factory chimneys belching out smoke every day. **Life expectancy** for the poor at this time in Bradford was 20 years. Cholera and other diseases frequently broke out in the cramped conditions.

In 1843 a local man, Samuel Lister, invented a wool-combing machine and thousands of wool combers soon found themselves unemployed. Titus Salt set up and paid for soup kitchens to help. He was chosen as the second mayor of Bradford in 1848 and tried to persuade the council and local factory owners to do something to improve living and working conditions in Bradford. He failed. He even paid for his 2000 workers to have a day out in the country using the newly opened railway. In 1850 Salt took the decision to move his factories out of Bradford and bought a site at Shipley, out in the country but adjacent to the railway, the Leeds and Liverpool Canal, and the River Aire. Here, he built the largest and most up-to-date mill in Europe. The mill opened in 1853 employing 3500 workers.

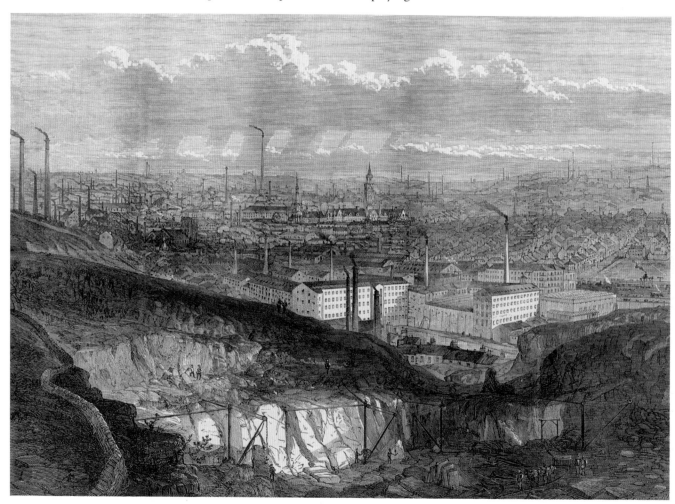

▲ Source H: Bradford 1873 engraving, view from Cliff Quarry

Saltaire

Not only did Salt build a mill, he also built a model village for his workers and called it Saltaire. His 11 children all had streets in the village named after them. There were over 800 houses (but no pubs) as well as wash houses with running water; bath houses; a hospital; an institute containing reading rooms, a library, a billiard room, a science lab and a concert hall; a school; a church; almshouses; allotments; a park; and a boathouse. He also donated land for a Methodist chapel to be built. He said he built the village 'to do good, and give his sons employment'. Saltaire is regarded as one of the best examples of nineteenth-century urban planning and is now a World Heritage Site.

Salt's motives

Historians argue about Salt's motives for building Saltaire. He claimed it was to help his workers lead 'healthy, virtuous lives'. Some say it was a matter of simple economics. Here he could control his workers better, and run his factories longer. It was also built beside the Leeds–Liverpool canal (visible in Source I) making it easy to move materials in and out. Others argued that it allowed Salt to show off his power and wealth. Another possible motive was tied up with his religious beliefs; that it was his Christian duty to try to make things better for those less fortunate than himself. When he died in 1876 an estimated 100,000 people lined the streets of Bradford to watch his funeral procession. The editor of the *Bradford Observer* wrote: 'Sir Titus Salt was perhaps the greatest captain of industry in England, not only because he gathered thousands under him, but also because, according to the light that was in him, he tried to care for all those thousands … he was upright in business, admirable in his private relations, he came without seeking the honour to be admittedly the best representative of the Employer Class in this part of the Country if not the whole Kingdom.'

> **THINK** ?
>
> 1 Look carefully at Sources H and I. Would you prefer to live in Bradford, or in Saltaire? Why?
>
> 2 Were the workers in Saltaire better off or worse off than they had been in Bradford?
>
> 3 Why do you think Titus Salt built a model village for his workers?
>
> 4 What does the life of Titus Salt tell us about public health in nineteenth-century Britain?

▲ Source I: Saltaire – engraving from *c.*1860

Birmingham and 'municipal socialism': a town acts to improve public health

As we have seen, throughout the 1840s and 1850s there was a gradual increase in local and central government intervention in public health, albeit reluctantly and always within the philosophy of voluntarism – even the 1848 Public Health Act allowed councils to improve conditions *if they wished*.

Birmingham provides an interesting case study of a local council that finally grasped the nettle of public health improvement. In the 1840s and 1850s the council was controlled by ratepayers who resisted demands to spend money. They blocked a move to purchase the Birmingham Waterworks Company (it was too expensive) and dismissed the borough engineer, replacing him immediately with his deputy at half the salary. They cut spending on roads by 50 per cent. In consequence, according to Thomas Carlyle, 'the streets are ill-built, ill-paved, always flimsy in their aspect – often poor, sometimes miserable. Not above one or two of them are paved with flagstones at the side.' The editor of the *Birmingham Daily Post* declared that citizens were so ashamed of their city that they refused to show the town centre to their visitors.

All that changed when Joseph Chamberlain became mayor in 1873. He devised what he called 'gas and water socialism', whereby the council would take over the gas and water companies, improve supplies, and use the profits to make the city a better place to live. He persuaded the council to borrow £2 million to buy the gas companies in 1875.

By 1879 the council had made £165,000 profit to spend on other projects, and built a public park on ten acres of derelict gas company land. By 1884 they had also reduced gas prices by 30 per cent. Water followed in 1876, and by 1880 the death rate in central Birmingham had dropped from 25.2 per thousand to 20.7 per thousand. The council also obtained a Birmingham Improvement Act in 1876 allowing it to clear 40 acres of slums in the centre of the city, removing 9000 people in the process, and replace these slums with a shopping centre (another source of income for the council), a council house, an art gallery, public library and new, broad, well-paved streets. Chamberlain wrote, in a letter to a friend in June 1876, that 'I think I have now almost completed my municipal programme. The town will be parked, paved, assised [magistrates courts], marketed, Gas-and-Watered and improved – all as the result of three years' active work.'

> **THINK** ?
>
> 1 How had attitudes to public health in Birmingham changed between the 1840s and the 1880s?
>
> 2 What was 'municipal socialism?' How did it work in Birmingham?
>
> 3 Do you think public health in Birmingham had improved by 1886?
>
> 4 Source I was published in 1886, at the time of the improvements in Birmingham. Does that make it reliable?
>
> 5 Which do you think had the most impact in Birmingham – the Public Health Act 1875 or Joseph Chamberlain? Why?

◄ **Source J:** A drawing by H.W. Brewer, taken from *The Graphic*, 1886. It shows Birmingham city centre in 1886 looking over Chamberlain Square with the newly extended council house and art gallery (in the centre), the town hall (the building with pillars on the right) and Christ Church between them

The need for fresh water: the building of reservoirs in Wales

All large towns and cities in Britain experienced an enormous increase in demand for water during the nineteenth century. The population of cities such as Liverpool and Birmingham was growing rapidly. What was needed was a clean water supply that would serve to counteract the diseases, such as cholera and typhoid, which spread as a result of contaminated water supplies.

Liverpool and Lake Vyrnwy

The first reservoir built in Wales by an English corporation was Lake Vyrnwy. Until the 1870s, Liverpool had obtained its water from sources in Lancashire, but as demand continued to grow the Corporation had to look further afield. A site in the Vyrnwy Valley in mid-Wales was found but in order to build the reservoir Liverpool Corporation had to buy up ten farms and the village of Llanwddyn. Work began on building the dam in 1881 and it was not completed until November 1889. It formed the largest masonry dam in Britain. As the dam filled, an aqueduct was built and pipes laid to transport the water to Liverpool. Water from Lake Vyrnwy first reached Liverpool in 14 July 1892 and the reservoir continues to supply the city with water to this day.

Birmingham and the Elan Valley

As Lake Vyrnwy was being built, the Birmingham Corporation was also looking towards Wales as a possible source for its water needs. In the early 1890s, the city of Birmingham bought land in the Elan Valley in the middle of Wales, with the aim of creating a series of man-made lakes from damming up the Elan and Claerwen Rivers within the Elan Valley. Water from the reservoirs would then be carried by gravity along a 116-kilometre pipeline to the rapidly expanding city of Birmingham.

The passing of the Birmingham Corporation Water Act in 1892 allowed the Corporation to acquire land by compulsory purchase within the Elan Valley. Over 100 people living in the valley had to move out and their homes were demolished. It included three manor houses, 18 farms, a school and a church. Work to construct four dams began in 1893 and the navvies (workers) had to live in temporary wooden huts near the construction site.

In 1904, the Elan Reservoir was opened by King Edward VII and Queen Alexandra. It supplied water to the city of Birmingham. Three dams were also opened at Craig Goch, Pen y Garreg and Caban Coch; a fourth at Dol-y-Mynach was never finished. An additional dam, the Claerwen Dam, was built much later and was opened in 1952 (see Figure 6.1).

With a regular supply of fresh water, public health within the cities of both Liverpool and Birmingham significantly improved.

> **THINK**
>
> 1   Describe how the cities of Liverpool and Birmingham managed to solve their problem of how to obtain a regular supply of fresh water.
>
> 2   What impact did the building of reservoirs have upon the Welsh communities living in the flooded areas?

▲ **Source K:** The Craig Goch dam in the Elan Valley. The reservoir behind it forms one of the main sources of water for the city of Birmingham

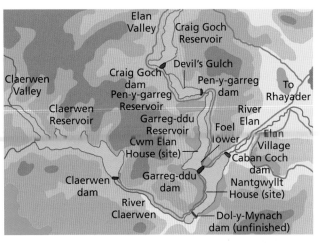

▲ **Figure 6.1:** The Elan Valley reservoirs and dams in mid-Wales. It shows the position of the two big mansion houses, Cwm Elan and Nantgwyllt, which were lost because of the flooding of the two valleys

Efforts to improve housing and pollution in the twentieth century

The twentieth century has seen a major shift in the role of government with regards to public health. The Victorian *laissez-faire* attitude has been replaced by an acceptance that it is the role of government to ensure people live healthy lives, but the extent of that role is still open to debate even today.

Identifying the problem

When the **Boer War** broke out in 1899, many volunteers for the army were unfit to serve. This was a shock to people at the time, and led to worries about the continued growth of the economy and strength of the British Empire. The state of these volunteers for the army provided the inspiration to investigate living conditions and the health of ordinary people in the new industrial cities, which eventually led to the changes introduced by the Liberal government from 1906. As a result, some social surveys were carried out in order to understand the extent of the problem. Charles Booth, in his *Life and Labour of the People* published in 1889 found that 35 per cent of London's population were living in abject poverty. His detailed survey had originally been designed to prove that the belief that 25 per cent of the population lived in poverty was far too high.

Seebohm Rowntree was inspired by Booth's work to do the same in York, where he lived. In 1897 and 1898 his researchers interviewed over 46,000 citizens of York, and his results were published in *Poverty, A Study in Town Life*, in 1901. He found that very nearly one-half of the working-class people in York lived in poverty. He is acknowledged as the inventor of the term 'poverty line', and became an adviser to the British Liberal politician Lloyd George after 1906.

A third book played an influential part in shifting opinion. In 1913 Maud Pember Reeves published *Round About a Pound A Week*, a detailed study of the way workers, many of them in regular employment like policemen, struggled to exist on an average wage of £1 a week. She had set out to prove that these families wasted money on drink but found that often women were going without food so the man (the wage earner) and the children could eat.

Progress after the First World War

The Housing Act 1919 proposed to build 500,000 homes 'Fit for Heroes', as the slogan at the time stated, but only half were built. Throughout the 1920s and 1930s there were subsidies for building council houses to rent to workers, and acts of parliament encouraging the demolition of slum properties, but economic difficulties between the wars limited progress. These were the first generation of houses to feature electricity, running water, bathrooms, indoor toilets and front and rear gardens. However, until well into the 1930s, some were being built with outdoor toilets. By 1939 over 1 million houses had been built by councils for workers to live in, but nearly 3 million had been built for better-off families. The damage and destruction during the Second World War made the demand for 'affordable' housing even greater. Clement Attlee's Labour government of 1945–51 built another 1 million homes. In the 1950s and 1960s emphasis changed to slum clearance from city centres.

Developments in Wales after the Second World War

Since the 1960s, surveys have been conducted in Wales to assess the state of repair of the nation's housing stock and also to identify homes deemed to be 'unfit' for living. The 1968 Welsh House Condition Survey found that 92,000 homes were unfit for human habitation, a figure which amounted to 10 per cent of the nation's housing stock. While later surveys saw this figure fall, down to 8.5 per cent (or 98,000 dwellings) in 1998, the figure remained high in comparison to England. At 12.5 per cent, Merthyr Tydfil had the highest percentage of unfit housing in 1998 and the Isle of Anglesey had the lowest at 4.4 per cent.

One consequence of such reports has been the introduction of improvement grants. By 1968, over 70,000 homes in Wales had been improved through such grants, with the money focused on houses built before 1945. Financial packages were also put in place to help stimulate the building of new homes and the 1960s saw a period of sustained growth in house building (see Table 6.1).

Table 6.1: Sustained growth in house building

Year	Houses built
1960	11,604
1961	12,669
1962	15,110
1963	14,080
1964	18,969
1965	19,524
1966	19,360
1967	20,158

THINK

1 Why were *Life and Labour of the People, Poverty, A Study in Town Life* and *Round About a Pound A Week* so influential at the time?

2 How similar, and how different, are the problems identified by the authors of these three books to those identified by Edwin Chadwick (page 96)?

3 What measures were put in place in the second half of the twentieth century to monitor and improve the quality of housing in Wales?

Clean air, new towns and tower blocks: the definitive answer to public health?

In December 1952, London was engulfed in what became known as the 'Killer Smog'. Air pollution and fumes from coal fires were trapped by an **anticyclone** over the city from 5–9 December. Recent estimates suggest over 12,000 people died and as many as 100,000 were taken ill as a result. It was the worst example of air pollution in Britain and led to the government passing Clean Air Acts in 1956 and 1968. This encouraged householders throughout the country to change from coal fires to the cleaner gas and electricity, or even burn coke and other smokeless fuels. There were further attempts to improve air quality in the Environment Protection Act 1990 and the Clean Air Act 1993. Both of these were focused on 'greenhouse gas' issues and aimed to limit both factory and motor car emissions. Latest research still shows that up to 27,000 people each year die prematurely from the impact of air pollution. Air pollution is an ongoing issue in many cities.

New towns and cities were also developed, such as Milton Keynes and Telford, in an attempt to move people out of dirty, overcrowded neighbourhoods into 'greener' settings, with industry and housing carefully segregated from one other. The first new town, at Letchworth, was the work of Ebenezer Howard, in 1903. Housing was meant to be attractive and spacious, gardens were an integral part of the plan, as were public parks and amenities. Cycle routes and pedestrian walkways were separated from traffic, to make it safer for all. By 2014 over 2.7 million people lived in new towns or cities in the UK.

In the 1960s, slum clearance took place in old towns and cities too, with a massive expansion of council-built housing in an attempt to provide everyone with a decent home to live in. Unfit housing was demolished and often replaced with 'modern' tower blocks; high-rise blocks of flats with all modern conveniences like central heating, bathrooms and fitted kitchens.

Towns like Chelmsley Wood, just outside Birmingham, sprung up overnight. From 1965 it was created on a greenfield site, with over 16,000 houses designed to house 50,000 people who were unable to find a home in the city. At the time it was the largest single residential development in Europe. Cumbernauld, just outside Glasgow, is another new town, started in 1956, and it is now the eighth largest town in Scotland.

Public reaction to the new towns is often mixed. Cumbernauld town centre, for example, was voted 'the worst building in Britain' in 2005, yet it was voted the 'Best Town' in Scotland in 2012. The new tower blocks were often built cheaply, from concrete and on out-of-town 'greenfield' sites. People usually liked the interiors, but often found themselves isolated from their community, missing their neighbours, the local shops and the pub on the street corner. Poor maintenance and cheap construction have led to many of these 'ideal' homes in the sky being demolished as people simply did not want to live in them.

ACTIVITIES ?

1 Carry out your own research on a new town that has been proposed or is being built near where you live.

2 How is it similar, and how is it different, to the new towns of the 1960s?

THINK ?

Why do you think so much emphasis was placed on building better housing for people?

◀ **Source L:** View of new town housing in Cumbernauld, 1970, built to solve the severe shortage of housing in post-war Glasgow

Local and national government attempts to improve public health and welfare in the twenty-first century: campaigns, fitness drives, healthy eating

Unhealthy lifestyles?

It seems stories such as the one in Source M appear in the news nearly every day. Scientists estimate that many of us are reducing our life expectancy by our lifestyle. We eat too much, often of the wrong foods, drink too much alcohol, do not take enough exercise and smoke too much. We also spend too much time sitting at a desk or playing computer games rather than exercising. All this adds up to a recipe for obesity and ill health. Obesity is one of the greatest causes of heart disease. So despite better diagnoses of illness, the availability of more effective medicines and skilled surgeons, it is all to no avail if we refuse to follow a healthy lifestyle.

> **Source M:** *Daily Telegraph*, 28 September 2015
>
> *Just one can of fizzy drink a day can increase the risk of heart attack by a third and dramatically raise the chance of diabetes and stroke, the largest ever study has found. The study … follows new official UK advice which says adults should restrict their sugar intake to just 30 grams – seven teaspoons – a day.*

THINK ?

1 How easy is it to live a healthier lifestyle?

2 Should money be spent on the prevention of disease rather than curing it?

Prevention or cure?

Throughout the twentieth century and today in the twenty-first century, governments have put more and more effort into health education, trying to persuade people to live healthier lifestyles and look after themselves better. Some people argue it is not the job of the government to do this; remember the letter to *The Times* newspaper at the time of the cholera outbreak in 1854 (see page 96)? Some people still think like that, arguing it is up to each individual to make their own choices. Others argue that there is a cost associated with poor lifestyle choices. For example, if people stopped smoking this would save the NHS millions of pounds each year. As fewer people would get sick, they would miss less time off work, and so it would also help the country get richer. This argument applies to almost every aspect of health. Some people argue it is better to spend money on prevention than having to spend money on curing diseases that could be prevented. These are the arguments that the Victorians were having (see page 96) when Chadwick and Southwood Smith were saying much the same thing.

ACTIVITIES ?

1 How is the Healthier Hackney Fund similar to other attempts at prevention mentioned in this section? How is it different?

2 Which, in your opinion, is more likely to be effective? Why?

3 Conduct some research to see if your local area has any schemes similar to Healthier Hackney

Hackney, in London, has adopted a different approach to prevention. It has set up the Healthier Hackney fund. Local communities and voluntary organisations can ask for grants to implement their own attempts to be healthier and to tackle health issues that are important to them. The fund was developed as a new approach for Hackney Council to work with the voluntary and community sector, and a new way to commission health services. The programme is based on the principle that organisations based in the heart of the community have strong connections to residents, know the issues, and often have fresh ideas for unique projects to deal with challenging health issues.

Fitness drives

In August 2009 the health secretary said, 'Promoting active lifestyles is the simple answer to many of the big challenges facing our country today. It can save us money and ease the burden on public services. The NHS has the green light to be bold and creative to help people to be fitter and more healthy.' 'Walking for health' (www.nhs.uk/Livewell/getting-started-guides/Pages/getting-started-walking.aspx) is typical of many fitness drives. It is a campaign designed to encourage people to take more exercise, to walk 10,000 steps a day, at moderate to fast pace. It provides support to gradually build up from no exercise to sufficient exercise. You can access cheap or free swimming classes and get reduced gym membership. 'Be Active' is Birmingham City Council's scheme to provide free leisure services to its residents. Participants register and are given a card which allows them to use a range of facilities from swimming pools and gyms to exercise classes and badminton courts for free during certain times. One-third of the local population has got involved since the project was launched in 2008. Research showed that three-quarters of users were not previously members of a leisure centre, gym or swimming pool and one-half were overweight or obese. It also had a knock-on effect in other areas with rises seen in the numbers seeking help over smoking and alcohol. Overall, for every £1 spent on the scheme £23 is estimated to have been recouped in health benefits.

Healthy eating

'Five-a-day' is perhaps the best known of all the government's health messages. The 'Five-A-Day' campaign is an attempt to get people to eat more fruit and vegetables (see Source N). It has been proven that eating more fruit and vegetables reduces your risk of heart disease and cancer.

The Eatwell Guide, issued in March 2016, is typical of national government campaigns. It depicts a healthy, balanced diet, which includes:

- eating at least five portions of a variety of fruit and vegetables every day
- basing meals on potatoes, bread, rice, pasta or other starchy carbohydrates, ideally wholegrain
- having some dairy or dairy alternatives (such as soya drinks), choosing lower fat and lower sugar options
- eating some beans, pulses, fish, eggs, meat and other proteins (including two portions of fish every week, one of which should be oily)
- choosing unsaturated oils and spreads and consuming in small amounts
- drinking six to eight cups or glasses of fluid a day
- if consuming foods and drinks high in fat, salt and sugar then have these less often and in small amounts.

> **THINK** ?
> Does this 'Eatwell' guide:
> a) explain clearly the benefits of healthy eating; and
> b) persuade you enough to change any unhealthy habits you might have?

▲ Source N: Campaign logo, to encourage us to eat better

FOCUS TASK REVISITED

1 At the beginning of this chapter, you were asked to create tables based on the actions and arguments of the nineteenth-century Clean and Dirty Parties. You will have worked through each section and made lists of actions that might have been, or were, proposed by the Clean Party and the Dirty Party and why they were proposed.

2 Prioritise each list, with the best arguments at the top.

3 Which of the two have, in your opinion, the best arguments? Why?

4 How have the arguments of the Clean Party and the Dirty Party changed over time?

5 Finally, return to the main question we started this chapter with – how effective have attempts been to improve public health and welfare over time? How are you going to measure 'effective'?

ACTIVITIES

1 In pairs, we would like you to produce a worksheet, with the heading, 'Improving public health and welfare.' The target audience is other students studying this course in the future.

2 You might like to consider these ideas:
   a) Why was public health and welfare an issue?
   b) When was the best time to live in towns and cities?
   c) When was the worst time to live in towns and cities?
   d) Whose job was it to improve conditions in towns and cities?
   e) How effective were attempts from the medieval period to today, to improve towns and cities?

Of course, these are only suggestions. It is entirely up to you how you devise your worksheet and what activities you ask other students to do. Have fun!

TOPIC SUMMARY

- In the medieval period towns were more unhealthy than rural areas – but sometimes made strong efforts to improve public health.
- Medieval attempts to clean up towns were not always successful.
- In the seventeenth century towns were healthier than ever.
- The Industrial Revolution completely changed things for the worse, and the government's belief in *laissez-faire* did not help.
- People seemed to split into the Clean Party and the Dirty Party.
- Some individuals worked hard to improve public health in the nineteenth century.
- In the twentieth century government made great efforts to improve public health.
- Many 'new towns' have been set up in an attempt to improve living conditions.
- Now, more emphasis is placed on prevention rather than cure. In particular, lots of emphasis is on healthy living.

Practice questions

1 Study Source A (page 91), Source E (page 94) and Source J (page 100). Use these sources to identify one similarity and one difference in public health over time. (*For guidance, see page 120–121.*)

2 Describe how some towns like Coventry attempted to improve public health during the fifteenth century. (*For guidance, see page 122.*)

3 Explain why the work of social reformers was important in improving public health during the second half of the nineteenth century. (*For guidance, see page 124.*)

4 To what extent was government action the most effective method of improving public health and welfare over time? (*For guidance, see page 126–128.*)

7 Study of a historic environment: Urban Cardiff in the nineteenth century

During the nineteenth century, as the Industrial Revolution gathered pace, the population of Wales and England expanded rapidly. Many small settlements grew into large industrial towns, employing many hundreds of workers in their factories. As travel was difficult, these workers needed to live close to their place of employment and this meant that lots of houses had to be built nearby. Health hazards soon emerged. Rubbish and raw sewage was thrown onto the street and the water supply was often contaminated. In such unhealthy living conditions outbreaks of disease were common. Diseases such as typhoid and cholera had a dramatic impact. During this period the then small town of Cardiff grew to become the largest town in Wales, and this rapid urban growth brought with it serious public health issues. In this unit you will investigate how Cardiff's dramatic growth caused major health concerns, and you will also examine how successful the authorities in the town were in addressing those public health issues.

FOCUS TASK

As you work through this chapter complete the table below which requires you to identify the main problems in public health, how the authorities attempted to tackle these health problems and then make a judgement as the degree of their success. Add a new row for each problem you identify.

What were the main public health problems resulting from the growth of industrial towns?	What attempts were made by the Victorians to overcome these problems?	To what extent did these changes bring about an improvement in public health?

The growth and development of Cardiff

The growth of Cardiff in the nineteenth century was dramatic. In the 1801 census its population was recorded as just 1,871 people, most of whom were Welsh-speaking and who engaged in small-scale trade and manufacturing, or in the import and export of goods from the town's small port. A century later in 1901 Cardiff had grown into the most populous town in Wales with a population of 164,333 people. This spectacular growth was the result of the development of its docks and the building of a railway that enabled the transport of coal mined in the South Wales valleys to the port at Cardiff, where it was then exported across the world (see Figure 7.1).

By 1901, Cardiff had become a thriving commercial centre where prosperous coal mine owners, ship owners, industrialists, merchants and bankers had helped develop the town into the coal metropolis of the world. Its population had become heavily anglicised and cosmopolitan.

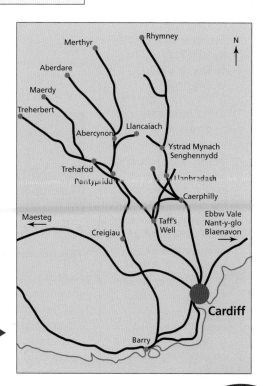

Figure 7.1: The geographical position of ▶ Cardiff and the coalmining towns of the South Wales valleys

Reasons for the growth of Cardiff

A number of factors influenced the growth and development of Cardiff.

Building of the Taff railway

The opening of the Glamorgan Canal in 1794 resulted in the slow development of the coal trade, with coal being transported to the docks and then shipped to markets across Britain. What jumpstarted the commercial development of Cardiff was the building of the Taff railway, which linked Merthyr Tydfil with Cardiff. This 26-mile railway, which opened in 1841, proved to be a turning point in Cardiff's development.

Branch lines into the Cynon and Rhondda valleys soon followed and by 1852 the railway line was linked to the Great Western Railway. This connected South Wales with the Midlands and London. The railway was able to transport the coal from the mines to the port and by 1900, South Wales had developed into the most important coal exporting area in Britain.

Development of the docks

The individual who played a significant role in developing the port at Cardiff was the Marquis of Bute who, in 1839, decided to build the Bute West Dock. As trade increased the docks had to be enlarged and in 1855 the East Dock was built. This was followed in 1874 by the digging of the Roath Basin and in 1887 by the building of the Roath Dock. While Cardiff was in competition with other ports along the coast of south-east Wales, such as Barry, Penarth and Newport, it successfully fought off this rivalry and by 1901 it had emerged as the main port for the export of coal from the Cynon, Rhondda and Rhymney valleys (see Table 7.1).

	1833	1851	1885	1905
Newport	440,492	451,491	2,684,111	4,186,430
Swansea	387,176	352,247	1,239,338	2,653,447
Cardiff	171,978	501,002	6,678,133	7,294,020

▲ Table 7.1: Export of coal and coke from ports in south-east Wales (figures are in tons)

Population growth

The building of the docks and other industrial sites caused large numbers of people to migrate from the small valley towns and rural villages of the Vale of Glamorgan and the west of England. Cardiff's population rose sharply and by 1841 a quarter of the town's residents had been born in England and more than ten per cent in Ireland. By 1871, Cardiff overtook Merthyr as the largest town in Wales. By the end of the century its population included immigrants from Italy, Germany, India and Somalia. As a result Cardiff became known as the 'Chicago of Wales' (see Table 7.2).

	1801	1851	1901
Merthyr Tydfil	7,750	46,378	69,228
Newport	1,087	19,323	67,270
Swansea	6,831	21,533	94,537
Cardiff	1,871	18,351	164,333

▲ Table 7.2: The population growth of towns in south-east Wales between 1801 and 1901

Trade, money and industry

Cardiff successfully fought off competition from rival ports, such as Barry, to become the dominant coal exporting port. It became the administrative centre of the coal trade, its Coal Exchange being the place where the price of coal on the British market was determined, and where the first million pound deal was struck in 1907. The town also developed into an important industrial centre with ironmaking and steelmaking plants, a shipbuilding industry, as well as a rope-making, brewing, milling and paper-making industry operating within the town.

THINK

1 How did each of the following developments help to make Cardiff the largest town in Wales by 1871?
   a) The railway
   b) The docks
   c) Population growth
   d) Industrial and commercial developments

2 Which of the factors listed in Question 1 do you consider to be the most important in explaining Cardiff's rapid development? Give reasons to support your answer.

3 Look at Tables 7.1 and 7.2. What does this information tell you about the growth of Cardiff in relation to its neighbouring towns?

Living conditions in Cardiff in the nineteenth century

As with many industrial towns in Victorian times, rapid expansion brought with it a catalogue of public health concerns. Cardiff was no exception to this trend.

Lack of regulation and planning

As Cardiff developed as a trading and industrial centre there was a need for housing to accommodate the workers who migrated into the town in increasing numbers. The lack of any official planning and regulation meant that many of the houses were of poor quality, having being built by builders more concerned with profit than with any health and safety consideration. Many of the houses were built back-to-back on the cheapest available site, without ventilation, drainage and an adequate water supply. The narrow streets were unpaved and often followed the lines of streams, which served as the means of transporting excrement and household waste (see Source A). There was no regulation of what was built or where it was built.

Health concerns

The 1848 Public Health Act (see page 113) introduced a system of inspection and these reports quickly identified serious health concerns in the rapidly expanding industrial towns. Common concerns were bad drainage, no provision for the disposal of sewage, a lack of adequate supplies of clear water, and squalid and overcrowded living conditions. Cardiff was no exception. It was a disease-ridden town and between 1842 and 1848 its mortality rate was 30 per 1,000, which compared badly to the UK average of 20 per 1,000, and deaths exceeded births by 4 per cent. Between 1847 and 1854 two cholera outbreaks accounted for 33 per cent of the total deaths that occurred during those years.

Poor sanitation

The local Medical Officer of Health's report on Cardiff for 1858 records that in the poorest area of the town there were 222 houses in which lived 2,920 people, the average house contained 26 inhabitants and the average for one street being 21 people per house. The worst area for overcrowding included Herbert Street, Stanley Street, Love Lane, Mary Anne Street and Little Frederick Street. In the late 1840s, Stanley Street had 18 houses and each house consisted of two rooms. Sanitation was primitive, each house containing a privy housed in a small room opening directly into the living room. The waste was infrequently emptied and it gave off a foul smell which drifted through the house. The street was barely four and a half metres wide and waste was strewn across it. Raw sewage flowed through many streets and sometimes seeped into the water supply.

▲ Source A: Mason's Arms Court, off Little Frederick Street. Typical housing in Cardiff in the mid-nineteenth century

Overcrowding and poor health

What added to the unhealthy environment was the chronic overcrowding, with most houses taking in lodgers to help pay the rent. The 1851 census reveals that 17 Stanley Street, kept by Michael Harrington, housed 54 men, women and children, while 15 Stanley Street, John Bryant's house, contained 36 people. Such crowded living conditions represented a serious risk to public health and the appearance of any disease spread rapidly through such areas. The denser the population the higher the risk of disease and death from illness, and this was the case with the cholera outbreaks of 1849 and 1854. Added to this was the poor diet, which weakened the body's defences and made it harder for the individual to fend off infection and illness (see Source B).

> **Source B: Extract taken from the *Annual Report of the Medical Officer of the Privy Council in Wales (1863)*, under the section 'Conditions of nourishment'**
>
> It must be remembered that shortage of food is very reluctantly accepted, and that, as a rule, great poorness of diet will only come when the lack of other basic necessities have come before it. Long before poor diet is a matter of hygienic concern ... the household will have been utterly without other material comfort: clothing and fuel will have been scantier than food – against bad weather there would have been no adequate protection ... There must be much direct causation of ill-health, and the associated causes of disease must be greatly strengthened by shortages.

Poor water supply

A factor that helped such outbreaks of disease was the polluted water supply. In Cardiff the locals obtained their water from either the Glamorganshire Canal, the Bute Dock, the River Taff or from town pumps and some private wells. Often this supply was poisoned by leakages from neighbouring cesspits, making the water unsuitable for drinking. A survey of the distribution of deaths following the two cholera outbreaks of 1849 and 1854 revealed that the middle and upper classes accounted for few of the deaths; the deaths were concentrated in the overcrowded areas of the town. Bute Docks recorded 33 deaths, the old workhouse 24, Stanley Street 19, Millicent Street 18, Mary Anne Street 13, yet the affluent Crockherbtown area recorded only one death.

With such overcrowding, poor sewage disposal and polluted water supplies it is not surprising that outbreaks of disease were common in Cardiff, and serious outbreaks of cholera and typhoid took a heavy toll upon the population.

> **THINK** ?
>
> 1 What do Sources A and B tell you about housing conditions in Cardiff in the mid-nineteenth century?
>
> 2 Study the information on pages 109 and 110. What would you consider to be the chief dangers to public health in Cardiff during the second half of the nineteenth century? Explain your points.

Outbreaks of cholera and typhoid

Outbreaks of typhoid were common in most industrial towns during the nineteenth century. It was a bacterial infection that spread throughout the body affecting many organs, often resulting in the death of the infected patient. It was spread through contaminated water or food, and was most likely to strike in the poorer areas of urban sites. Cardiff experienced a number of typhoid outbreaks but they were never as severe as those of cholera.

Asiatic cholera was an infectious disease which had a high mortality rate. Its symptoms were violent vomiting and diarrhoea. The diarrhoea was often referred to as 'rice water'. The outbreak of the disease was usually the result of a contaminated water supply. It affected all ages, and those already weak due to lack of food and living in unhygienic surroundings were particularly prone to infection.

Wales experienced four significant outbreaks of cholera, in 1832, 1849, 1854 and 1866. The disease first appeared in the UK in Sunderland in north-east England on 23 October 1831. It then spread across England and Wales resulting in around 21,832 deaths. It arrived in Cardiff via a sailor who was taken ill on board the ship *The Traveller* which had sailed from Gloucester. On this occasion Cardiff was lucky and less than half a dozen people died from the disease in the town.

The 1849 cholera outbreak

Cholera reappeared in Britain in September 1848 and over the following two years it caused 52,293 deaths.

On this occasion Cardiff was badly affected. The first recorded case of cholera in Wales was in Cardiff on 13 May 1849, when a nineteen-year-old canal worker died after an attack lasting less than 24 hours. In the subsequent months the disease spread among the South Wales valleys, reaping a very heavy toll.

During the summer months of 1849 the disease increased in severity. The greatest number of deaths were recorded between June and September (see Table 7.3) and by the time the last death occurred in November, 396 people had died from cholera, 206 men and 190 women. It had a devastating impact upon the town.

Month	Deaths
May	39
June	135
July	69
August	91
September	55
October	3
November	1

▲ Table 7.3: Deaths from cholera in Cardiff during 1849

Attempts to manage the outbreak

Responsibility for trying to curb the spread of the disease fell upon the Board of Guardians. At a meeting on 26 May, the town was divided into three districts and on 8 June a committee was appointed to implement the cholera precautions ordered by the General Board of Health. The Board of Guardians was given the power to appoint additional officers who were used to make house-to-house visits twice a day in the poorer districts. They had the power to order the 'frequent and effectual cleansing and whitewashing and the removal of all filth, odours and nuisances.' Lodging houses were inspected and landlords were required to ventilate them. As the death toll increased the town was further sub-divided into seven smaller districts and medical officers were appointed to each. Dispensaries were opened across the town where 'remedies' were issued as well as advice on how to deal with bowel complaints.

There was some disagreement among medical officers as to the exact cause and reasons for the spread of the cholera outbreak in Cardiff. Dr John Sutherland, the medical inspector to the General Board of Health, believed that it was caused by contaminated water as a result of the draining of part of the Glamorgan Canal (see Source C), while the medical registrar of Cardiff believed it was due to chronic overcrowding (see Source D).

> **Source C: Comments made by Dr John Sutherland, Medical Inspector to the General Board of Health, which were recorded in the *Report of the General Board of Health on the Epidemic Cholera of 1848 and 1849*, published in 1850**
>
> On the 26 of May the end of the canal nearest the sea was emptied in order to admit repairs to the lock. By this process, a large surface of black stinking mud was exposed to the direct action of a hot sun, and the result was that very offensive fumes were immediately smelled.

> **Source D: The observations of the registrar of Cardiff which were quoted in the *Report on the Mortality of Cholera in England, 1848-49* published in 1852**
>
> [The infection was due] ... to the very crowded state of the streets and houses of the poorer localities to which the disease has thus far chiefly confined itself.

Blame for the outbreak

One alarming feature of the 1849 epidemic was the anti-Irish feeling it aroused since the disease had had a particularly devastating impact in their locality. As part of this xenophobia, the Irish became the scapegoats who were blamed for spreading the disease. A claim was made that the disease had increased by between 5 and 8 per cent because of the 'immense Irish invasion into the town' (see Source E). Other causes were blamed on evils such as drunkenness and the irresponsible spending habits of the poorest classes.

> **Source E: An account in the *Cardiff and Merthyr Guardian* on 16 June 1849, which blamed the Irish community for spreading the disease**
>
> We are accustomed to associate notions of filth, squalor and beggarly destitution with everything Irish from the large number of lazy, idle and wretched natives of the sister island who are continually crossing our paths.

The 1854, 1866 and 1893 outbreaks

Cholera reappeared in Cardiff in August 1854 and by the time it had faded away in the early Autumn, 225 people had died from the disease. While this was a high figure it was considerably less than Merthyr Tydfil which experienced 455 deaths, making it the worst hit town in Wales. The next major outbreak of cholera occurred in 1866 when Cardiff experienced 76 deaths. The last time cholera gained a footing in the UK was during the summer months of 1893. Cardiff was affected, experiencing three deaths but by then improvements such as piped water and sewers limited the impact of the infection.

> **THINK** ?
>
> 1 Study Sources C, D and E. Use the information in the sources and your knowledge to complete this table.
>
> | | What reason is given for the cholera outbreak? | What evidence can you find to support this reason? |
> |---|---|---|
> | Source C | | |
> | Source D | | |
> | Source E | | |
>
> 2 Can you think why the cholera outbreaks of 1866 and 1893 resulted in less deaths in Cardiff than the outbreaks of 1849 and 1854 did? Explain your conclusions.

Attempts at improving public health

A number of government acts from the mid-nineteenth century onwards attempted to bring about improvements in the health of the nation. In 1847, a severe outbreak of typhoid occurred in Cardiff which killed nearly 200 people. A doctor in the town, Henry James Paine, investigated the outbreak and after examining 283 cases he concluded that there was a direct connection between unsanitary conditions and the intensity of the disease. He found that the majority of cases were centred upon the poor and overcrowded areas of the town. However, little notice was taken of Dr Paine's findings and it was not until the passing of public health legislation by the government that Cardiff began to take action to improve the health of its citizens.

The Public Health Act, 1848

The Public Health Act of 1848 was in many respects the starting point for the gradual improvement in public health. It granted permission for towns to set up Local Boards of Health where there was a significant demand. These Boards were to be responsible for:

- sewers and drains
- wells and supplies of water
- refuse and sewage systems
- control of slaughterhouses
- removal of nuisances
- control of housing unfit for human habitation
- providing burial grounds, recreation parks, public baths and other amenities.

A petition was set up in Cardiff, signed by more than one-tenth of the people who lived there, calling for the setting up of a Board of Health in the town. One of the Board's first actions was to appoint Dr Henry James Paine as the town's first Medical Officer of Health, a post he occupied from 1853 to 1889.

The Rammell Report, 1850

In 1849, Thomas Rammell, the Superintendent Inspector of the General Board of Health, carried out an inquiry into the state of public health in Cardiff. He published a report in 1850 and it catalogued a list of health concerns – open sewers, unclean public water supply, inadequate housing, high rents and overcrowding. He recommended a number of key changes in order to improve public health within the town:

- a safe supply of pure water
- a system of drainage
- a system to deal with sewage
- the collection of refuse
- increased and improved housing for the poor
- the opening of a new cemetery on the edge of the town.

It took several decades for Cardiff Corporation (council), to carry out these improvements but change was initiated by its first Medical Officer of Health, Dr Paine.

The work of Dr Henry James Paine

In 1850, the Cardiff Waterworks Act granted permission for the drilling of wells to secure the supply of drinking water for the town. By 1856, with Dr Paine pushing the scheme, a new system of sewerage and drainage was completed at a cost of £200,000. As a result of this improved water supply, when another cholera outbreak occurred in 1866, the number of deaths was only 66, a significant reduction upon previous outbreaks. In an effort to reduce the threat of cholera entering the town from sailors in the docks, Dr Paine was instrumental in buying and fitting out the HMS *Hamadryad* hospital ship which was moored in the docklands, an area which later became known as Tiger Bay (see page 79). As Medical Officer Dr Paine took action to reduce the effects of smallpox in Cardiff through inoculation. He also passed bylaws to stop the tipping of rubbish and sewage into the River Taff.

It has been estimated that through his pioneering efforts to keep Cardiff free from disease and improve sanitation, Dr Paine may have saved over 15,000 lives by the time of his retirement in 1889.

▲ Source F: Dr Henry James Paine, Medical Officer for Cardiff between 1853 and 1889. He played a leading role in improving public health in the town

The supply of clean water

The passing of the Sanitary Act in 1866 made local authorities responsible for the sewers, water supply and street cleaning. In Cardiff, action had been taken prior to this to improve the water supply. The Cardiff Waterworks Act of 1850 led to the building of a pumping station at Ely and the laying of mains water pipes across the town during the 1850s to supply filtered water. As the town grew the company built a storage reservoir at Llanishen.

In 1879, Cardiff Corporation took over the water supply to the town and additional water storage reservoirs were constructed in the late 1880s.

The town infirmary

Urban growth was often the trigger for the building of hospitals during the eighteenth and nineteenth centuries. In 1823, a dispensary was set up in Cardiff to provide medical aid to the poor. This led to pressure to build a hospital and it was through the donation of £3,550 by a prosperous solicitor, Daniel Jones of Beaupré Castle, that an infirmary was built. Opened in 1837, the Glamorgan and Monmouth Infirmary and Dispensary treated the 'deserving poor' for free but charged those who could afford to pay.

The rapid growth of Cardiff put increasing pressure on the hospital to expand and extensions were built frequently. A new hospital was opened in 1883 but it soon proved too small to meet the needs of the rising population, and an extension was added in 1894 (see Source G). In 1895, it was renamed the Cardiff Infirmary. The population served by this single hospital had increased from 65,811 in 1831 to 885,000 in 1914.

Source G: A comment on a new plan to extend Cardiff Infirmary made by the Reverend W.E. Winks in *Programme, Guide and Souvenir of a Grand Bazaar in Aid of the Building Fund of Cardiff Infirmary, 1896*

It seems that no building belonging to any public institution in this town, is adequate to its needs for more than ten years or so. The town is like a youth who grows so rapidly that his clothes become too small for him, while they are yet comparatively new.

Table 7.4: The number of beds in Cardiff Infirmary

Year	No. of beds
1837	20
1862	50
1873	60
1883	120
1903	154
1911	270

Public baths and wash houses

The Public Baths and Wash-houses Act 1846 enabled local authorities to raise money through rates to build public baths. The Victorians realised that improvements in public health resulted from providing people with opportunities to wash themselves and their clothes.

In May 1862, the Cardiff Baths Company opened new facilities at Guildford Street. It contained two large swimming pools, hot water baths and a Turkish bath. However, due to low attendance and a failure to make a profit, it was forced to shut down by the early 1870s. Many poor people could not afford the entrance fees. It was then taken over by the Cardiff Corporation and by the end of the century the baths had grown in popularity, necessitating major remodelling between 1895 and 1896.

Source H: Dorothy Scannell describes a visit to the public baths in the 1890s, an event performed by thousands of people each week

When we were too old for mother to bathe us in the little tin bath, we would join the older ones every Friday and go to the public baths. We would have to go early for a large crowd collected in the waiting room when the young people came home from work. It was impossible for a girl to pop in the baths before a dance, for sometimes it was necessary to wait over two hours for one's bath. We always saw the local brides there the night before their wedding.

Other public health improvements

The Public Health Act of 1875 built upon previous laws and ordered local authorities to cover sewers, keep them in good condition, supply fresh water to their citizens, collect rubbish and provide street lighting.

THINK ?

1 Did government legislation help to improve public health in Cardiff during the nineteenth century? Support your answer with specific examples.

2 How important was Dr Henry James Paine to improvements in public health in Cardiff during this period?

3 Study Source H. How did the opening of public baths and wash houses improve public health?

Effectiveness of attempts to improve public health

While repeated typhoid and cholera outbreaks raised the profile of the squalid living conditions in many parts of Cardiff, they did little to bring about permanent improvements in public health in the town. After any infection, there was an initial push to purify houses, reduce overcrowding, whitewash buildings and collect refuse, but this was too often just a short-term reaction and conditions soon drifted back to what they were prior to the outbreaks of disease.

As we have seen, the real trigger for more permanent change came from government inquiries and the passing of specific legislation:

- The Public Health Act 1848. This resulted in Cardiff setting up a Local Board of Health and appointing a Medical Officer (Dr H.J. Paine) to oversee public health.
- The Rammell Report 1850. This highlighted the need to take action to improve public health. Dr H.J. Paine used this report as the basis for the changes he introduced.
- The Sanitary Act 1866. This forced local authorities to take responsibility to ensure that there was a safe supply of water. Cardiff Corporation took on this responsibility from private companies in 1879.
- Public Baths and Wash-houses Act 1846. This enabled local authorities to build public baths. Cardiff Corporation took over responsibility for operating the town baths from private companies in the early 1870s.

Another trigger for improvement came from changed attitudes towards public health. During the second half of the nineteenth century local authorities adopted a more philanthropic approach, introducing measures specifically intended to improve living conditions for its inhabitants. Cardiff Corporation took on this responsibility, ensuring that public parks were opened across the town: Roath Park in 1894, Victoria Park in 1897 and Cathays Park in 1897. It also took action to ensure the streets were paved and lit at night, Cardiff Gas Works having been set up as early as 1821. A new cemetery, Cathays Cemetery, was opened in 1859. Other facilities, such as a public library that was opened in 1861, and public baths were made available. Planning regulations were introduced as well as annual medical reports on the state of public health.

The extent to which such improvements had an impact can be gauged from the decline in the death toll from each cholera epidemic, at a time when Cardiff's population was rising sharply (see Table 7.5). By 1900, Cardiff had the fourth lowest infant mortality rate of a town its size in Britain (compared with a quarter of the children dying before their first birthday in the 1840s). This marked a significant improvement.

Cholera outbreaks	Number of deaths in Cardiff	Population of Cardiff
1849	396	18,351 (1851 census)
1854	225	18,351 (1851 census)
1866	76	48,965 (1861 census)
1893	3	128,915 (1891 census)

▲ Table 7.5: The number of deaths in Cardiff during each cholera epidemic, in relation to its population size

> **THINK** ?
>
> Use the information in Table 7.5 and your own knowledge to identify any links between cholera outbreaks and improvements in public health in Cardiff.

By 1905, when Cardiff became a city, the town had a university, sports stadiums and open parks in the centre of the town, and fine grand baroque buildings such as the City Hall and the National Museum had been built. The town was developing a civic pride in its appearance (see Source I). However, some areas were still squalid and pockets of deprivation existed well into the early twentieth century. Older streets such as Stanley Street showed little sign of improvement and, as late as 1891, the local newspaper reported on the unhealthy environment of the older industrial housing (see Source J).

▲ **Source I:** Cardiff City Hall and National Museum which were completed in 1905

> **Source J:** An account of the squalid living conditions in Stanley Street as reported in the *Cardiff Argus* newspaper on 10 January 1891
>
> Stanley Street … is only a few feet wide, having in the centre of it a narrow channel into which is poured all the liquid refuge, slops etc., from the houses on each side. The stench from the lower portion of this open gutter is, in summer, often terrible. The street, or rather pitched footway, forms the drying ground of the occupants of the houses. A clothesline, common to all, extends from one end of the alley to another and this is, in fine weather, constantly in use.

To what extent, therefore, had public health improved in Cardiff by 1900? While there had been a significant improvement in the quality of housing through the introduction of planning laws and building regulations and inspections, there still remained pockets of deprivation such as Stanley Street. A greater impact had resulted from the securing of a safe supply of pure drinking water through the laying of underground pipes. This significantly reduced the risk of contamination, which was a major cause of cholera. Alongside this was the improvement in the disposal of sewage through the building of underground sewers and the collection of household rubbish. Improved medical facilities, such as an infirmary to hold infectious individuals and the opening of public baths and laundry facilities, all helped to improve the overall standard of public health, making the town of Cardiff a healthier environment to live in.

> THINK ?
>
> 1 Study Sources I and J. What do they suggest about public health in Cardiff by 1905?
> 2 How successful was Cardiff Corporation in improving public health within the town by the end of the nineteenth century?

FOCUS TASK REVISITED

Look over the focus task you have completed while working through this chapter. Working in pairs, discuss the following:

1 What, in your opinion, were the most significant public health problems facing the people of Cardiff in the middle of the nineteenth century?

2 To what extent were those problems overcome by the end of the nineteenth century? Give specific examples to illustrate your answer.

ACTIVITIES

Divide into groups of four or five to complete the following task.

In today's world we are told that there is an increasing chance of the emergence of a disease that is resistant to treatment from antibiotics. If such a disease, which proved to be highly contagious and had a high rate of death following infection, was to break out in a large city such as Cardiff, what action do you think the government should take to:

1 limit the spread of the disease

2 reduce the high rate of death?

Share and compare the recommendations of the different groups in your class.

TOPIC SUMMARY

- The population of Cardiff grew rapidly during the nineteenth century.
- From a small town of 1,871 inhabitants in 1801, Cardiff became Wales' largest town by 1901, with a population of 164,333.
- Cardiff's rapid growth was due to a combination of factors – the Taff railway, the docks, migration, and industrial and commercial developments.
- Living conditions in the rapidly expanding town were squalid due to poor-quality housing, overcrowding, lack of clean water, open sewers, and no collection of refuse.
- Outbreaks of disease were common, especially typhoid and cholera, which were spread by contaminated water.
- Cardiff experienced four outbreaks of cholera, in 1849, 1854, 1866 and 1893.
- The government passed legislation which aimed at improving living conditions: the Public Baths and Wash-houses Act, the Public Health Act and the Sanitary Act.
- In response to the Public Health Act of 1848 Cardiff set up a Local Board of Health.
- Dr Henry James Paine was appointed Medical Officer of Health for Cardiff in 1853, a post he held until retirement in 1889.
- The Cardiff Infirmary was opened in 1837 and a new replacement hospital was opened in 1883.
- The Cardiff Bath Company opened a public swimming pool and wash house at Guildford Street in 1862.
- Cardiff Corporation carried out improvements, opening parks, a new cemetery, a public library, undertook the laying of pavements and arranged for the collection of refuse.
- There were improvements in public health, which was evidenced by the decline in deaths when there was a cholera outbreak, but pockets of deprivation existed in parts of the town.

Practice questions

1 Describe living conditions in Cardiff during the time of the cholera outbreaks of 1849 and 1854. (*For guidance, see page 122.*)

2 Explain why public health had improved in industrial towns like Cardiff by the end of the nineteenth century. (*For guidance, see page 124.*)

WJEC Examination Guidance

This section will give you step-by-step guidance on how best to approach and answer the types of questions that you will face in the exam. Below is model exam paper with a set of exam-style questions (without the sources).

Unit three: thematic study

> **In Question 1 you have to** provide a specific historical term to complete the sentence. It may be a name, date, specific method or medical term.

> **In Question 2 you have to** compare and contrast what you can see in three sources. You need to pick out features that are the same/similar and also points of difference/contrast.

> **In Question 3 you have to** demonstrate your own knowledge and understanding of a key feature, and include specific information relating to the historic environment named in the question.

> **In Question 4 you have to** demonstrate your own knowledge and understanding of a key feature. You should aim to include specific factual detail.

> **In Question 5 you have to** identify a number of reasons to explain why a key development/ issue was important or significant. You should aim to include specific factual detail.

> **In Question 6 you have to** use your knowledge to explain the importance/significance/ effectiveness of a key issue, supporting your answer with specific factual detail. This will enable you to develop a reasoned and substantiated judgement.

> **In Question 7 you have to** develop a two-sided answer which provides specific evidence to support and counter the key issue named in the question. You must cover three historical time periods and you **must** provide detail on the **Welsh context**. Remember to check your spelling, punctuation and grammar.

3B Changes in Health and Medicine, c.1340 to the present day

Time allowed: 1 hour and 15 minutes

1 Complete the sentences below with an accurate term.

   a) James Lister is best known for his work with ....

   b) William Harvey wrote a book about the circulation of the ....

   c) The National Health Service was set up after World War ....

   d) An influential report on public health was written in 1842 by Edwin .... **[4 marks]**

2 Look at the three sources which show living conditions over time and answer the question that follows.

Use Sources A, B and C to identify one similarity and one difference in living conditions over time. **[4 marks]**

[Use at least two of the sources to answer the question]

3 Describe the living conditions in industrial towns such as Cardiff that led to cholera outbreaks in the mid-nineteenth century. **[6 marks]**

4 Describe traditional herbal remedies that were used before the modern era. **[6 marks]**

[In your answer you are advised to refer to herbal remedies that were used in Wales]

5 Explain why developments in vaccination were important in the prevention of illness and disease in the nineteenth and twentieth centuries. **[12 marks]**

6 How effective was the development and use of scanning techniques in the twentieth century? **[12 marks]**

7 To what extent has the development of modern anaesthetics been the most effective method of treating and curing illness over time? **[16 marks]**

In your answer you should:

■ assess the effectiveness of modern anaesthetics as a method of treating illness

■ discuss the effectiveness of other methods of treating illness over three historical eras

■ include direct references to the history of Wales.

Marks for spelling, punctuation and the accurate use of grammar and specialist language are allocated to this question. **[4 marks]**

Total marks for the paper: 64

Examination guidance for the WJEC examination

Examination guidance for Question 1

This section provides guidance on how to answer the factual knowledge questions. Look at the following question:

Complete the sentences below with an accurate term.

a) Medieval doctors based their medical knowledge on the theory of the four ....
b) The seventeenth century saw the outbreak in London of the Great ....
c) Florence Nightingale brought about important changes in modern ....
d) An important report on welfare provision was written in 1942 by William ....

How to answer

- Make sure you revise your notes well – these questions require good factual knowledge.
- In your revision concentrate upon key issues such as:
  - ☐ the names of important individuals who advanced medical knowledge
  - ☐ the names of the different methods of treating illness and disease
  - ☐ the names of key health and medical reports and acts of parliament
  - ☐ key medical terms
  - ☐ key developments in the history of health and medicine.
- If in doubt, have a guess – never leave the space blank.

Example

---

a) Medieval doctors based their medical knowledge on the theory of the four humours.
b) The seventeenth century saw the outbreak in London of the Great Plague.
c) Florence Nightingale brought about important changes in modern nursing.
d) An important report on welfare provision was written in 1942 by William Beveridge.

Now try answering the following question:

Complete the sentences below with an accurate term.

a) The Black Death was spread by fleas living on ....
b) Edward Jenner is best known for his work with ....
c) Addenbrookes and Guys are examples of endowed ....
d) The link between germs and disease was investigated by Louis ....

Examination guidance for Question 2

This section provides guidance on how to answer the 'similarity and difference' question. You will have to pick out information from three sources to identify both similarities and differences. Look at the following question:

> Look at the three sources below which show the treatment of illness over time. Use Sources A, B and C to identify one similarity and one difference in the treatment of illness over time.

▲ **Source A:** A man being bled using leeches during medieval times

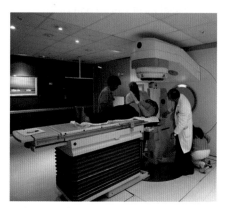

▲ **Source C:** A patient undergoing radiation therapy

▲ **Source B:** Professor Alexander Fleming and Penicillin

How to answer

- Study the three sources – pick out features that are the same or similar.
- Pick out points that contrast – which show things that are different.
- Make sure you refer to both similarity **and** difference in your answer.

Example

All the sources show attempts by medical persons to treat illness. Within their own time period they were all considered to be medical experts – Source A shows a physician treating a patient during medieval times, Source B shows a professor of medicine and Source C shows a specialist doctor.

> **Step 1:** Identify features of similarity – things which are the same across the sources

However, the sources differ in the type of treatment shown. Source A shows primitive methods of bleeding the patient using leeches. Source B shows the development of specialist drugs to fight illness and disease, and Source C shows the use of modern scanning machines to detect illness and disease. It shows how the methods of treating illness have changed over time.

> **Step 2:** Identify features of difference – things which contrast and are not the same across the sources

Now try answering the following question:

Look at the three sources below, which show public health over time. Use Sources A, B and C to identify one similarity and one difference in public health over time.

▲ Source A: A medieval town scene

▲ Source B: The Public Health Act 1848

▲ Source C: A housing development of the 1970s

Examination guidance for Question 3

This section provides guidance on how to answer the question that relates the study of a historic environment connected with health and medicine. It is a 'describe' question which requires you to demonstrate your own knowledge and understanding of a key feature. Look at the following question:

> Describe the attempts made in industrial towns such as Cardiff to improve public health during the second half of the nineteenth century.

How to answer

- You need to identify and describe at least two key features.
- Only include information that is directly relevant.
- Be specific, avoid generalised comments.
- Provide specific detail relating to the historical environment named in the question.

Example

Step 1: Identify and develop a key reason/ feature. Include specific information relating to the historic environment named in the question.

> Poor living conditions and the constant threat of disease meant that improvements in public health became a major concern during the second half of the nineteenth century. Following the passing of the Public Health Act in 1848, Cardiff Corporation responded by appointing Dr Henry James Paine as the town's first Medical Officer. Dr Paine encouraged the setting up of the Cardiff Waterworks Company which laid water pipes to provide clean and safe drinking water, thereby reducing the threat of an outbreak of cholera. Underground sewers were laid to carry away the town's sewerage. Dr Paine also pressed to ensure that people were inoculated against smallpox. He bought and fitted out a hospital ship in Tiger Bay to treat sailors with infectious diseases so that the disease did not spread into the town. By such actions he helped to secure improvements in public health in the town.

Step 2: Identify and develop other key reasons/ features. Aim to cover two to three reasons/ features which are specific to the named historic environment.

> Cardiff Corporation also played its part in securing improvements. It provided land for the creation of public parks at Roath and Cathays, and encouraged the setting up of the Cardiff Baths Company to provide swimming pools and hot water baths for the people of the town. A new cemetery was opened at Cathays in 1859 and the town's infirmary was rebuilt in the 1880s. Areas of poor housing were demolished to make way for new civic buildings, such as the City Hall and National Museum. Planning regulations were introduced and the annual Medical Reports on the State of Public Health reveal that many steps had been taken to improve public health in towns like Cardiff between 1848 and 1900.

> **Now try to answer the following question:**
>
> Describe the impact on industrial towns, such as Cardiff, of the cholera outbreaks during the second half of the nineteenth century.

Examination guidance for Question 4

This section provides guidance on how to answer a 'describe' question. You will have to demonstrate your own knowledge and understanding of a key feature. Look at the following question:

> Describe the development of methods used to combat the spread of the plague during the Black Death.

How to answer

- You need to identify and describe at least two key features.
- Only include information that is directly relevant.
- Be specific, avoid generalised comments.

Example

The Black Death spread rapidly across Europe during 1348–49 causing the death of up to 40 per cent of the population. It was highly contagious and various methods were developed to try and prevent its spread. One common method was that of quarantine. Travellers were placed in quarantine zones before being allowed to enter a town. Another method adopted to stop the spread of disease from dead bodies awaiting individual burial was to speed up the process by taking the dead away to be buried in one large plague pit outside the town walls. They needed to be buried as quickly as possible. Infected families had to board up doors and windows to prevent infecting neighbours.

Step 1: Identify and develop a key reason/feature, supporting it with specific detail.

Other methods developed included the increasing use of potions like theriac or the carrying of scented flowers and herbs, in the belief that they would kill off the plague. The clothes of diseased people were burnt in the hope it would kill off the infection. In an attempt to appeal to God for salvation flagellants whipped themselves in a display of suffering, hoping this penance would cause the disease to pass them by. In an attempt to stop catching the plague doctors developed protective clothing, wearing gowns and hoods when making house calls, their hood containing a beak which was stuffed with herbs.

Step 2: Identify and develop other key reasons/features. Aim to cover two to three reasons/features in some detail.

> ### Now try to answer the following question:
> Describe the development of the theory of the four humours during the medieval period.

Examination guidance for Question 5

This section provides guidance on how to answer the explanation question. This requires you to identify and discuss a number of reasons to explain why a key development/issue was important or significant. Look at the following question:

> Explain why the work of Pasteur and Koch was important in the advancement of medical knowledge during the nineteenth and twentieth centuries.

How to answer

- You should aim to give a variety of explained reasons.
- Try to include specific details such as names, dates, events, developments and consequences.
- Always support your statements with examples.
- Remember that you need to provide a judgement, evaluating the importance or significance of the named individual, development or issue.

Example

Step 1: Provide several reasons to support the view that the factor mentioned in the question was important or significant. Include specific factual detail to support your judgement.

The work of Louis Pasteur and Robert Koch was very important in the development of medical knowledge in the nineteenth and twentieth centuries. Pasteur developed the 'germ theory', which suggested that germs were the cause of disease. Through examining the causes of diseases he discovered that the process of heating liquids helped to kill germs, a process that came to be known as pasteurisation. He also built upon the work of earlier pioneers such as Edward Jenner who had experimented with vaccination against smallpox using the cowpox disease, taking this a stage further. Using Jenner's model he developed vaccines for diseases such as avian cholera, anthrax and rabies, and experimented in methods of vaccination and immunisation. His research had a significant impact upon the treatment of illness.

Step 2: Add additional factors or reasons to help build up a strong case. Make sure your information is accurate and relevant – it answers the question.

Koch developed Pasteur's work further by isolating the bacteria responsible for tuberculosis, cholera and anthrax. He pioneered the new science of bacteriology, proving that a specific germ caused a specific disease, and he discovered that antibodies help the body fight against germs by destroying the bacteria and in so doing they enable the body to build up an immunity against disease. In 1905, he was awarded the Nobel Prize for his research work.

Step 3: Make sure you provide a reasoned judgement upon the degree of importance or significance. Make links to the longer-term impact.

Through their experiments with germs, both Pasteur and Koch played a very important and significant role in the development of medical knowledge. Later scientists were able to use their methods to develop a vaccine for diphtheria and syphilis.

Now try to answer the following question:

Explain why the work of Edwin Chadwick was important in the improvement of public health in the nineteenth and twentieth centuries.

Examination guidance for Question 6

This section provides guidance on how to answer a question which requires explanation and analysis of a set issue, together with a judgement.

> How effective was the development and use of antiseptics as a method of treating and curing illness in the nineteenth century?

How to answer

- Use your knowledge to place the key issue in context.
- Explain what was happening at that time.
- Include specific factual detail to help construct an informed explanation.
- Make regular links to the key issue, providing some judgement.
- Conclude with a reasoned judgement, making clear links to the question.

Example

A major advancement in the treatment of illness in the nineteenth century was the discovery and use of antiseptics in surgery. While surgeons were improving their skills on the operating table many patients died after surgery because their wounds became infected with sepsis or hospital gangrene. This was an infection caught during or after surgery from which few people survived. What was not known at the time was that dirty clothes worn by the surgeon and the use of unsterile equipment actually increased the risk of infection to the patient. While many patients might survive the operation, many would die later from infection resulting from the operation.

Step 1: Begin by placing the key issue into context, providing some background detail.

One surgeon who pioneered new techniques which greatly reduced the risk of infection and improved the chances of patients surviving operations was Joseph Lister. Learning from Pasteur's germ theory, Lister began to experiment using carbolic acid as a means of sterilising his surgical equipment. Through experiments he discovered that by soaking the wound with carbolic acid and by using dressings that had been sterilised, he greatly reduced the risk of infection setting in after the operation. In 1871, he invented a machine that sprayed carbolic acid over the entire room, surgeon, patient and assistants during an operation. His methods of using antiseptics to sterilise the environment proved to be highly effective, reducing the number of his patients who died after an operation from 47 per cent to 15 per cent in just three years.

Step 2: Continue to develop the explanation, provide specific detail and make links to the key issue, attempting some judgement.

Lister's methods were quickly followed by other surgeons and the widespread use of antiseptics by the end of the nineteenth century had a dramatic impact upon the survival rates of patients post operation. Lister came to be known as the 'father of antiseptic surgery' and his pioneering use of antiseptics proved to be highly effective in the treating and curing of illness during the Victorian era.

Step 3: Conclude with a reasoned and well supported judgement upon the key issue.

Now try to answer the following question:

How effective was the development and use of anaesthetics as a method of treating and curing illness in the nineteenth century?

Examination guidance for Question 7

This section provides guidance on how to answer the synoptic question, which requires you to use your knowledge to analyse and evaluate the importance of a key issue against other issues. Look at the following question:

> To what extent had the development in voluntary and endowed hospitals been the most effective means of improving patient care over time?

How to answer

- You need to develop a two-sided answer which has balance and good support.
- You should start by discussing the key issue mentioned in the question, using your knowledge to explain why this factor was most effective, important or significant.
- You then need to consider the counter-argument, discussing a range of other relevant factors.
- Make sure your answer covers three historical time periods – the medieval, early modern and modern era.
- You must include a number of specific references to the Welsh context, i.e. say what was happening in Wales.
- Conclude your answer with a reasoned and well-supported judgement.

Example

Step 1: Introduce the topic to be analysed and discussed in the answer.

> The care and treatment of patients has improved significantly over the centuries. At some times the pace of change has been faster, particularly in recent centuries and, to an extent, these changes have resulted in an improvement in the quality of patient care. Among the most important developments in this area was the establishment of voluntary and endowed hospitals during the seventeenth and eighteenth centuries.

Step 2: Discuss the key issue identified in the question – this should relate to one time period. Provide specific factual detail, remembering to make links to what was happening in Wales.

> Following the dissolution of the monasteries in the 1530s, which closed most of the medieval hospitals run by the church, the role of caring for the sick fell upon voluntary charities and private individuals to organise. Although these charities were often religious based, their primary role was no longer to provide spiritual guidance but to treat patients for their specific illness and to provide a centre of medical care. In London, hospitals such as Saint Bartholomew's, Saint Thomas's and Saint Mary's were set up, their upkeep being paid for through endowments, sometimes from the king but more often from private individuals. Even some towns outside London, such as Norwich and Cambridge, set up endowed voluntary hospitals. These institutions were developed further during the eighteenth century through the endowments of wealthy individuals such as Thomas Guy and John Addenbrooke, which resulted in the founding of Guy's hospital in London in 1724 and Addenbrooke's hospital in Cambridge in 1766. In Wales, the move towards voluntary hospitals was slightly later, the setting up of a Dispensary at Denbigh in 1807 being among the first. Swansea opened an infirmary in 1817, as did Cardiff and Wrexham in the 1830s. However, many towns in Wales were without any voluntary form of patient care. These institutions marked a turning point in the development of patient care. They employed doctors to treat patients and nurses to care for them on wards. They also issued medicine. This was a significant improvement upon the type of care offered during the medieval period.

Before the introduction of voluntary and endowed hospitals, it was the church who was the main provider of patient care. During the medieval period over 1,100 hospitals had been set up across Wales and England, most of them being attached to monasteries. Wales had a number of monasteries such as those at Valle Crucis, Strata Florida, Margam and Tintern, all of which provided care for the sick. Most monasteries had infirmaries which tended to the sick but they were not like later hospitals. They provided a place of 'hospitality' which was a place of rest and recuperation rather than a place to be cured from illness and disease. Some specialised in looking after certain types of people such as lepers, unmarried pregnant women, young orphaned children and the elderly. At Ysbyty Ifan the Knights of Saint John established a hospital to serve as a hostel for pilgrims travelling along the pilgrim route to Holyhead. Such establishments did not treat the sick and people who were seriously ill and in need of constant care were often not allowed into the hospital. The quality of care in these hospitals was not based upon treating the nature of the illness but upon saving the soul of the patient. The endowed and voluntary hospitals of the sixteenth and seventeenth centuries, which actually attempted to treat the sick, were therefore a more significant improvement upon the medieval monastic hospitals which were more concerned with religion than medical treatment.

Step 3: Begin to develop a counter-argument – this should relate to a different time period. Make links to other time periods to show improvement/changes or lack of improvements/changes that have taken place. Make links to Wales.

However, the biggest change in patient care came in the nineteenth and twentieth centuries with the building of purpose-built hospitals, such as Great Ormond Street in 1852, the development of surgical procedures, the advancement of medical knowledge and the creation of a professional nursing staff. Of these, one that had a dramatic impact upon the quality of patient care was the work of Florence Nightingale who pioneered new methods in nursing. Upon her return from treating the wounded soldiers in the Crimean War, Florence Nightingale set up the Nightingale School of Nursing. This created a professional nursing corps, a move which revolutionised how patients were looked after in hospital. She was also heavily involved in the design of new hospitals. Working in the Crimea with Nightingale was the Welsh nurse, Betsi Cadwaladr. She ran a hospital at Balaclava where she worked tirelessly to improve the quality of care for the wounded soldiers. In this respect it can be said that the development of nursing played an important part in improving patient care.

Step 4: Continue with the counter-argument, selecting other time periods to illustrate change or improvement. Remember to provide links to what was happening in Wales.

As the twentieth century dawned the government began to take on some of the responsibility for tending to the sick and injured. The 1911 National Insurance Scheme devised by the Welshman Lloyd George enabled members to receive treatment if they contributed into the National Insurance Scheme. The Beveridge Report of 1942 forced the government to take on a more direct control of looking after the nation's health and in 1948 the National Health Service was created. The establishment, the NHS was the responsibility of Welshman Aneurin Bevan, MP for Ebbw Vale, who had been appointed Minister of Health in 1945. The son of a miner, Bevan was well aware of the hardships that faced working class families in obtaining medical treatment and he wanted to set up a system of medical care that was free for all people, regardless of background and wealth. The introduction of the NHS was a radical change which brought about significant improvement in the care of patients.

Step 5: Aim to cover a range of factors, making judgements about the importance or significance of these developments. Make direct links to the question.

Step 6: Write a conclusion which contains a reasoned judgement upon the question. Remember to check through your answer for correct spelling, punctuation and grammar.

While the creation of voluntary and endowed hospitals during the seventeenth and eighteenth centuries bought about a significant improvement in patient care when compared to the monastic hospitals of the medieval period, developments in hospital and nursing care during the nineteenth and twentieth centuries saw greater improvements. However, it could be argued that the most significant improvement in patient care has resulted from the intervention of the government which led to the creation of the Welfare State and a National Health Service.

Now try to answer the following question:

To what extent has the development of modern antiseptics been the most effective method of treating and curing illness over time?

Changes in crime and punishment, c.1500 to the present day

This chapter focuses on the key question: What have been the main causes of crime over time?

Crime has been present in society across the ages, and it is possible to detect continuity in the causes of common crimes, such as theft and murder. Petty theft, such as the stealing of clothing, food or small sums of money, has remained the most common type of crime across the period of our study – c.1500 to the present day – and a common cause of petty theft is poverty. However, at certain times there has been a sudden increase in particular types of crime, mostly due to the introduction of new laws. During the sixteenth century, for example, changes in the official religion of the land resulted in an increase in crimes such as **heresy** and **treason**, while in the eighteenth century the introduction of high taxes on imported goods resulted in an increase in the crime of smuggling. As you advance through this chapter you should consider which causes of crime have remained the same across all the centuries, and which causes are specific to a certain century or time period. You should also consider whether they were the result of specific changes of policy or are due to political, social and economic factors.

FOCUS TASK

As you work through this chapter you need to gather together information to enable you to record instances of 'continuity' and 'change' in the causes of crime across the period c.1500 to the present day. At the end of this chapter you will be able to use this information to make a judgement upon the degree of continuity and change, and provide reasons why certain periods of time saw the emergence of new types of crime, or the rapid growth in crimes that were common to all time periods.

Time period	Crimes common to all these periods	Causes of these crimes	Crimes which are specific to certain time periods	Causes of these crimes
Sixteenth and seventeenth centuries				
Eighteenth and nineteenth centuries				
Twentieth century				
Twenty-first century				

Causes of crime during the sixteenth and seventeenth centuries

While the sixteenth and seventeenth centuries saw the continuance of traditional crime common during the medieval period, such as theft and murder, this period also witnessed a sudden increase in specific crimes. Changes in economic conditions caused a sharp increase in poverty and unemployment, which in turn resulted in an increase in crimes associated with **vagrancy**. Changes in the official religion caused some people to commit the crimes of heresy and treason which became quite common during this period.

The growth of economic pressures in the Tudor period

During the sixteenth century, and especially during the reign of Elizabeth I (1558–1603), there was a sharp rise in poverty and the number of people classified as poor. This was brought on by a number of economic changes and pressures. For some of these people the only way they could survive was by resorting to crime.

Who were the poor?

Society has always had a proportion of the population classified as poor and in need of help and support from others. Throughout the medieval period the church had played a key role in looking after the poor and destitute, providing shelter and relief in **alms houses** or in the monasteries. The rich and better off had also made donations to help relieve the poor.

Tudor governments came to classify the poor and destitute into one of two categories:

1. The **impotent poor** – those who were genuinely unable to work due to age, hardship or some other ailment. It was recognised that these individuals were in need of poor relief.
2. The **able-bodied** poor – those considered capable of work but who were either unable or unwilling to find employment. It was thought that these individuals needed to be encouraged or even forced to find work in order to prevent them from resorting to begging.

Reasons for the growth in poverty

This rise in the number of poor was the result of a combination of factors resulting from changes within society, a sharp rise in population and the pressures this brought, and the effects of increasing economic hardship.

> **Interpretation 1: Historian Chris Culpin, from his book, *Crime and punishment through time* (1997)**
>
> Social tension was bitter in Norfolk. The richest six per cent of the population owned 60 per cent of the land. This meant they were able to get richer while the poor grew poorer. In particular, they used their right to graze huge flocks of sheep and cattle on the commons, then bought the land and enclosed it.

Year	Wales and England	Wales
1500	2.9 million	225,000
1550	3.2 million	250,000
1600	4.3 million	300,000

▲ **Table 1.1:** Population figures for Wales and England during the sixteenth century

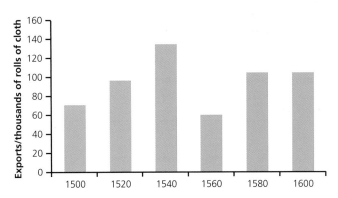

▲ **Figure 1.1:** Wool exports between 1500 and 1600

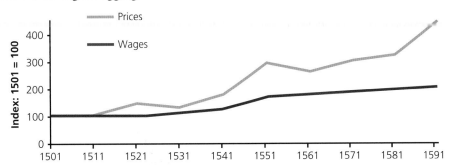

▲ **Figure 1.2:** Relative increase in wages and prices, 1501–91

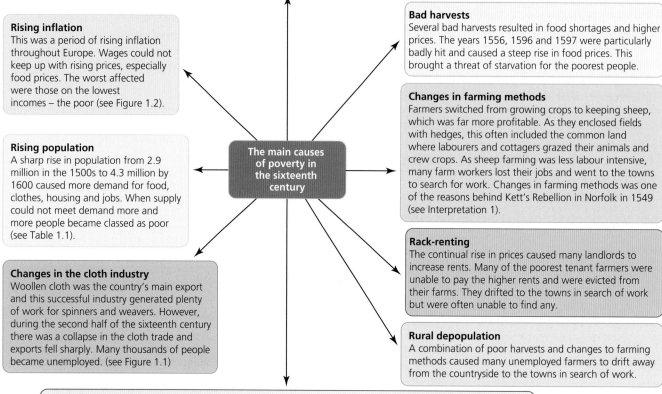

Dissolution of the monasteries
Monasteries had served a vital function in helping the poor people, providing them with food, clothing and money. When Henry VIII closed the monasteries between 1536 and 1540, this charity relief was no longer available. Monks, servants and labourers who had worked in the monasteries became unemployed, and many were forced to drift towards the towns in search of new work.

Rising inflation
This was a period of rising inflation throughout Europe. Wages could not keep up with rising prices, especially food prices. The worst affected were those on the lowest incomes – the poor (see Figure 1.2).

Bad harvests
Several bad harvests resulted in food shortages and higher prices. The years 1556, 1596 and 1597 were particularly badly hit and caused a steep rise in food prices. This brought a threat of starvation for the poorest people.

Changes in farming methods
Farmers switched from growing crops to keeping sheep, which was far more profitable. As they enclosed fields with hedges, this often included the common land where labourers and cottagers grazed their animals and crew crops. As sheep farming was less labour intensive, many farm workers lost their jobs and went to the towns to search for work. Changes in farming methods was one of the reasons behind Kett's Rebellion in Norfolk in 1549 (see Interpretation 1).

Rising population
A sharp rise in population from 2.9 million in the 1500s to 4.3 million by 1600 caused more demand for food, clothes, housing and jobs. When supply could not meet demand more and more people became classed as poor (see Table 1.1).

The main causes of poverty in the sixteenth century

Rack-renting
The continual rise in prices caused many landlords to increase rents. Many of the poorest tenant farmers were unable to pay the higher rents and were evicted from their farms. They drifted to the towns in search of work but were often unable to find any.

Changes in the cloth industry
Woollen cloth was the country's main export and this successful industry generated plenty of work for spinners and weavers. However, during the second half of the sixteenth century there was a collapse in the cloth trade and exports fell sharply. Many thousands of people became unemployed. (see Figure 1.1)

Rural depopulation
A combination of poor harvests and changes to farming methods caused many unemployed farmers to drift away from the countryside to the towns in search of work.

Costly foreign wars and demobbed soldiers
During the 1540s Henry VIII was at war with France and Scotland and during the 1590s Elizabeth I was at war with Spain. The cost of fighting such campaigns led to higher taxes, and Henry was forced to lower the value of the coinage by using inferior metals to mint coins. When these wars were over soldiers and sailors were left without jobs, and many wandered around the countryside in gangs in search of work.

▲ Figure 1.3: The main causes of poverty in the sixteenth century

THINK ?

1 Explain the difference between 'impotent poor' and 'able-bodied' poor.

2 Study the nine boxes in Figure 1.3 that shows the causes of poverty. Use this information and your own knowledge to complete the table below. The first key cause has been done for you.

3 Study the table you have completed in question 2.
   a) Identify three factors that you consider to be the most important reasons that caused an increase in poverty during the sixteenth century. Justify your choices.
   b) How do your choices compare with those of the student sitting next to you? Note the differences.

Key cause/factor	How it contributed to the increase in poverty in the sixteenth century
Growing population	This put added pressure on limited food supplies and a shrinking jobs market. More and more people were classed as being poor.

The impact of religious change in the sixteenth and seventeenth centuries

Many of the major crimes of this period were linked to the problems associated with religious change and the change of monarch. (All four monarchs in the Tudor period can be seen in Source A.) The majority of people living in the sixteenth and seventeenth centuries were very religious, attended church regularly and followed the advice of their parish priest to ensure that they would ascend to heaven when they died. In 1500, most people in Wales and England were Catholic but some were paying attention to the calls for a reform of some of the bad practices and abuses within the Catholic Church made by a German monk, Martin Luther. This resulted in the emergence of the **Protestant Reformation**, a movement that made its initial impact in England during the reign of Henry VIII. Disputes over religion were to dominate the reigns of all the Tudors, as the official religion switched between the Catholic and Protestant faiths with each new monarch. This period saw a growth in the crime of **heresy**.

The impact of religious change – heresy

Henry VIII (1509–47)

Henry VIII ruled as a Catholic monarch but when the Pope refused to grant him a divorce from his first wife, Catherine of Aragon, Henry broke away from the Roman Catholic Church and created the Church of England. Henry made himself head of this Church and, although it was still Catholic, the Pope no longer had any power over it. Henry tolerated some of the Protestant beliefs, but he did not embrace them.

Edward VI (1547–53)

When Henry died in 1547, his son and heir, Edward, was only nine years old, so two of his uncles, the Earl of Northumberland and the Duke of Somerset, were appointed regents to rule in his name. These two men had embraced the new religion started by Luther and were strong Protestants. They persuaded Edward to introduce religious changes, making Protestantism the official religion of the land.

The population was forced to embrace these changes and those who refused and continued with the Catholic faith were accused of being heretics. By going against the official religion they had committed treason and would be condemned to death.

Mary I (1553–58)

Edward died while still a teenager and he was succeeded as ruler by his elder sister, Mary, who was a devout Roman Catholic. Mary hated the Protestant beliefs and reversed all the religious changes that had been introduced during her brother's reign. She was determined to restore the Roman Catholic faith as the official religion of Wales and England. The religious pendulum had swung in the opposite direction and those who remained faithful to the Protestant religion during Mary's reign were accused of being heretics and would be condemned to death.

Elizabeth I (1558–1603)

When Elizabeth became queen the country was bitterly divided over religion. During the previous reigns of Edward and Mary, many ordinary people had been put to death as heretics because of their religious faith. Elizabeth therefore attempted to reach a compromise by adopting a 'middle road'.

- She made herself Supreme Governor rather than Head of the Church of England.
- She made Protestantism the official religion.
- She brought back some of the changes introduced during Edward's reign.
- She tolerated Catholics to some degree – crosses and candles could be used in churches and priests could wear their official robes.
- However, Catholics were expected to attend the Church of England services and were fined for not doing so.

Any Catholics or Protestant extremists (Puritans) who refused to accept this settlement were treated as heretics and punished accordingly.

▼ Source A: The family of Henry VIII, painted in c.1545. From left to right: Mary, Edward, Jane Seymour and Elizabeth

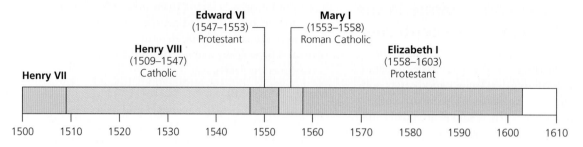

▲ Figure 1.4: Timeline showing religious change during the reigns of the Tudor monarchs

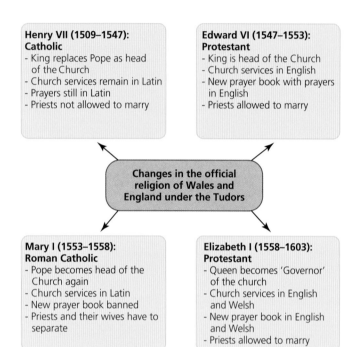

Henry VII (1509–1547): Catholic
- King replaces Pope as head of the Church
- Church services remain in Latin
- Prayers still in Latin
- Priests not allowed to marry

Edward VI (1547–1553): Protestant
- King is head of the Church
- Church services in English
- New prayer book with prayers in English
- Priests allowed to marry

Changes in the official religion of Wales and England under the Tudors

Mary I (1553–1558): Roman Catholic
- Pope becomes head of the Church again
- Church services in Latin
- New prayer book banned
- Priests and their wives have to separate

Elizabeth I (1558–1603): Protestant
- Queen becomes 'Governor' of the church
- Church services in English and Welsh
- New prayer book in English and Welsh
- Priests allowed to marry

▲ Figure 1.5: Changes in the official religion of Wales and England under the Tudors

Interpretation 2: An explanation of why heresy became a serious crime during the sixteenth century. Taken from a school history website.

In the reign of Mary, Protestants were executed for refusing to accept that the Pope was the head of the Church. Others were executed for reading the English Bible. However, the most common cause of heresy concerned something called transubstantiation. Catholics believed that the bread and wine used at communion became the body and blood of Jesus Christ. Protestants who refused to believe this miracle happened during communion were in danger of being executed.

The impact of religious change – treason

At a time when religious change dominated people's lives, when the ruling monarch insisted on people worshiping in the way that he or she did, and when economic hardship was causing a rise in the number of vagrants, outbreaks of riots and rebellions became quite common. When such riots, rebellions or planned plots attempted to betray or illegally overthrow a monarch or government, then those involved were said to have committed the crime of treason.

Following his break with Rome and his attempts to divorce his first wife, Catherine of Aragon, Henry VIII attempted to silence opposition by introducing a new set of treason laws. These stated that:

■ Anyone who said or wrote things against the king, his wife and/or his heirs, or who displayed support for the Pope, was guilty of treason.

■ Anyone who said that the beliefs of the king went against the teachings of the church, or said that the king was using his power unjustly, was guilty of treason.

■ Anyone who kept silent when questioned on what were the rights and authority of the king was guilty of treason.

This meant that political as well as religious opinions could now be classed as treason. The punishment for those found guilty of treason was death. In many instances this involved being **hung, drawn and quartered**.

THINK ?

1 Use Interpretation 2 and your knowledge to explain why heresy became more widespread during the sixteenth century.

2 Why did treason emerge as a serious crime during the sixteenth and seventeenth centuries?

ACTIVITY ?

Copy out and complete the table below to show how the causes of religious crime changed during the Tudor period.

Tudor monarch	Official religion	Reasons why an individual could be accused of being a heretic during that reign	Was there a change of reason from the previous reign?

The pressures of industrialisation and urbanisation in the eighteenth and nineteenth centuries

The eighteenth and nineteenth centuries were times of great change due to the **Agricultural** and **Industrial Revolutions**. The increasing use of new methods and machinery on farms led to a fall in demand for agricultural labourers, many of whom were forced to leave the countryside and migrate to the rapidly expanding industrial towns like Merthyr Tydfil in South Wales. Here they found work in the factories, mines and ironworks.

As more and more people moved away from the countryside, the towns grew rapidly and some, such as Liverpool, Manchester, Leeds and Birmingham, became cities during the early nineteenth century. This process of industrialisation and **urbanisation** dramatically changed the way people lived and worked. The increased population in towns and cities led to a rise in the levels of crime and, in some instances, resulted in the emergence of new types of crime.

Development of large towns

Historians have identified a range of 'push and pull' factors to explain the dramatic increase in the size of towns and cities during the nineteenth century. The push factors were those that drove people to leave the countryside, while the attractions of working in the new industrial towns acted as the pull factors.

- Due to the introduction of new methods of farming and farm machinery, it was becoming increasingly difficult to get work in the countryside.
- The wage of an agricultural labourer was considerably less than that of an industrial worker.
- After bad harvests many poorer people living in the countryside were near starvation.
- The rural population was growing and there were not enough farming jobs to go around.
- The development of the railways made transport easier and cheaper.
- Factories, mines and ironworks were labour intensive, requiring large numbers of workers who needed to live close by.
- Industrialists built houses for their workers next to their factories, mines and iron works.
- Industrial jobs offered employment throughout the year, unlike agriculture, which was seasonal.
- Industrial jobs offered jobs to the whole family – men, women and children.

- The multiplier effect – once one member of a family had migrated to the towns and found employment, this often attracted other family members to do the same.
- Young people in towns married earlier than they would have in the country and they tended to have larger families.

An important factor contributing to the rise in crime during this period was the social and economic change linked to the dramatic growth of industrial towns and cities. London experienced the biggest growth, with its population increasing from 675,000 in 1750 to 2.3 million in 1851. This resulted in overcrowding and squalid living conditions, particularly in the East End. Life in these areas was very hard and crime became an increasing problem. Criminals liked to live in places that were full of narrow, twisting, crowded alleys that enabled them to slip away quickly from any pursuer.

City	1750	1801	1851
Liverpool	35,000	82,000	376,000
Birmingham	30,000	71,000	233,000
Manchester	45,000	75,000	303,000
Leeds	14,000	53,000	172,000
Merthyr Tydfil	400	7,705	46,378

▲ **Table 1.2:** The dramatic increase in population size of the new industrial towns and cities

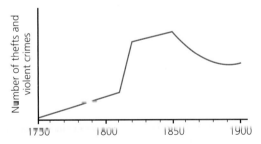

▲ **Figure 1.6:** The trends in crime, 1750–1900

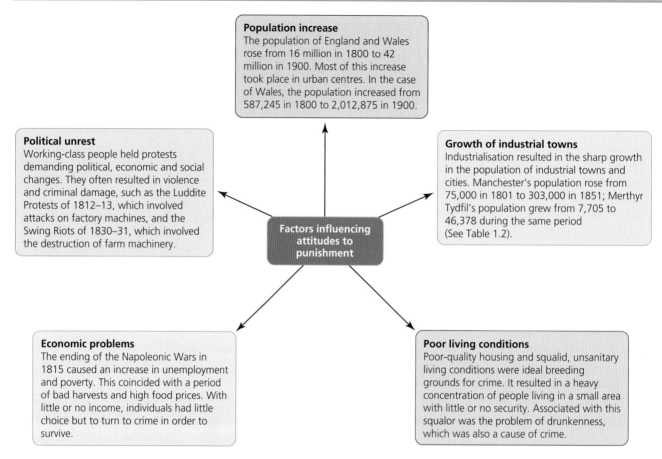

Population increase
The population of England and Wales rose from 16 million in 1800 to 42 million in 1900. Most of this increase took place in urban centres. In the case of Wales, the population increased from 587,245 in 1800 to 2,012,875 in 1900.

Political unrest
Working-class people held protests demanding political, economic and social changes. They often resulted in violence and criminal damage, such as the Luddite Protests of 1812–13, which involved attacks on factory machines, and the Swing Riots of 1830–31, which involved the destruction of farm machinery.

Factors influencing attitudes to punishment

Growth of industrial towns
Industrialisation resulted in the sharp growth in the population of industrial towns and cities. Manchester's population rose from 75,000 in 1801 to 303,000 in 1851; Merthyr Tydfil's population grew from 7,705 to 46,378 during the same period (See Table 1.2).

Economic problems
The ending of the Napoleonic Wars in 1815 caused an increase in unemployment and poverty. This coincided with a period of bad harvests and high food prices. With little or no income, individuals had little choice but to turn to crime in order to survive.

Poor living conditions
Poor-quality housing and squalid, unsanitary living conditions were ideal breeding grounds for crime. It resulted in a heavy concentration of people living in a small area with little or no security. Associated with this squalor was the problem of drunkenness, which was also a cause of crime.

▲ **Figure 1.7:** Factors that contributed to the increase in crime during the nineteenth century

THINK

1 Compare and contrast Table 1.2 and Figure 1.6. What information can be obtained from this data to explain the trend in crime levels between 1750 and 1850?

ACTIVITY

Use the information from this section to identify the reasons for the development of large towns and cities during the nineteenth century. Copy out and complete the table below, dividing your reasons into 'push' and 'pull' factors.

Push factors	Pull factors

Twentieth-century pressures, including changing technology

Many of the crimes that had occurred in previous centuries, such as theft, robbery, assault and murder, continued into the twentieth century and, in many instances, the causes of these traditional crimes remained the same. However, changes in society, particularly those relating to developments in technology, also provided criminals with new opportunities for crime. The development of the motor car gave rise to a wide range of transport crimes (see Chapter 2), while the growth in computer technology has given birth to cybercrime.

Did crime really increase during the twentieth century?

Crime figures have risen sharply since 1900 but much of the increase can be accounted for by the increased reporting and recording of crime, improved policing methods, and improved use of scientific technology to detect crime.

While Figures 1.8 and 1.9 would appear to show a sharp rise in crime, such figures can be misleading and in reality the crime rate has not risen as dramatically as it would seem. The apparent rise must be examined in context and several factors need to be considered before a final judgement can be made:

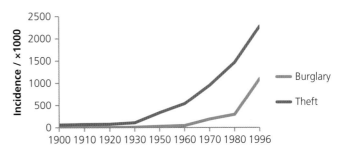

▲ **Figure 1.8:** Recorded instances of burglary and theft between 1900 and 1996

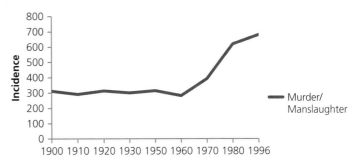

▲ **Figure 1.9:** Recorded instances of manslaughter between 1900 and 1996

- **Actual increases in some crimes:** While the numbers of some crimes did increase during the twentieth century, others fell. Violent crime remained the same, although the ration of murders to population fell. In the 1880s there were fifteen murders per million people and by the 1980s the figure had fallen to eleven, a reduction of 26 per cent. Men were still responsible for around 85 per cent of crime, with over half of these committed by men aged 25 or younger. The crime rate among juvenile boys rose faster during the twentieth century than for any other age group.

- **Increased reporting of crime:** The reporting of crime by the media helps to sell newspapers and attract television audiences. Crimes involving violence or attacks on the elderly or the very young receive wide media coverage. Such reporting can present a distorted picture, helping to suggest that the late twentieth century experienced a dramatic crime wave. Also significant is the fact that more victims of crime now report it.

- **Increased recording of crime:** While there has always been a substantial 'dark figure' of unreported and unrecorded crime, the gap between the actual crime and reported crime has narrowed during the past half-century. This is because more people are now reporting crime for insurance purposes and the growth in mobile phone ownership has meant that the majority of people now have access to a phone, which makes it easier to inform the police. Developments in computer technology have enabled the police to improve their methods of recording crime and a change in the type of data collected has increased the number of different crimes being recorded.

Increased crime

However, despite such explanations there was an increase in crime during the twentieth century and a number of suggestions have been put forward to explain this rise (see Figure 1.10).

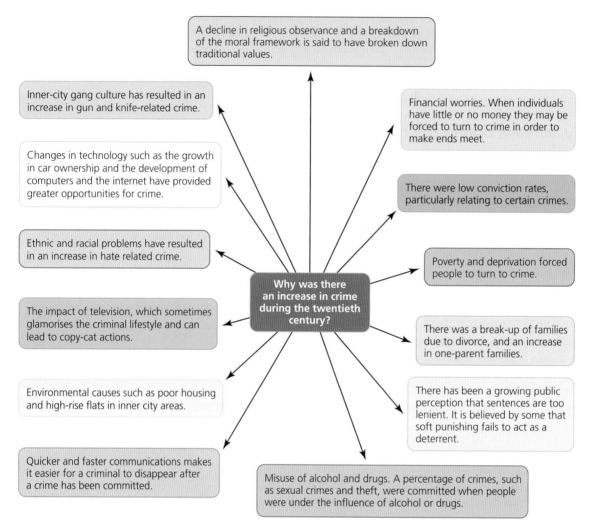

A decline in religious observance and a breakdown of the moral framework is said to have broken down traditional values.

Inner-city gang culture has resulted in an increase in gun and knife-related crime.

Changes in technology such as the growth in car ownership and the development of computers and the internet have provided greater opportunities for crime.

Ethnic and racial problems have resulted in an increase in hate related crime.

The impact of television, which sometimes glamorises the criminal lifestyle and can lead to copy-cat actions.

Environmental causes such as poor housing and high-rise flats in inner city areas.

Quicker and faster communications makes it easier for a criminal to disappear after a crime has been committed.

Why was there an increase in crime during the twentieth century?

Financial worries. When individuals have little or no money they may be forced to turn to crime in order to make ends meet.

There were low conviction rates, particularly relating to certain crimes.

Poverty and deprivation forced people to turn to crime.

There was a break-up of families due to divorce, and an increase in one-parent families.

There has been a growing public perception that sentences are too lenient. It is believed by some that soft punishing fails to act as a deterrent.

Misuse of alcohol and drugs. A percentage of crimes, such as sexual crimes and theft, were committed when people were under the influence of alcohol or drugs.

▲ **Figure 1.10:** Suggested reasons for the apparent rise in crime during the twentieth century

ACTIVITY ?

Study Figure 1.10. Working in pairs, divide the causes of crime into two types, before copying out and completing the table below.

Cause of crime common to all centuries	Causes of crime unique to the twentieth and twenty-first centuries

New causes of crime

Motoring offences

As car ownership has increased there has been more opportunity for people to commit motoring crimes. In 1902 Harold Bater, the chauffeur of the Marquis of Anglesey, was among the first drivers in Wales to be fined for speeding. A witness claimed he had been travelling at more than 25 mph. By 1939, 60 per cent of all cases presented before magistrates involved motoring offences. In 1996, there were over 1.3 million recorded motoring offences, including the theft of over half a million cars.

As a result of increased car ownership motoring offences have grown into one of the biggest categories of offending, involving people from across all social classes. A range of crimes specific to motoring has emerged, such as joyriding and carjacking (see Chapter 2).

Rise of computer crime

The dramatic increase in the use of computer technology in the late twentieth century provided criminals with new opportunities for crime. As business is now dependent on the use of information technology, computer crimes have become common. As with motoring, the development of computers has resulted in the emergence of new crimes such as hacking, phishing scams and cyberterrorism. In May 2017, the NHS was seriously affected by a global ransomware cyberattack which caused many hospital computer systems to be shut down for several days.

Football hooliganism

Hooligans are often members of gangs and being a member of a gang is like belonging to a tribe. Violence is often associated with gang culture. Football hooliganism is not a new threat to society but it became a particular problem from the 1970s onwards. There are a number of reasons for this:

- It often involved gangs of supporters from rival football teams, often under the influence of alcohol, fighting each other or attacking property.
- Membership of such gangs was like belonging to a tribe and violence was accepted as the norm.
- Many of these gangs were well organised and run by middle-class men aged between 18 and 25 years, who had the money and the knowledge to outwit police attempts to contain them.

Drug-related crime

Drug-related crime is not new but it has become much more prominent during the second half of the twentieth century. Throughout history, the **smuggling** of banned or highly taxed goods has encouraged criminals to break the law in the hope of making a profit. In the past, goods like tobacco, rum, brandy and tea have been smuggled. In more recent times, the ban on particular drugs, such as cocaine, has resulted in increased instances of smuggling. Drug smuggling has become an international business with well-organised international drug dealers using sophisticated methods to smuggle drugs into the UK. Gangs use planes, drones, boats, trucks and people to smuggle drugs across the Channel into the country.

At the other end of the operation, the drug users have caused an increase in crime. Drug addiction has resulted in higher instances of certain crimes, particularly burglary, mugging and robbery. Addicts need a constant supply of money to feed their drug habit and if they cannot obtain this by holding down a steady job they are often forced to turn to crime to obtain money.

> **Source B: A report on the dramatic rise in gang-related drugs crime, which appeared in** *The Sunday Times* **newspaper, 24 October 1993**
>
> The culture of drug-related violence now taking hold in London and other British cities mirrors that which has already wrought havoc on the streets of New York, Miami, Toronto and Kingston, Jamaica. The open use of guns, the motivation and even many of the individuals involved are the same … Their principal activity is peddling crack cocaine, and their operations are characterised by the use of extreme violence in pursuit of huge profits.

▲ **Figure 1.11:** Knife crime

Gun and knife crime

Closely associated with the increase in drug-related crime has been the growth of gun and knife crime, which is often linked to juvenile gangs. The rise in gang culture, particularly in inner city areas, has provided youngsters with a sense of belonging. Members of the gang carry knives, or even guns, for protection. The result has been a huge increase in gun and knife crime. In areas dominated by gang culture, gangs are being used to settle scores between rivals as well as 'turf wars' between rival drug dealers.

Several reasons have been suggested to account for the increase in juvenile gang culture:

- poverty
- lack of opportunity
- 'must have now' culture
- the growing divide between rich and poor
- breakdown of family values and discipline.

Source C: A report on youth gangs and the associated knife and gun crime, produced by the British Library in 2009.

More than 70 youngsters died at the hands of gangs in Britain in 2008. In London, 26 were stabbed to death. More than 170 gangs, with members as young as ten have been identified by police in London alone. Many are loose affiliations of friends from the same area intent on controlling a 'turf' or territory, often defined by a postcode. The penalty for straying into the wrong area is to be robbed, beaten or stabbed. Many teenagers now routinely carry a knife out of fear, in order to defend themselves if attacked.

THINK

Study Sources B and C. What do these sources tell you about the changing nature of crime in Britain during the late twentieth century?

ACTIVITY

Use the information in this section to identify the chief causes of new crime in the twentieth century. Copy out and complete the following table.

Type of crime	Reasons for the growth of this type of crime during the twentieth century	To what extent is this a new crime, or a traditional crime which has been given a new name? Think: continuity/change
Motoring offences		
Computer crime		
Football hooliganism		
Drug-related crime		
Gun and knife crime		

The growth of terrorism in the twenty-first century

Modern crimes such as motoring offences and computer crime have continued to grow in the twenty-first century and, in the case of the latter, become international in scope. Since the attack on the World Trade Center in New York in September 2001, the world has witnessed the growth of another crime, that of international terrorism.

Between 1969 and 2005 the IRA was engaged in terrorist activities in Northern Ireland in an attempt to break away from the United Kingdom and join with the Republic of Ireland. In Wales the Welsh nationalist group Meibian Glyndŵr (Sons of Glyndŵr) carried out arson attacks on English property in Wales between 1979 and 1994. (For more on terrorism, see pages 163–4.)

▲ **Source D:** The wreckage of a London bus following a terrorist attack on the capital by Muslim extremists in July 2005

Belief in violent action
A belief by terrorist groups that they can only get what they want through acts of violence.

Terrorist groups willing to work together
Improved communications such as the internet allow radical groups to work more closely and co-ordinate attacks.

Media attention
Violent attacks result in extensive media coverage and raise the profile of the terrorist group. It can also inspire copy-cat actions by other groups.

Strong beliefs
Most terrorists have strong political or religious beliefs, to the extent that they become fanatical. Some terrorists are prepared to die while carrying out their mission.

Why has there been a growth in terrorist activities?

A form of direct action
It shows that a terrorist group can hurt their 'enemies'.

Growth in fundamentalism
There has been a growth in religious fundamentalism, particularly among Islamist groups.

Putting pressure on governments/organisations
Violent actions can cause governments/organisations to agree to the demands of the terrorists.

New technology
Advances in technology have made the world vulnerable to terrorist attacks.

▲ **Figure 1.12:** Reasons for the growth in terrorist activities in the twenty-first century

THINK ❓

- Explain why there has been a growth in terrorism since the 1970s.

- Use Figure 1.12 and your knowledge to explain why terrorists carry out such violent crimes.

FOCUS TASK REVISITED

As you have worked through this chapter you have completed a chart which has recorded examples of the causes of crime across the period c.1500 to the present day. Some of these causes have been common to all time periods, others have been specific to a particular period. Use your findings to answer the following questions:

1 What would you consider to be the three most consistent causes of crime across the years c.1500 to the present day?

2 Identify three causes of crime which are specific to a particular time period and explain why this crime emerged at that time.

3 Which time periods saw the greatest increase in new causes of crime? Suggest reasons to support your answer.

TOPIC SUMMARY

- Crime has been present across all ages, the most common crimes being theft and murder.

- The causes of common crimes have been consistent across time and are often linked to poverty, changes in the law or social and economic influences.

- Economic pressure during the sixteenth century resulted in the rise of poverty, which in turn caused increased instances of crime connected to vagrancy.

- Religious change during the sixteenth century resulted in rise of heresy as a common crime.

- The sixteenth and seventeenth centuries saw an increase in the crime of treason, as individuals refused to accept religious and/or political changes.

- Industrialisation and population increase resulted in the growth of large towns and cities, and these often squalid urban settlements became the breeding grounds for increased opportunities for crime.

- Crime statistics appear to indicate that there was a sharp rise in crime during the twentieth century, but these figures are not as dramatic as they first appear and they can be explained in part due to the increased reporting and recording of crime.

- Technological changes during the twentieth century have resulted in the emergence of new types of crime such as computer crime.

- The twenty-first century has been plagued with increased instances of terrorism, some of it on an international scale and often linked to the growth of fundamentalism.

Practice questions

1 Complete the sentences below with an accurate term:
 a) The most common cause of vagrancy in the sixteenth century was ....
 b) The desire to avoid the paying of customs duties during the eighteenth century resulted in the rise of ....
 c) Industrialisation was a cause of increased crime during the .... century.
 d) The growth in fundamentalism has been a major cause of the growth of international ....
 (For guidance, see page 252.)

2 Describe the main causes of poverty during the sixteenth century. (For guidance, see page 255.)

3 Describe the main causes of highway robbery in the eighteenth century. (For guidance, see page 255.)

4 Explain why opportunities for crime increased during the second half of the twentieth century. (For guidance, see page 257.)

5 Explain why urbanisation was significant in causing an increase in crime during the nineteenth century. (For guidance, see page 257.)

6 To what extent have laws passed by government been the main cause of crime over time?
 In your answer you should:
 - show how government laws have been a cause of crime over three historical eras
 - discuss the importance of other causes of crime over three historical eras
 - include direct references to the history of Wales.
 (For guidance, see page 260.)

2 Nature of crimes

This chapter focuses on the key question: How has the nature of criminal activity differed and changed over time?

During the period c.1500 to the present day there has been continuity in the types of crime committed, the most common throughout this long period were minor crimes such as petty theft together with less common but more violent crimes of robbery, assault and murder. However, it is also possible to identify the appearance of particular types of crime during specific time periods. During the sixteenth century, for example, changes in the official religion of the land resulted in an increase in crimes such as heresy and treason, while in the eighteenth century the introduction of high taxes on imported goods resulted in an increase in the crime of smuggling. Changing methods of transport during the twentieth century has resulted in the dramatic growth in motoring crimes, while the late twentieth and early twenty-first centuries has witnessed the growth of more violent crime associated with terrorism and especially international terrorism. As you advance through this chapter you should consider what types of crime are common to all time periods and which types of crime have been associated with particular time periods and why this has been so.

FOCUS TASK

As you work through this chapter make a 'Crimes common to this century' card – you will need six cards to cover the centuries between 1500 and the present day. On each card, make bullet points to record:

■ common crimes during that century
■ the nature of the crimes being committed
■ which crimes are specific to that century.

The first card has been started for you.

The sixteenth century
- Common crimes – vagrancy, heresy, treason, petty crime, violent crime
- Vagrancy – range of crimes associated with vagabonds – vagrants were named according to the crimes they specialised in (You complete the rest of this card)

Crime during the sixteenth and seventeenth centuries

While minor crimes such as petty theft and some violent crime remained common, this period witnessed the growth of specific crimes associated with vagrancy and heresy.

Vagrancy in the sixteenth century

Vagrancy became a significant problem during the sixteenth century, particularly during the reign of Elizabeth I. Vagrants were generally associated with an increase in crime and criminal activity.

Growth in the number of vagrants

We have seen in Chapter 1 that the sixteenth and seventeenth century experienced rising levels of unemployment and economic hardship (see pages 131–2). This resulted in an increase in homeless beggars who toured the country in wandering bands or gathered in towns, causing problems for the authorities. Contemporaries referred to them as 'sturdy beggars' or vagabonds and sometimes as 'rouges', the latter being a person who survived through a life of crime.

In 1560, London's Bridewell Prison dealt with 69 vagrants, by the 1570s this figure had increased to an average of 200 a year and by 1600 it stood at over 550. Even a small town like Salisbury saw an increase from about 20 vagrants a year in mid-century to 96 vagrants in 1598. As there was little in the way of **poor relief** the vagrants were forced to beg for food and money. Many had little choice but to resort to crime to keep themselves alive.

Types of vagrants

The Tudor clergyman William Harrison estimated that during the mid-sixteenth century there were about 10,000 vagabonds touring the countryside, causing problems in towns and villages, especially when they resorted to crime (see Sources A and B). In 1566 Thomas Harman published a study of vagabond life, which he called *A Caveat or Warning for Common Cursitors, vulgarly called vagabonds,* in which he identified 23 different categories of vagabonds and described them according to the methods they used to seek out a living. The most common types were:

Clapper dudgeon (a) – tied arsenic on their skin to make it bleed, hoping to attract sympathy while begging.

Hooker or angler (b) – carried a long wooden stick and knocked on the doors of houses seeking charity during the day to see what may be stolen. After dark they would return and use their hooked stick to reach in through windows to steal clothes and valuables, which they later tried to sell.

Doxy (c) – a devious female beggar who would carry a large bag on her back and at the same time she would be knitting to make it look like what she was knitting was going into her bag, but what she was really doing was walking around and picking up anything that would be worth money, putting it into her bag and running off with it. One of her common tricks was to steel chickens by feeding them bread tied to a hook, carrying the birds away in the large sack on her back.

Abraham man (d) – pretended to be mad, hoping that their threatening behaviour would result in charity donations through pity.

Ruffler (e) – former soldiers who had become vagabonds and who survived by robbing, using threats or by begging, as opportunity arose.

Dummerers (f) – they pretended to be deaf and unable to speak in order to beg for charity from passers-by.

Counterfeit crank (g) – dressed in tatty clothes and pretended to suffer from 'falling sickness' (epilepsy), sucking soap to fake foaming at the mouth.

(a) (b) (c) (d) (e) (f) (g)

> **Source A: The case of Griffith Jones of Flint, which was recorded in the Caernarfon Court Records, 1624**
>
> Griffith Jones of Flint, vagrant and beggar, is charged with the stealing of a cloak, belonging to David Lewis. He is also suspected of stealing various purses the same day which he strongly denied.

> **Source B: An account of the crimes of two vagabonds recorded in the town records of Warwick during the reign of Elizabeth I**
>
> Two vagabonds from the north confess to stealing ducks, geese and pigs on their travels, which they either ate there and then or sold to buy somewhere to stay.

> **THINK**
>
> Use Sources A and B, as well as your own knowledge, to describe the types of crime commonly associated with vagabonds.

Fear of vagabonds

Ordinary people viewed such false beggars with suspicion as they were associated with the increase in crime. These vagabonds even had their own slang language called 'canting', which added to their sinister nature. One notorious counterfeit crank was Nicholas Blunt who often disguised himself as the vagabond Nicholas Jennings to avoid being recognised (see Source D).

> **Source C: An extract from a letter sent from Edward Hext, a Somerset JP, to Lord Burghley, Queen Elizabeth's Chief Minister, on 25 September 1596**
>
> I may justly say that the infinite numbers of idle, wandering people and robbers of the land are the chief cause of the problem because they labour not and yet they spend doubly much as the labourer does for they lie idly in the alehouses day and night eating and drinking excessively. The most dangerous are the wandering soldiers and other stout rogues. Of these wandering idle people there are three or four hundred in a shire and though they go two and three in a company yet all or the most part in a shire do meet either at a fair or market or in some alehouse once a week.

▲ Source D: Nicholas Blunt or Jennings, disguised as a gentleman. He was interviewed by Thomas Harman for his book on vagabonds

THINK

1 How useful is Source C to a historian studying the problem of vagrancy during late Tudor times?

2 Why did people living during the second half of the sixteenth century grow to fear vagabonds?

Heresy in the sixteenth century

We have seen in Chapter 1 that during the sixteenth century religion changed in accordance with the change of monarch (see pages 133–4). Freedom of religion did not exist at this time, especially during the middle decades of the sixteenth century. Individuals had to accept and follow the religion chosen by the ruler – the Protestant faith under Edward and the Catholic faith under Mary. Failure to accept the official religion was regarded as treason, with individuals being accused of heresy and put on trial. During their trials heretics were given the opportunity to **recant**. If they did this they would receive a prison sentence, but if they refused then they would be found guilty of heresy and sentenced to death. It was a crime that reached its height during the mid-sixteenth century (see Table 2.1).

It was believed that heretics had rebelled against God, so their bodies had to be destroyed by burning. An alternative belief held by some was that burning the body would free the soul and allow it to ascend to heaven.

Monarch	Reign	Heretics executed
Henry VII	1485–1509	24
Henry VIII	1509–1547	81
Edward VI	1547–1553	2
Mary I	1553–1558	280
Elizabeth I	1558–1603	4

▲ **Table 2.1:** The number of people executed for heresy in Wales and England during the reign of the Tudor monarchs

During the short reign of 'Bloody Mary', 280 ordinary men and women were put to death because they refused to renounce their Protestant faith. Of these, the two best known were the bishops Hugh Latimer and Nicholas Ridley, who were burned as Protestant heretics in 1555 (see Source E).

In Wales three Protestants were put to death during Mary's reign for refusing to convert to the Catholic faith:

- Robert Ferrar, Bishop of St. David's who was burned at Carmarthen in 1555
- Rawlins White, a fisherman, who was burned at Cardiff in 1555
- William Nichol, a labourer, who was burned at Haverfordwest in 1558.

Even though Queen Elizabeth I attempted to steer a 'middle course' (adopting both Protestant and Catholic practices)

her advisers were constantly vigilant against religious extremism. During her reign it was the turn of Catholics to be watched and the first Catholic to be executed in Wales was Richard Gwyn, a schoolteacher from Llanidloes, who was executed at Wrexham in 1584 for spreading Catholic ideas. This was followed by the execution of Denbighshire-born Catholic priest William Davies of Beaumaris in 1593. He was accused of helping to publish Catholic literature using a secret printing press hidden in a cave at Rhiwledyn on the Little Orme, Llandudno. Extreme Protestants, known at Puritans, were also closely watched and in 1593 the Welshman John Penry was found guilty of spreading Puritan ideas and was executed in London.

▲ **Source E:** The burning of the Protestant bishops Latimer and Ridley in 1555

> **THINK**
>
> 1 Study Table 2.1. What does it tell us about the crime of heresy during the sixteenth century?
>
> 2 What does Source E tell you about the crime of heresy during the sixteenth century?
>
> 3 'In Wales, as in England, the crime of heresy was most common during the reigns of Mary and Elizabeth'. What evidence can you find to support this statement?

Crime during the eighteenth and nineteenth centuries

Minor crime remained the most common of all crimes during the eighteenth and nineteenth centuries, but this period also witnessed the appearance of specific crimes associated with smuggling and highway robbery.

The growth of smuggling during the eighteenth century

Smuggling is the crime of secretly importing or exporting goods in order to avoid paying custom duties. In the eighteenth century many people did not regard smuggling as a 'real' crime. They disliked the harsh import and export duties and regarded smuggling as a lawful way of making a living and an acceptable means of avoiding unfair taxation. This period is often referred to as the 'Golden Age' of smuggling and a number of reasons have been put forward to explain why there was a dramatic increase in this specific crime.

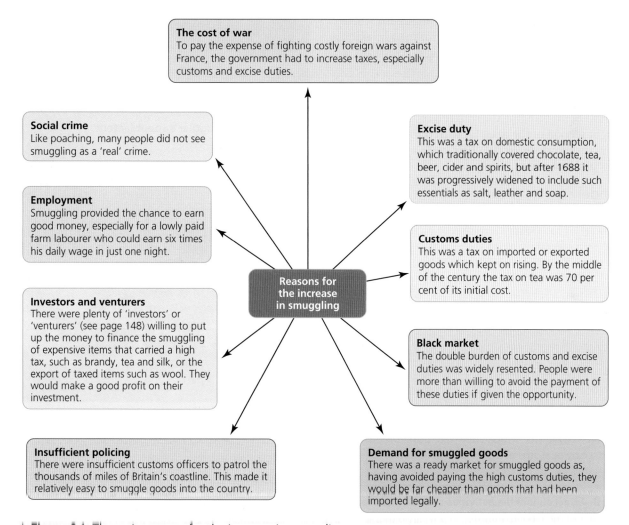

The cost of war
To pay the expense of fighting costly foreign wars against France, the government had to increase taxes, especially customs and excise duties.

Social crime
Like poaching, many people did not see smuggling as a 'real' crime.

Employment
Smuggling provided the chance to earn good money, especially for a lowly paid farm labourer who could earn six times his daily wage in just one night.

Investors and venturers
There were plenty of 'investors' or 'venturers' (see page 148) willing to put up the money to finance the smuggling of expensive items that carried a high tax, such as brandy, tea and silk, or the export of taxed items such as wool. They would make a good profit on their investment.

Insufficient policing
There were insufficient customs officers to patrol the thousands of miles of Britain's coastline. This made it relatively easy to smuggle goods into the country.

Reasons for the increase in smuggling

Excise duty
This was a tax on domestic consumption, which traditionally covered chocolate, tea, beer, cider and spirits, but after 1688 it was progressively widened to include such essentials as salt, leather and soap.

Customs duties
This was a tax on imported or exported goods which kept on rising. By the middle of the century the tax on tea was 70 per cent of its initial cost.

Black market
The double burden of customs and excise duties was widely resented. People were more than willing to avoid the payment of these duties if given the opportunity.

Demand for smuggled goods
There was a ready market for smuggled goods as, having avoided paying the high customs duties, they would be far cheaper than goods that had been imported legally.

▲ Figure 2.1: The main reasons for the increase in smuggling

Source F: Comments made on smuggling made by John Taylor, the keeper of Newgate prison, in 1747

The common people of England in general fancy there is nothing in the crime of smuggling ... the poor feel they have a right to shun [avoid] paying any duty on their goods.

THINK

Study Figure 2.1. What do you think were the FOUR most important reasons for the increase in smuggling during the eighteenth century? In each case give reasons for your choice.

The organisation of smuggling

By the middle of the century smuggling was big business. Large gangs like the Hawkhurst and Hadleigh gangs, who operated along the south coast of England, dealt with several cargo loads of smuggled goods every week. Each gang employed between 50 and 100 individuals, the bulk of the work being undertaken by farm labourers looking for a quicker way to make money. Smuggling had evolved into an organised operation, involving operators at every level:

The venturer

Heading a smuggling operation was an investor or venturer – an unseen wealthy individual or group of individuals, who would put up the initial money to finance the whole operation. They would receive payment for their investment when the goods had been sold after being successfully landed ashore.

The spotsman

Responsibility for bringing the ship full of smuggled goods to the right section of the coast lay with the spotsman. He had intimate knowledge of the cliffs, coves and beaches along his patch of coast.

The lander

On shore the lander would be responsible for arranging for a number of tub-boats to row out to pick up the cargo from the ship several miles off shore, usually at night. Contact was often made using a special 'spout lantern' (see Source H), which could shine a light to signal a ship at sea but which could not be seen from the shore. The lander organised ponies, horses and carts and the manual labour needed to carry the goods once they were landed on the shore.

Tubmen and batsmen

The men who did the heavy manual lifting and carrying were the tubmen or tub-carriers. These men were protected by batsmen – hired thugs who were equipped with strong oak clubs or handguns, which they were quite prepared to use against any customs officials who attempted to break up the operation.

▲ Source H: A smuggler's spout lantern

▲ Source I: A group of smugglers landing their cargo at a bay

> **THINK** ?
> Describe how smuggling gangs were organised.

> **Source G: An account of the activities of smugglers made in a 'Report to the Excise Commissioners' in 1734**
>
> The smugglers pass and re-pass, to and from the seaside, 40 and 50 in a gang, in the daytime, loaded with tea and brandy. Above 200 mounted smugglers were seen one night upon the sea-beach there [Lydd, in Kent], waiting from the loading of six boats. They went in a body from the beach about four miles into the country and then separated into small parties.

Smuggling along the Welsh coast

With its extensive coasts Wales was particularly prone to smuggling activity:

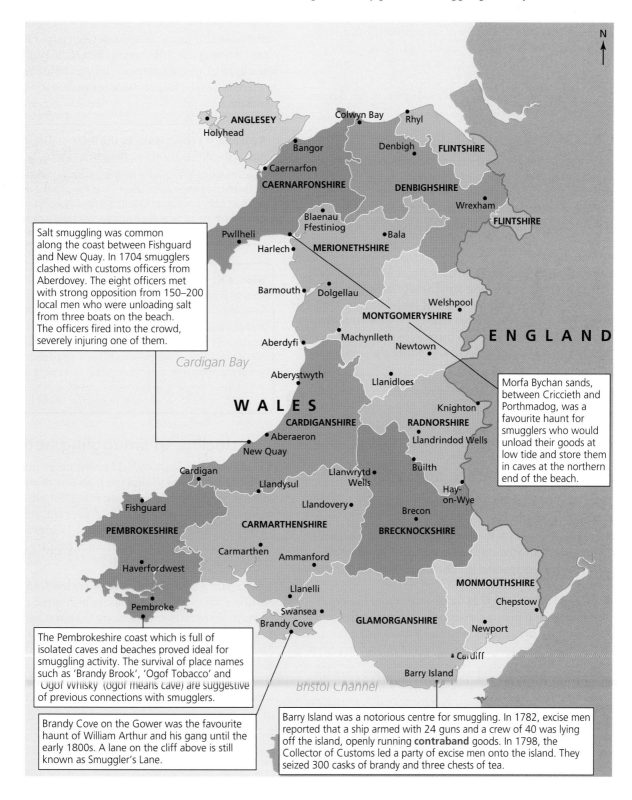

Salt smuggling was common along the coast between Fishguard and New Quay. In 1704 smugglers clashed with customs officers from Aberdovey. The eight officers met with strong opposition from 150–200 local men who were unloading salt from three boats on the beach. The officers fired into the crowd, severely injuring one of them.

Morfa Bychan sands, between Criccieth and Porthmadog, was a favourite haunt for smugglers who would unload their goods at low tide and store them in caves at the northern end of the beach.

The Pembrokeshire coast which is full of isolated caves and beaches proved ideal for smuggling activity. The survival of place names such as 'Brandy Brook', 'Ogof Tobacco' and 'Ogof Whisky' (ogof means cave) are suggestive of previous connections with smugglers.

Brandy Cove on the Gower was the favourite haunt of William Arthur and his gang until the early 1800s. A lane on the cliff above is still known as Smuggler's Lane.

Barry Island was a notorious centre for smuggling. In 1782, excise men reported that a ship armed with 24 guns and a crew of 40 was lying off the island, openly running **contraband** goods. In 1798, the Collector of Customs led a party of excise men onto the island. They seized 300 casks of brandy and three chests of tea.

There were many notable Welsh smugglers, including:

William Owen

He wrote his autobiography while in Carmarthen Goal, awaiting trial for the murder of an accomplice during a botched robbery. He operated a smuggling gang along the Welsh coast during the 1720s and 1730s, running contraband brandy and salt from his base on the Isle of Man, landing it at various places along Cardigan Bay and the Llŷn Peninsula. He was executed in 1747.

Siôn Cwilt

A smuggler who operated in the mid-eighteenth century, so called because of the colourful patches on his coat. He lived in a tŷ unnos (a house built in one night) near Synod Inn, Ceredigion, a district known to this day as Banc Siôn Cwilt. It is said that he stored his smuggled goods in sea caves.

The Lucas family

Living at Stout Hall on Gower, members of this family were engaged in smuggling activities for over 200 years. Their reign ended with the death of John Lucas in 1703. His home, Salt House, possessed cellars that were large enough to drive a horse and cart into them. A secret path led from the cellars to a cave at Culver Hole, where the smuggled goods were landed.

> **THINK** ?
>
> To what extent was smuggling a problem in Wales?

Attempts to reduce smuggling

The government passed several laws designed to limit the extent of smuggling:

- **Hovering Act 1718** – this made it illegal for vessels smaller than 50 tons to wait within six miles of the shore; transportation to the colonies was introduced as a penalty for smuggling.
- **Act of Indemnity 1736** – this introduced the death penalty for injuring preventative officers in the course of their duty, heavy fines for bribery and a free pardon to a smuggler who revealed the names of fellow smugglers.

Those responsible for apprehending smugglers were the preventative officers who were officially known as the Revenue Men of the Customs and Excise Service. Their task was to patrol the coastline of Wales and England, which was divided into 33 areas, each with its own collector, customer and controller. Each port was staffed by an additional five officials. Teams of riding officers were based every few miles to patrol the coastal paths, with a supervisor for every six men. However, with smuggling being so widespread, it was a difficult task to stop all

transactions, and when faced with large gangs protected by batsmen the preventative officers were almost powerless.

Even if smugglers were apprehended it often proved difficult to secure a conviction. Faced with threats against their life from powerful gangs, magistrates were often too afraid to convict smugglers. Informers also ran the risk of attack or even death. Coastal communities were often tight-lipped, with many in the locality heavily involved in the smuggling business.

> **Source J: A report made by the Duke of Richmond in 1749 about the difficulty of catching smugglers**
>
> The smugglers reigned a long time uncontrolled ... If any of them happened to be taken, and the proof ever so clear against him, no magistrate in the county durst commit him to gaol. If he did he was sure to have his house or his barns set on fire, if he was so lucky to escape with his life.

> **Source K: Information given by Abraham Walter, a tea dealer who had been a smuggler, to a Commission of Enquiry into smuggling set up by the government in 1748**
>
> It is extremely dangerous for the Custom House Officers to attempt to seize goods in the coast counties because smugglers are very numerous there and can assemble a great number whenever they need. Nine persons in ten in the area would give them assistance and do lend the smugglers their horses and teams to convey their goods.

The decline of smuggling activity

A Committee of Enquiry held by the government in the early 1780s concluded that the high rate of smuggling was due to the levying of high duties. In 1784, the duty on tea was cut from 119 per cent to 12.5 per cent, thus making tea an unprofitable cargo for smugglers. Duties on other items were reduced in the early nineteenth century signalling the end of smuggling on this scale.

The impact of the **Napoleonic War** (1804–15) added to this decline. Fear of a French invasion prompted the building of Martello (watch) towers along the coast of south-east England and these served as ideal lookout posts for the forces of law and order. The Royal Navy patrolled the English Channel and blockaded French ports, all of which served to restrict trade with France. A further hindrance for smugglers was the establishment of the Coast Guard service in the 1820s.

> **THINK** ?
>
> 1 Study Sources J and K. Explain why the authorities found it difficult to capture and convict smugglers.
> 2 Explain why smuggling declined during the late eighteenth and early nineteenth centuries.

The growth of highway robbery

The eighteenth century saw the growth of a more mobile society. The development of industry, the sharp rise in population and the growth of towns, caused people to move around the country more frequently. However, better transport links and an increased volume of traffic also brought with it more opportunities for crime (see Source L).

Highway robbery had been present in the sixteenth and seventeenth centuries, but it became much more common in the eighteenth century. Many roads secured reputations for being particularly unsafe due to an increased risk of being attacked by armed robbers. For several reasons this period became the age of the highwayman.

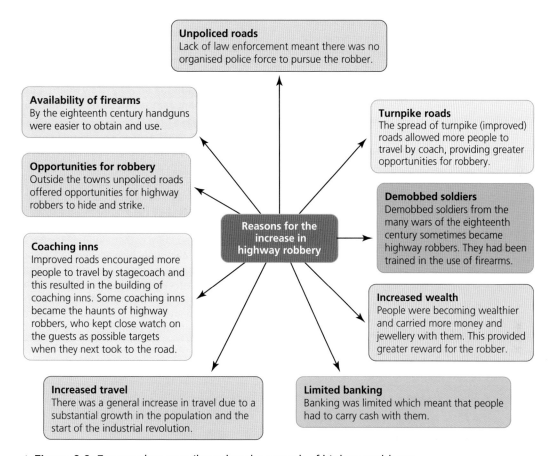

Unpoliced roads
Lack of law enforcement meant there was no organised police force to pursue the robber.

Availability of firearms
By the eighteenth century handguns were easier to obtain and use.

Opportunities for robbery
Outside the towns unpoliced roads offered opportunities for highway robbers to hide and strike.

Coaching inns
Improved roads encouraged more people to travel by stagecoach and this resulted in the building of coaching inns. Some coaching inns became the haunts of highway robbers, who kept close watch on the guests as possible targets when they next took to the road.

Reasons for the increase in highway robbery

Turnpike roads
The spread of turnpike (improved) roads allowed more people to travel by coach, providing greater opportunities for robbery.

Demobbed soldiers
Demobbed soldiers from the many wars of the eighteenth century sometimes became highway robbers. They had been trained in the use of firearms.

Increased wealth
People were becoming wealthier and carried more money and jewellery with them. This provided greater reward for the robber.

Increased travel
There was a general increase in travel due to a substantial growth in the population and the start of the industrial revolution.

Limited banking
Banking was limited which meant that people had to carry cash with them.

▲ Figure 2.2: Factors that contributed to the growth of highway robbery

THINK ?

Compare and contrast Source L and Figure 2.2. What factors are common to help explain why highway robbery became more widespread during the eighteenth century?

Source L: Rev. John Evans describing improvements in road transport in *The Beauties of England and Wales* (1812)

The country [Wales] may now be traversed in almost every direction, and few towns are devoid of the accommodating vehicle, a post-chaise. Many of the roads of the interior are narrow, and abound with frequent and long ascents and descents; but they are no longer what formerly they were ... Numerous roads have been widened, shortened, and otherwise ameliorated [improved] by the addition of drains, arches, bridges, etc. to the great accommodation of travellers, and general benefit of the inhabitants.

Highway robbers

Highway robbery caused great alarm, as it involved stealing using violence or the threat of violence, and sometimes resulted in murder. There were two types of highway robber – the footpad and the highwayman.

Footpads

They attacked their victims on foot and, because they did not have a horse, they tended to specialise in robbing pedestrian travellers who could not escape as easily as mounted travellers. They lacked the glamorous image of the highwayman and were considered to be more lowly criminals. Their attacks on the unsuspecting traveller could often be quite brutal.

Highwaymen

These were mounted robbers who, because they rode a horse, were able to attack stage coaches and travellers on horseback. Such travellers tended to be richer and, as the raid often resulted in bigger takings, highwaymen were considered to be socially superior to the lowly footpads. Many such robberies involved the use of firearms. Some robbed alone, but most operated in pairs or in small groups. Private coaches and public stagecoaches were the most common targets, as well as postboys carrying the mail.

The most frequent instances of highway robbery took place on the roads leading in and out of London. The isolated spot of Hounslow Heath, which was crossed by the roads from London to Bath and Exeter, was a favourite haunt.

Finchley Common on the Great North Road was another area prone to attacks.

> **Source M:** An account of a highway robbery contained in *The Proceedings of the Old Bailey*, 12 September 1781.
>
> Evidence of John Mawson: 'As I was coming home, in company with Mr. Andrews, within two fields of the new road that is by the gate-house of Lord Baltimore, we were met by two men; they attacked us both: the man who attacked me I have never seen since. He clapped a bayonet to my breast, and said, with an oath, Your money, or your life! He had on a soldier's waistcoat and breeches. I put the bayonet aside, and gave him my silver, about three or four shillings.

> **Source N:** A contemporary account of an armed attack on Lord Eglington on Hounslow Heath, London, by the highwayman, James MacLaine in June 1750
>
> On the 26 June, as his Lordship was going over Hounslow Heath early, MacLaine and his companion, knowing they should have a good booty, resolved to rob him. But as he was armed with a blunderbuss some contrivance was necessary. They therefore agreed that one should go before the post-chaise and the other behind it; he before the chaise stopped the Postilion, and screened himself in such a manner that his Lordship would not discharge his blunderbuss at him without killing his own servant; at the same time MacLaine, who was behind, swore if his Lordship did not throw the blunderbuss out of the chaise, he would blow his brains through his face. His Lordship, finding himself thus beset, was forced to comply and was robbed of his portmanteau and 50 guineas. His Lordship had two servants half a mile behind.

An Exact Representation of MACLAINE the Highwayman Robbing LORD EGLINGTON on Hounslow Heath on the 26ᵗʰ of June 1750.

(From a Contemporary Engraving.)

▲ **Source O:** A contemporary illustration showing the highwayman James MacLaine stopping the coach of Lord Eglington on Hounslow Heath, June 1750

> **THINK** ?
> 1 How useful is Source M to an historian studying highway robbery in the eighteenth century?
> 2 Use Sources N and O, and your own knowledge, to describe the crime of highway robbery.

Case study: Richard 'Dick' Turpin (1706–39)

Dick Turpin is probably the best remembered highwayman of the eighteenth century, whose daring deeds were celebrated in the romantic novels of the nineteenth century. Historians have now shown that many of the glamorous stories attached to Turpin are more myth than historical fact. In reality his career was violent and brutal.

Turpin was born in Essex in 1706 and trained as a butcher. In his teens he took to cattle-stealing before joining a gang of violent house-breakers. During a raid on a house in Loughton, Essex, in 1735, Turpin was said to have threatened to put the widow on the fire if she did not disclose where her money was hidden. When some of his gang were arrested and hanged, Turpin turned to highway robbery and joined up with Tom King, carrying out attacks on travellers on the Cambridge Road. Their crimes resulted in a reward of £100 for their capture, forcing the pair to live in a cave in Epping Forest. In May 1737, Turpin and King were cornered during an attack. Turpin escaped but King was killed by a shot fired from Turpin's gun. Turpin fled to Yorkshire where, using a false name, he set up a business buying and selling horses. In February 1739, he was arrested on suspicion of horse-stealing, found guilty and hanged at York on 7 April 1739. He was thirty-three years old.

Contrary to popular belief Turpin never owned a horse called Black Bess, neither did he ride from London to York in the near impossible time of 16 hours, a journey that took a stagecoach three days. In fact, this ride was actually undertaken by John Nevison who in the 1680s attacked a sailor at Gadshill in Kent at 4.00 a.m. and tried to establish an alibi by reaching York at 7.45 p.m. In a novel called *Rockwood* written in 1834, the ride to York was attributed to Turpin not Nevison.

Reasons for the decline in highway robbery

By the early nineteenth century, attacks on the highway were becoming less common and the last recorded robbery by a highwayman occurred in 1831. Several factors contributed to the decline in highway robbery:

- London was growing rapidly and some of the most dangerous open spaces near the city, such as Finchley Common and Hounslow Heath, were being covered with buildings. This made it more difficult to ambush coaches.
- A greater use of banknotes, which were more traceable than gold and silver coins, made it more difficult for robbers.
- London was becoming better policed. The Fielding brothers (see page 171) had set up a horse patrol to stop highwaymen and in 1805 a new patrol of 54 men was set up to guard the roads leaving the capital.
- The spread of turnpike roads with their manned tollgates, made it more difficult for a highwayman to escape notice while making his getaway.
- Justices of the peace refused to licence taverns that were popular with highwaymen.

THINK

'By 1831 instances of highway robbery had declined sharply.' Why was this?

ACTIVITY

Write an obituary notice for the highwayman Dick Turpin, as it might have appeared in a London newspaper in 1739.

Crimes connected with urbanisation in the nineteenth century

As urban settlements grew rapidly in both size and population, this afforded greater opportunities for crime to emerge and develop.

The criminal class

Nineteenth-century writers such as Henry Mayhew identified a 'criminal class' who lived in criminal areas of large cities known as rookeries. In London the most notorious rookery was that of St Giles at the eastern end of Oxford Street, where criminals haunted the narrow alleyways and over-crowded tenement blocks. Mayhew even classified criminals according to their crimes and identified over 100 different types, including:

- buzzers – stole handkerchiefs from gentlemen's pockets
- thimble-screwers – stole pocket-watches from their chains
- prop-nailers – stole pins and brooches from ladies
- till-friskers – emptied tills of their cash while the shopkeeper was distracted
- drag-sneaks – stole goods or luggage from carts and coaches
- snoozers – waited in railway hotels to steal passengers' luggage and property.

While crimes such as highway robbery declined, new crimes such as railway crime emerged to take their place. Over 90 per cent of crime was against property, the most common being small-scale theft. Pickpocketing became common, particularly among juveniles. In 1876, Dr Barnardo estimated that 30,000 children were sleeping rough, many of whom had to resort to crime to survive.

Oliver amazed at the Dodger's Mode of 'going to work'

▲ **Source Q:** The Artful Dodger picking pockets in an etching by George Cruikshank from a first edition of *Oliver Twist* by Charles Dickens, 1837–38

> **Source P: A contemporary, John Binny, described how children were trained in the craft of pickpocketing during the mid-nineteenth century**
>
> A coat is suspended on the wall with a bell attached to it, and the boy attempts to take the handkerchief from the pocket without the bell ringing. Until he is able to do this with proficiency he is not considered well trained. Another way in which they are trained is this: The trainer – if a man – walks up and down the room with a handkerchief in the tail of his coat, and the ragged boys amuse themselves abstracting it until they learn to do it in an adroit manner.

> **THINK** ?
>
> Use Source P and your own knowledge to describe the nature of crime in the expanding urban settlements of nineteenth-century Britain.

Industrial and agrarian disorder during the Industrial Revolution

The early years of the Industrial Revolution brought hardship for ordinary people. Many craftspeople lost their jobs due to the arrival of new machines. Farm labourers found themselves replaced by new technology, such as threshing machines. Wages were low especially in farming and the high price of food, particularly after a bad harvest, resulted in misery and hardship for many. Ordinary people could do little, and some turned to violence as a last resort.

Between 1790 and 1840 there was a real threat of revolution and the government responded by issuing harsh punishment for any unrest. In 1799 and 1800 it passed the Combination Acts, which made it illegal for workers to combine together in order to improve their situation. This period witnessed the appearance of a number of popular protests.

Industrial disorder

The Luddites

The introduction of new machines, called stocking frames, spelt disaster for the traditional handloom weavers. Machine produced cloth, although of inferior quality, was much cheaper than hand woven cloth. The price of a roll of hand woven cloth in 1797 was 27 shillings but by 1827 a roll of machine produced cloth cost just 3 shillings. As a last resort, workers who had lost their jobs ganged together and broke into the new factories at night to smash the hated stocking-frames. To begin with they sent letters asking mill owners to destroy the machines and they signed these letters 'Nedd Lud'. For this reason the machine breakers became known as 'Luddites'.

The attacks began in Nottingham in 1812 and soon spread to Lancashire and Yorkshire. In April 1812, 150 armed Luddites attacked Rawfolds Mill near Huddersfield and in Yorkshire mill owner William Horsfall was murdered. The government responded by sending 12,000 troops into the troubled areas and passed a law making frame-breaking punishable by death. In 1813, 17 Luddites were executed, including three for the murder of Horsfall and five for the attack on Rawfolds Mill. Many were fined while others were transported. Such harsh punishments caused Luddism to fade away, but the new machines remained.

▲ Source R: Luddites destroying a textile machine

> **Source S: An account of a Luddite attack which appeared in the *Manchester Gazette* newspaper on 2 May 1812**
>
> On Monday afternoon a large body, not less than 2,000, commenced an attack, on the discharge of a pistol, which appeared to have been the signal; vollies of stones were thrown, and the windows smashed to atoms; the internal part of the building being guarded, a musket was discharged in the hope of intimidating and dispersing the assailants. In a very short time the effects were too shockingly seen in the death of three, and it is said, about ten wounded.

Chartist protests in Wales, 1839

Chartism was a movement for democratic rights which had been started in London in 1838 with the publication of the 'People's Charter'. This demanded the reform of parliament and the granting of the vote to all men over the age of 21. Chartism appealed mainly to working-class people and the first Working Men's Association (which is what Chartists called their local groups) in Wales was set up in Carmarthen in 1837.

During 1839 chartist protests occurred in several areas across mid and south Wales:

The Llanidloes disturbances, April 1839

During 1838 Henry Hetherington, the leader of the Birmingham chartists, toured the area of mid-Wales, encouraging the setting up of Working Men's Associations in towns like Llanidloes and Welshpool. On 3 April 1839 a chartist uprising took place in Llanidloes when an attack was made on the Trewythen Arms hotel which housed some police constables who had been sent down from London to keep the peace. On 3 May, troops arrived in the town to restore order and over the next few weeks 32 alleged chartists were arrested. They were all put on trial, found guilty and sentenced to either imprisonment or transportation.

The Newport Rising, November 1839

The most serious outbreak of chartist violence occurred in Newport in south-east Wales. Local chartists led by John Frost, Zephaniah Williams and William Jones, planned to lead a march of 20,000 men from Blackwood, Ebbw Vale and Pontypool, down through the valleys to Newport. In the event only 5,000 actually went on the march. On the morning of 3 November they gathered outside the Westgate Hotel in Newport. The authorities had placed 30 soldiers inside the hotel. As the crowd gathered shots were fired and the result was the death of eight chartists and many wounded. Frost and the other leaders were eventually rounded up, put on trial and found guilty of treason. They were sentenced to death but this was later changed to transportation.

Scotch Cattle, 1830s

The Scotch Cattle protests took place in the industrial districts of south Wales, especially near the heads of the valleys. Members of the movement were mostly young Welsh-speaking colliers who often disguised themselves by blacking their faces and wearing animal skins. Their leader was called the Tarw Scotch (Scotch Bull). They were angry at the truck system, the high rents and the continual wage reductions. They called for strikes and sent warning notes to blacklegs who ignored their calls to stop work. They attacked the property of the industrialists and intimidated any potential informers. Events reached a climax in 1835 when a young miner called John Morgan was found guilty of killing a woman during a raid on a house at Bedwellty. He was hanged at Monmouth. Events died down after this incident.

▲ Source T: An artist's impression showing the attack on the Chartists outside the Westgate Hotel in Newport, November 1839

Source U: An account of violence associated with the Scotch cattle movement, which appeared in *The Monmouth Merlin* newspaper on 12 May 1832

We have to record further acts of outrage and violence by the 'Scotch Cattle' ... On Wednesday last, at midnight, about 200 men from Pontypool district ... began injuring houses by hurling immense stones at them ... It seems the men are determined to be paid weekly for their labour in the current coin of the realm, and will not be compelled, as heretofore, to deal in the shops of their employers.

Agrarian disorder

The Swing riots, 1830–32

Between 1830 and 1832 gangs of protestors attacked the property of rich farmers, setting fire to hayricks and smashing up farm machinery, in riots that spread across southern and eastern England. The protestors were mostly agricultural labourers who were angry about poverty and the increasing use of machines. Wages were much lower for farm labourers than industrial workers and the work was seasonal. During the winter months they were kept employed by threshing, but the introduction of threshing machines robbed them of this work.

The harvests of 1828 and 1829 were bad and this led to increased food prices. In frustration the protestors turned to violence. Threshing machines and the hated workhouse were obvious targets. Many attacks were preceded by a threatening letter signed by the fictional 'Captain Swing'. Between January 1830 and September 1832 there were 316 reported cases of arson and 390 attacks on threshing machines. The authorities cracked down hard and issued harsh punishments to those caught. Several hundred were sent to prison, 481 were transported and 19 were hanged.

> **Source W: An account of an attack on the farm of Mr Ellerby in 1831, taken from the memories of Caleb Rawcombe, a Wiltshire shepherd**
>
> Mr Ellerby had been the first to introduce the new methods. He did not believe the labourers would rise against him for he knew he was regarded as a just and kind man... One day, the villagers got together and came to Mr Ellerby's barns, where they set to work to destroy his new threshing machine. When he was told, he rushed out and went in hot haste to the scene. As he drew near, some person in the crowd threw a hammer at him, which struck him on the head and brought him senseless to the ground.

▲ Source V: A contemporary engraving showing Swing rioters in Kent setting fire to hayricks

The Rebecca riots, 1839–43

Between 1839 and 1843 gangs of poor farmers, disguised in women's clothing and led by 'Rebecca', attacked tollgates on roads across south west Wales. It is possible that the name was taken from a passage in the Bible referring to a Rebecca and her children, and instructing them to 'possess the gate of those that hate them'.

The farmers were angry at the high rents, the payment of the tithe to the Church of England (even though many of them were non-conformist chapel goers) and changes to the operation of the Poor Law after 1834, which saw the building of new workhouses. The spark that finally ignited their anger was the building of more tollgates on roads around Carmarthen and the charging of tolls for carrying lime, which was used to fertilise their land. When the Whitland Turnpike Trust put up a new gate at Efailwen it was attacked three times between May and July 1839. After the third attack the magistrates ordered that the gate was not to be rebuilt.

The harvests of 1839–41 were bad and in 1842 trouble reignited, spreading into neighbouring areas. By May 1843, 20 tollgates had been destroyed and the rioters then turned their attention to other targets. In June 1843, the Carmarthen workhouse was attacked. In September 1843, Sarah Davies, a 75-year-old tollgate keeper, was killed in an attack. Troops and special constables were sent into the area and rewards were offered for information as to the identity of the Rebecca rioters. Eventually the ringleaders were caught and for their attacks on Sarah Davies. David Davies (Dai'r Cantwr) received 20 years' imprisonment while John Jones (Shoni Sgubor Fawr) was transported for life. In 1844, the government set up a Royal Commission of Enquiry and as a result of its findings toll charges were standardised. By the mid-1840s south-west Wales was peaceful again.

> **Source X: The activities of Rebecca reported in the newspaper *The Carmarthen Journal* on 16 December 1842**
>
> The leaders of the mob were disfigured by painting their faces in various colours, wearing horsehair beards and women's clothes … All the doors of all the houses in the neighbourhood were locked and the inhabitants locked within, not daring to exhibit a light in their windows … the mob stopped all drovers coming in the direction of Carmarthen and levied a contribution from them, stating they had destroyed all the tollgates.

Source Y: A cartoon that appeared in *Punch* magazine in 1843 showing Rebecca rioters attacking a list of grievances listed on the tollgate

---

THINK

1 Use Sources R to Y to complete the following table to record the causes, events and outcomes of the popular protests of the early nineteenth century.

Source	Name of protest movement	Type of protest: industrial or agricultural?	Main causes of the protest	Summary of the main events	Result of the protests
Source R					
Source S					
Source T					
Source U					
Source V					
Source W					
Source X					
Source Y					

2 Study the table you have completed in Question 1 above. Which of the protests were the most serious threat to law and order? Give reasons to support your answer.

The growth of crime in the twentieth and twenty-first centuries

The twentieth century was a time of tremendous change particularly in terms of advances in technology and transport, advances which have continued into the twenty-first century. It has resulted in the appearance of new types of crime such as motoring offences, cybercrime and terrorism.

Development of transport crime

Motor cars first made their appearance on British roads in 1894. The Locomotive Acts (or Red Flag Acts) introduced during the late nineteenth century set speed limits and safety procedures for self-propelled vehicles. A law of 1865 set a maximum speed of 4 mph in the country and 2 mph in towns and each vehicle had to have a person carrying a red flag or lantern walking sixty yards in front of it. A further Act in 1896 increased the speed limit to 14 mph and removed the need for a person to walk in front of the vehicle.

One of the first recorded fatalities in Wales caused by a car accident occurred in Llanishen, Cardiff, in 1903, when a 75-year-old woman was knocked down and killed by a car travelling at between 5 and 8 mph driven by a learner driver.

At first only the wealthy upper classes could afford to buy cars. However, as motor manufacturers such as William Morris and Herbert Austin introduced mass-production techniques during the 1920s, the cost of cars fell. By the 1930s there were many thousands of cars on the roads. Between 1924 and 1936 car prices fell by over 50 per cent, making them affordable to the middle classes. As more and more cars appeared on the roads, so specific laws had to be introduced to regulate motorised transport. In 1933 and 1934 there were over 7,000 fatal accidents a year, so the Ministry of Transport took action and introduced a range of safety measures, such as speed limits, tests for new drivers and Belisha Beacons at pedestrian crossings. The safety campaign reduced the number of deaths to around 6,500 per year.

▲ **Source Z:** Under the rules of the Red Flag Act of 1865 a person had to walk in front of a motor car warning pedestrians of an approaching vehicle

Creation of new motoring crimes

As car ownership increased there has been more opportunity for people to commit motoring crimes.

During the first half of the twentieth century it brought the police up against the middle classes, who made up most of the car owners. Before this, four-fifths of all crime had involved working-class offenders.

1908	Road signs introduced
1924	White lines on roads introduced
1925	It became an offence to be drunk in charge of motorised vehicle
1926	Traffic lights introduced
1930	Compulsory motor insurance brought in
1934	Speed limit of 30 mph was set for roads in built-up areas
1935	Compulsory driving test introduced for new drivers
1956	Yellow lines introduced to restrict parking
1960	Traffic wardens allowed to issue fines for illegal parking
1967	Introduction of breathalysers to test for alcohol level in motorists' breath
1977	Speed limit of 70 mph on dual-carriageways and 60 mph on single carriageways
1983	Compulsory for drivers and front-seat passengers to wear a seatbelt
1991	Compulsory for back-seat passengers to wear a seatbelt
1991	New law of 'Causing death by driving under the influence of alcohol or drugs'
2003	Illegal to use a hand-held mobile phone or similar device while driving

▲ Table 2.2: Examples of road traffic legislation

Motor offences range from drunk driving to minor traffic offences and they involve a huge amount of police and court time (see Figure 2.3).

Once a person is responsible for a vehicle they have to fulfil several legal requirements before they take to the road:

- The vehicle needs to be taxed, insured and, if it is more than three years old, possess a valid MOT certificate.
- The driver must have passed their driving test and hold a driving licence.
- Once on the road the driver must drive according to the laws of the road, following the Highway Code and obeying signs and speed limits.
- They must not drive while under the influence of drugs or alcohol.

Failure to comply with any of the above makes the driver liable for prosecution.

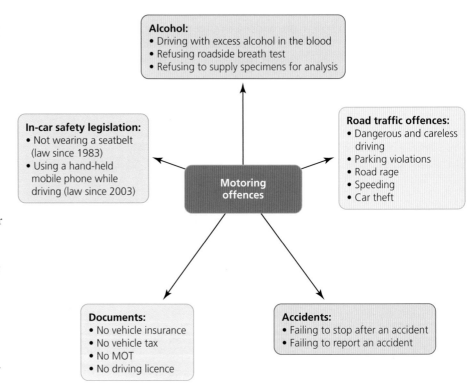

▲ Figure 2.3: The most common types of motoring offences today

Types of motoring crimes

Theft of vehicles

Car theft has traditionally been one of the biggest categories of crime. Poor locks and a lack of any security fittings made cars easy targets for thieves, either to gain access to the car to steal possessions or to 'hotwire' the car and drive it away. In 1996, over half a million cars were stolen in the UK, but since the 1990s car manufacturers have made significant improvements in security measures such as fitting better locks, car alarms, immobilisers and tracking devices. This has made it harder for thieves and as a result the number of cars stolen has fallen each year.

However, as car security has improved thieves have adapted and one consequence has been an increase in house burglary solely to get car keys. Cars can be towed or put on trailers and engine controls can be bypassed using a laptop to re-programme car processes. High-value cars are often stolen to order and within a few hours of the theft they can be in a container; within 24 to 72 hours they will be on a ship to destinations such as Europe and the Middle East.

An extreme form of car theft is car-jacking. Car-jackers have been known to 'accidently' bump into another car forcing the driver to get out, upon which a thief jumps into the car and drives it off. Increasingly thieves are avoiding breaking into locked vehicles in favour of getting their hands on the ignition key. In some extreme cases drivers have been threatened at gunpoint to hand over the keys.

Theft from vehicles

During the late 1980s and early 1990s a new type of car crime emerged – the theft of mobile phones from vehicles. Thieves would often press buttons at pelican crossings to stop the traffic and steal phones from drivers waiting at the lights. Over 145,000 phones were stolen in 1993. In many modern vehicles all doors are now automatically locked once the engine is started and the car moves off.

Joyriding

Driving a car without the consent of the owner is known as joyriding and it is a crime commonly associated with young males. Around 10,000 cases are reported each year and while the age of joyriders is usually between 17 and 25 years, children of a much younger age have been caught driving motor vehicles. In May 2012, a schoolboy of 11 became Britain's youngest joyrider.

Alcohol and drug-related driving offences

Prosecutions for drink driving offences have increased since the breathalyser, which tests blood and alcohol levels, was introduced in 1967. On average 3,000 people are killed or seriously injured each year in the UK as a result of drink driving collisions. Nearly one in six of all deaths on the roads involve drivers who are over the legal alcohol limit. This crime is particularly common among men aged between 17 and 29. Deaths from drink driving rose during the early years of the twenty-first century but then fell significantly from 2004 onwards. In 2004, the maximum sentence for causing death by drink driving was raised to 14 years.

A new trend in motoring offences has been the increased instances of drivers being caught while under the influence of drugs. In 2011, almost a quarter (22 per cent) of those killed in road traffic accidents in the UK had illegal drugs in their bloodstream, the most common being cannabis. Drug driving is most common among 20- to 24-year-olds.

Speeding offences

Motorists can be prosecuted for a range of traffic offences. The most common motoring offence is that of speeding. Since 1934 a speed limit of 30 mph has been in force in built-up areas and since then a range of other speeding restrictions have been introduced to suit different driving environments. The punishment for speeding is normally a fine and penalty points put on the licence. When 12 points have been awarded the driver will be banned from driving for six months. The 1990s saw the introduction of permanent speed cameras as well as mobile speed detection systems. New technology means that speed cameras can record offences without a police officer having to be present (see Source AA).

Source AA: Since the late 1990s permanent speed cameras as well as mobile speed camera vans have been introduced across the UK

ACTIVITY ?

Copy and complete the chart below, using your knowledge to fill in each section.

Type of car crime	Description of the crime	When this crime became common	Examples from this section
Theft of vehicles			
Theft from vehicles			
Car-jacking			
Joyriding			

The development of technology and computer crime

Using the internet, criminals can access computers remotely to commit crimes without having to enter the victim's home or office.

Some computer crimes are new; others are just new versions of old crimes. For example, using the computer to obtain passwords to illegally transfer money out of a person's bank account is fraud, a very old crime.

A growing computer crime is that of identity theft and fraud. Phishing scams are used to trick people into revealing important information, such as passwords or credit card details. Both firms and individuals are increasingly getting targeted by online fraud attacks, and during 2015 recorded phishing attacks increased by 21 per cent upon the previous year, costing cybercrime victims in the UK over £174 million.

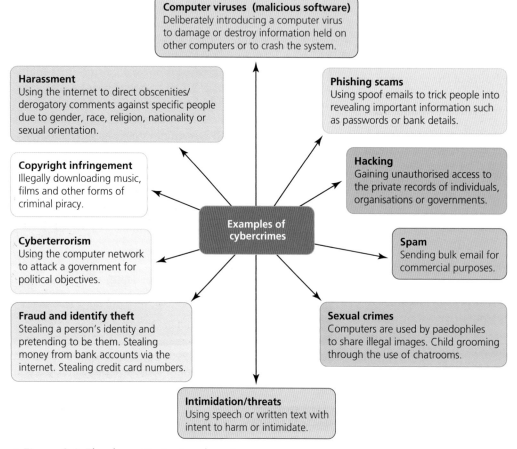

Computer viruses (malicious software)
Deliberately introducing a computer virus to damage or destroy information held on other computers or to crash the system.

Harassment
Using the internet to direct obscenities/derogatory comments against specific people due to gender, race, religion, nationality or sexual orientation.

Phishing scams
Using spoof emails to trick people into revealing important information such as passwords or bank details.

Copyright infringement
Illegally downloading music, films and other forms of criminal piracy.

Hacking
Gaining unauthorised access to the private records of individuals, organisations or governments.

Examples of cybercrimes

Cyberterrorism
Using the computer network to attack a government for political objectives.

Spam
Sending bulk email for commercial purposes.

Fraud and identify theft
Stealing a person's identity and pretending to be them. Stealing money from bank accounts via the internet. Stealing credit card numbers.

Sexual crimes
Computers are used by paedophiles to share illegal images. Child grooming through the use of chatrooms.

Intimidation/threats
Using speech or written text with intent to harm or intimidate.

▲ **Figure 2.4:** The dramatic rise in cybercrime

> **Source BB: Reference to the problems caused by cybercrime contained in 'Cyber Crime Strategy', a document presented to Parliament in March 2010 by the Home Secretary.**
>
> The nature of the internet not only allows criminals to be located in a different country to the victim, but they can target many thousands of victims at once. A phishing email can be sent easily to hundreds and thousands of people from one computer, and a single person can infect many computers with malicious software.
>
> Individuals are targeted primarily for user names and passwords to enable criminals to access, and in some cases to control online accounts. These are usually bank accounts.

ACTIVITY ?

Study Figure 2.4. Working in pairs, work out which of the cybercrimes shown in the diagram are new crimes and which are old crimes committed in a new way.

THINK ?

Study Source BB. Explain why cybercrime is now one of the fastest-growing areas of criminal activity in many countries.

The development of terrorism

Terrorism involves the use of violence and intimidation to obtain political demands. Britain has lived with the fear of terrorist activity since the 1960s, and various terrorist groups have carried out operations in the UK.

The actions of terrorists during the early twenty-first century have resulted in increased security measures, which have had an impact on everyday life, whether it be through the installation of CCTV in most cities and major towns, the placing of concrete barriers to prevent vehicles from getting close to public buildings, the security searches and body scans at airports and ports, or the restrictions on what can be carried in hand luggage on planes.

Some of the methods used by terrorist groups have included:

- hijackings
- assassinations/killings
- hostage taking
- bombings
- suicide bombings/attacks
- arson attacks and criminal damage to property
- use of chemical weapons
- cyber attacks.

Terrorist attacks within the UK

A number of terrorist groups have operated within the UK, both home grown groups and branches of international terrorist organisations.

'The Troubles' in Northern Ireland, 1969–98

One of the most serious threats of the twentieth century has come from the Irish Republican Army (IRA). A largely Catholic group, the IRA have used violence to try to end British rule in Northern Ireland. They opposed the Protestant majority in Northern Ireland and their violent actions led to the emergence of Protestant terrorist groups such as the Ulster Defence Association (UDA). Between 1969 and 2001, a period known as 'The Troubles', over 3,500 people were killed in the violence in Northern Ireland as the IRA targeted members of the armed forces, police and prison services and the Protestant community, while the Protestant loyalist terrorist groups attacked members of the Catholic community.

The number of deaths is much higher if the IRA attacks on the British mainland are counted in the statistics. These have included assassination of politicians and exploding bombs in pubs, railway stations and shopping centres, as the following examples illustrate:

- November 1974 – the IRA planted bombs in two public houses in Birmingham, killing 19 people
- March 1979 – Shadow Northern Ireland Secretary Airey Neave was killed by a car bomb as he left the House of Commons car park
- August 1979 – the IRA assassinated Earl Mountbatten, the Queen's cousin, by exploding a bomb on his boat
- October 1984 – an attempt to blow up members of the British Cabinet by exploding a bomb in the Grand Hotel in Brighton in which the Prime Minister, Margaret Thatcher, and her senior ministers were staying during their Annual Party Conference
- February 1991 – mortar shells were fired into the grounds of No.10 Downing Street in an attempt to assassinate the Prime Minister, John Major, and his War Cabinet, who were meeting to discuss the Gulf War
- March 1993 – an IRA bomb exploded in Warrington High Street, killing two small boys
- June 1996 – an IRA bomb exploded in the Arndale Shopping Centre in Manchester, injuring 212 people, but there were no fatalities. It was the largest peacetime bomb detonated in Great Britain causing damage to the value of £600 million.

The Good Friday Agreement signed in 1998 ended the 30-year cycle of violence and gave Northern Ireland its own power-sharing assembly. While peace returned to Northern Ireland, groups such as the 'Continuity IRA', a breakaway IRA group, have continued to carry out some violent attacks.

The actions of Mudiad Amddiffyn Cymru (MAC), 1963–69

Between 1963 and 1969 the Mudiad Amddiffyn Cymru (Movement for the Defence of Wales), a paramilitary Welsh nationalist organisation, was responsible for a number of bombing incidents. In 1967, MAC blew up a pipe carrying water from Lake Vyrnwy to Liverpool and in 1968 they exploded bombs outside the tax office and Welsh Office buildings in Cardiff.

The campaign peaked at the time of the investiture of Prince Charles in Caernarvon Castle on 1 July 1969. On that day, two MAC activists, Alwyn Jones and George Taylor, were killed when a bomb they were carrying to blow up civic offices in Abergele in north-east Wales exploded prematurely. This resulted in a massive hunt for the leader of MAC, John Jenkins, its Director General. He was caught later that year and was charged with 19 offences, was found guilty and sentenced to ten years' imprisonment. His removal destroyed the MAC organisation.

The actions Meibion Glyndŵr (Sons of Glyndŵr) in the 1980s and 1990s

This Welsh nationalist movement strongly opposed what they felt was the decline of the Welsh language and culture in areas where Welsh is widely spoken, due to non-Welsh speakers moving into these areas. Between 1979 and 1994 they carried out an arson campaign, setting fire to English-owned holiday homes in Wales, which, they claimed, were responsible for rising house prices, making homes unaffordable to locals. About 220 properties were damaged by the arson campaign over a 15-year period.

▲ **Source CC:** Sion Aubrey Roberts, a member of the Meibion Glyndŵr, being led into Holyhead Police Station after his arrest in December 1990

International terrorist groups operating within the UK

During the last decades of the twentieth century a number of international terrorist groups have carried out attacks on the British mainland.

The Lockerbie Bombing, 1988

On 21 December 1988, Pan Am Flight 103 left London Heathrow Airport to fly to New York when a bomb exploded while the plane was flying over Lockerbie in Scotland. The explosion killed all 243 passengers and 16 crew members, as well as 11 people on the ground. It is believed the explosion was the work of two Libyan terrorists, one of whom was jailed for the bombings in 2009.

Islamist terrorist attacks

Since the events of 11 September 2001 in New York, terrorist groups with connections to al-Qaeda and other Islamist groups have carried out attacks:

- On 7 July 2005 (often referred to as the 7/7 attacks) a series of co-ordinated suicide attacks in London targeted civilians using public transport during the morning rush hour. Four Islamist terrorists detonated four bombs, three on the London Underground and a fourth on a double-decker bus in Tavistock Square. The explosions killed 52 civilians as well as the four bombers and injured 700 people.
- On 30 June 2007, a jeep loaded with propane gas canisters was driven into the glass doors of Glasgow International Airport terminal and set ablaze, injuring five members of the public. Police caught the two terrorists who carried out the attack, although one, Kafeel Ahmed later died of his burn injuries. The other, Bilal Abdullah, was found guilty of conspiracy to commit murder and sentenced to 32 years in prison.
- In May 2013, two Islamist extremists brutally attacked and killed an off-duty soldier outside Woolwich Barracks.
- In March 2017, a lone attacker, Khalid Masood, drove a vehicle at speed across Westminster Bridge in London, knocking down pedestrians before he crashed the vehicle into the railings of the Palace of Westminster. He got out of the vehicle and fatally stabbed a police officer as he attempted to enter the grounds of the Houses of Parliament. His actions injured over 40 persons and killed five.

> **THINK** ?
>
> 1. Explain why groups like Mudiad Amddiffyn Cymru and Meibion Glyndŵr used violence as part of their campaign.
>
> 2. To what extent has the UK been affected by terrorism since the 1970s?

FOCUS TASK REVISITED

1 Your focus task was to make a 'Crimes common to this century' card for every century between 1500 and the present day.

2 Look through your completed cards and use the information to:
- ☐ identify which crimes were common across all the centuries
- ☐ identify which crimes were very common during certain times periods but much less common at other times.

3 What patterns can you discover in the types of crimes being committed between c.1500 and the present day?

4 Think of reasons why some crimes are only common during certain periods of time.

TOPIC SUMMARY

- During the sixteenth century vagrancy was a particular problem and many vagrants resorted to crime.
- Some vagrants were named after the crimes they specialised in, such as the Abraham man, the Counterfeit crank and the Angler.
- Religious crimes were common during the sixteenth century, with those who refused to follow the official religion being accused of heresy.
- A sharp rise in customs and excise duties during the eighteenth century caused an increase in smuggling.
- William Owen, Sion Cwilt and the Lucas family were engaged in smuggling along the Welsh coast.
- Improved transport, more frequent travel and an increase in personal wealth, helped to make highway robbery an attractive crime during the eighteenth century.
- Dick Turpin was the most famous highwayman of this period.
- Urbanisation resulted in the emergence of a new criminal class and crimes such as pickpocketing became common.
- The industrial and agricultural revolutions resulted in a number of popular protests during the early nineteenth century, such as the Luddite, Swing, Chartist and Rebecca protests.
- The twentieth century saw the emergence of new types of crime associated with developments in transport and technology.
- Motoring offences became increasingly common during the twentieth century, involving people from all social classes and backgrounds.
- Technological changes involving the development of the computer and the internet have resulted in the emergence of cybercrimes.
- Instances of terrorism have grown during the late twentieth century and continue to be a major concern to the security of the country and its inhabitants in the twenty-first century.

Practice questions

1 Complete the sentences below with an accurate term:
- **a)** A vagabond who used a long wooden pole to steel items was called a ....
- **b)** The most famous highway robber of the eighteenth century was Dick ....
- **c)** The Newport Rising took place in 18........ .
- **d)** Drivers suspected of drunk driving are required to breathe into a ....
  (*For guidance, see page 252.*)

2 Look at Source D [vagabonds, page 145], Source Q [highway robbery, page 152] and Source CC [terrorism, page 164] to identify one similarity and one difference in the nature of crime over time. (*For guidance, see pages 253–4.*)

3 Describe the main features of religious crime during the sixteenth century. (*For guidance, see page 255.*)

4 Explain why opportunities for crime increased during the late twentieth and early twenty-first centuries. (*For guidance, see page 257.*)

5 To what extent has criminal activity remained the same over time? In your answer you should:
- show how some criminal activity has remained the same over three historical eras
- discuss how some types of criminal activity are common to particular historical eras
- include direct references to the history of Wales.
  (*For guidance, see page 260–1.*)

3 Enforcing law and order

This chapter focuses on the key question: How has the responsibility of enforcing law and order changed over time?

As Britain has changed over time there has been a need for law enforcement methods to change. Throughout the medieval period the main responsibility for enforcing law and order lay with the community itself, the emphasis being upon self-policing. A small group of unpaid amateurs who held office for short periods were the law enforcers but they could call upon fellow citizens for support in the detecting and apprehending of criminals. This system worked well in small communities and continued into the sixteenth and seventeenth centuries, but the growth of towns in the eighteenth century put increasing strain upon this system and made it less effective. By the end of the century, private police forces had been established and this was taken a stage further with the formation of the **Metropolitan Police force** in 1829. The success of this model caused the government to take action to order the establishment of police forces across the country. By the twentieth century people had come to see a formalised police service as an essential tool in the fight against crime and in the enforcement of law and order. As you advance through this chapter you need to think about how and why the responsibility for enforcing law and order has changed over time and what factors have brought about those changes and contributed towards changes in attitudes.

FOCUS TASK

As you work through this chapter gather together information to enable you to complete the table below. In each section make bullet points to spell out the key features of that time period. At the end of the chapter you will be able to use this information to outline who had responsibility for law enforcement at a particular point of time, and to make a judgement upon the degree of change and continuity in the enforcement of law and order over the centuries.

Centuries	What was the attitude towards law enforcement during this period?	Who were the main law enforcement officers at this time?	Was this a change or continuity from the previous century?
1500 to 1700			
1700 to 1800			
1800 to 1900			
1900 to present day			

The growth of civic and parish responsibilities in the sixteenth century

In today's world governments have well-equipped police forces to catch criminals and, in times of emergency, the army can be called upon to help maintain law and order. There are also many prisons in which to house those found guilty of serious crimes. However, during the sixteenth century things were very different. There was no police force, no full-time army and few prisons. Law and order was expected to be maintained by a small group of unpaid, amateur officials.

Continuance of the medieval system

From the medieval period through to the Tudor and Stuart periods, keeping the peace was mainly the responsibility of **justices of the peace (JPs)**, **parish constables** and **town watchmen**, with the emphasis very much upon 'self-policing'. (For more information on JPs, constables and watchmen see Chapter 4.) It was a continuation of the medieval system of direct community involvement in maintaining day to day law and order.

In his quest to apprehend a criminal a parish constable could raise the '**hue and cry**'. This was a 'cry' or summons to all able-bodied men in the area to join in the search to track down the criminal. The downside to this method was that the constable could not continue with the search beyond his own parish. Another avenue open to the constable was to call together a *posse comitatus* which was a summons to every male over 15 to catch criminals or help put down a riot.

Development of civic responsibility

During the sixteenth century there was a growth in **civic responsibility**. The Tudor gentry, who in social standing were below the wealthy aristocracy but still substantial landowners themselves, began to take on more and more responsibility for law enforcement. They occupied the important position of justice of the peace, a post which afforded them status within the community and reflected their local importance. Indeed, they came to see this unpaid duty acting as a magistrate in the local courts and supervising the local law enforcement officers as part of their social responsibility (see Source A).

> **Source A:** At the end of the sixteenth century Sir Henry Killigrew wrote to Robert Cecil, Secretary of State to Elizabeth I, recommending that William Treffry of Fowey in Cornwell should be appointed a JP
>
> I know the gentleman to be of very sufficient living, of sound religion and judgement to execute such authority and no justice to the west of his house within thirty miles, nor to the north within twelve, nor to the east within six; the town where he dwelleth being a place subject to many disorders through the common recourse of men of war to that harbour.

The system law enforcement coming under increasing strain

While the post of JP commanded social standing, it was very time consuming and by the seventeenth century there were complaints over the excessive workload imposed upon JPs, particularly those working in the expanding towns. Similarly, due to urbanisation, the posts of parish constable and watchman were also becoming rather burdensome and increasingly less effective.

▲ **Source B:** A Tudor JP had many duties. In this contemporary illustration the JP is licensing a pedlar

> **THINK** ?
>
> 1 Using Source A and your own knowledge, explain why there was a growth in the number of JPs during the sixteenth century.
>
> 2 How useful is Source B to a historian studying the growth of civic responsibility during the sixteenth century?
>
> 3 'During the sixteenth and seventeenth centuries the enforcement of law and order in both town and countryside fell upon a small number of unpaid private individuals.' What evidence can you find to support this statement?

The concept and development of organised police forces by the nineteenth century

The population of England and Wales grew steadily during the sixteenth and seventeenth centuries. In 1500, the figure stood at roughly 2.5 million people, by 1600 it had grown to 4 million and by 1700 it stood at 5 million. This meant a doubling in the size of the population over the 200-year period. With such a growth the inherited medieval system of community self-policing came under increasing strain. This was especially true in large urban centres like London where, by the end of the seventeenth century, the town watchmen were proving to be no match in dealing with the sharp rise in organised crime that had taken place. By 1800, the population of England and Wales had doubled again, rising to 10 million by the end of that century. Such a dramatic increase ultimately forced a change in the methods used to enforce law and order.

▲ Source C: A watchman patrolling the streets of London in the early eighteenth century

Changing attitudes to law enforcement in the eighteenth century

The largest growth in population occurred in the expanding industrial towns and cities associated with the development of the Industrial Revolution. In 1700, it was estimated that 500,000 people lived in London but that figure had doubled by 1800. Manchester's population was just 6,000 in 1700 but had risen to over 50,000 by 1788. Due to the growth in iron making, by the early nineteenth century Merthyr Tydfil had developed into Wales' largest town, with a population of over 30,000, yet it was still policed by only two JPs.

Despite this population growth, law and order in these expanding industrial towns was still maintained by getting everyone to serve as a constable for a year, overseen by overworked JPs. This system had remained almost unchanged since Anglo-Saxon times. Watchmen still operated under laws passed by Charles II, but they were regarded as being of little use in preventing crime or catching criminals (see Sources C and D). The eighteenth century writer JP Henry Fielding described them as 'poor, old decrepit people who are for want of bodily strength rendered incapable of getting a livelihood by work.' Such failings eventually prompted some individuals to experiment in setting up more organised systems of crime prevention and detection.

> **Source D:** An account of London watchmen made by a French traveller, Eugene Lami, writing in his book *Voyages en Angleterre* (1829)
>
> As dawn breaks the watchmen ... crawl home after their all-night vigil over the safety of London. They are for the most part ailing old men, armed only with a pole or a walking stick ... At the slightest alarm each man can summon his nearest colleague by sounding a rattle, but normally their only duty is to cry the hour every twenty minutes as though they were clocks walking in the silent darkness.

THINK

1 Explain why population growth during the period 1500 to 1700 made the enforcement of law and order more difficult.

2 What do Sources C and D tell you about the effectiveness of town watchmen as law enforcers?

The appearance of 'thief-takers'

The emergence of daily newspapers in the early eighteenth century helped to bring crime and criminals to the attention of the public. One consequence was the appearance of private individuals known as '**thief-takers**' who captured criminals and claimed the reward money. In the absence of a formal police force they acted as unofficial law officers, operating as 'go-betweens', negotiating the return of stolen goods for a fee. They saw themselves as public-spirited crime fighters. However, they were often corrupt, demanding protection money from the crooks they were supposed to catch.

Two powerful thief-takers operating in London during the early eighteenth century were Charles Hitchen and Jonathan Wild.

Case study: Charles Hitchen (c.1675–1727)

Although from a poor background, Hitchen was able to use his wife's inherited wealth to purchase the position of Under City Marshal for London. With a staff of six men, Hitchen was expected to police the city for prostitutes, vagrants and unlicensed tradesmen. However, he quickly abused his position and demanded bribes from brothels and pickpockets to prevent arrests. He also pressurised thieves to fence their stolen goods through him. Hitchen would then act as 'finder' of the stolen goods and negotiate a fee for their return to the original owner. He enlisted Jonathan Wild to help him keep control of his thieves, and once these thieves had served their usefulness to him he would turn them in, hence the title 'thief-taker'. In 1727, he was arrested for sexual crimes and died shortly after serving a six-month prison term.

Case study: Jonathan Wild (1683–1725), 'Thief-taker General of Great Britain and Ireland'

Born in Wolverhampton, Jonathan Wild was 12 years old when he was apprenticed to a buckle maker in Birmingham. In 1706, he moved to London and quickly became drawn into the underworld of crime, making a living out of thieving and fencing. In 1713, he became one of Hitchen's assistants in thief-taking. However, within a short time he was running his own empire of crime from Cripplegate, in direct competition with Hitchen.

When a thief came to him with stolen goods for sale, Wild would find out where they had come from and then pay the victims a visit. He would promise to 'make enquiries' about the missing property and would persuade them to offer a reward for their return. After a few days Wild would return the goods, claim the reward and pay off the thief.

London was divided up into districts, each the home territory of one of his gangs. He received information from a network of spies as to where the rich pickings were to be had. He planned robberies, trained and organised the burglars and employed forgers and craftsmen to work on any property that could not be returned to its owner.

Apart from dealing in stolen goods, Wild also blackmailed criminals and then accepted money from the courts when he eventually turned them in. As a result of these 'policing duties' he acquired the title 'Thief-taker General of Great Britain and Ireland'. The corrupt activities of Wild greatly angered the government, but it was difficult to gather evidence about his empire of organised crime. However, in February 1725, he was arrested on various charges, tried at the Old Bailey, found guilty and hanged at Tyburn on 24 May 1725.

> **Source E:** An advert placed by Jonathan Wild in the *Daily Post* newspaper in London in 1724
>
> Lost, the 1st of October, a black shagreen Pocket-Book, edged with Silver, with some Notes of Hand. The said Book was lost in the Strand, near Fountain Tavern, about 7 or 8 o'clock at Night. If any Person will bring aforementioned Book to Mr Jonathan Wild, in the Old Bailey, he shall have a Guinea reward.

▲ **Source F:** A gallows ticket to view the hanging of Jonathan Wild, 'Thief-taker General'. The execution attracted a very large crowd

> **THINK** ?
>
> Study the careers of Charles Hitchen and Jonathan Wild.
>
> a) Describe the role and purpose of thief-takers.
>
> b) 'A public-spirited crime fighter.' Do you agree with this description of Jonathan Wild? Give reasons to support your answer.

Experiments with private police forces

During the second half of the eighteenth century, several JPs began to experiment in trying to reduce crime through the setting up of private police forces. The most successful were two brothers, Henry and John Fielding, who created a small force of paid law officers who patrolled the streets of central London from their base at Bow Street. These 'Bow Street Runners', as they became known, did achieve success in lowering crime levels (see Chapter 4), but they only covered a relatively small area of the city and elsewhere crime continued to increase. The ancient post of watchman, the main law officer on the street, was increasingly criticised for their ineffectiveness in enforcing law and order (see Source G).

Source G: Information given during a House of Commons Committee hearing in 1817 into law enforcement in the area of Soho in London

[Question] Do the watchmen in your parish consider it their duty to assist the watchmen in an adjoining parish?

[Answer] No they do not. It is a difficulty which frequently occurs.

[Question] So that if any disturbance occurs in the same street, if out of his parish, the watchman would not think it his duty to interfere?

[Answer] No, he would not. Perhaps he would stand and look on.

Opposition to the idea of creating a formal police force

The development of a formal police force in England and Wales was not the result of steady progress, a natural progression from the Bow Street Runners through to the Metropolitan Police and then on to the establishment of a national countrywide force. This was not the case at all, and in reality, the police system grew in a very haphazard fashion with wide regional variations.

One reason for this slow piecemeal development was fierce opposition from several quarters to an established police force. The arguments against were based on a number of reasons:

- A strong belief that it was not the government's business to operate preventative policing, people should do this themselves.
- Many viewed a police force as an invasion of privacy and an end of the freedom to express opinions, which included the ability to criticise the government.
- It was the view held by many liberals that the police would be used by the government to stamp out any political opposition. The police in some countries, such as France, acted as spies (see Source H).
- There were objections on the grounds of cost – such measures would be very expensive and cause taxes to rise. Instead many people preferred to rely on constables and thief-takers to deal with crime, especially in the towns.
- The belief that such a system just would not work. It was thought that the best way to deter crime was to make the punishment very severe, hence the **Bloody Code**. As criminals were not afraid of constables then they had to be made aware of the severe punishments that they would receive if they got caught.

THINK ?

1 Use Source G and your own knowledge to explain why law enforcement was still a cause of concern at the start of the nineteenth century.

2 Use Source H and your own knowledge to write a speech that might have been delivered in the early 1800s, explaining why you would oppose the setting up of a police force.

Source H: An MP, speaking in 1811, explaining why he was against the introduction of a police force

They have admirable police in Paris, but they pay for it dear enough. I had rather half a dozen men's throats should be cut in Radcliffe Highway every three or four years than be subject to house raids, spies and all the rest of it.

The development of organised police forces during the nineteenth century

By the middle decades of the nineteenth century, professional police forces had been set up, starting with the Metropolitan Police in 1829, followed by the compulsory setting up of police forces across the country after 1856 (see Chapter 4). Village constables and overworked JPs had struggled to deal with the rising crime rates associated with the Industrial Revolution and the growth of industrial towns. Now the constables were replaced by a professional police force whose sole job was to prevent crime and catch criminals.

Several factors helped bring about a change of public opinion and overcome the fierce opposition that had been present at the end of the eighteenth century.

Fear of revolution

The French Revolution of 1789 and the long period of war with Revolutionary and Napoleonic France between 1793 and 1815 caused both the government and landowners in Britain to fear that a similar revolution might break out here. The serious possibility of a French invasion only added to this fear.

As we have already seen in Chapter 2 a series of events made revolution seem likely:

- Luddite protests 1812–13 – these involved weavers and textile workers who destroyed machinery that they thought was putting them out of work
- Peterloo 1819 – a mass meeting held at St Peter's Field in Manchester in August 1819 to demand the right to vote for ordinary working men
- Swing Riots 1830–31 – these involved attacks on farm machinery and buildings by agricultural workers angry at low wages and high food prices
- Merthyr Rising 1831 – violent disturbances by industrial workers who took to the streets to protest against the lowering of wages, rising unemployment and to demand political reform
- Chartists 1838–50s – people who campaigned for the right to vote for working men
- Newport Rising 1839 – angry chartists marched through the streets of Newport, clashing with troops.
- Rebecca riots 1839–43 – protests by farmers in south-west Wales against high tolls on the new turnpike roads.

The government was forced to call out the army to deal with most of these disturbances. The main concern of the authorities was to maintain law and order and not give in to the protestors. The old methods of law and order relied on local support, but this was sometimes not forthcoming if the local population refused to co-operate with the constable. During this period the government was forced to rely on the **Riot Act** and the army to deal with such protests.

> **Source I: In 1769, an American staying in Britain, Benjamin Franklin, commented upon the increase in riots and civil disturbance. Such riots continued well into the nineteenth century**
>
> I have seen within a year, riots in the country about corn; riots about elections; riots about workhouses; riots of colliers; riots of weavers; riots of coal heavers; riots of sawyers; riots of political reformers; riots of smugglers in which custom-house officers and excise men have been murdered and the King's armed vessels and troops fired at.

Increased crime and increased fear of crime

Many people in authority feared that crime and especially violent crime was on the increase and was getting out of control. Statistics reveal that the crime rate had risen in the years following the French Wars (see Figure 3.1).

Inadequacies of the existing system

In the larger urban settlements the JPs, constables and watchmen were unable to cope with the rise in crime. Their efforts increasingly proved to be ineffective in the battle to reduce crime, apprehend wrongdoers and bring them to trial (see Sources J and K).

Source J: In 1817 there had been a riot at the port of Amlwch on Anglesey. A mob of local people had stolen the rudder from a ship loaded with grain to prevent it from leaving. A magistrate described the scene in letter to the Home Office

The constables were no sooner sworn in than they seemed to consider their duty at an end and disappeared except five or six who were totally inactive. ... Not a single person could be found to assist the constable to convey the offenders to gaol ... and the ringleader would have escaped ... had not Mr Wm Jones of Amlwch, Surgeon, volunteered ... to attend the constable.

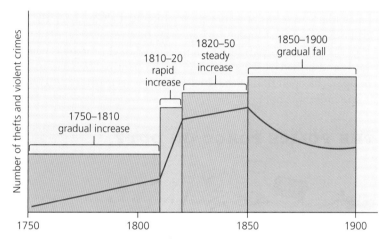

▲ Figure 3.1: The trends in crime between 1750 and 1900

Growth of towns

The rapid growth of towns and cities like London had made the old system of constables and watchmen seem out-of-date and ineffective. There were simply too many people, crammed into closely packed houses and streets, to police in the old ways.

Increasing government involvement

Governments during the nineteenth century became increasingly involved in reforming and changing life in Britain. Governments began to raise more money in taxes and they allowed local authorities to raise local taxes to pay for basic services such as the setting up of a police force.

Source K: A report submitted to a House of Commons committee in 1839 from Glamorganshire magistrates concerning the use of constables to enforce law and order

The present constabulary force of this part of the country cannot by any possibility be worse than it is ... All the constables in the rural districts with very rare exceptions are perfectly illiterate.

ACTIVITIES

1 Copy out and complete the table below.

Source	Key message of the source	How might this source be used to support the argument for the creation of a police force?
Source H		
Source I		
Source J		
Source K		

2 Study Sources A to F on pages 167–70. Which do you think are the three strongest reasons that could be used to justify the setting up of an organised police force?

Changing attitudes: overcoming opposition to the police forces

The idea of a formal police force had been resisted for a long time and to begin with there was opposition and ridicule of the police forces established after 1829 (see Sources L and M). Gradually, however, as the benefits of having an organised force of law officers came to be appreciated, the reputation of the police steadily improved over the course of the nineteenth century (see Source N).

By the end of the nineteenth century responsibility for enforcing law and order had fallen upon a force of paid, full-time, professional police officers. By 1900, England and Wales had 46,800 policemen and 243 separate forces. Their presence on the streets had deterred criminal activity, particularly in terms of minor theft which had always been the most common form of crime. Some of the toughest urban areas now received regular police patrols and the role of the police was particularly appreciated in poorer areas where shopkeepers, landlords and skilled workers were exposed to criminal behaviour. This was a major improvement upon the operation of the thief-takers two centuries earlier where the enforcement of law and order was poor.

THE POLICE FORCE ON DUTY.

◀ Source L: An anti-police cartoon published in 1832 showing the 'Peelers' in action

Source M: An extract from the weekly magazine *Fun* in 1868 following the Reform Riots in Hyde Park. Richard Mayne was the chief of the Metropolitan Police

Richard Mayne is the leader of an organised gang of ruffians who for some time have annoyed all respectable people by 'playing at soldiers' on various occasions in public places. The miscreants wear helmets and commit other absurdities.

Source N: James Grant, commenting on the impact of the new Metropolitan Police in his book *Sketches in London* (1838)

There has been a great lessening of the amount of crime committed in London, since the setting up of the new police. The great organisations of criminals have been broken up and scattered in all directions.

THINK ?

1 How useful is Source L to a historian studying attitudes towards the police during the first half of the nineteenth century?

2 Using Soures M and N as well as your own knowledge, explain why attitudes towards the police changed during the second half of the nineteenth century.

The changing nature and purpose of policing in the twentieth and twenty-first centuries

Since 1900, the police force in England and Wales has undergone considerable changes, especially as a result of the introduction of new technology and the growth of specialist units to manage particular issues. However, in a number of areas it is possible to detect continuity in the enforcement of law and order.

Areas of continuity

Despite considerable changes in organisation and resources, the principal duties of a police officer have remained the same since the setting up of the Metropolitan Police force in 1829:

- dealing with minor and major crimes
- maintaining public order.

The powers they possess have changed very little during the century:

- **arrest**: police officers have the power to arrest somebody they suspect of committing an offence
- **search**: normally the police need a warrant issued by a magistrate to search a property, unless a breach of the peace is occurring
- **detention**: police officers can hold a suspect for up to 24 hours before charging or releasing them; they can apply for an extension of up to 96 hours
- **fines and reporting**: police can issue on-the-spot fines or report a suspect who will later be called to court.

The public still view the police as 'thief-catchers' but dealing with crime is now only a small part of their work. They are far more likely to be called out to deal with a road traffic accident, a noisy neighbour or antisocial behaviour as they to spend time on dealing with theft and burglary.

Areas of change

Some of the most substantial changes in policing have been in its organisation, in the introduction and utilisation of technology and in training and specialisation.

Organisation

One noticeable trend has been the consolidation of forces into larger units. In 1900, there were 243 separate forces. The Police Act of 1946 pushed forward the merging of smaller town forces with county constabularies, reducing the number of forces to 117. This process was taken further by the Police Act of 1964 which reduced the number of forces in England and Wales to 47. Today the figure stands at 43. A key argument for this reduction has been that larger forces have greater resources and manpower and are more cost effective. The downside is that a bigger force can lose touch with local communities and can result in criticism and resentment building against the police as they are seen as an outside body.

A Chief Constable heads each force and the work of the forces is co-ordinated by the Association of Chief Police Officers, which was formed in 1948. Forces share information through the National Police Computer. In 2016 the total number of police officers stood at 124,066, of which 35,498 (or 29 per cent) were women officers.

Some people have argued for the creation of a single national police force but there has been strong opposition to this idea. Opponents claim that this would place too much power in the hands of the government.

Year	1900	1939	1964	1966	1990	2017
Number of forces	243	183	117	49	43	43

▲ **Table 3.1:** The development of the police force in Wales and England, 1900 to 2017

Pay and recruitment

At the start of the twentieth century there were no women police officers. First introduced in 1919 they now account for 29 per cent of the total number of officers in England and Wales, and there is also representation from ethnic groups.

In order to attract and retain well-qualified officers, the police have been awarded regular pay rises and they are now well-paid in relation to other professions. They have a good pension and can retire at a relatively young age (between 55 and 60). In 1947, a National Police College was set up to ensure quality training was given to all new recruits, who now receive at least 14 weeks of basic training before starting work.

> **Source O:** The *Police Service Advertiser* for 29 November 1872 contained an account by PC Green, addressing a meeting of Birmingham police officers in 1872, in which he said that when he first joined the police:
>
> … the rate of wage was such that he would never have accepted had he not been driven to it. It was the very last employment he would have sought, for … police duties not only deprived them of their comfort, but of their liberty, and when they put on their uniform they became the scoff of every low blackguard in town.

Transport and communications

In 1900, policemen carried out their duties on foot, walking their beat. Constables spent their day on the beat, walking up to 20 miles a day. They patrolled alone and had only a whistle with which to summon help. Each police officer had his own 'patch' which he was expected to know well. This had the advantage of having regular contact with the locals and building a relationship of trust and a network of informers.

Since the Second World War police officers have been more mobile, originally on motorbike but now more in the patrol car. This took them off the beat, eventually leading to criticism that the police had become too remote and had drifted away from community policing. It was felt by some that they had lost touch with the locality they served. The result was that by the late twentieth century some forces had reintroduced the 'bobby on the beat'.

In recent decades the police have made use of helicopters to help with the pursuit of criminals, crowd control and traffic problems. They also use horses, mountain bikes, boats and light aircraft if they are required.

Community policing

The late twentieth century saw the introduction of a number of initiatives designed to return to the traditional method of enforcing law and order by asking the community itself to help with policing duties. The result was the setting up of Neighbourhood Watch schemes and the introduction of community liaison officers. Police community support officers (PCSOs) were introduced in 2002 to support the work of the police in the community. They provide a visible presence in communities, tackle antisocial behaviour and gather evidence when dealing with minor incidents.

Specialisation

Developments in technology and science have brought about substantial changes to help the enforcement of law and order. The radio, the internet and computer technology have speeded up communication and allowed for improved record keeping and helped streamline detective work. Camera technology has improved crime detection and helped secure convictions. Advances in forensic science, such as DNA profiling and genetic engineering, have revolutionised detective work.

Attitudes towards the police

Although most people have confidence in the police, the level of trust has wavered. A number of factors have been suggested to account for this:

- The police have to enforce unpopular laws, such as motoring laws (not wearing a seatbelt or driving while using a mobile phone).
- Some people see the police as being too powerful and too intrusive.
- The police are sometimes accused of 'picking' on certain sections of society, such as ethnic minorities or young people.
- A few policemen have been shown to be corrupt, dishonest or incompetent, and the rest have been tarred with the same brush.

THINK ?

1 Study Source O. To what extent have the duties of a police officer changed since the 1830s?

2 Copy out and complete the table below using the information on pages 175–6.

Areas of change	Main changes in policing during the twentieth and twenty-first centuries	In what ways have these changes improved the enforcement of law and order?
Organisation		
Pay and recruitment		
Transport and communication		
Community policing		
Specialisation		

3 Explain why some people believe trust in the police force has declined in recent decades.

FOCUS TASK REVISITED

As you have worked through this chapter you have completed a table which has identified key areas of continuity and change in law enforcement across the period c.1500 to the present day. This will have provided you with a good overview of the key changes in the responsibility for law enforcement over time. It is important that you use this fact file to build up a picture of the developments in law enforcement over time.

Use this table to help you answer the following questions:

1 How have attitudes towards the enforcement of law and order changed from c.1500 to the present day?

2 Which centuries saw the least degree of change in the methods of law enforcement? Give reasons to support your answer.

3 Which centuries saw the greatest changes in the methods of law enforcement? Provide reasons to justify your choice.

TOPIC SUMMARY

- In 1500 there was no police force.

- Law enforcement was undertaken by a small group of unpaid, amateur 'law officers' – the JP, constable and watchman.

- The emphasis at this time was upon civic responsibility – each person had a duty to help with crime detection and the apprehension of criminals.

- Population growth and urbanisation during the seventeenth and eighteenth centuries put great strain on this system of law enforcement and the result was a rise in crime.

- Some private individuals set up as thief-takers, promising to apprehend criminals and return stolen property. Many of them, like Charles Hitchen and Jonathan Wild, were corrupt.

- During the 1750s and 1760s, the Fielding brothers experimented with the setting up of a small force of paid constables operating from their base at Bow Street in London.

- There was strong opposition to the idea of the government becoming involved in the creation of a police force, the main argument being that it took away people's liberty.

- Several factors brought about a change of attitude such as the fear of revolution, the growth in crime and urbanisation which showed up the inadequacies of the existing system.

- During the second half of the nineteenth century, the government took charge and ordered the setting up of police forces across England and Wales.

- During the twentieth century, the number of separate police forces has consolidated.

- Major changes in policing in the twentieth century have resulted from improvements in transport and communication, training, recruitment and the development of specialist units to deal with particular areas of crime.

- The attitude of the public towards the police has changed over time.

Practice questions

1 Complete the sentences below with an accurate term.
   a) During the Tudor period the main law enforcement officer was the ....
   b) A famous eighteenth century thief-taker was Jonathan ....
   c) During the first half of the nineteenth century the trend in crime levels was ....
   d) In 2017, the number of separate police forces was ....
   (For guidance, see page 252.)

2 Describe the system of law enforcement during the sixteenth and seventeenth centuries. (For guidance, see page 255.)

3 Explain why the system of law enforcement came under increasing strain during the eighteenth and early nineteenth centuries. (For guidance, see page 257.)

4 Explain why the methods of law enforcement underwent change during the second half of the twentieth century. (For guidance, see page 257.)

4 Methods of combating crime

This chapter focuses on the key question: How effective have methods of combating crime been over time?

During the period c.1500 to the present day there has been continuity in the methods of combating crime but also substantial change, particularly since the formation of regional police forces from the mid-nineteenth century onwards. During the sixteenth and seventeenth centuries the emphasis upon catching the criminal and bringing the apprehended suspect to trial was very much placed upon the individual and the community. Things began to change during the eighteenth century with the first experiments in private police forces such as the Bow Street Runners. This experiment was taken a stage further in the nineteenth century with the setting up of the Metropolitan Police force and, after 1856, in regional police forces across the country. During the twentieth century, a major change resulted from the development of specialist units such as the **Criminal Investigation Department (CID)** and forensics to deal with particular aspects of crime detection. As you advance through this chapter you should consider the extent to which the methods of combating crime have changed over time but also whether it is possible to detect any continuity of approaches and methods.

FOCUS TASK

As you work through this chapter gather together information to enable you to complete this time chart. In each section make bullet points to spell out the key features of that time period. At the end of the chapter you will be able to use this information to make a judgement upon the degree of change and continuity in the methods used to combat crime, as well as evaluate the reasons for the changes and the degree to which they were effective.

Time period	Continuity in the enforcement of law and order	Changes in the enforcement of law and order	Reasons for these changes	The impact of these changes
Sixteenth and seventeenth centuries				
Eighteenth century				
Nineteenth century				
Twentieth and twenty-first centuries				

The role and effectiveness of Tudor justices of the peace, constables and watchmen

The early sixteenth century witnessed some continuity in the methods used to combat crime, particularly in relation to the use of the hue and cry. The community was still expected to police itself and if the hue and cry was raised, citizens were obliged to turn out and help search for and catch the criminal. The constable would lead the search and, if necessary, the local *posse comitatus* could be called out to help. While this medieval system worked reasonably well in smaller communities it proved to be less effective in the growing towns where population increases resulted in increased crime. This resulted in the adoption of new methods.

By the end of the sixteenth century the real work of maintaining law and order at local level fell upon the shoulders of a number of unpaid amateurs, without whom the Tudor monarchs would have found it extremely difficult to ensure that royal instructions were carried out and peace was maintained. Chief among these local officials was the justice of the peace, or JP, and below them, the parish constable and the town watchman.

The role of the justice of the peace

Under the Tudors the JP was made supreme over all other local officials, from the sheriff to the constable, and they became the chief agent of royal power at local level. JPs were responsible for a wide range of duties. They were chosen from among the landowners of the county and they were men whose social status enabled them to command obedience by respect rather than by force.

Although they were only meant to be part-time, by the end of Elizabeth I's reign, JPs were responsible for enforcing over 300 different laws. They were often given instructions from the Privy Council and they were expected to enforce new laws issued from Parliament. In 1581 William Lambarde wrote a book called *Eirenarcha: Or, Of The Office of the Justice of Peace*, which at over 600 pages, acted as a manual to help JPs do their job. He divided the role of the JP into different areas of responsibility (see Figure 4.1). By the end of the sixteenth century the heavy workload had become a burden for these unpaid local amateurs (see Sources A, B and C).

Maintaining law and order

The primary role of the JP was to act as a magistrate, administering justice. During Tudor times it was common for a JP to try minor cases such as petty theft, drunkenness and fighting, on his own, often from his own house. For other minor cases, however, it was expected two or three JPs met at the Petty Sessions, and all the JPs in the county met four times a year at the Quarter Sessions.

The Quarter Sessions could handle such cases as murder, assault, theft, witchcraft, poaching and rioting, as well as a range of other offences. In 1554, JPs were given the right to detain suspects for up to three days while their case was being investigated and then, if they thought there was a case to answer, commit them for trial. They could give a range of punishments such as issuing fines, sentencing guilty persons to time in the stocks or pillory, or to be whipped. Serious cases had to be passed onto the Assize Court to be examined before a judge and jury.

▲ **Figure 4.1:** The duties of the justice of the peace

Administering local government

Tudor monarchs required JPs to undertake a number of roles to ensure the efficient administration of local government. They were expected to:

- regulate alehouses and supervise inns
- insure that bridges were kept in a good state of repair
- check regulations on weights and measures were enforced
- issue genuine vagrants with a licence to beg
- supervise the maintenance of roads
- regulate the wages of manual workers
- supervise the relief of the poor
- establish and manage houses of correction
- keep a register of all persons entitled to receive poor relief and then tax the community to raise money to care for them
- under the Elizabethan Poor Law of 1601 they had to appoint overseers of the poor to supervise the distribution of poor relief.

Supervise the work of the other law enforcement officers

To help them enforce the law in the rural areas JPs could rely on Constables. In the sixteenth century JPs appointed a High Constable in every hundred to supervise local constables. The following century the system changed and JPs were now expected to appoint a constable in every parish. In the towns, watchmen were expected to patrol the streets at night. The sheriff, who came under the control of the JP, was responsible for looking after the county gaol and its prisoners.

Carry out the orders of the Privy Council

JPs were expected to act as the enforcer of royal authority at local level, ensuring that the acts passed by the Privy Council were obeyed. In Wales this also included the acts passed by the **Council in the Marches**, which sat at Ludlow.

Source A: An extract from the book *De Republica Anglorum* written by Sir Thomas Smith, one of Queen Elizabeth's Privy Councillors, in 1556. It outlines the range of duties expected of the JP

The Justices of the Peace are those in whom ... for repressing [the punishment] of robbers, thieves, and vagabonds, of ... conspiracies, of riots, and violence, and all other misdemeanours [bad behaviour] in the country, the Prince puts his special trust. Each JP has authority upon complaint made to him of any theft, robbery, manslaughter, murder, violence, ... riots, unlawful games, or any such disturbance of the peace, and quiet of the Realm, to commit the persons ... to the prison. A few lines signed in his hand is enough for that purpose: these JPs meet four times in the year, that is, once in each quarter, to enquire of all the misdemeanours.

Source B: Extracts from the Quarter Sessions held in West Yorkshire between 1597–98 that detail the varied work of the JP

From the information given to this court by the constables, Adam Hutchonson and Thomas Hodgson of Barnsley, ale keepers, are men of bad behaviour and do maintain ill rule in their houses. It is therefore ordered that they shall not run any alehouses. It is ordered that no brewers in this area shall brew any ale or beer to be sold at a greater price than a penny per quart, unless they possess a special licence from a justice of the peace.

The highway leading from Leeds to Wikebrigg is in great decay to the great hindrance of all Her Majesty's subjects who travel that way. Therefore the justices here present do order every person occupying land in Leeds to send labourers to repair the highway before August 25.

Source C: A list of some of the laws a JP was expected to enforce, taken from an order of the Council of the Marches in Wales, issued on 21 April 1576

Statutes for the maintenance of Archery and debarring of Unlawful Games, the Statute for Punishment of Rogues and Vagabonds and Relief of the Poor, diverse Statutes for the Preservation of the Spawn of Fish, the Statute for the Amending of the High Ways and the Statute for Alehouses and Tipping Houses.

THINK ?

1 Using information from Figure 4.1 and your own knowledge, describe the chief duties of a JP during the second half of the sixteenth century.

2 a) Copy out and complete the table below, using Sources A to C to identify and record the specific duties performed by Tudor JPs.

	Source A	Source B	Source C
Duties expected of a JP			

b) What evidence is there from these Sources to support the claim that by the end of the sixteenth century the workload of the JP had become 'a heavy burden'?

English law enforcement in Wales resulting from the Acts of Union

The Acts of Union of 1536 and 1543 resulted in Wales formally coming under the political control of England. The English legal system was now imposed upon Wales, replacing the medieval system based upon the laws of Hywel Dda, under which the Welsh legal system had been based since the tenth century. Wales was divided into shires and the English structure of local government was introduced. At the local level this resulted in the introduction of JPs, with many of the Welsh gentry quickly valuing the social status to be gained from taking on this role (see case study).

Case study: Sir Edward Stradling (1529–1609), a Welsh JP during the reign of Elizabeth I

Sir Edward Stradling was a landowner who lived at St Donat's Castle in the Vale of Glamorgan (see Source D). As a wealthy Tudor gentleman he was expected, as part of his social standing, to play a full part in the affairs of the community. In 1554, at the age of just 25, he became an MP and over the coming decades served as sheriff of the county on three occasions – 1573–74, 1582–83, 1595–96. Most of Sir Edward's commitment to the local community, however, came through his role as a JP, a post he held through most of his adult life.

As a JP Sir Edward was responsible for ensuring that individuals obeyed the laws of the land and that they were brought to justice and punished accordingly when they broke them. Below are some examples of the duties carried out by him while acting as a JP:

- 1575: John Wadham asked Sir Edward to find two thieves who had escaped from Somerset to Glamorgan, a task he completed quite quickly.
- 1578: the Privy Council asked Sir Edward and his fellow JPs to investigate the price of butter. The government had been buying Glamorgan butter for shipment to Ireland but the local merchants had got wise to this and put up their prices.
- 1582: the Earl of Pembroke requested that Sir Edward and another JP examine a case of riots involving the Basset family of Beaupre in Glamorgan.
- 1590: a London court instructed Sir Edward and four other JPs to sell the property of a merchant named Anthony Morley who had recently died, in order to pay his debts of £450.

Sir Edward was responsible for issuing summonses against local individuals on a regular basis and for finding tenants who had escaped from their masters. On one occasion he was asked to recover stolen goods taken by locals following the wreckage off the Glamorgan coast of a ship belonging to Bristol merchants. On another, he was asked to help hunt down the thieves who had attacked the household chaplain of Sir Arthur Champernowne of Devon while he was travelling through Glamorgan, and had robbed him of £3.13s.0d.

> **ACTIVITY** ?
>
> Working in pairs, prepare an interview with Sir Edward Stradling, with one of you playing the role of Sir Edward and the other one being the interviewer. You should aim to ask between six to eight questions that focus upon his role and responsibilities as a JP, and also his additional civic duties serving as a sheriff and MP.

▲ Source D: St Donat's Castle, the home of Sir Edward Stradling, JP

The role of the parish constables

As a continuance of the medieval system of community self-policing, the duty of the maintaining law and order fell upon the shoulders of the JP but to help him with the day-to-day policing duties he could call upon the services of lessor officials, namely the parish constable and the town watchman.

The office of constable first appeared in the 1250s and over the centuries it had evolved into that of a law enforcement officer. The parish constable was appointed from among the tradesmen or husbandmen (farmers) living in the area. They were expected to hold the unpaid post for one year and were given a range of duties under the close supervision of the JP (see Figure 4.2). They had to carry out this extensive range of duties on top of their existing job. For many this was an unwanted extra burden, making the job unpopular.

In theory every able-bodied male in the village had to serve as a constable, but in many instances wealthier people paid others to take their turn. Those who refused to do their duty could be fined and placed in the stocks. In 1721, the author Daniel Defoe paid ten pounds to be excused from constable duties in Stoke Newington, Middlesex, complaining that 'it takes up so much time that his own affairs are frequently totally neglected, too often to his ruin.'

The constable was not expected to undertake all these tasks alone and he could call on any townsmen to give assistance in time of need, and people were duty-bound to help (similar to the medieval system of hue and cry).

In the towns constables were helped in their duties by the night watchman.

Deal with illegitimate children

Keep an eye on apprentices

Make arrests and convey the accused to prison, making sure they were held there until their trial

Ensure that taxes were paid punctually

Figure 4.2: The duties of the parish constable

Fig. 58.—" Whipping at the Cart's Tail."

▲ **Source E:** A Tudor woodcut showing a parish constable punishing a vagabond by whipping him through the streets

Source F: The duties of the constable as described by the Tudor author and JP, William Lambarde, in his work *Eirenarcha: Or, Of the Office of the Justices of Peace* (1581)

First, in foreseeing that nothing be done that tendeth either directly or by means, to the breach of the peace; secondly in the quieting and pacifying those that are occupied in the breach of the peace; and thirdly, in punishing such as have already broken the peace.

THINK

Study Figure 4.2 and Sources E and F. What would you consider to be the three most important functions of the parish constable? Rank and order your findings, giving reasons for your choice.

▲ Source G: A contemporary woodcut showing a bellman on his rounds in London in 1616

The role of the town watchman or bellman

The town equivalent of the parish constable was the night watchman or bellman. In 1285, King Edward I ordered that all towns had to be patrolled at night by a number of watchmen who had the power to arrest strangers and wrong doers. They were expected to walk the streets at night calling out the hours (see Source G). They handed over any suspected wrongdoers to the constable in the morning. They did not wear any uniform but dressed in thick, heavy clothing to keep out the cold night air. They carried a bell, a lantern and a staff or sometimes a weapon called a halberd. Their presence may have deterred thieves and given some reassurance to the townsfolk that law and order was being maintained.

Development of the watchmen: charlies

In 1663 King Charles II passed an Act of Council creating a force of paid night watchmen who were quickly nicknamed 'charlies'. Their job was to patrol the streets and keep a lookout for anything suspicious (see Source H). Although they were paid it was only a very small amount and so only those who could not get other work tended to take on the job. In most places they proved to be of limited use only and, by the early eighteenth century, they had become objects of fun and pity.

> **Source H: A job description of the night watchman written in 1677**
>
> A Watch is to be kept in every Town, Parish, Village, and Tything, every night from Ascension till Michaelmas, from Sunset to Sunrise, which the Constables, etc., must constantly cause to be set, and that by two or four men, according to the greatness of the place. These Watchmen are to apprehend and examine all strangers that pass by them in the night, and if they find cause of suspicion in them, then they may secure them till the morning, and if the parties refuse to obey the Watchmen, they may levy hue and cry to take them, and upon their Resistance the Watchmen may justify the beating of them, and set them in the stocks and Cage till morning.

How effective were parish constables and night watchmen?

While the constable and watchmen represented the front line of policing during the sixteenth century, their effectiveness can be questioned.

- The fact that the post of parish constable was unpaid naturally made it unpopular among those who had to perform the duty, a factor which might not produce the best outcome.
- As the duties of constable had to be performed alongside an existing day job it often proved to be very burdensome and few occupants could devote sufficient time and attention to perform the job properly.
- In the absence of a professional police force the parish constable did serve a useful role – as the main law enforcement officer they helped to maintain law and order across the country.
- In the urban environment the watchman served as the principal law enforcement officer and their presence gave reassurance to locals that the streets were being patrolled at night.
- A development of the watchman was the charlie. Although they were paid a wage, it was generally too low to attract decent applicants and many contemporaries complained that the watchmen were either too old or too lazy to perform their duties to the highest standard.

> **THINK**
>
> Study Sources G and H. Use the information in the sources and your own knowledge to describe the duties of a town watchman.

ACTIVITY

Use your knowledge of this topic area to evaluate the effectiveness of constables and watchmen by copying and completing the table below:

Aspects of the role of the constable and watchman which were effective in the task of combating crime	Aspects of the role of the constable and watchman which were not effective in the task of combating crime

The establishment and influence of the Bow Street Runners

The rapid growth of London's population in the eighteenth century resulted in a corresponding growth in crime and criminal activity. This led to the appearance of thief-takers who made a living from tracking down criminals and collecting rewards. However, they were often former criminals themselves and many proved to be corrupt in their actions (see Chapter 3). More success came from individuals who had become so concerned with the increasing level of crime that they took measures into their own hands and set up their own private police forces. The shopkeepers of the Burlington Arcade, for example, grouped together to employ **beadles** as uniformed security guards to watch over their shops. Another example was for magistrates to become much more proactive in the apprehending and punishing of criminals.

Thomas de Veil and his work at Bow Street

In 1729, Thomas de Veil, a retired army officer, was appointed justice of the peace for the city of Westminster. He set up his office in Bow Street near Covent Garden, an area that had a very bad reputation for criminal activity, and over the coming years he made a real effort to reduce crime. Not only did he try offenders, he also went out with his constables to investigate crimes and make arrests, often endangering his own life. In carrying out this work he set the example for the more successful schemes of the Fielding brothers.

Henry Fielding and the establishment of the Bow Street Runners

The first serious attempt to tackle crime in London's streets was a result of the efforts of two half-brothers, Henry and John Fielding. Henry was a successful novelist and in 1748 he was appointed Chief Magistrate at Bow Street. He was horrified at the number of crimes being regularly committed in the city and was determined to do something to try and stop it.

Henry made a careful study of the causes of crime and criminal habits, which he published in 1751 under the title *An Enquiry into the Late Increase of Robbers &c.* This was one of the first attempts in Britain to analyse the causes of crime. He identified several problems:

- too many people moving to London expecting an easy life
- corruption in the government
- people choosing crime rather than hard work
- constables were mostly useless and he considered that only six of the 80 in London were worth keeping on.

He kept a record of all reported crimes and sent lists of stolen property to pawnbrokers and innkeepers. He also placed adverts in newspapers asking people to help him (see Source I). In 1752, he started a bi-weekly magazine called *The Covent-Garden Journal* to pass on information about crimes and criminals.

With the help of Saunders Welch, High Constable of Holborn, Henry established a new force of six law officers to act as full-time 'runners' or 'thief-takers' and he paid them a guinea a week each, together with a share of the reward money for each criminal successfully prosecuted. He trained these men in the proper duties of a constable, until they were efficient and reliable. They were known as 'Mr Fielding's People' and it was not until later in the century that they became known by the more popular name of Bow Street Runners.

To begin with the officers did not wear any uniform. They were plain clothed to enable them to blend in on the streets. Now for the first time the criminal gangs of London found themselves up against a real police force, which, although small, was well organised. Henry's motto for success against crime was 'Quick notice and sudden pursuit'. If people told him straight away when crimes were committed, his runners were instantly ready to hunt down the criminals.

> **Source I: An advertisement placed in London newspapers by Henry Fielding**
>
> To the PUBLIC
> All persons who shall for the Future suffer by Robbers, Burglars, &c. are desired immediately to bring, or send, the best Description they can of such Robbers, &c. with the Time and Place, and Circumstances of the Fact, to Henry Fielding, Esq; at his House in Bow Street.

Sir John Fielding develops the Bow Street Runners

After three years' hard work at Bow Street, Henry's health began to fail and his half-brother, John was appointed magistrate to assist him. John Fielding had been blinded in an accident when he was 19 but despite this challenge he went on to become a very able magistrate. It was John who carried on the work of the Runners after Henry's death in 1754.

He was 33 when he took charge at Bow Street and he stayed there for 26 years. He was nicknamed 'Blind Beak' and it was said that his hearing was so sharp he could recognise over 3,000 thieves by their voices.

Sir John copied his brother's appeals to the public at large to send him information on the whereabouts of criminals. In 1772 he established a newspaper, *The Quarterly Pursuit*, which was published four times a year. In 1786 it started appearing every week and renamed *The Public Hue and Cry*, which referred to the tradition of calling on everyone available to help chase and catch criminals when a crime had been committed.

During his time as Chief Magistrate, Sir John put forward a number of suggestions to the government and city authorities to improve the policing of the streets of London, some of which were acted upon (see Table 4.1). In 1761, in recognition of his work of helping to develop a force of paid police officers to protect the lives and property of individuals and to keep the peace, the government awarded him a knighthood.

Figure 4.3: A portrait of 'blind' Sir John Fielding

▼ **Table 4.1:** Sir John Fielding's proposals for improving the policing of London

Sir John Fielding's proposals for improving policing	The outcome of his suggestions
1. 1755: 'A Plan for Preventing Robberies within Twenty Miles of London'. Sir John proposed that people living on the outskirts of London should join together to pay a subscription. This would be used to provide fast riders who would react to crime as soon as it was reported.	The idea was not taken up. People were reluctant to pay for the scheme.
2. 1763: Sir John suggested dividing London into six areas each under the control of a salaried JP who would supervise police stations and paid patrols, together with strong guards on the main roads entering London and a regiment of light horses at the ready.	The government rejected the idea but granted £600 to establish a Bow Street Horse Patrol of 8 (later 10) men in 1763. This proved highly successful and by 1764 they had virtually put an end to highway robbery on the main roads into London. As a result government funding stopped and consequently the highway robbers returned. There was no patrol again until 1805 because it was considered too expensive.
3. 1772–73: 'General Preventative Plan'. JPs and mayors across the country were asked to supply Sir John with details about crimes and suspects, and gaolers were requested to keep descriptions of prisoners brought into their prisons.	The government granted £400 to set-up the scheme and to print the details in a 'Hue and Cry' news-sheet. Every half-year Sir John issued lists of offenders still at large and asked JPs to make parish constables search for wanted criminals. In the 1800s this became the Police Gazette and it marked the beginning of a national crime information network.
4. 1775: Sir John suggested that all High Constables within 160 kilometres of London should live on the main road to enable them to chase offenders.	The plan failed as High Constables refused to live along the roadside and considered themselves too important to chase after criminals.

Patrick Colquhoun and the expansion of the Bow Street scheme

Following Sir John Fielding's death in 1780, the work at Bow Street was continued by other magistrates, such as Patrick Colquhoun.

- In 1792, the government passed the Middlesex Justices Act which extended the Bow Street scheme by funding seven other magistrates in the London area, each with six full-time constables at their disposal to combat crime. London was now divided into seven police districts.
- In 1798, the Thames River Police was set up to prevent thefts from ships and the docks. Two magistrates, John Harriot and Patrick Colquhoun, convinced ship owners to contribute funds and in their first year the 50 officers recovered £122,000 worth of stolen property from criminal gangs.
- In 1800, the government began funding the River Police.
- By 1800, there were 68 Bow Street Runners.
- In 1805, a horse patrol of 54 officers armed with swords, truncheons and pistols was set up to patrol the highways in and out of London. They became known as 'Robin Redbreasts' because of their red waistcoats. By 1822, they numbered 60 men.

How effective where these experiments in policing?

While there was opposition to the idea of a police force, which it was claimed would limit individual freedom, the work of Henry and John Fielding did make an important contribution in the development of the methods of crime prevention:

- They introduced the idea of 'preventative policy' by attempting to stop crime from being committed rather than dealing with the consequences of crime.
- In creating the Bow Street Runners the Fielding brothers set up a system of policing without the need for new officials – they used local JPs and existing law officers.
- The Bow Street Runners, and later the Thames River Police, served as deterrents to crime by their very presence.

By 1829, London had 450 constables and 4,000 watchmen to serve a population of 1.5 million. However, something bigger was needed to serve a growing population and a high crime rate.

▲ Source J: A contemporary print showing the Bow Street Runners in action, capturing two muggers in 1806

THINK

1 Copy out the following table and use your knowledge of this topic to complete each column.

The enforcement of law and order on the streets of London between 1729 and 1754

Methods used by Thomas de Veil	Methods used by Henry Fielding

2 Study Table 4.1. To what extent was Sir John successful in implementing his proposals for improving the enforcement of law and order in central London?

3 The eighteenth century witnessed several experiments in policing. Using your knowledge of this topic, identify the problem areas of policing that still needed to be resolved in 1800.

Sir Robert Peel and the setting up of the Metropolitan Police in 1829

While there was strong opposition to any extension of a police force, the growth in population and the increase in crime on London's streets during the early nineteenth century, finally helped to convince MPs that change was needed (see Sources K and L). The man who brought about this change was the Home Secretary, Sir Robert Peel.

> **Source K: A comment made in 1821 by John Hopkins Warden, a constable in Bedford, on the inefficient system of using constables to keep law and order**
>
> '[A part-time constable] who is perhaps new to his office every year and cannot be aware of criminals' habits and plans also has his own business to take care of. He knows that his term of office as constable will soon expire so he does not give it the attention it requires.'

> **Source L: A comment made in 1829 by the Prime Minister, the Duke of Wellington, on the occasion of the formation of the Metropolitan Police force**
>
> In one parish, St Pancras, there are now no fewer than 18 different establishments, not one of which has any communication with another. The consequence is that the watchmen of one district are content with driving thieves from their own particular neighbourhood into the adjoining district.

▲ Source M: Sir Robert Peel was Home Secretary between 1822 and 1830 during which time he was responsible for the setting up of the Metropolitan Police force. The first constables were called 'Peelers' after their founder

Sir Robert Peel becomes Home Secretary

In 1822, Sir Robert Peel became Home Secretary and one of his principal responsibilities was law and order. He believed that the existing police forces were inefficient, patchy and mostly inadequate in their attempts to combat crime and apprehend criminals. Peel set about putting pressure on the Prime Minister, the Duke of Wellington, to introduce reform and in 1828 a House of Commons Committee recommended that a new police force should be set up for London under the control of the Home Secretary.

The Metropolitan Police Act, 1829

The result of Peel's campaign was the Metropolitan Police Act in 1829. The Home Secretary was in overall charge of the new Metropolitan Police force but two Commissioners, Charles Rowan, a former soldier, and Richard Mayne, a lawyer, ran it. The two Commissioners had equal authority and they quickly established a strong working relationship.

The new Metropolitan Police force:

- covered an area up to seven miles from Charing Cross, but it excluded the City of Westminster
- set up its headquarters at Scotland Yard
- London was divided into 17 divisions, each with a company of 144 constables under a superintendent
- within a year over 3,300 men had joined the force and all 17 divisions were fully manned
- police officers had to be less than 35 years old, at least 5 feet 7 inches tall, healthy and able to read and write
- the wage was one guinea (£1.05) a week
- constables were required to work a seven-day week
- they operated a beat system, patrolling a set area, which involved walking over 20 miles a day
- uniforms were blue, rather than the red of military uniforms. Constables did not carry a gun or sword but were supplied with a wooden truncheon and a rattle to summon assistance (this was replaced by a whistle in 1884). They wore top hats.

Many of the initial recruits were ex-soldiers and many proved unsuitable. Over 2,200 were sacked (mostly for drunkenness) or resigned due to the long hours and low pay.

The Metropolitan Police Act, 1839

A further Metropolitan Police Act, issued in 1839, extended the area covered by the force to a 15-mile radius from Charing Cross and established more uniformity. This resulted in the end of the Bow Street Runners, their Horse Patrol and the Thames Police as separate forces under the control of JPs.

The growth of the Metropolitan Police force after 1839

During the second half of the nineteenth century the Metropolitan Police force increased in size considerably:

- 1850: Commissioner Rowan retired and was replaced by Captain Hay. While Commissioners Rowan and Mayne had worked well together, Hay and Mayne did not. The quarrel between the two became a scandal, and when Hay died in 1852 the Home Secretary decided to operate with just one Commissioner.
- 1862: Police strength was about 7,800 men.
- 1882: Police strength was about 11,700 men.
- 1890: Headquarters moved to New Scotland Yard.
- 1900: Police strength about 16,000 men, organised into 21 divisions.

> **Source N:** A description of the duties of a constable from *Sketches in London* by James Grant, 1838
>
> He must make himself perfectly acquainted with all the parts of the streets, courts, thoroughfares, outhouses, &c ... of the section of the metropolis constituting his beat. He is also expected ... 'to possess such a knowledge of the inhabitants of each house as will enable him to recognise their persons'. He is further expected to see every part of his beat once every ten, or at least fifteen minutes.

▲ Source O: Metropolitan policemen in the 1850s

ACTIVITIES ?

1 What arguments are put forward in Sources K and L in favour of establishing a police force?
2 Using Source N, as well as your own knowledge, describe the main duties of a police constable in the Metropolitan force.
3 Describe the growth and development of the Metropolitan Police force between 1829 and 1900.
4 What does Source O tell you about the policing in London in the 1850s?

The extension of the police forces in the nineteenth century

After the success of the Metropolitan Police in London the government passed a series of laws in the mid-nineteenth century which were designed to set up police forces in other parts of the country.

The creation of network of police forces

The creation of a nation-wide police force took several decades to achieve.

The Municipal Corporations Act, 1835

This act reformed some of the **rotten boroughs** and laid down regulations that boroughs could, if they wished, set up a police force under the control of the borough Watch Committee. Very few boroughs seemed keen to implement the law and by 1837 only 93 out of 171 boroughs had organised a police force. In an attempt to speed up the process the government was forced to pass the Rural Police Act.

The Rural Police Act, 1839

This Act, which is sometimes referred to as the County Police Act, enabled justices of the peace to establish police forces in their counties. The Act was not compulsory and police forces had only been established in 55 counties by 1856. Many rural areas objected to the cost and refused to introduce the scheme.

▲ **Source P:** William Hughes, Constable of Pwllheli Borough Police, 1869-79

Both the 1839 and 1835 Acts were 'permissive Acts' since they permitted counties and boroughs to create police forces but did not compel them to do so. Essex was the first to do so, quickly followed by the neighbouring counties of Hertford, Cambridge and Suffolk. In Wales, Denbighshire and Montgomeryshire were among the first counties to establish a Constabulary in 1840, followed by Glamorgan in 1841.

The County and Borough Police Act, 1856

This Act made it compulsory for a police force to be established in any county that had not previously formed a constabulary. The new forces that were set up varied considerably in detail, especially over size, wages, hours and conditions of work. To make sure that law was obeyed the Home Secretary appointed Inspectors of Constabulary. They inspected every force and reported to the Home Secretary. Those that were rated 'efficient' were given a government grant of 25 per cent towards their running costs.

Establishment of town and county police forces in Wales

As in England, the setting up of police forces in Wales was piecemeal. During the 1840s five of the thirteen counties – Cardiganshire, Carmarthenshire, Denbighshire, Glamorganshire and Montgomeryshire – set up constabularies. Some boroughs also set up their own police units – Swansea established a force of seven officers, Cardiff had five and Neath and Pwllheli had one each (see Source P). After 1856 constabularies were set up in the remaining shires.

Attitudes towards the new police

At first, the new forces were poorly received outside London, and there was widespread public resentment at having to fund them when it was felt that they were hardly needed (see Source Q). Gradually, however, as the police grew more successful at tackling crime, suspicion and hatred of the force died down and they became better accepted as part of the community (see Source R).

Source Q: A series of break-ins in the village of Marchwiel outside Wrexham resulted in criticism of the Denbighshire constabulary in the *Wrexham Advertiser* newspaper in 1855

Our police we shall dismiss very summarily. They can neither catch a thief, nor keep him when he is caught. Of bone and muscle and fat and big sticks there is more than enough, and to give them their due, they are docile and active and affable. What is wanted is not so much 'guts' as brains, and these they have not got. They cost us £1,000 a year and the inadequacy of the quid to the quo must be apparent to everyone.

Source R: Following the Great Exhibition in London in 1851, an article in *Punch* magazine praised the Metropolitan force for its policing of the capital's streets

The police are beginning to take that place in the affections of the people – we don't mean the cooks and housemaids alone but the people at large – that the soldiers and sailors used to occupy. The blue coats – the defenders of order – are becoming the national favourites. The taking of a foreign fort seems to sink into insignificance before the taking of an unruly cabman's number. Everyone has been charmed during the Great Exhibition by the way in which this truly civil power has been effective.

THINK

1 Study Sources Q and R, both of which were written in the 1850s. Can you suggest reasons why they hold such differing viewpoints on the usefulness of the police force?

2 Describe the process which led to the creation of a nationwide system of police forces across England and Wales by the 1860s.

The development of specialist units

As police forces expanded in size, one consequence was the creation of specialist units to tackle particular aspects of crime detection.

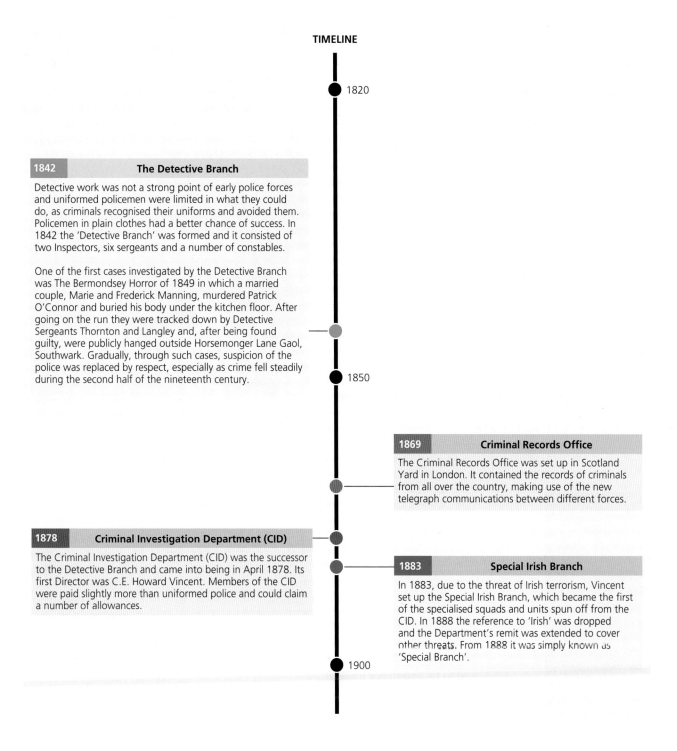

TIMELINE

● 1820

1842 — The Detective Branch

Detective work was not a strong point of early police forces and uniformed policemen were limited in what they could do, as criminals recognised their uniforms and avoided them. Policemen in plain clothes had a better chance of success. In 1842 the 'Detective Branch' was formed and it consisted of two Inspectors, six sergeants and a number of constables.

One of the first cases investigated by the Detective Branch was The Bermondsey Horror of 1849 in which a married couple, Marie and Frederick Manning, murdered Patrick O'Connor and buried his body under the kitchen floor. After going on the run they were tracked down by Detective Sergeants Thornton and Langley and, after being found guilty, were publicly hanged outside Horsemonger Lane Gaol, Southwark. Gradually, through such cases, suspicion of the police was replaced by respect, especially as crime fell steadily during the second half of the nineteenth century.

● 1850

1869 — Criminal Records Office

The Criminal Records Office was set up in Scotland Yard in London. It contained the records of criminals from all over the country, making use of the new telegraph communications between different forces.

1878 — Criminal Investigation Department (CID)

The Criminal Investigation Department (CID) was the successor to the Detective Branch and came into being in April 1878. Its first Director was C.E. Howard Vincent. Members of the CID were paid slightly more than uniformed police and could claim a number of allowances.

1883 — Special Irish Branch

In 1883, due to the threat of Irish terrorism, Vincent set up the Special Irish Branch, which became the first of the specialised squads and units spun off from the CID. In 1888 the reference to 'Irish' was dropped and the Department's remit was extended to cover other threats. From 1888 it was simply known as 'Special Branch'.

● 1900

THINK

How significant was the development of specialist units in improving the methods of combating crime during the second half of the nineteenth century?

Developments in policing in the twentieth century

During the twentieth century the police force continued to evolve, one of the key areas of change being the introduction of female police officers, as well as significant advances in the methods of transport and communication. There was also growth in specialist units and at the end of the century a return to community policing.

Developments in women police officers

In 1914, at the start of the First World War, Nina Boyle, a suffragette, formed the Women Police Volunteers but it was not until 1919 that the first female police officers appeared. They were not allowed to carry handcuffs nor make arrests until 1923. They were distinguished from male officers by having the prefix 'woman' before their rank, such as 'Woman Police Constable' (WPC) and 'Woman Police Sergeant' (WPS). Until 1939 they were given only limited duties, such as patrol work (especially in parks and open spaces), escort duty (looking after children and female prisoners) and hospital duty.

Since the Second World War the number of female police officers has increased and the scope of their work has widened. However, it was not until the 1970s that they were fully integrated into the police service and, while they now take on a similar role to male officers, they are much fewer in number. By the end of the twentieth century some female officers had risen to occupy senior positions, such as Pauline Clare who, in 1995, became the first woman to be appointed a Chief Constable (see Table 4.2).

▲ Source S: Women police officers, 1930

1919 (February)	First Women Officers in the Metropolitan Police came into service
1923	Women officers given the power to make arrests
1931	Women officers required to resign once they got married
1937	Women officers allowed to take fingerprints
1946	Marriage rule abolished
1948	Women officers allowed to join the Police Federation
1969	Sislin Fay Allen became the Metropolitan Police's first black female officer
1970	Women allowed to join the mounted branch
1971	Women allowed to be appointed dog handlers
1972	Women allowed to be appointed to the Traffic Division
1973	Women granted equal opportunities
1995	Pauline Clare became the first female Chief Constable (for Lancashire)
2009	Cressida Dick became the first female Assistant Commissioner at Scotland Yard

▲ Table 4.2: Key dates in the history of women police officers

THINK

1 Describe how the role of women police officers has changed since 1919.

2 Study Table 4.2. What do you consider to be the three most important developments in improving the role and status of women in the police force? Rank your decisions in order of importance, giving reasons for your choices.

Developments in transport

One of the biggest changes in policing during the first half of the twentieth century resulted from new methods of transport. Bicycles were first introduced for use by police officers in 1909 but it was the introduction of the motor car in 1919 that allowed police officers to get to the scene of a crime much faster. However, few forces could afford police patrol cars before the 1930s. Motorbikes, which became common in the 1930s, greatly improved police speed and effectiveness (see Source T).

▲ **Source T:** Police motorbikes became common in the 1930s. This photograph shows PC John Marshall Jones of the Flintshire Constabulary in North Wales on patrol in the early 1930s

▲ **Source U:** This police helicopter based at St Athan is shared by the South Wales Police and Gwent Police forces. It is fitted with TV cameras, searchlights and public address system

By the 1970s the patrol car had become an essential tool in policing and many police forces began to change their methods of working, replacing the 'bobby on the beat' with rapid response teams in cars, who could travel quickly to the scene of a crime. However, due to public pressure, police forces in the late twentieth century re-introduced foot-patrols, reassuring local communities that police officers were on hand.

Since the 1970s the police have used helicopters and light aircraft to help with the surveillance of criminals, to monitor large crowds and events, to track stolen vehicles, to direct police on the ground and to help with the search of missing persons (see Source U). Helicopters and aircraft have proved highly effective in crime detection:

■ Police helicopters are equipped with daytime and night vision video equipment, and radio equipment to track suspects and liaise with officers on the ground.

■ Small aircraft can be used for higher and quieter surveillance, making it less likely that suspects will become aware they are being watched.

■ With scramble times of just four minutes for helicopters, aerial units can be faster than ground units and can often be the first on the scene to reported incidents.

■ Aerial units are often tasked to assist in vehicle pursuits – they allow ground units to follow at a distance, set up road blocks and deploy spike strips.

■ Aerial units can be highly useful in managing large crowds such as at football matches.

■ Aerial units can be used to locate missing persons.

THINK

1 Using Sources T and U, and your own knowledge, explain how transport has helped the police to improve their methods of catching criminals.

2 Why have developments in transport been important in policing methods during the twentieth and twenty-first centuries?

Developments in communication

Improvements in communication and technology have revolutionised police methods in detecting crime.

Telegraph and radio

Improvements in communication have made it easier to report issues and call for backup.

- By 1880, most London police stations were linked to headquarters by telegraph.
- In 1910, a radio message from SS *Montrose*, on its way to Canada, enabled police to arrest Dr Crippen. Crippen was wanted for the murder of his wife and was fleeing to Canada on a liner with his mistress. The captain of the SS *Montrose* radioed Scotland Yard, who sent a detective out by fast boat and he was able to arrest Crippen as soon as the ship docked in Canada.
- Police telephone boxes began to appear in the 1920s.
- In 1923, the Metropolitan Police experimented with mobile radio, fitting Morse code transmitters into police cars and telephone boxes soon after.
- In 1934, some police cars were fitted with two-way radios, but the radio reception was often very poor.
- In 1937, the 999 emergency number was introduced.
- In 1963, the first miniature police radios were introduced.
- Today, all police officers carry a two-way radio for instant communication with their police station or headquarters. It uses a special system to ensure unbroken communication.

Source V: Dr Crippen being escorted off the SS *Montrose* on 31 July 1910, having been arrested for the murder of his wife. He was the first criminal to be caught through the use of wireless telegram (radio) message

Camera and video technology

The use of photography proved to be a great help in combating crime. The photographing of prisoners started in the 1850s and its value was soon realised. It provided a visual record and images could be circulated across the country. Since the employment of the first police photographer in 1901, photographic and visual recording have played an important role in crime investigation.

- Images of suspects can be circulated and have resulted in positive identification and arrests.
- Most police cars now have cameras fitted, including automatic vehicle number plate recognition systems and cameras to record a driver's behaviour and check car speeds.
- Evidence from security cameras and CCTV has helped to solve many crimes.
- Camera technology is also built into police helicopters and light aircraft, relaying an aerial image to officers on the ground and providing heat-seeking night vision when pursuing criminals in the dark.

Computer technology

Computers have greatly improved police record-keeping, allowing for the speedy communication of information. They help to sort information, find patterns and match evidence, thereby saving police time. The Police National Computer first went live in 1974, holding records of stolen vehicles. Today, the system holds records on over 25 million people, with databases covering fingerprints and DNA records, motor vehicle details and information about missing persons. It is available 24 hours a day, providing police access to information of national and local significance. It can alert police to criminals who have committed crimes similar to the ones being investigated. It can monitor websites and emails, and has a major role to play in antiterrorist activities.

Most police cars are now fitted with advanced computer technology, providing officers with direct access to specific information such as car insurance, MOT records, and individual driver convictions.

ACTIVITIES ?

1 Use Source V and your own knowledge to explain how new technology, such as the use of the radio, assisted police work during the twentieth century.
2 How important was the use of technology in developing policing methods in the twentieth century?

The creation of larger integrated police forces in Wales

In May 1966 the Home Secretary, Roy Jenkins, announced that the number of police forces in England and Wales was to be reduced from 177 to 49. This was to be achieved through the amalgamation of existing police forces to create larger integrated forces. In Wales this resulted in the creation of the current set-up of four major police forces, the argument being that the creation of larger forces was more cost effective and allowed for the sharing of resources, thereby improving efficiency. Since 1969 the number of forces across England and Wales has been reduced further to the current figure of 43. In Wales proposals were put forward in 2006 to amalgamate all four forces into one but nothing came of this.

Date of merger	New force created	Merged forces
April 1967	Gwent Constabulary	Newport Borough Police; Monmouthshire Constabulary
June 1967	South Wales Constabulary (This was renamed the South Wales Police in 1996.)	Glamorgan Constabulary; Cardiff City Police; Merthyr Tydfil Borough Police; Swansea Borough Police
October 1967	Gwynedd Constabulary (This was renamed the North Wales Police in 1974.)	Gwynedd Constabulary; Denbighshire Constabulary; Flintshire Constabulary
April 1968	Dyfed-Powys Constabulary	Carmarthenshire and Cardiganshire Constabulary; Mid-Wales Constabulary; Pembrokeshire Constabulary

▲ Table 4.3: The consolidation of police forces within Wales during 1967–68

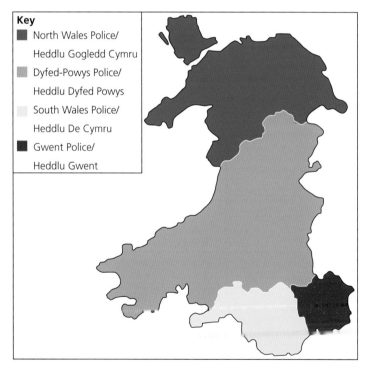

Key
- ■ North Wales Police/ Heddlu Gogledd Cymru
- Dyfed-Powys Police/ Heddlu Dyfed Powys
- South Wales Police/ Heddlu De Cymru
- ■ Gwent Police/ Heddlu Gwent

▲ Figure 4.4: Map showing the four police forces which currently serve Wales

---

THINK

Describe the changes to the structure of the police forces in Wales during the second half of the twentieth century.

Specialisation of policing

Developments in science and technology during the twentieth century have greatly improved the police's ability to track down criminals and link them to the scene of a crime. Such developments have resulted in the growth and development of specialist branches within the police force, each having a particular area of responsibility (see Table 4.4).

Developments in forensic science

In 1900, a Home Office Committee, chaired by Lord Belper, met to discuss new methods of aiding the detecting of crime.

Fingerprinting

A fingerprint is the skin-pattern on the tip of a person's finger, which can be used for identification. By inking the finger an impression of the ridges can be recorded on paper and compared with fingerprints left at a crime scene. As every fingerprint is unique, this is a secure method of identifying a person.

Sir Edward Richard Henry, who had set up the Fingerprint Bureau in Calcutta in 1897, pioneered the system in India and in 1900 he gave a successful demonstration to the Belper Committee. In response, Scotland Yard set up a Fingerprint Department in 1901, and the first person to be successfully prosecuted using fingerprints was Harry Jackson, who was convicted for burglary in 1902. A national register of fingerprints was set up and since then such evidence has helped identify many suspects and solve many crimes. Since 1995 a National Automatic Fingerprint Identification System has enabled police forces across England and Wales to compare records of fingerprints.

Forensic scientists

The job of forensic scientists is to help eliminate individuals or link suspects to the scene of a crime. They attempt to do this by carrying out a variety of forensic tests such as analysing hair, skin, dust, fibres on clothing and traces of blood or other body fluids found at the scene of a crime, and trying to match them with those belonging to or found on the suspect.

Specially trained experts called Scenes of Crimes Officers (SOCOs) attend crime scenes to examine and gather forensic evidence. Recent years have seen the development of specialist Crime Scene Investigators (CSIs).

DNA and genetic fingerprinting

DNA is a chemical present in all living things, which provides the unique genetic code of that body. Forensic scientists can use DNA from blood, skin, saliva or hair found at a crime scene to identify individuals with matching DNA. This process is called DNA profiling or 'genetic fingerprinting'. DNA profiling was developed in 1984 by the British geneticist Sir Alec Jeffreys and was first used in forensic science to convict Colin Pitchfork in the 1988 Enderby murders case. Since the late 1980s police have depended a great deal on DNA to solve serious crimes and to help reinvestigate old crimes. In 1995 the DNA National Database was set up to store DNA evidence.

Year founded	Specialist unit	Principal function
1883	Special Irish Branch (later became the Special Branch (SO12))	Deals with terrorism
1919	Flying Squad (later became the Central Robbery Squad)	Deals with serious theft; originally equipped with cars for the quick pursuit of criminals
1946	Fraud Squad	Investigates fraud and other economic crimes
1946	Dog Handlers	Officers trained to work with dogs; the dogs are used to trace people, property, drugs and explosives; they are also used to deal with hooligans
1965	Special Patrol Group (became the Metropolitan Patrol Group in 1987)	Deals with inner-city disturbances and threats to public order
1972	Anti-terrorist Squad (SO13)	Aimed to prevent terrorist activity
1998	National Crime Squad (NCS)	Targets serious and organised crime such as kidnapping, international drug smuggling, people smuggling, contract killing
2001	National Hi-Tech Crime Unit (NHTCU)	Deals with serious and organized cybercrime of a national or international nature
2002	Immigration Crime Team (ICT)	Deals with illegal immigration into the UK by organised criminals
2006	Counter Terrorist Command (SO15)	Formed out of the merger of the Anti-Terrorist Branch (SO13) and Special Branch (SO12), its key function is to prevent terrorist related activity and domestic extremism

▲ Table 4.4: The development of specialist units: examples of specialist units within the police force

Developments in community policing

During the late twentieth century, following on from the criticism of the police handling of serious civil disturbances such as the Brixton riots in London in 1981 and the Miners' Strike of 1984–85, attempts have been made to improve relations between the police and the communities they serve. More police officers have returned to the beat to provide a visible presence and help make people feel more secure.

A range of other initiatives have been introduced to try to improve police–community relations:

Community Relations Branch (1968)

In 1968, a Community Relations Branch was set up at New Scotland Yard. It was an attempt by the Metropolitan Police to develop closer ties with immigrant communities but it had limited success.

Neighbourhood Watch schemes (1982)

The Neighbourhood Watch scheme is made up of organised groups of local people who work together with the police to prevent crime within their locality (see Source W). The UK's first Neighbourhood Watch scheme was set up in Mollington in Cheshire in 1982 and there are now over ten million members of this nationwide scheme.

The aims of the Neighbourhood Watch scheme are:

- To help people protect themselves and their properties.
- To reduce the fear of crime by means of improved home security and greater vigilance.
- To assist the police in detecting crime by promptly reporting suspicious or criminal activity.
- To improve police/community relations by promoting better communication and using the Neighbourhood Watch co-ordinators as a link with the police.

With the support of the police, members run their own Neighbourhood Watch schemes under the guidance of a co-ordinator. The police pass on information about local crime trends to the co-ordinators, who then share this information with scheme members. They also act as the link to inform the police of incidents when they occur.

Police community support officers (2002)

Police community support officers (PCSOs) were first introduced by the Metropolitan Police in 2002 and have since been incorporated into all 43 forces. Being civilian members of the police staff they are not as well trained as full officers, have a modified uniform and carry less equipment. The main job of the PCSO is to provide a visible presence in the community, tackle antisocial behaviour, deal with minor incidents, gather criminal intelligence and support front-line policing (see Source X). There are currently nearly 16,000 PSCOs in England and Wales and they account for nearly seven per cent of the total police force.

Crime prevention schemes

In their drive to make people more aware of the fight against crime the police offer advice on crime prevention strategies. These include advice on such issues as personal safety, home and vehicle security and on how to avoid being the victim of fraud. They also work closely with community groups such as Neighbourhood Watch schemes to help prevent crime.

Victim support schemes

The victim support scheme is a national organisation that exists, through local branches, to help victims of crime by offering advice, counselling and reassurance.

▲ **Source W:** A Neighbourhood Watch sign illustrating the partnership between the police and the community

▲ **Source X:** One police community support officer and one Metropolitan police officer on duty in the community

> ### THINK
>
> 1 What does Source W show you about modern policing methods?
> 2 Use Source X and your own knowledge to explain the role of PCSOs.
> 3 Describe the attempts to improve police and community relations since the 1980s.

FOCUS TASK REVISITED

As you have worked through this chapter you have completed a time chart which has identified the major changes in combating crime across the period c.1500 to the present day. This will have provided you with a good overview of the key changes, when they occurred, why they occurred and the impact they had. It is important that you use this fact file to build up a picture of the developments on policing across time. Use this time chart to help you answer the following questions:

1 What areas of continuity did you discover in the methods used to combat crime across the period c.1500 to the present day?

2 What do you think were the most significant changes in the methods used to combat crime during this period?

3 Which of these changes would you consider to be the most effective in combating crime? Give reasons to justify your answer.

TOPIC SUMMARY

■ The medieval system of community self-policing continued into the sixteenth century.

■ During the Tudor period the chief responsibility for law enforcement lay with the justice of the peace, aided by the parish constable and town watchman.

■ By the eighteenth century this system of law enforcement was coming under increasing strain, especially in the rapidly expanding industrial towns.

■ Some individuals in London, such as Thomas de Veil, began to experiment with the setting up of private police forces, but the first significant change was the setting up of the Bow Street Runners during the 1750s by Henry Fielding, who was soon joined by his half-brother John.

■ John Fielding expanded the Bow Street Runners, establishing a newspaper to record criminal activity and also a horse patrol to deal with highway robbery.

■ In 1829, the Home Secretary, Robert Peel, set up the Metropolitan Police force to tackle crime in central London.

■ The government passed Acts to persuade other areas to set up their own police forces – Municipal Corporations Act 1835 and Rural Police Act 1839. The County and Borough Police Act of 1856 made it compulsory for a police force to be established in every county.

■ Specialist units such as CID were introduced to help with crime detection.

■ During the twentieth century, key developments in policing have resulted from improvements in transport and communication, especially cars and the radio and developments in specialist units such as fingerprinting, forensics and DNA analysis.

■ In recent decades the emphasis has been upon a return to community-based policing, with the introduction of Neighbourhood Watch schemes and PCSOs.

Practice questions

1 Complete the sentences below with an accurate term.
   a) Tudor JPs were helped in their day-to-day policing duties by the parish ....
   b) Henry Fielding was responsible for the setting up of the Bow Street ....
   c) The first women police officers came into service in 19 ....
   d) In 1901, Sir Edward Henry was responsible for introducing ....
   (*For guidance, see page 252.*)

2 Use Source C [watchman, page 183], Source J [Bow Street Runner, page 186] and Source O [Metropolitan Police, page 188] to identify one similarity and one difference in the methods of combating crime over time. (*For guidance, see pages 254–5.*)

3 Describe the role of a Tudor parish constable in combating crime. In your answer you are advised to refer to the Welsh context and provide examples from Wales. (*For guidance, see page 256.*)

4 Describe the work of Sir Robert Peel in the establishment of a police force in central London. (*For guidance, see page 255.*)

5 Explain why developments in transport and communication were significant in the methods of combating crime during the twentieth century. (*For guidance, see page 257.*)

6 To what extent have the actions of private individuals been the most important factors in combating crime over time? In your answer you should:
   – show how the work of private individuals has been important in combating crime over three historical eras
   – discuss the importance of other factors in the combating of crime over three historical eras
   – include direct reference to the history of Wales.
   (*For guidance, see page 260–1.*)

5 Attitudes to punishment

This chapter focuses on the key question: Why have attitudes to punishment changed over time?
Attitudes to punishment have evolved over time to reflect developments in society, changes in social attitudes, and the role and purpose of government in protecting individuals and their property. From the sixteenth through to the nineteenth century, the commonly accepted view was that punishment needed to be severe in order to act as a deterrent. For this reason it was felt necessary for punishment to be administered in full public view. However, during the nineteenth and twentieth centuries attitudes towards the severity and public nature of such punishments began to change. This has resulted in the ending of both **corporal** and **capital punishment**, with the result that prison is now seen as the most effective means to punish wrongdoers. In this chapter you will investigate how and why attitudes have changed over the centuries.

FOCUS TASK

The key focus of this chapter is to examine how and why attitudes towards punishment have changed or remained the same across the centuries. As you work though the chapter you need to gather evidence to enable you to complete a time chart. In each section make bullet points on the attitude towards a particular punishment at a specific period of time. At the end of the chapter you will be able to use this information to make judgements upon the extent to which attitudes have changed or remained the same.

Attitudes across the centuries towards the following punishments:	Sixteenth and seventeenth centuries	Eighteenth century	Nineteenth century	Twentieth and twenty-first centuries
Punishment to deter				
Punishment to reform				
Punishment in public				
Use of banishment				
Use of prison				
Use of capital punishment				
Treatment of young offenders				

Retribution and deterrence as purposes of punishment over time

Why do we punish those we consider having done wrong by the accepted standards of our society? This is a question which is often asked and one for which there is no one set answer. Society punishes wrongdoers for a variety of reasons (see Figure 5.1).

In Britain today imprisonment is the normal punishment for serious crime and the prison population is currently at its highest ever level. Less serious crimes could be punished through fining the individual, giving them some form of community service, tagging them or giving them a suspended sentence dependent upon their good behaviour. In the past serious crime was punished through the death sentence, usually by execution, and in earlier times through public humiliation in the stocks or pillory, whipping or fining.

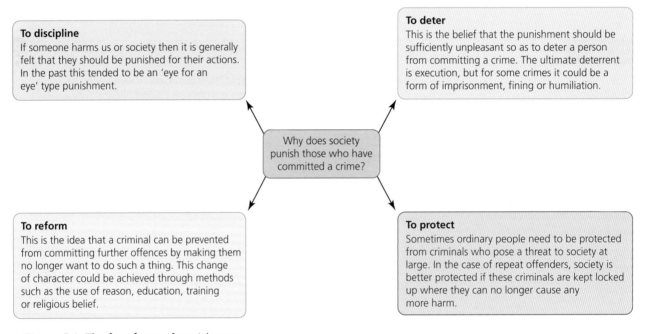

To discipline
If someone harms us or society then it is generally felt that they should be punished for their actions. In the past this tended to be an 'eye for an eye' type punishment.

To deter
This is the belief that the punishment should be sufficiently unpleasant so as to deter a person from committing a crime. The ultimate deterrent is execution, but for some crimes it could be a form of imprisonment, fining or humiliation.

Why does society punish those who have committed a crime?

To reform
This is the idea that a criminal can be prevented from committing further offences by making them no longer want to do such a thing. This change of character could be achieved through methods such as the use of reason, education, training or religious belief.

To protect
Sometimes ordinary people need to be protected from criminals who pose a threat to society at large. In the case of repeat offenders, society is better protected if these criminals are kept locked up where they can no longer cause any more harm.

▲ **Figure 5.1:** The four faces of punishment

> **THINK** ?
>
> Study Figure 5.1. Which of the four faces of punishment do you think is the most dominant attitude today? Give reasons to support your answer.

Factors which have influenced attitudes to punishment

Many factors have influenced attitudes to punishment over time. As society has changed, so the attitudes of people living in society have changed, and this in turn has put pressure on leaders and governments to respond and alter the ways in which punishment has been delivered. Almost all changes in punishment have stemmed from government decisions, and these decisions have been influenced by a number of factors (see Figure 5.2).

Social change
The closing of the monasteries combined with agricultural changes resulted in the growth of poverty during the late Tudor period and with it an increase in crime. The Industrial Revolution caused a sharp rise in population and a growth in the size of towns, thereby increasing the opportunity for crime. In such instances, people felt the need to be protected against the increase in crime.

Ideas and attitudes to punishment
Religious views have influenced the type of punishment imposed, such as burning at the stake for the crime of heresy during the sixteenth century. During the eighteenth and nineteenth centuries some people became influenced by the progressive ideas of the **Enlightenment** which offered more humane attitudes to punishment. An outcome was the belief that prisons should reform as well as punish the criminal and that it was not always appropriate to impose the death penalty.

Attitude of government
It is the laws passed by government which determine which actions are designated as 'crimes' and what measures are to be used to 'punish' those who have committed an offence. Governments can change old laws to reflect changes in social attitudes towards punishment, and also introduce new types of punishment to accommodatechanges in society.

Factors influencing attitudes to punishment

Wealth and poverty
Increased poverty during Tudor times resulted in a rise in vagrancy and laws being passed to punish vagrants. Increased wealth during the seventeenth and eighteenth centuries caused landowners to protect their property by introducing the 'Bloody Code', with over 225 crimes being classed as capital crimes, the punishment for which was execution by hanging.

The role of the media
The more widespread circulation of newspapers during the eighteenth century resulted in the increased reporting of crime, helping to give the impression that crime was on the increase. Newspapers have had a strong influence on people's attitudes to punishment, especially in the mid-twentieth century during the intense debate surrounding the abolition of the death sentence.

Actions of individuals
The actions of key individuals have resulted in major changes in the methods of punishment. Prison reformers like John Howard and Elizabeth Fry campaigned during the late eighteenth and early nineteenth centuries for improved prison conditions, while Sir Samuel Romilly and Sir Robert Peel were largely responsible for dismantling the 'Bloody Code' in the 1820s and 1830s (see Chapter 6).

Fear of crime
Fear of crime waves can lead to calls for tougher punishments. Governments have traditionally responded by making punishments more severe. It was the fear of a sharp increase in crime in the late seventeenth century that resulted in the introduction of the 'Bloody Code'.

▲ Figure 5.2: Factors which have influenced attitudes to punishment

THINK

Study Figure 5.2. What two factors would you consider to be the most important in influencing attitudes to punishment? Justify your choice.

Changing attitudes to punishment over time

Over the centuries various factors have caused attitudes to punishment to change:

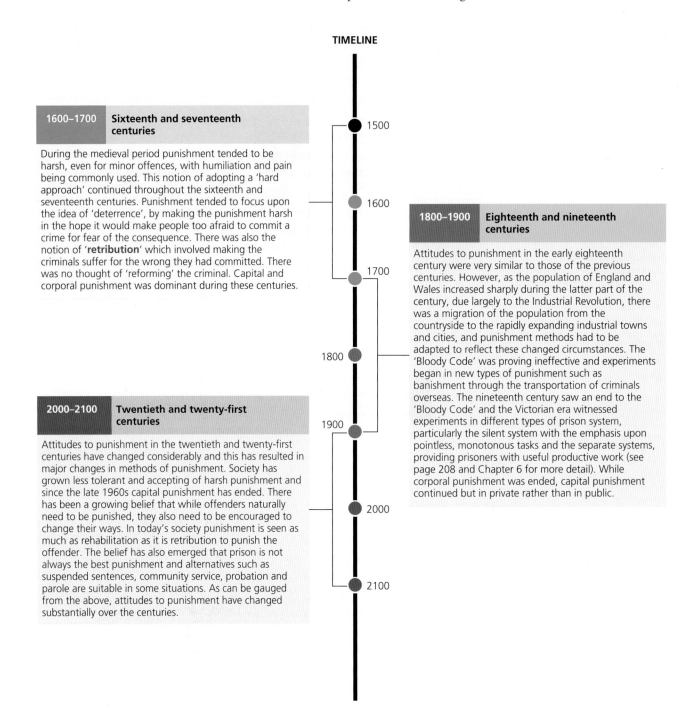

TIMELINE

1600–1700   Sixteenth and seventeenth centuries

During the medieval period punishment tended to be harsh, even for minor offences, with humiliation and pain being commonly used. This notion of adopting a 'hard approach' continued throughout the sixteenth and seventeenth centuries. Punishment tended to focus upon the idea of 'deterrence', by making the punishment harsh in the hope it would make people too afraid to commit a crime for fear of the consequence. There was also the notion of '**retribution**' which involved making the criminals suffer for the wrong they had committed. There was no thought of 'reforming' the criminal. Capital and corporal punishment was dominant during these centuries.

1800–1900   Eighteenth and nineteenth centuries

Attitudes to punishment in the early eighteenth century were very similar to those of the previous centuries. However, as the population of England and Wales increased sharply during the latter part of the century, due largely to the Industrial Revolution, there was a migration of the population from the countryside to the rapidly expanding industrial towns and cities, and punishment methods had to be adapted to reflect these changed circumstances. The 'Bloody Code' was proving ineffective and experiments began in new types of punishment such as banishment through the transportation of criminals overseas. The nineteenth century saw an end to the 'Bloody Code' and the Victorian era witnessed experiments in different types of prison system, particularly the silent system with the emphasis upon pointless, monotonous tasks and the separate systems, providing prisoners with useful productive work (see page 208 and Chapter 6 for more detail). While corporal punishment was ended, capital punishment continued but in private rather than in public.

2000–2100   Twentieth and twenty-first centuries

Attitudes to punishment in the twentieth and twenty-first centuries have changed considerably and this has resulted in major changes in methods of punishment. Society has grown less tolerant and accepting of harsh punishment and since the late 1960s capital punishment has ended. There has been a growing belief that while offenders naturally need to be punished, they also need to be encouraged to change their ways. In today's society punishment is seen as much as rehabilitation as it is retribution to punish the offender. The belief has also emerged that prison is not always the best punishment and alternatives such as suspended sentences, community service, probation and parole are suitable in some situations. As can be gauged from the above, attitudes to punishment have changed substantially over the centuries.

Timeline: 1500, 1600, 1700, 1800, 1900, 2000, 2100

THINK ?

Identify and explain the dominant attitudes towards punishment in each of the following periods:

1   The sixteenth and seventeenth centuries
2   The eighteenth and nineteenth centuries
3   The twentieth and twenty-first centuries.

The purpose of punishment in public over time

In the centuries before the formation of an organised police force and a formal prison system in the nineteenth century, society was self-regulating in terms of maintaining law and order. The most effective method society had of trying to reduce the level of crime was by making sure that the punishment was sufficiently harsh to dissuade people from committing such crimes. This was often best achieved through delivering the punishment in public, to the full view of the community so that they could see that justice had been done.

The use of corporal punishment

Many of the medieval methods of punishment continued to be used during the sixteenth and seventeenth centuries including corporal punishment, where pain was inflicted upon the offender. The word 'corporal' comes from the Latin word for body, *corpus*, so corporal punishment was punishment of the body. The aim was to teach offenders how wrong they were and to discourage others from following their example.

Corporal punishment, which normally involved either whipping or flogging, usually took place on a market day, in an open area such as a market place, so that it was as public as possible. It was used as a punishment for minor offences such as drunkenness, petty theft, begging and vagrancy. The ultimate aim was the public humiliation of the wrong doer. Whipping had become less common by the eighteenth century and was eventually abolished as a punishment for women in 1820. An Act of 1948 finally ended corporal punishment.

Public humiliation – the stocks and pillory

The stocks and the pillory were common forms of punishment during the sixteenth and seventeenth centuries (see Chapter 6 for more detail). Their main purpose was to humiliate offenders of minor crimes in public, to the full view and amusement of their fellow citizens (see Source A). It was widely believed that a day spent in the stocks or pillory was sufficiently humiliating to prevent any further re-offending. The pillory continued to be used until its abolition in 1837 and the stocks until its abolition in 1872.

▶ Source A: Two individuals who committed a minor crime in the early eighteenth century and placed in the stocks as a form of public humiliation

Capital punishment and the criminal code

Capital punishment involved putting the convicted criminal to death by execution in the hope that it would deter those watching from committing similar offences. Between 1688 and 1815 the number of crimes carrying the death penalty increased dramatically, rising from 50 to 225 (see Figure 5.3).

This sharp increase in capital offences became known as the Criminal Code or by its more popular name the 'Bloody Code'. It was a very harsh period of punishment which made excessive use of the death penalty. Among the eventual list of 225 capital crimes were:

- stealing horses or sheep
- destroying turnpike roads
- pickpocketing goods worth one shilling (5p) or more
- shoplifting goods worth five shillings (25p)
- being out at night with a blackened face
- stealing from a rabbit warren
- sending threatening letters
- rioting against high food prices.

Reasons for the development of the 'Bloody Code'

Attitude to punishment

There was a common belief that punishment needed to be harsh to deter others from committing crime. It was thought harsh punishments were effective in controlling crime.

Social change made it harder to enforce law and order

From the late seventeenth century onwards the social structure of Britain was changing. Migration from the countryside to the growing industrial towns resulted in a more mobile society. There was an increase in protest and social unrest. Such changes made it more difficult to enforce the law.

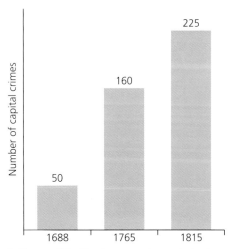

▲ **Figure 5.3:** The increase in capital crimes

Fear over the rise in crime

The late seventeenth century witnessed a sharp rise in crime and crime rates remained high throughout the first half of the eighteenth century.

Increase in new crimes

There was a sharp increase in new crimes such as vagrants wandering the streets threatening the public, highway robbery, smuggling and poaching.

Increased media reporting of crime

Pamphlets and newspapers began to report crime, giving the inflated impression of crime levels, providing lurid details of robberies and murders, forcing the government to add to the increasing number of capital crimes.

Influence of landowners

After 1688 rich landowners had the power through parliament to pass laws, which they did to protect their property and wealth. For example, in 1723 the Black Act made the hunting of deer, hare and rabbits illegal. Poaching was now to be punished by death. It was believed it had been introduced to protect the interests of the landowners.

The attitude among the ruling classes was that capital punishment was there to frighten the masses into obedience and so must be regularly used. Executions became great public events, attracting large crowds especially at Tyburn in London.

However, by the mid-nineteenth century attitudes towards public execution were changing. The large unruly crowds were themselves proving to be a threat to the maintenance of law and order. A Royal Commission on Capital Punishment was established in 1864. It carried out a two-year investigation and in 1866 recommended that executions should no longer take place in public. In 1868 an Act officially put an end to public executions.

The last public hanging in Wales took place in Swansea on 12 April 1866 when Robert Coe was executed for the murder of John Davies. Michael Barrett was the last prisoner to be hanged in public in England outside Newgate Prison on 26 May 1868. This marked a major turning point in methods of punishment and between 1868 and 1965, when capital punishment was abolished; all executions took place out of public view inside prisons.

> **THINK**
>
> 1 Explain why punishments before the nineteenth century were often delivered in public.
>
> 2 The 'Bloody Code' was mainly introduced because there was a sharp increase in crime.' To what extent do you agree with this statement?

The use of banishment in the eighteenth and nineteenth centuries

Throughout the eighteenth century there was a growing feeling, especially among enlightened thinkers, that punishments were far too brutal. There was an argument that punishment should more accurately fit the actual crime committed, and there was a move towards experimenting with alternative methods of punishment such as **banishment** through transportation.

Problems with public executions

In 1783, a London magistrate commented upon the failures of the Bloody Code: 'all the aims of public justice are defeated. All the effects of example, the terrors of death, the shame of punishment, are lost.' Public executions had lost their effectiveness. They drew large unruly crowds who, far from being in horror of the proceedings, mocked the executioner and laughed at the events (see Source B). Furthermore, such gatherings were the perfect opportunities for pickpockets, thereby increasing rather than reducing crime.

> **Source B: Bernard Mandeville, describing the impact of public executions in London in 1725.**
>
> All the way, from Newgate to Tyburn, is one continued fair for rogues and whores of the meaner sort ... instead of giving warning, they are exemplary the wrong way, and encourage where they should deter.

The search for alternative punishments – banishment through transportation

Attitudes towards using such extreme punishment as hanging for minor crimes were changing and an alternative to execution was needed. The answer came in the form of transportation as it was seen as the 'middle' punishment between the extremes of execution on the one hand and the milder whipping or use of the stocks and pillory on the other. Banishing the criminal into the unknown had an advantage in common with hanging in that it reduced crime by completely removing the criminal (see Source C). It was hoped the fear of such banishment would deter people from committing crime, and for those who were transported they would be reformed by being forced to work and learn new skills.

> **Source C: Summing up the sentence passed upon the criminal, one judge summarised the punishment of banishment to Australia as:**
>
> I sentence you, but to what I know not; perhaps to storm and shipwreck, perhaps to infectious disorders, perhaps to famine, perhaps to be massacred by savages, perhaps to be devoured by wild beasts. Away – take your chance; perish or prosper, suffer or enjoy; I rid myself of the sight of you.

The 1717 Transportation Act was a major turning point in the methods of and attitudes towards the punishment of criminals. It was used as a less severe form of punishment than hanging and, in certain instances, it allowed the individual to return once they had completed their sentence. However, there was little consistency between the punishments issued by courts (see Source D).

Source D: Sentences imposed upon criminals at the Gloucester Assizes in August 1826

Criminal	Sentence
Thomas Jones, for breaking open the house of John Nichols, of St James', Bristol and stealing shirts, etc.	Death sentence
William Jones, for breaking open the house of John Cox, of St Philip's, Bristol, and stealing 20 lbs weight of cheese	7 years' transportation
George Gwilliam, for intent to commit rape on Mary Gwilliam, of Stanton, against her will	3 years' imprisonment
William George, Thomas Parker and Elizabeth Parker, for house-breaking, at Old Sodbury, and stealing a bed quilt	7 years' transportation
Robert Hudson, for assaulting Jane Neale, at Stroud, with intent to commit a rape	2 years' imprisonment
John Mico and Robert Shackle, for stealing 2 sacks and 3 casks, from J. Staite, of Bristol	7 years' transportation
Richard Fowler, for stealing hay, at Winterbourne	12 months' imprisonment
George Cootle, for housebreaking at Dursley, and stealing a tea caddy, and other articles	7 years' transportation
Richard Mee, for stealing a bottle of brandy at Cheltenham	7 years' transportation
Elizabeth Jones, for stealing calico, the property of W. Mumford, also for various other felonies, at Tewkesbury	Transportation for life

THINK

1 Using Source B and your own knowledge, explain why there was growing criticism of public execution.

2 Study Source D. Do you think the sentences imposed by judges at the Gloucester Assizes in 1826 were fair in relation to the crimes committed? Give reasons and examples to support your answer.

ACTIVITY

Write a short speech, putting forward the arguments in favour of using transportation as an alternative punishment to execution.

Abolition of the Criminal or 'Bloody Code'

Despite there being 225 crimes punishable by death, the Criminal or 'Bloody Code' was not working. By the early nineteenth century, juries had become increasingly unwilling to convict people for some offences that carried the death penalty because they thought that the punishment was too harsh. Between 1770 and 1830 over 35,000 death sentences were passed in England and Wales but only 7,000 offenders (just 20 per cent) were actually hanged. By the early nineteenth century the rate of execution had fallen to just ten per cent, even though the level of crime was higher at that time. The Criminal Code was undermining the law because juries were finding offenders not guilty to avoid public execution.

In parliament MPs began to question the effectiveness of the Criminal Code and whether it was too extreme (see Source E). One man who campaigned vigorously for a reform of the Criminal Code was the lawyer and later MP Sir Samuel Romilly (1757–1818). He achieved his first success in 1808 when he had the death penalty for pickpocketing abolished. In 1810, Romilly wrote *Observations on the Criminal Law in England* in which he criticised the working of the Criminal Code. He also voiced his criticism in parliament.

The greatest success occurred when the Home Secretary, Sir Robert Peel, also took up the campaign. Like Romilly and other critics, Peel believed that the Code was savage and too extreme (see Figure 5.4). In 1823, he abolished the death penalty for more than 100 capital offences. In 1832 the Criminal Code was further reformed and the Punishment of Death Act reduced the number of capital crimes by a further two-thirds. By 1861, the number of capital crimes had been reduced to just five:

- murder
- treason
- espionage
- arson in royal dockyards
- piracy with violence.

The Criminal Code had finally been abolished.

> **Source E: From a speech in parliament delivered by Sir Willaim Meredith, MP, in 1770**
>
> A man who has picked a pocket of a handkerchief worth 18 pence is punished with the same severity as if he had murdered a whole family. None should be punished with death except in cases of murder.

> **Source F: Observations upon the failings of the Criminal Code made by Cesare Beccaria in his book *Of Crimes and Punishments* (1767)**
>
> Current punishments do not stop crime. Instead of making a terrifying example [by hanging] a few criminals we should punish all criminals and punish them fairly. We need punishments that fit the crimes. Instead of relying on the death penalty, criminals should be imprisoned and do hard labour that is visible to the public.

> **ACTIVITY** ?
>
> Using information from Sources E and F, as well as Figure 5.4, write a report justifying the need to end the 'Bloody Code'.

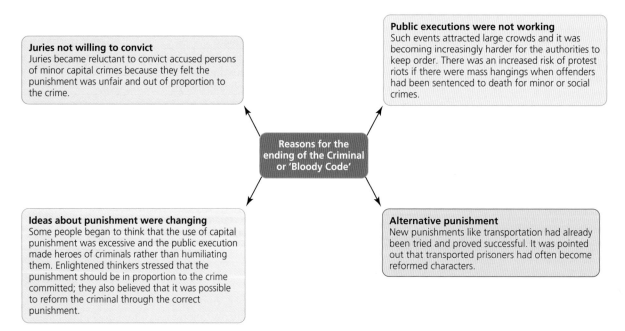

Juries not willing to convict
Juries became reluctant to convict accused persons of minor capital crimes because they felt the punishment was unfair and out of proportion to the crime.

Public executions were not working
Such events attracted large crowds and it was becoming increasingly harder for the authorities to keep order. There was an increased risk of protest riots if there were mass hangings when offenders had been sentenced to death for minor or social crimes.

Reasons for the ending of the Criminal or 'Bloody Code'

Ideas about punishment were changing
Some people began to think that the use of capital punishment was excessive and the public execution made heroes of criminals rather than humiliating them. Enlightened thinkers stressed that the punishment should be in proportion to the crime committed; they also believed that it was possible to reform the criminal through the correct punishment.

Alternative punishment
New punishments like transportation had already been tried and proved successful. It was pointed out that transported prisoners had often become reformed characters.

▲ Figure 5.4: Reasons for the ending of the Criminal or 'Bloody Code'

The use of prisons to punish and reform in the nineteenth century

Britain entered the nineteenth century with a prison system dating back centuries. In 1750 prisons played only a minor part in the system of punishment yet, by the 1860s, over 90 per cent of serious offenders were sent to prison. By this time attitudes towards the use of prison had changed dramatically. The main purpose of punishment had shifted towards the reform of the criminal, rather than a deterrent impact, designed to warn others away from the crime. The aim was to change the prisoner, rather than getting rid of them.

During the course of the nineteenth century three major changes affected the development of the use of prisons as a form of punishment:

1 Imprisonment became the normal method of punishing criminals – transportation ended in 1868, the number of capital crimes was greatly reduced, and there was a change in public attitudes towards punishment.
2 The reform of prisoners became the key aim of the punishment – this resulted in great debates over contrasting systems to be used within prisons (the Separate and Silent Systems).
3 The huge increase in the prison population forced the government to take over the running of the prison system and to supervise the construction of new, purpose built prisons. In the 1770s prisons were run by towns and counties with no rules about their organisation; by the 1870s government inspectors checked every aspect of prison life.

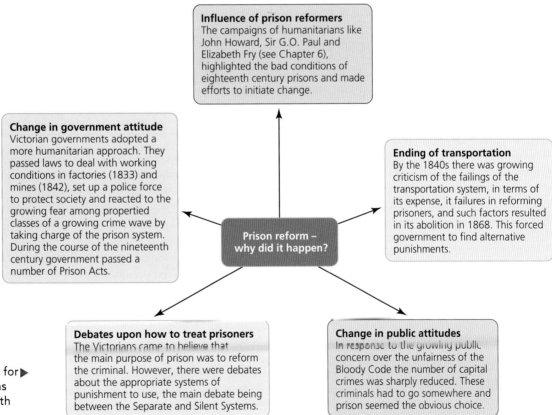

Influence of prison reformers
The campaigns of humanitarians like John Howard, Sir G.O. Paul and Elizabeth Fry (see Chapter 6), highlighted the bad conditions of eighteenth century prisons and made efforts to initiate change.

Change in government attitude
Victorian governments adopted a more humanitarian approach. They passed laws to deal with working conditions in factories (1833) and mines (1842), set up a police force to protect society and reacted to the growing fear among propertied classes of a growing crime wave by taking charge of the prison system. During the course of the nineteenth century government passed a number of Prison Acts.

Ending of transportation
By the 1840s there was growing criticism of the failings of the transportation system, in terms of its expense, it failures in reforming prisoners, and such factors resulted in its abolition in 1868. This forced government to find alternative punishments.

Prison reform – why did it happen?

Debates upon how to treat prisoners
The Victorians came to believe that the main purpose of prison was to reform the criminal. However, there were debates about the appropriate systems of punishment to use, the main debate being between the Separate and Silent Systems.

Change in public attitudes
In response to the growing public concern over the unfairness of the Bloody Code the number of capital crimes was sharply reduced. These criminals had to go somewhere and prison seemed the obvious choice.

Figure 5.5: Reasons for ▶ the reform of prisons during the nineteenth century

The campaigns of prison reformers

By the end of the nineteenth century prisons had been completely reformed from chaotic, squalid, unhealthy environments, to efficient, tightly controlled institutions. The initiation for this change resulted from the actions of a small number of penal reformers who, through visiting prisons and gathering evidence, were able to report on the harsh and squalid conditions they found (see Chapter 6 for further detail), pointing out that prisons were cruel and unfair institutions, which were inefficiently run.

Debate over how to treat prisoners – punish or reform?

The Victorian period witnessed the 'great debate' about how best to treat prisoners and the arguments centred around two differing methods, one intending to punish, the other to reform:

- The **Separate System**: this system operated under the central belief that criminals were bad because they had been exposed to wicked influences and if they could be exposed to good influences they could be changed for the better (see Source G). They needed to be separated from others and given time through Christian teaching to reflect upon the evils of crime. The criminals should be put to work with worthwhile tasks such as making boots, mats, prison clothes, sewing mailbags or coal sacks.
- The **Silent System**: others believed that prisoners' wills could only be broken through exposing them to a tough, hardened regime of strict discipline, harsh punishment, and complete isolation. The emphasis was not upon the reform but punishment. Prisoners had to perform daily monotonous tasks of a pointless nature, such as oakum picking or walking the tread wheel in the belief that this constant punishment would cause them not to re-offend.

> **Source G: Rev. John Clay, a prison chaplain, describing the effects to the Separate System**
>
> A few months in the solitary cell renders the prisoner strangely impressible. The chaplain can then make the brawny navvy [labourer] cry like a child; he can work on his feelings in almost any way he pleases.

Changing attitudes by the late nineteenth century – the Gladstone Committee, 1895

After the Prisons Act of 1865 Prison Commissioner, Edmund du Cane, ordered that prisons were run in accordance with the principles of 'hard labour, hard fare and hard board'. However, by the end of the century, public opinion was turning against this 'hard' approach. Critics argued that prison conditions were too brutal and had not succeeded in reforming criminals or reducing instances of re-offending. Far from reforming criminals, many prisoners had gone insane and there had been an increase in the suicide rate (see Source H).

> **Source H: Comments made upon prison life by the playwright and poet Oscar Wilde, who served two years in Reading Gaol between 1895–97**
>
> Prison life, with its endless restrictions makes one rebellious. The most terrible thing about it is not that it breaks one's heart, but that it turns one's heart to stone. It is only with a front of brass and a lip of scorn that one can get through the day.

Concerns over the effects of harsh treatment of prisoners resulted in the setting up of a government investigation. It was called the Gladstone Committee and in 1895 it reported its findings (see Source I), the main points of which were:

- Long periods of isolation were not reforming prisoners but were having a negative impact upon their mental health.
- Juvenile prisoners, aged between 16–20 years, should not be subjected to the harsh treatment given to the older prisoners.
- To provide them with some worthwhile skills, younger prisoners should be given education and training while in prison.

> **Source I: One of the recommendations from the Gladstone Report, 1895**
>
> Prison discipline should be designed to awaken prisoners' moral instincts, to train them in orderly and industrious habits, and, whenever possible, to turn them out of prison better men and women, physically and morally, than when they went in.

The government responded to these recommendations by passing the Prisons Act of 1898, and by making a number of important changes to prison life:

- Reduction in the time prisoners were kept isolated.
- Prisoners were allowed more free time to communicate with each other.
- Unproductive hard labour was abolished in 1898.
- The first prison designed for young offenders was opened at Borstal in Kent in 1902.

> **THINK**
>
> 1 Using Sources G and I describe how attitudes towards the treatment of prisoners changed during the nineteenth century.
>
> 2 What do Sources G and H tell you about the impact of the Victorian prison system upon prisoners?
>
> 3 How important was the Gladstone Committee of 1895 in changing attitudes towards the treatment of prisoners?
>
> 4 'The nineteenth century marked a turning point in attitudes towards the role and function of prison as a punishment.' How far do you agree with this statement?

Changes in attitudes to punishment in the twentieth century

Source J: Rev. Sydney Turner, who was in charge of Redhill Reformatory in the late nineteenth century, believed in severely punishing boys by locking them up alone

... for a few days in unheated cells on a bread and water diet and whipping them with as much solemnity as possible.

Attitudes to punishment in the twentieth and twenty-first centuries have changed considerably and this has led to major changes in the types of sentence imposed upon convicted criminals, and in the treatment of prisoners in prison. Corporal and capital punishment disappeared during the twentieth century, and were replaced with the realisation that offenders should not only be punished for their acts, but that they should also be encouraged to change their ways. This has meant that punishment is now seen as a form of rehabilitation as well as retribution.

Changing attitudes towards prison

The Gladstone Report of 1895 showed a swing in public opinion away from harsh punishments towards reform and it resulted in a move towards an end to the Silent System. During the early twentieth century, under the direction of two reforming Prison Commissioners, Sir Evelyn Ruggles-Brise (1895–1921) and Sir Alexander Paterson (1921–1947), major changes took place in the treatment of prisoners.

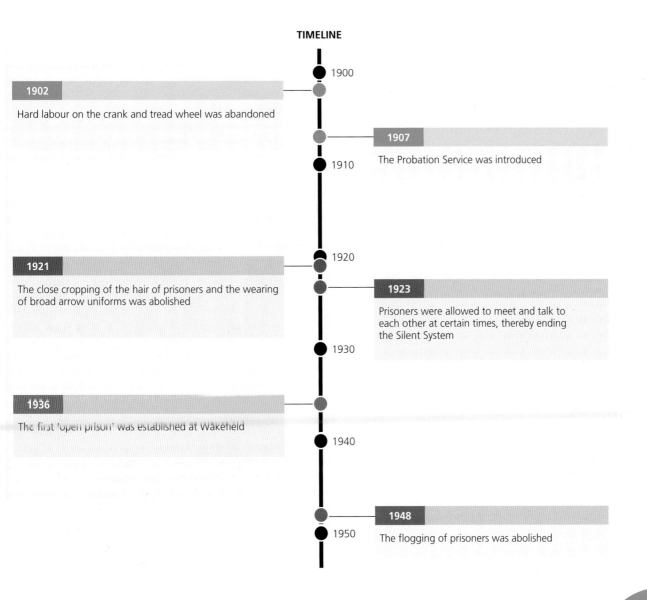

TIMELINE

1900

1902
Hard labour on the crank and tread wheel was abandoned

1907
The Probation Service was introduced

1910

1921
The close cropping of the hair of prisoners and the wearing of broad arrow uniforms was abolished

1920

1923
Prisoners were allowed to meet and talk to each other at certain times, thereby ending the Silent System

1930

1936
The first 'open prison' was established at Wakefield

1940

1948
The flogging of prisoners was abolished

1950

The old belief that criminals inherited their criminal tendencies was declining, to be overshadowed by the belief that prisoners could be reformed by better treatment and education in prison.

Dealing with young offenders

During the nineteenth century, young offenders, or juveniles as they were then referred to, were treated no differently to adults and they could be sentenced to be hanged, transported, imprisoned or fined. In 1880 there were 6,500 children under the age of 16 in adult prisons, 900 of whom were aged under 12. The Victorians operated a harsh approach, believing that this would prevent such offenders from re-offending (see Source J). During the twentieth century, attitudes were changing, swinging more towards reform. The belief became more widespread that young people were suitable for reform as their characters were not yet fixed. With positive influences and a good environment they could be turned away from a life of crime. The starting point for change was the separation of young offenders from adult criminals. In 1902, in Kent the first 'borstal' was opened for offenders under the age of 21 as a juvenile alternative to prison. The purpose was to reform the young person through a combination of training and specialist care (see Source K). The establishments were run like boarding schools.

In 1908, separate juvenile courts were set up, operating a much less formal approach than normal courts. Here an attempt was made to provide emphasis upon the reform of the young offender. In 1932, Approved Schools were set up for offenders under 15 in the hope that education would better prepare them for life after release.

During the last quarter of the twentieth century the tide began to turn against the borstal approach. Statistics showed that over 60 per cent of young people released from borstal or Approved Schools offended again. In 1982, borstals were closed and replaced by Youth Detention Centres (see Chapter 6 for further detail). By the 1980s public opinion was moving towards the use of a tougher system of punishment, the so-called 'short, sharp, shock' approach. This involved lots of military drills and discipline in the belief that it would scare inmates off future re-offending. This tougher approach proved less successful than borstals, with a re-offending rate of 75 per cent. As the twenty-first century has dawned new types of youth punishments have been introduced:

- ASBOs (antisocial behaviour orders) were first used in 1999
- Tagging and curfew orders were introduced in 2003.

Attention has also turned towards punishing the parents, fining them if they cannot keep their children under control and, as an ultimate punishment, removing the child from the parental home if fining has no impact. What such experiments demonstrate is that as society's attitudes change so to do punishments.

▲ Source K: A blacksmith's workshop at a borstal, 1945. Such facilities aimed to teach boys a trade to better prepare them for life after borstal

> ### THINK ?
>
> 1 Describe how attitudes towards the treatment of prisoners changed during the first half of the twentieth century.
> 2 What do Sources J and K tell you about attitudes towards the treatment of young offenders during the first half of the twentieth century?
> 3 To what extent did the methods of punishing young offenders during the twentieth century prove to be successful?

Abolition of the death sentence

The ending of public executions in 1868 was an indication that public attitudes towards the use of the death sentence were changing. The use of the death penalty had declined during the nineteenth century. Opposition to capital punishment gradually grew during the early twentieth century with several failed attempts being made by MPs to abolish it:

■ 1930 – A government Select Committee recommended ending the death penalty for five years, but the Home Secretary did not accept the recommendation
■ 1948 and 1956 – MPs voted to abolish capital punishment but on each occasion the House of Lords overturned their decision

A breakthrough came in 1957 when capital punishment was restricted to five types of murder:

■ murder of a police officer or prison officer
■ murder by shooting or explosion
■ murder while resisting arrest
■ murder while carrying out a theft
■ murder of more than one person.

Arguments for and against the use of capital punishment

By the 1950s the arguments both for and against the use of capital punishment were being actively debated. A number of miscarriages of justice helped to further the debate and by the 1960s the topic was regularly debated both on television and in the newspapers. Opinion was still divided between those who saw execution as barbaric, uncivilised and unchristian practice and those who thought it was a necessary deterrent, a means to protect society from violent crime (see Table 5.1 below).

Arguments against abolition	Against in favour of abolition
• A dead murderer cannot kill again. • Hanging is the ultimate deterrent. • Keeping a murderer in prison is expensive. • A hanged murderer gets what he/she deserves. • Hanging satisfies the victim's family and the public generally. • Hanging protects police and prison staff. • Murderers who have completed their sentence might kill again once released. • Criminals are more likely to carry guns if there was no danger of the death sentence.	• The wrong person may be hanged. • Hanging is not really a deterrent, as most murders happen on the spur of the moment. • Hanging is barbaric; no one has the right to take a life. • Even the worst person may be reformed. • Other countries have abolished capital punishment and the crime rate has not increased there. • Hanging can make martyrs of criminals such as terrorists. • Execution is against the teachings of different religions and the Christian idea of forgiveness. • Some people are mentally ill or do not understand the seriousness of their actions.

▲ Table 5.1

> **Source L: Reginald Paget, MP, speaking in parliament in 1947**
>
> Let the dictators have their gallows and their axes, their firing squads and their lethal chambers. We, the citizens of a free democracy, do not have to shelter under the shadow of the gallows tree.

> **Source M: Comments made by Albert Pierrepoint, Britain's last official executioner. He hanged over 430 criminals**
>
> I have come to the conclusion that executions solve nothing ... it did not deter them then and it had not deterred them when they committed what they were convicted for. All the men and women I have faced at that final moment convince me that in what I have done I have not prevented a single murder.

THINK ?

Do Sources L and M support or counter the argument for abolishing the death penalty? Give reasons to justify your answer.

The impact of controversial cases and miscarriages of justice

Three cases in the 1950s caused a great deal of controversy and highlighted the debate about capital punishment.

The case of Timothy Evans

Timothy Evans was born in Merthyr Tydfil in 1924 and was hanged for murdering his baby daughter in 1950. In November 1949 Evans confessed to the police that he had accidentally killed his wife, Beryl and had gone to Wales to stay after arranging for his daughter to be looked after. When police found the bodies of his wife and daughter, he confessed to killing both. However, he changed his statement several times before his trial.

During the investigation the police lacked forensic expertise and a lot of evidence had been completely missed, such as human bones in the back garden of 10 Rillington Place, London, the house where Evans and his wife lived. In court, Evans claimed that the police had threatened him with violence and forced him to make false statements. Based on his confessions, however, he was found guilty and hanged at Pentonville Prison on 9 March 1950.

In 1953, the remains of six other women, including the wife of a downstairs neighbour, John Christie were found hidden in and around the house were Evans and his family had lived in Rillington Place. It soon became evident that Christie was a serial killer and he was convicted for the murder of his wife and hanged. He also confessed to killing Beryl Evans, but an inquiry at the time decided that his statement was unreliable.

▲ **Source N:** Timothy Evans on his way to trial

Timothy Evans was given a posthumous pardon in 1966.

The case of Derek Bentley

Derek Bentley (1933–53) was hanged at Wandsworth Jail in London. He had been found guilty of being an accomplice in the murder of a police officer during a burglary. His 16-year-old friend, Christopher Craig, committed the actual murder, but Bentley was reported to have shouted 'Let him have it' to Craig before he shot the policeman. As Craig was classified as a juvenile he could not be sentenced to death. He was ordered to be detained 'at Her Majesty's Pleasure', which meant indefinite imprisonment.

The hanging of Bentley on 28 January 1953, at the age of 19, caused great controversy, especially as he had learning difficulties and a mental age of 11. The trial was widely reported and provoked a public outcry, with many newspapers suggesting that the use of the death penalty was outdated. Following his sentence over 200 MPs signed a memorandum asking the Home Secretary to cancel the execution. Many argued that it was a miscarriage of justice and it resulted in a 45-year campaign to win a posthumous pardon for him. In 1993 a partial pardon was granted, followed by a full pardon in 1998. This meant that Bentley was no longer considered to be guilty.

▲ **Source O:** Members of the public being asked to sign a petition calling upon the government to reconsider the sentence given to Derek Bentley

The case of Ruth Ellis

Ruth Ellis was born in Rhyl, North Wales, and was the last woman to be hanged in the United Kingdom. She was convicted of the murder of her lover, David Blakely, who she shot in cold blood after a stormy affair during which she had been violently assaulted by him on several occasions. He had proved to be disloyal during their relationship by going out with other women. Despite appeals that this was 'a crime of passion' this was not accepted as provocation and Ellis was hanged at Holloway Prison, London, on 13 July 1955.

▲ **Source P:** Crowds protesting against the execution of Ruth Ellis

THINK

1 Explain how each of the following cases contributed towards the debate which eventually resulted in the ending of capital punishment:
   a) Timothy Evans
   b) Derek Bentley
   c) Ruth Ellis.

2 Do you think that any one of these three cases played a greater role in influencing public opinion than the other two? If so, which one and why?

ACTIVITY

Working in groups of four or six, divide into two groups. One group should prepare an argument to keep using capital punishment and the other group should prepare an argument to abolish capital punishment. Once you have completed your case, ask your teacher for time for you to debate both sides to the argument in front of the rest of the class.

The ending of capital punishment

On 13 August 1964 at 8.00 a.m., two men in different prisons were both executed – Peter Allen in Walton Prison, Liverpool, and Gwynne Evans in Strangeways Prison, Manchester. They had been convicted of the murder of John Alan West and they became the last two people to be executed in the United Kingdom. In 1965, the Murder (Abolition of the Death Penalty) Act was introduced for a trial period of five years. In 1969 the Abolition of the Death Penalty Act was made permanent, abolishing capital punishment for murder but it remained on the statute book for the crimes of treason and piracy until 1999. A hundred years after the abolition of public executions, capital punishment in England and Wales had finally come to an end.

The last person to be hanged in Wales was Vivian Teed. He was hanged at Swansea Jail on 6 May 1958 for the murder of William Williams, the sub-postmaster of Fforestfach Post Office, Swansea.

Attempts to rehabilitate and make restitution

During the late twentieth and early twenty-first century attitudes towards punishment have tended to steer towards the lines of rehabilitation of offenders and the restitution of their crimes. Rehabilitation is the idea that the offender should be educated and helped to be put back upon the correct path. That might mean teaching them new skills to prepare them for a return to society, putting them through a programme to wean them off drug or alcohol addiction, or providing them with suitable education and counselling.

Restitution takes this a stage further through the process of restorative actions. These might mean facing the person who has been wronged, repairing the criminal damage to physical property, or carrying out some form of community service to pay back society for their wrongdoing.

Over the previous 60 years various schemes have been introduced to accommodate the process of rehabilitation and restitution:

- **Parole** was introduced in 1967 as a way to rehabilitate prisoners, releasing them early from prison due to good behaviour providing they demonstrated that they no longer posed a threat to society.
- **Community orders** were introduced in 2003 as an alternative to prison. Such sentences require the offender to attend drug or alcohol treatment programmes, work on community projects, work for charities or repair damage to property and remove graffiti (see Source Q). The aim of such programmes is to make offenders understand the effect of their crimes.
- **Probation Centres** were set up in the 1980s as alternatives to prison. Within such centres group meetings take place, allowing offenders to discuss issues which result in crime, explore ways to use leisure time in a positive and constructive way, and allow probation officers the opportunity to monitor and control the behaviour of offenders. (For more on parole, community service and probation, see page 232.)

Social changes and changing attitudes to punishment have therefore resulted in alternatives to imprisonment, and such factors serve as a clear indication that punishment, and attitudes to punishment is an evolving process and will continue to change as society changes.

▲ **Source Q:** Convicted offenders working on a Community Service project during the early 2000s. Such schemes are used as alternatives to a prison sentence

ACTIVITIES

1 What does Source Q tell you about attitudes to punishment in the twenty-first century?

2 What have been the major changes in the attitudes to punishment over the past 60 years? Can you suggest why such changes have occurred?

FOCUS TASK REVISITED

As you have worked through this chapter you have completed a time chart which has outlined how attitudes towards punishment have changed or remained the same across the centuries. This will have provided you with an overview of the dominant attitudes in each century. Use your time chart to identify:

1 Which centuries witnessed the most dramatic changes in attitudes towards punishment?

2 The reasons why these changes in attitudes occurred when they did.

3 What you consider to be the most significant change in attitude towards punishment across the period c.1500 to the present day, supporting your answer with evidence.

TOPIC SUMMARY

- There are four main reasons why society punishes those who have committed a crime – to discipline, to deter, to reform and to protect.

- Attitudes to punishment have changed over the centuries to reflect changes in society, changes in social attitudes, and the role of government.

- Between c.1500 and the mid-nineteenth century both corporal and capital punishment was administered in public, including whipping, flogging, use of the stocks and pillory, and hanging.

- Fear over an increase in crime led to the development of the Criminal or 'Bloody Code'– between 1688 and 1815 the number of capital crimes rose from 50 to 225.

- Attitudes during the time of the 'Bloody Code' favoured severe punishment as the best way to control and deter criminal activity.

- Concern over the brutality of the 'Bloody Code' resulted in the introduction of alternative punishments during the eighteenth century, such as banishment through transportation.

- By the early eighteenth century, social attitudes were changing and this resulted in the abandonment of the

'Bloody Code' and the growth in the use of prison as a punishment.

- During the nineteenth century prison was the dominant form of punishment, although different methods of treating prisoners were used – the Separate and Silent Systems being the main ones.

- The Gladstone Report of 1895 was a major turning point as it reflected changed attitudes towards a less strict and severe form of prison system.

- New types of punishments were introduced for young offenders during the early twentieth century such as borstals and Approved Schools.

- During the 1950s and 1960s there were intense debates about whether or not to abolish capital punishment.

- Three controversial cases intensified the debate – the cases of Timothy Evans, Derek Bentley and Ruth Ellis.

- Capital punishment officially came to an end in 1969.

- The last 60 years have seen social attitudes shift towards alternatives to prison sentences through a focus upon rehabilitation and restitution.

Practice questions

1 Complete the sentences below with an accurate term:
   a) Between 1688 and 1815 over 225 crimes carried the death penalty and formed part of the .... Code.
   b) The system of punishment which involved banishment overseas was known as ....
   c) A type of prison for young offenders which first opened in 1902 was called ....
   d) Capital punishment finally came to an end in 19... (For guidance, see page 252.)

2 Look at Source A [stocks, page 203], Source L [Borstal, page 210] and Source R [prison, page 226], to identify one similarity and one difference in attitudes to punishment over time. (For guidance, see pages 253–4.)

3 Describe the work of the Gladstone Committee of 1895. (For guidance, see page 255.)

4 Describe how the punishment of young offenders changed during the early twentieth century. In your

answer you are advised to refer to the Welsh context and provide examples from Wales. (For guidance, see page 256.)

5 Explain why attitudes towards capital punishment changed in the mid-twentieth century. (For guidance, see page 257.)

6 Explain why the Criminal or 'Bloody Code' developed during the seventeenth and eighteenth centuries. (For guidance, see page 257.)

7 To what extent have changes in social attitudes been the main reason for changes in punishment between c.1500 and the present day? In your answer you should:
   - show how changes in social attitudes have been the cause of changes in punishment across three historical eras
   - discuss the importance of other causes of changed attitudes towards punishments over three historical eras
   - include direct references to the history of Wales. (For guidance, see pages 260–1.)

6 Methods of punishment

This chapter focuses on the key question: How have methods of punishment changed over time?

Society has always felt the need to protect itself by punishing wrongdoers. As shown in Chapter 5, the punishment inflicted very much depended upon the social attitudes of the day and until the last century, it focused upon the severity of punishment, believing that only a harsh system would serve as a deterrent to crime. During the sixteenth and seventeenth centuries hanging was used as the ultimate punishment, but for lesser crimes some form of public humiliation such as the stocks and pillory or whipping was the norm. Change began in the eighteenth century with the introduction of transportation and continued into the nineteenth century with experimentation in differing prison systems. During the twentieth century society has become less tolerant of physical forms of punishment, such as corporal and capital punishment, both of which were eventually banned. Alternatives replaced them such as life sentences, suspended sentences and community service orders. In this chapter you will investigate continuity and change in the methods of punishment across the centuries, thereby enabling you to make a judgement as to how and why methods of punishment have changed or remained the same over time.

FOCUS TASK

When working through this chapter you need to focus on how methods of punishment have changed over time, but also make a judgement as to which types of punishment have continued and remained in use virtually unchanged. To help you build up a picture of this continuity and change you need to complete each section of this chart. In each section make lists of the types of punishment in use at a particular period of time. At the end of this chapter you should then be able to make an overall judgement about which methods of punishment have changed/remained the same over time.

	Main types of punishment in use during this period	Punishments which have stayed the same since the previous time period	New types of punishment introduced during this period	Overall conclusion: change or continuity during this period?
Sixteenth and seventeenth centuries				
Eighteenth century				
Nineteenth century				
Twentieth and twenty-first century				

The treatment of vagabonds during Tudor times

Unemployment was a major problem in England and Wales during the second half of the sixteenth century and this, along with the religious changes of the time, led to high levels of crime. Punishment tended to be harsh, even for minor offences, with public humiliation and physical pain often being used. One of the most widespread crimes during this century was vagrancy.

Whipping was a common form of punishment and in 1530–31 an Act was passed to deal with the huge increase in robberies and thefts, much of which was associated with the growing problem of begging and vagrancy (see Source A). The latter became an increasing problem during the Tudor period. People who were unemployed but fit to work were considered criminals if they were caught being idle or begging. Unemployment was high and there was no support for people who were out of work in England and Wales from the 1530s. The Dissolution of the Monasteries between 1536 and 1539 not only made most monks unemployed and homeless; it also deprived poor people of the charity they would have received by way of poor relief from the monastery.

During the reign of Elizabeth I (1558–1603), unemployment became even more of a problem. Changes in farming practices caused many Elizabethans to move to the towns in search of work. When they failed to find any they often turned to crime. London in particular suffered from bands of wandering beggars. Not all of the poor were helpless and some were known as 'sturdy beggars', which meant that they were fit enough to work but too lazy to do so. An Act of Parliament was passed in 1572 to punish these sturdy beggars or vagabonds (see Source B).

Quarter Session courts would commonly order anyone found guilty to be flogged (see Source C). However, punishment could be even more severe and often involve mutilation such as burning through the 'gristle' of the right ear with a hot iron. The aim of these severe punishments was to deter people from begging or turning to crime.

Whipping, or flogging, continued to be used as a form of punishment into the following centuries and was often used against those taking part in rebellions. By the eighteenth century it had become less common. It was eventually abolished as a punishment for women in 1820 but continued for men until the 1830s. However, it was still used as a punishment for offences in prison into the twentieth century.

▲ Source B: A woodcut from Holinshed's *Chronicle* of 1577 which shows a vagabond being whipped through the streets. On the left is another vagabond being hanged, the final penalty for begging

Source C: An extract from the Quarter Session records for 1574 held at Middlesex County Records Office

On 29 March, in the sixteenth year of the reign of Queen Elizabeth (1574), at Harrow-on-the-Hill in the County of Middlesex, on the said day, John Allen, Elizabeth Turner, Humphrey Foxe, Henry Bower and Agnes Wort, being over 14 years old, and having no lawful means of livelihood, were vagrants and had been vagrants in other parts of the country. Sentenced to be flogged severely and burned on the right ear.

THINK

1 Copy out and complete the following table which relates to the types of punishment common during Tudor times.

	Date of the source	What type of punishment was given?	What were the reasons for this punishment?
Source A			
Source B			
Source C			

2 Use the information from the table you have completed to answer the following:
   a) Did the punishment for rogues and vagabonds change during Tudor times?
   b) Do you think such punishments had much impact on reducing the level of crime associated with rogues and vagabonds? Give reasons to support your view.

Source A: A section from the Vagabonds Act of 1572

Where all the parts of the realm of England and Wales be presently exceedingly pestered with rogues, vagabonds and sturdy beggars, by means whereof daily happeneth horrible murders, thefts and other outrages, be it enacted that all persons above the age of fourteen years, being rogues, vagabonds or sturdy beggars ... shall be grievously whipped and burnt through the gristle of the right ear with a hot iron.

The use of public punishment up to the nineteenth century

Physical and public punishments continued to be used from Tudor times through the centuries up to the nineteenth century, with a few continuing into the twentieth century.

The stocks and pillory

The main purpose of the **stocks** and **pillory** was to humiliate offenders in public so that they would serve as an example to others.

The stocks

The stocks consisted of a wooden framework in which petty criminals were confined by the ankles and were put on public show. An Act of 1351 had required stocks to be set up in villages to hold and punish runaway servants and labourers and they were used regularly to punish villagers for committing minor crimes. An Act of 1406 further stated that every town should have a set of stocks to punish drunkards, profaners (those who spoke against sacred things like the Christian religion), gamblers and vagrants. People who failed to pay their fines could be put in the stocks for between three and six hours.

The main emphasis of the punishment was the element of public disgrace and humiliation, when the villagers could shout abuse and throw objects at the person being punished (see Source D). Stocks continued to be used until they were finally abolished in 1872. Stocks were a common sight in all large Welsh towns and some, like those on Denbigh town square, are still on display today. The last recorded use of the stocks in Wales was at Newcastle Emlyn in the year they were abolished, 1872.

▲ **Source D:** Found guilty of a minor crime, this person is receiving his punishment in the stocks during Tudor times

The pillory

The pillory, which was a wooden framework in which the criminals were held by the neck and wrist, was also based on the idea of punishing offenders through public humiliation and had been used even before the Normans came to Britain in 1066. Dishonest traders who, for example, sold underweight goods, people who swore persistently and even those who cheated at cards were punished in this way.

Some criminals sentenced to the pillory could be savagely treated, as crowds pelted them with stones and rotten fruit. Criminals who had been convicted of sexual crimes, especially involving children, were likely to be attacked and some were actually killed in the pillory (see Source E).

Like the stocks, the pillory continued to be used as a form of punishment throughout the sixteenth, seventeenth and eighteenth centuries, until it was finally abolished in 1837.

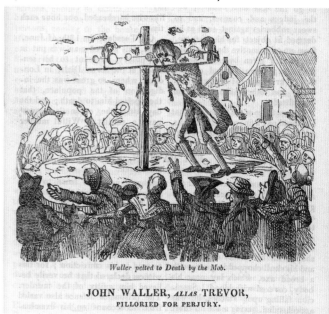

Waller pelted to Death by the Mob.

JOHN WALLER, *ALIAS* **TREVOR,**
PILLORIED FOR PERJURY.

▲ **Source E:** John Waller was pilloried for perjury and pelted to death by a hostile mob in 1732

By the early nineteenth century the stocks and pillory were used less and less as they were being replaced by alternative methods of punishment.

> **THINK**
>
> Use Sources D and E, as well as your own knowledge, to explain why the stocks and pillory were common forms of punishment up to the nineteenth century.

The use of ceffyl pren in Wales

Ceffyl pren (or wooden horse) was a type of community self-policing through a means of public humiliation. A person suspected of a crime such as domestic violence or assault would be carried on a pole or ladder for the purpose of public ridicule. It usually took place during the hours of darkness and involved men dressing in women's clothes; a mock trial would take place followed by a procession around the town, accompanied by the beating of drums. The practice continued to be used until the early nineteenth century and it proved to be an effective means of exercising social control before the establishment of a police force.

Public execution

Execution had been used as a form of punishment in Wales and England for many centuries. In the sixteenth, seventeenth and eighteenth centuries the death penalty continued to be used for major crimes such as murder, where it was felt that the punishment should fit the crime. The death penalty was also used for treason, counterfeiting and arson. Hundreds of people were hanged every year in England and Wales for committing these offences.

During the Tudor and Stuart periods, thieves who stole goods valued at over one shilling (5p) would also be executed. In fact, the number of minor crimes punishable by execution increased throughout this time so that, by the end of the seventeenth century, 50 different crimes carried the death penalty. By the end of the eighteenth century the figure stood at over 200 capital crimes, ranging from murder, horse-stealing, making false coins, stealing from a shop and stealing anything from a person's pocket.

Case study: the work of Rowland Lee restoring law and order in Wales

Two Acts of Parliament, in 1536 and 1542–43, had been passed in order to unite Wales with England. The Council of Wales and the Marches, with its headquarters in Ludlow, was in charge of maintaining law and order in Wales and Bishop Rowland Lee was Lord President of this Council from 1534 to 1543. Lee considered the Welsh to be 'lawless' and governed Wales and its borders very strictly. His policy was based on fear and he used the death penalty in order to enforce law and order in preparation for union with England. It is believed that he ordered the hanging of over 5,000 criminals in just nine years, but in doing so, he did help to restore law and order along the Welsh borders. Public execution sites existed in those Welsh towns associated with Assize Courts such as Beaumaris, Carnarvon, Flint, Carmarthen, Cardigan, Pembroke, Brecon and Monmouth.

Tyburn

Executions were carried out in public mainly to deter onlookers from committing similar crimes. During the eighteenth century, 'hanging days' attracted vast crowds as shopkeepers and tradesmen closed their businesses; many of their employees took the day off to go and watch the public executions. In London the place of execution was Tyburn, where Marble Arch is situated today. The gallows was nicknamed the 'Tyburn Tree' and it consisted of a large framework capable of executing a number of criminals at the same time. Of the 1,232 people hanged at Tyburn between 1703 and 1792, only 92 were women. It has been estimated that 90 per cent of all those executed were young men aged under 21. Over 200,000 people watched the execution of Jack Sheppard in 1724, the notorious thief famous for his multiple escapes from prison. Such large crowds showed the popularity of public punishment at this time (see Source F).

▲ Source F: A satirical print by William Hogarth entitled *The Idle Prentice Executed at Tyburn* (1747)

> ### THINK
>
> 1 How useful is Source F to a historian studying public executions in the eighteenth century?
>
> 2 'Executions were carried out in public to deter others from committing crime.' What arguments can you put forward to (a) support, and (b) challenge this statement?

The use of transportation from the 1770s to the 1860s

Transportation meant punishing criminals by sending them overseas. An Act of 1678 allowed for the sending of criminals to the British colonies of Virginia and Maryland in North America, as well as the West Indies. It proved to be a simple and quick solution to the problem of prison overcrowding and of disposing of the criminal element of society.

The reasons for transportation

- It was an alternative to hanging, which was felt to be too extreme for some crimes.
- It would reduce crime in Britain by completely removing the criminals.
- Imprisonment was too costly.
- It was believed that hard work and learning new skills would reform the criminals.
- A belief that criminals would benefit from the prospect of starting afresh with a new life after they had served their punishment.
- It would help Britain to colonise her Empire abroad.

Transportation to North America

In 1717, the Transportation Act was passed. This was a major turning point in the methods of punishment. It allowed convicts to choose transportation to America instead of branding, whipping or sometimes hanging. The sentence was for seven years, fourteen years or for life. Between 1718 and 1776 more than 30,000 British prisoners were transported to America.

A profitable trade in transporting convicts developed. Firms such as Messrs. Stephenson and Randolph, felon dealers, Bristol were created. Such firms took the prisoners, shipped them to the American colonies and recovered their expenses by selling them. In 1740, a good healthy convict could sell for up to £80 in the West Indies.

However, transportation came to a sudden end in 1776 when the American War of Independence broke out. This caused a crisis in the British prison system, as the prisons could not cope with the resulting overcrowding.

Prison hulks

After the loss of the American colonies the government was faced with the problem of what to do with the large number of criminals. Until a new location could be found, it was decided to take old warships and merchant ships and convert them into floating prisons. These disused ships were known as 'hulks' and their primary function was to serve as emergency prison accommodation and to hold prisoners awaiting transportation (see Source G).

Keeping a crowd of prisoners healthy in an old rotting ship was challenging. When hulks were first used, conditions were very bad. The 'captains', as jailers were called, made no effort to keep the ships clean and healthy. As a result, between 1776 and 1778, more than a quarter of the prisoners died. There was also a lack of supervision on board and this led to considerable disorder, fighting and even rioting (see Source H).

The government was concerned and ordered a public enquiry. As a result, conditions were much improved by the early nineteenth century. On board the hulk, each day started at 5.30 a.m. with breakfast at 6 a.m. Convicts left the hulk for work at 7 a.m. Some worked at Woolwich Arsenal in the Thames Estuary. Here they did heavy, unskilled work – clearing rubbish, carrying coal, pulling carts, scraping shot and building fortifications.

▲ **Source G:** The prison hulk *York* which was moored off Gosport near Portsmouth in Hampshire. It was converted into a prison hulk in 1819 and eventually broken up in 1854

Source H: The report of a prison chaplain after visiting a hulk in the late 1770s

On one prison hulk in the Medway Estuary in Kent, one prisoner was killed and 24 were desperately wounded. The hulk was a shambles. A mere handful of warders were powerless to deal with the armed mob below decks. All that could be done was to fasten down the hatches and when the work of butchery and carnage was over, descend below to fetch up the dead and wounded.

THINK

1 Which, in your opinion, were the two most important reasons why Britain chose to transport its criminals overseas? Give reasons to support your answer.

2 Study the section on hulks and then complete the following table. For each column think of three reasons.

Advantages of using hulks to house criminals	Disadvantages of using hulks to house criminals
1.	1.
2.	2.
3.	3.

Transportation to Australia

The hulks were not a satisfactory or effective way of dealing with such large numbers of prisoners and, following the discovery of Australia by Captain Cook in 1770, it was decided that convicts would be transported to populate this new part of the British Empire, located the other side of the world. The first convicts to be transported to Australia left Portsmouth harbour in Britain in May 1787, when Captain Arthur Phillip set sail with 11 ships packed with 736 convicts, of whom nearly 200 were women. More than 40 died on the voyage. On 26 January 1788, after a nine-month voyage, the ships reached Botany Bay (near modern-day Sydney) in New South Wales, establishing Britain's first penal colony in Australia. Between 1788 and 1868, 160,663 convicts (including 24,960 women) were transported there. During that period, 2,200 of the convicts had been sentenced in Wales. By the 1820s, an average of five ships per year were sent, which amounted to over 2,000 convicts per year.

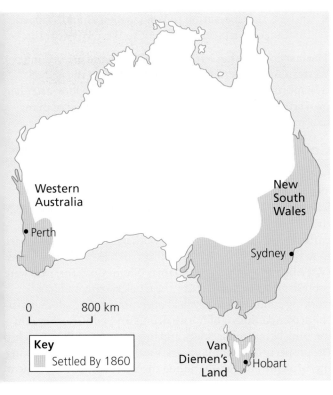

▲ **Figure 6.1:** The main areas of convict settlement in Australia by 1868

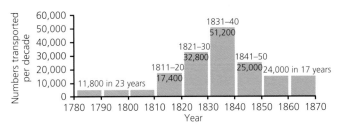

▲ **Figure 6.2:** The total number of people transported to Australia between 1787 and 1868

Spotlight on Wales

Between 1787 and 1868 over 2,200 criminals from Wales were transported to Australia; it amounted to about 15 in every 1,000 convicts. The great majority were convicted for offences against property such as horse or sheep stealing, burglary, house-breaking, or the theft of items from a person. Once found guilty by Welsh courts, convicts had to be taken by road to the hulks moored on the Thames.

The case of Frances Williams

Of the 24,960 women who were transported, just 283 were Welsh, one of whom was Frances Williams who sailed on the First Fleet which left for Australia on 13 May 1787. She had been found guilty of breaking into the house of Moses Griffith of Whitford in Flintshire, at midnight on 1 August 1783, and stealing freshly-ironed laundry. After appearing before the local magistrate, Thomas Pennant, she was ordered to be held in Flint gaol until the Mold Assizes later that year. At her trial she was found guilty of 'Feloniously and Burglariously did steal and taking away diverse pieces of wearing apparel' and sentenced to be executed. This was later changed to seven years' transportation. She spent the next four years in Flint gaol while the government arranged a new destination for transportation and once the decision had been made to use Australia to set up a penal colony, Frances was ordered to be taken in irons to Portsmouth to board the First Fleet. She was placed on board the one ship of eight of the fleet which contained female convicts. The voyage took eight months to complete and when the ships dropped anchor at Botany Bay on 26 January 1788 we know that Frances had survived the voyage; however, what became of her serving her time in the first penal colony in Australia is unknown.

Welsh transportees involved in popular disturbances

Only 1.2 per cent of all transportees came from Wales but among them were a number of individuals who had been involved in popular disturbances:

- Merthyr Rising 1831 – for his role as one of the leaders of the Merthyr Rising (see Chapter 7), Lewis Lewis (Lewsyn yr Heliwr or Lewis the Huntsman) was sentenced to death. He was found guilty of directing the crowd to attack the soldiers based in the Castle Inn in Merthyr. His sentence was later changed to transportation for life to Australia.
- Newport Rising, 1839 – for their part in the Chartist Rising at Newport (see Chapter 2) the three Welsh leaders, John Frost, Zephaniah Williams and William Jones, were each sentenced to death for treason, but this was later commuted to transportation for life.
- Rebecca Riots, 1839-44 – for their part in the attacks on tollgates in West Wales (see Chapter 2) eight of the rioters were sentenced to transportation to Australia. David Thomas received 20 years for 'persuading and procuring' other rioters to attack the tollhouse at Porthhyfryd; David Davies (Dai'r Cantwr) was also sentenced to 20 years, while John Jones (Shoni Ysgubor Fawr) was transported for life.

Punishment and conditions in Australia

Life in the new settlement was very harsh and many convicts died as a result of the harsh treatment. Soon other convict colonies were established at Norfolk Island and Van Diemen's Land (now the island of Tasmania). An assignment system was set up in some colonies, whereby convicts were assigned to work for private individuals. The convicts were made to do whatever work their master chose to give them:

- Farm workers were the least fortunate as they might find themselves on a remote and isolated farm, at the mercy of their master.
- Domestic workers were usually well treated and lived as members of the family.
- Skilled workers – blacksmith, carpenter, cooper, gardener, mason or wheelwright – were the most fortunate; their skills were put to good use and they were regarded as the most valuable of the servants.
- Others were made to work in labour gangs.

In some cases good conduct by convicts could lead to rewards:

- Ticket of Leave – this was a document given to convicts before the end of their sentence, giving them the freedom to work and live in a particular district of the colony. Convicts could apply for a Ticket of Leave after serving a certain amount of their sentence.
- Conditional Pardon – this meant that the convict was set free but not allowed to return to his or her native country.
- Absolute Pardon – this meant that the convict's sentence had been cleared and that they were allowed to return home.
- Certificate of Freedom – these were introduced in 1810 and given to convicts at the end of their sentence.

If a convict committed further crimes while serving a sentence in Australia, they would be either flogged or sent to a harsh penal settlement such as Norfolk Island far out in the Pacific Ocean. Here they could be put to work in **chain gangs**, stone-breaking and road-building.

The ending of transportation

A Parliamentary Committee of Enquiry reported on the transportation system in 1838. It concluded that it was not enough of a deterrent and that it was very expensive. At the same time, the Australians themselves made it clear that they resented their country being used as a human dumping-ground for the criminal elements of society.

As a result of this change in attitude:

- In 1839 the government of New South Wales refused to accept any more convicts.
- After this date they were sent to Van Diemen's Land instead.
- In 1853 transportation to Van Diemen's Land stopped. Instead, convicts were now sent to Western Australia.

The last convict ship left Britain in 1867 and arrived in Western Australia in January 1868, marking the end of transportation. After this date Britain had to look after her own criminals, and this resulted in the building of many new prisons.

Community punishment in Wales – the Scotch Cattle

The Scotch Cattle was the name given to bands of workers who, in the valleys of south-west Wales, during the years 1820 to 1835, attacked those they held grievances against or to enforce solidarity among fellow workers. Most who took part were young, Welsh-speaking colliers such as William Jenkins (Wil Aberhonddu) and John James (Shoni Coal Tar) who were protesting against wage cuts, the truck system and harsh working conditions. They held open-air meetings at night to the accompaniment of horns, drums and gunfire, they sent warning letters to blacklegs and informers, and they attacked the property of their managers, breaking windows, smashing up furniture and manhandling their victims. The movement had died out by the early 1840s.

> ### ACTIVITY
>
> Write a report outlining the key features of transportation to Australia. Make sure you mention the following:
>
> a) the reasons why Australia was selected as the location for transportation
>
> b) the treatment of the criminals in the penal colony in Australia
>
> c) the rise and fall in the numbers of criminals transported to Australia (see Figure 6.2).

The need for prison reform: Howard, Paul and Fry

Before the eighteenth century, prisons were mainly used for holding offenders who were awaiting trial. As trials were so infrequent, offenders could be held in jail for a long time, in appalling conditions, in prisons which had no set plan and no uniformity of regulation. This resulted in overcrowding, unhygienic and unhealthy conditions in almost all prisons.

Conditions in prisons in the eighteenth century

As prisons were only supposed to house suspects and convicts temporarily, no one seemed to care very much what conditions inside them were like. In 1729, a government committee was appointed to examine these conditions and to report to parliament on what they found. They were shocked at their discoveries. These included the fact that over 300 prisoners in the Marshalsea Prison in London were on the point of starvation and that over 100 prisoners actually died from lack of food in the same prison.

These prisons were privately owned and their owners naturally wished to make a profit out of them. The gaoler made money by charging fees from the inmates for food, bedding, and anything else they needed (see Source I). This was especially hard on debtors who formed a large percentage of the prisoners as they could not be released until they had paid off their debts and paid the gaoler to free them.

Source I: A selection of the fees, to be taken by the Gaoler or Keeper of the Prison of Newgate, charged to prisoners in Newgate Prison in London in 1729 [Shillings (s) Pence (d)]	
Every prisoner shall pay to the Keeper for his Entrance Fee	3s 0d
Every prisoner shall pay for use of bed, bedding, and sheets, to the Keeper, there being two in a bed, and no more, each per week	1s 3d
Every prisoner who, at his own desire, shall have a bed to himself, shall pay to the Keeper for chamber-room, use of bed, bedding, and sheets per week	2s 6d
Every Debtor shall pay to the Keeper, for his discharge fee	6s 10d

> **THINK** ?
>
> What does Source I tell you about the conditions for prisoners in gaol during the eighteenth century?

John Howard, 1726–90

John Howard was born in London in 1726. His mother died when he was very young and when his father died in 1742 he inherited a large sum of money. In 1755, while travelling abroad the ship on which he was sailing was captured by French pirates and he was imprisoned in France. Although he was soon released the incident had a lasting effect on him. In 1773, he became High Sheriff of Bedfordshire, and one of his responsibilities was to supervise the county jail. He was so shocked by the conditions that he decided to visit other jails in England, but found the situation very similar wherever he went.

In 1775, John Howard made the first of several journeys to examine prisons all over Europe. His survey of the prisons of England and Wales in 1776 showed that the majority of prisoners were debtors and that only about a quarter had committed serious crimes. He followed up this survey with a book, *The State of the Prisons in England and Wales* (1777) (see Source J).

▲ **Figure 6.3:** A portrait of John Howard, prison reformer, painted in 1789

Criminals convicted of minor offences	16%
Serious offenders awaiting trial, transportation or execution	24.3%
Debtors	59.7%

▲ **Table 6.1:** The different types of offenders, by percentage, held in prisons in England and Wales in 1776

Source J: Extracts taken from John Howard's book *The State of the Prisons in England and Wales* (1777)

Many prisoners who were found not guilty could not get out of prison because they could not afford the discharge fee set by the gaoler. Debtors' prisons had few warders and the prisoners could not be chained or forced to work. In Marshalsea prison in London, butchers and other tradesmen came into the prison to sell food or play skittles with the prisoners in the prison drinking room. In prisons were debtors were mixed with serious criminals, the warders let the criminals have the same privileges as the debtors. There were not enough warders to keep them separate. Prisoners already in a cell forced new prisoners to pay a fee to them known as 'garnish'. Warders did little to stop this.

In 1773, Howard gave evidence before a Parliamentary Committee and he made four suggestions:

- sound, roomy, sanitary buildings
- salaries for gaolers
- training for prisoners to help them reform
- inspection of prisons.

Howard believed that prisons should reform criminals and that clergymen should visit regularly to help guide prisoners to a better life. He also believed that prisoners should be kept in solitary confinement so that they could not learn more about crime from more hardened criminals.

Howard's suggestions were acted upon by one MP, Alexander Popham, who introduced two bills. The first, the Gaol Fever Bill, called for prisons to be cleaned regularly, receive annual whitewashing, ventilation, the appointment of a regular doctor, and the provision of separate sickrooms. The downside was that the Act did not say how these things were to be enforced and so little was done. Popham's second bill was more effective. This did away with the jail release fee, ensuring that any person found not guilty was to be released immediately.

By the end of the eighteenth century the need for change in the prison system had become urgent. The overcrowded prisons of England and Wales were filthy and disease-ridden and there were frequent outbreaks of **jail fever**. John Howard died in 1790 after catching jail fever while visiting a prison in Russia.

Spotlight on Wales: Howard's visits to Welsh prisons

In his work *The State of the Prisons in England and Wales* (1777) John Howard records visits to several Welsh prisons, including those at Caernarvon, Swansea and Wrexham. All of these prisons he considered to be in a terrible state, both in terms of their accommodation and the treatment of the prisoners within them. He described Caernarvon County Jail as being particularly derelict, lacking drainage and a fresh water supply, and housing its inmates, debtors and criminals alike in tiny dark rooms (see Source K). Conditions in Swansea Castle gaol and the Wrexham Bridewell (see Source L) were no better, with inmates being mixed together and confined into small cells with little daylight and no water supply.

> **Source K: Howard's description of conditions in Caernarvon County Gaol which appeared in his *The State of the Prisons in England and Wales* (1777)**
>
> This gaol, is in a ruinous condition. Two rooms for debtors, and two for felons; one of the latter down 11 steps, with an aperture [window] 18 inches by 3; the other under the stairs only 9 feet by 7, with no window: all of them very dirty, and never white-washed. .... A court, but no sewer; no water.... The gaolor has £5 a year as keeper of bridewell. He stops from each felon's allowance six-pence per week for (what he calls) his trouble of weekly payments. No table of fees.
>
> Among the various improvements that are making in this town, may it not be hoped, that the county-magistrates will think of a better prison.

THINK

To what extent did John Howard's findings into the state of prisons in Wales mirror conditions in English prisons?

> **Source L: Howard's description of conditions in Wrexham Bridewell which appeared in his *The State of the Prisons in England and Wales* (1777)**
>
> The prison has – on the ground floor the keeper's rooms and stable; and for prisoners, two dark offensive rooms, with apertures [windows] in the doors 10 inches by 7; a wall within 6 feet of the doors; prisoners have, with just cause, complained of being almost suffocated; and begged to be let out for air into the keeper's garden. Upstairs are three rooms for those who can pay. The prison out of repair. No pump.

Sir George O. Paul, 1746–1820

During his time as High Sheriff of Gloucester, Sir George Onesiphorous Paul became very concerned with the poor conditions in prisons, particularly Gloucester Prison. In 1784, he wrote *Thoughts on the Alarming Progress of Jail Fever*, which led to the prison reform movement in Gloucestershire.

Paul badgered parliament into passing the Gloucestershire Prison Act in 1785 which allowed for the building of new prisons. He worked with the architect William Blackburn to achieve new designs which were later copied in other parts of England and Wales. These new prisons had to meet three requirements:

- security – the perimeter wall should be 5.4 metres high and the buildings were to be arranged so that the staff could easily see what was happening around the prison.
- health – there was to be an isolation section for newly-admitted prisoners where they could be bathed, their clothes fumigated and their health checked. There were to be exercise yards and the whole prison was to be well ventilated.
- separation – prisons were to be divided into a gaol for offenders who were awaiting trial, a House of Correction for minor offenders and the Penitentiary for the more serious criminals. Each area would have sections for male and female prisoners. There was to be a chapel and workrooms, as well as darkened cells for punishment.

Elizabeth Fry, 1780–1845

Sir George O. Paul had highlighted the need to separate male and female prisoners and this suggestion was taken a stage further by mother of 11, Elizabeth Fry. Fry was a very religious Quaker and did a lot of work helping the poor. In 1813 she visited the women's section of Newgate Prison and was horrified at what she saw (see Source M). After her visit to Newgate, Fry began a campaign to improve prison conditions for women. She felt that this would help to reform them and give them a better chance in life after being released.

In 1817, she formed the Association for the Improvement of Women Prisoners in Newgate. She was convinced that women in prison needed education, discipline, useful work and, above all, religion (see Source N). Fry travelled the country, gaining as much publicity as possible and created Ladies' Prison Committees to visit prisons and make changes to the way they were run.

▲ **Figure 6.4:** Elizabeth Fry

> ### Source M: Extract from Elizabeth Fry's report on conditions in Newgate Prison, 1813
>
> Nearly 300 women, sent there for every grade of crime, some untried and some under sentence of death, were crowded together in two wards and two cells. Here they saw their friends and kept a multitude of children, and they had no other place for cooking, washing, eating and sleeping.
>
> They all slept on the floor. At times 120 in one ward without so much as a mat for bedding and many of them very nearly naked. They openly drink spirits and swearing is common. Everything is filthy and the smell quite disgusting.

> ### Source N: The aims of the Association for the Improvement of Female Prisoners in Newgate
>
> … to provide for the clothing, the instruction, and the employment of these females, to introduce them to knowledge of the holy scriptures, and to form in them as much as lies in our power, those habits of order, sobriety, and industry which may render them docile and perceptible while in prison, and respectable when they leave it.

Thanks to Fry, conditions for women in Newgate Prison were greatly improved. Similar changes were later introduced to other prisons:

- Rules were drawn up for women to follow.
- Female warders were appointed.
- Schools were created for women prisoners and their children, focusing strongly on religious education and readings from the Bible.
- Regular work, such as needlework or knitting, was introduced.

However, the changes resulting from the campaigns of these pioneers were slow and piecemeal. What was needed to overhaul the prison system was direct action from the government.

ACTIVITIES

1 How useful are Sources M and N to an historian studying the state of prisons in England and Wales during the eighteenth and early nineteenth centuries?

2 Use your knowledge of eighteenth and early nineteenth-century prisons to complete the table below:

Prison reformer	Their proposals to secure improved conditions in prison	What was achieved as a result of their campaigning?
John Howard		
Sir George O. Paul		
Elizabeth Fry		

3 Of the three prison reformers you have studied (Howard, Paul and Fry), which of these individuals, in your opinion, made the greatest contribution to prison reform? Give examples to justify your choice.

New prisons in the later nineteenth century: the Separate and Silent Systems

One of the first serious attempts from the government to address the need for a reform of the prison system resulted from the actions of the Home Secretary, Sir Robert Peel, who in 1823 was successful in passing the Gaols Act. Peel was influenced by the work of Howard and Fry.

The Gaols Act, 1823

The Gaols Act of 1823 introduced a number of important reforms:

- A prison was to be established in every county and each large town, which was to be administered by local magistrates and maintained out of local rates.
- Justices of the peace were to inspect the prisons and report their findings to the Quarter Sessions, and also send an Annual Report to the Home Office.
- A system of discipline was to be enforced in all prisons.
- Prisons had to be secure and healthy.
- The gaoler was to receive a salary from the local authority.
- Prisoners were to be classified according to age, gender, offence and length of sentence.

These reforms were the first step in bringing some order to the prison system but they were limited in their impact. The Act also only dealt with 130 prisons in London, the counties and 17 large towns, and it was often ignored. There were only five Inspectors (who were not appointed until 1835) and they had only limited powers.

Building new prisons

During the early nineteenth century the government built new prisons at Milbank, Portland, Dartmoor, Portsmouth, Chatham and Borstal and many local authorities rebuilt local prisons. Between 1842 and 1877, 90 new prisons were built in Britain. One of the most famous was that built at Pentonville in London in 1842.

In Wales, the architect John Nash designed new county jails in Carmarthenshire in 1792 and in Cardiganshire in 1796. John Howard had visited the town of Carmarthen in 1788 and Nash's plan for Carmarthenshire Jail applied Howard's reforming ideas. He created a prison that was well ventilated, with separate night-cells and day rooms for the different classes of prisoners – felons, debtors and petty offenders. These were arranged around separate exercise courtyards. There was also a chapel, workshop and infirmary, all contained within the perimeter wall of the old castle.

William Blackburn, who was one of the leading prison architects in the late eighteenth century, had submitted plans for a new prison at Cardigan but had died before the work began. John Nash took over the work and adopted the idea of Blackburn's polygonal, or radial, plan. Prisoners were separated in individual wings that radiated from a central hall, or observatory. Prison staff could watch prisoners in the courts between the wings through windows set in the angles of the octagonal observatory. Nash also designed Herefordshire County Gaol. New prisons were also built in Beaumaris in 1829, Cardiff in 1832 and Swansea in 1861. The first 'Pentonville-style' prison in Wales was built at Ruthin and opened in 1878.

While there was some agreement on the actual design of these new prisons, there was little agreement on how to treat the prisoners within who came to occupy them.

THINK **?**
Identify the key strengths and weaknesses of the Gaols Act, 1823.

Experiments in differing prison systems

During the first half of the nineteenth century there was considerable argument about how prisoners should be treated. Some, like the Rev. Sydney Smith, believed that prison life should be as harsh and unpleasant as possible so as to deter criminals from reoffending.

The reformer Jeremy Bentham, in contrast, believed that prisoners should be made to work, the results of which could be sold to help with running costs. He also believed in efficient planning and running of prisons, favouring prisons with blocks radiating out from the centre so that only a few warders would be needed to supervise the whole prison. Others, such as the prison chaplain, the Rev. Kingsmill, believed that the principal aim of imprisonment should be the reform of the prisoners, which he believed was best achieved through solitary confinement.

During the second half of the nineteenth century prisons experimented with using either the separate or the silent system. Both of these systems, which were based upon ideas from the USA, tried to ensure that prisoners did not communicate with one another.

The Separate System

The key focus of this system was an attempt to reform prisoners through isolation, religious teaching and productive work. Prisoners were kept in individual cells, where they worked, prayed and received religious teaching from a visiting clergyman. It was believed that separate confinement would lead to the prisoner breaking down, after which he or she would be ready to listen to advice from the clergyman. Prisoners would only leave their cells for religious services in the chapel's separate cubicles, or for exercise. They were not allowed to see other prisoners on those occasions and were made to wear masks so they could not recognise or communicate with each other if they met. During exercise time they had to hold a knotted rope, each knot being 4.5 metres apart so that prisoners were too far away from each other to talk (see Figure 6.5).

Prison reformers believed that the Separate System would help prisoners to obtain work such as making boots, mats, prison clothes and sewing mailbags and coal sacks. However, the Separate System was very expensive as prisons had to be rebuilt to provide separate cells. The system also had a high death rate, and in its first eight years 22 prisoners at Pentonville went mad, 26 had serious breakdowns and three committed suicide.

Pentonville Prison was built on a radical design

Features of the Separate System

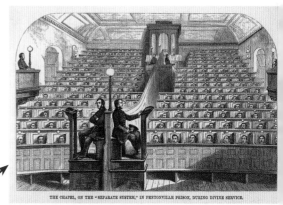

THE CHAPEL, ON THE "SEPARATE SYSTEM," IN PENTONVILLE PRISON, DURING DIVINE SERVICE.

Individual pews in the chapel

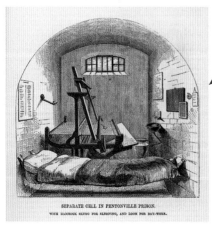

SEPARATE CELL IN PENTONVILLE PRISON.
WITH HAMMOCK SLUNG FOR SLEEPING, AND LOOM FOR DAY-WORK.

Work in individual cells

CONVICTS EXERCISING IN PENTONVILLE PRISON.

Exercising in the yard wearing hoods

▲ **Figure 6.5:** Features of the Separate System

Case study: Pentonville Prison

Pentonville Prison, known to inmates as 'The Ville' was built in 1842 as a model prison for the Separate System. It was based upon Cherry Hall Penitentiary in Pennsylvania, USA. The design of the prison was symmetrical. The cell blocks radiated from a central point. A warden standing in the centre could see down all corridors. Each of the four wings contained 130 cells, and each cell was 14 feet long and 9 feet high. The prison was perfectly clean and good order was everywhere. To complete the security a high wall surrounded the prison. By the 1850s, over 50 prisons were using the separate system.

The Silent System

The key focus of this system was an attempt to deter prisoners by making prison life as unpleasant as possible. It was based upon the system used in Auburn Prison, New York, USA. The job of the warders was to enforce silence so that prisoners could not have a bad influence on each other. Under this system prisoners were allowed to see each other in the workshops or dining room, for example, but they did so in silence. In this way prisoners could not influence each other. They system depended upon fear and hatred. To achieve these goals, prison life had to be as unpleasant as possible and so prisoners were set boring, pointless tasks, the most common being the tread wheel, the crank, oakum-picking and shot drill (see Figure 6.6)

The Silent System was cheaper that the Separate System. It was believed that prisoners would hate the Silent System so much that they were less likely to commit crimes in order to avoid returning to prison. However, as with the Separate System, silence combined with isolation, led to suicide or insanity and prevented the system from working effectively.

THINK ?

1 Use your knowledge of the Separate and Silent Systems to complete the following table:

The Separate System		
Key features of this system	The advantages of this system	The disadvantages of this system

The Silent System		
Key features of this system	The advantages of this system	The disadvantages of this system

2 Describe how the Prisons Acts of 1865 and 1877 increased government involvement over the running of prisons.

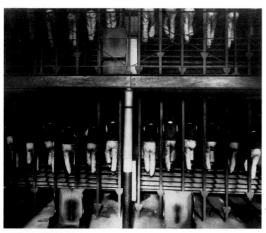

The treadmill

The crank

Features of the Silent System

Oakum picking

Shot drill

▲ **Figure 6.6:** Features of the Silent System

Government takes control of prisons

A number of Acts during the late nineteenth century increased government control over the prisons:

- Prisons Act, 1865 (also known as the Penal Servitude Act) – this can be summed up by 'Hard labour, hard fare and hard board':
  - hard labour: at least three months of tread wheel, crank, shot drill, oakum-picking and stone breaking;
  - hard face: diet of bread and water for three days, which could be increased to a month, as well as corporal punishment;
  - hard board: hammocks were replaced with board beds.
- The aim of this Act was to enforce strict punishment, not to reform. The Act also abolished the distinction between gaols and houses of correction. About 80 small prisons were closed, leaving about 113 prisons in England and Wales under the control of the government.
- Prisons Act, 1877 – this placed all prisons under Home Office control. A three-person Commission was set up to run all of the prisons in England and Wales. Fifty-three smaller prisons were closed. The prison system was now centrally organised and changes 'across the board' were now possible.

Alternative methods of dealing with prisoners in the twentieth century

The early twentieth century was a time of considerable change in the prison system in England and Wales. The abolition of capital punishment in 1969 meant that the system had to adapt even further. These changes have continued into the twenty-first century.

The use of borstals

Juvenile crime had been a problem in Victorian times and attempts had been made to address the issue at that time, focusing on reform, rather than retribution. This was reflected by the attempts to address youth crime in the early twentieth century. In 1902 an experiment in reformatory treatment was undertaken in Rochester Prison in the village of Borstal in Kent in the treatment of young offenders. The experiment was thought to be successful and in 1908 the Prevention of Crime Act ordered the setting up of 'borstals' for young people aged between 15 and 21 years of age. Inmates would be released only when satisfactory progress had been made.

The borstal system was designed to be educational, rather than punishing. It was a very rigid system and was organised according to a strict set of rules. The focus was on routine, discipline and authority (see Source O). There was limited use of corporal punishment – the birch – but this was abolished in 1962.

In 1969 the minimum age for borstal was raised to 17 years. Borstals were abolished in 1982. Further change was needed and alternative methods of punishing and reforming young offenders were introduced to replace the borstal system.

▲ Source O: Physical drill at a borstal, 1937

Detention centres, young offender institutes and youth custody sentences

When borstals were abolished in 1982 they were replaced with short sentences at detention centres or with longer youth custody sentences. The new system was for boys aged 15 to 20 and for girls aged 17 to 20. The average sentence at a detention centre was for six months, followed by supervision for three to twelve months. Youth custody was used for violent young people and for those dependent upon alcohol or drugs. It aimed to instil self-respect and self-discipline in young offenders. In 1988, young offenders' institutes replaced detention centres. They cater for 18-to 21-year olds and are run by Her Majesty's Prison Service.

Parc Young Offenders' Institute, Bridgend

Parc Prison in Bridgend is now a Young Offenders' Institution, the only such institution in Wales, and was opened in 1987. It has its own education department, offering a range of academic and vocational subjects to enable its inmates to gain qualifications up to Open University standard. It has nine workshops, including facilities for the study of carpentry, metalwork, graphic design and industrial cleaning. It also has a library, a gymnasium and fitness room, as well as a chapel for religious faiths. The aim is to prepare young offenders for life after prison.

Open prisons

Experimentation with open prisons first occurred in 1936 with the opening of New Hall Camp as an annexe to Wakefield Prison in West Yorkshire. The male inmates were put to work on neighbouring farms or making boots. The experiment proved a success and after the Second World War other open prisons were set up in an attempt to relieve pressure on overcrowded prisons.

Leyhill Open Prison in Gloucestershire was one of the earliest open prisons when it was set up in 1946 in a former United States military hospital. Today it accommodates 532 prisoners. Ford Open Prison, at Ford in West Sussex, is based in a former Royal Naval Air Station and was converted into an open prison in 1960. It houses non-violent offenders (Category D prisoners) with a low risk of escaping. Prisoner accommodation at Ford is never locked and there are no bars on the windows. Work opportunities are provided such as market gardening, vocational work in workshops, as well as work in the local community. Vocational and academic courses are also provided so that prisoners can try to achieve qualifications that will help them to secure employment on release.

Wales has one open prison and is situated just outside Usk at Prescoed. Originally opened in 1939 as an open borstal, it was converted into an open youth custody centre in 1983. In 1988, Prescoed became a Category D Open Prison for men. Prisoners are normally transferred to Prescoed from other prisons to serve out the latter part of their sentences, the aim being to integrate them back into the community before their final release.

Open prisons have been criticised as being a 'soft option', but they are cheaper to run than closed prisons.

> ### THINK
> 1 Describe how punishment for young offenders changed during the early twentieth century.
> 2 Explain why open prisons were introduced.

Alternative methods of punishment

The prison system is very expensive to run and currently prisons in England and Wales are very overcrowded. The number of offenders is at a record high and in December 2016 the prison population in England and Wales stood at 84,300 inmates. As a consequence of such pressure, alternative methods to imprisonment have been experimented with during the twentieth century.

Probation and parole

The probation service began in 1907. From that time courts could put offenders on probation instead of into prison. The offender then had to follow a set of rules, or orders, keep in touch with the probation officer and report regularly to the police. If the probationer did not re-offend during the probation period, there would be no further punishment.

From 1982, offenders on probation had to perform set activities and attend day centres for up to 60 days. Here the offender's problems could be discussed and help could be given. The National Probation Service continues it supportive work throughout England and Wales.

In 1967, the Parole Board was created and the system of parole was started. The granting of parole meant a prisoner was let off gaol before the end of their sentence for good behaviour, but must promise to follow a set of rules. They are monitored by probation officers who will work with them on release. Six months before a prisoner can get parole, they are asked if they wish to apply for early release. Their case is then discussed. If they are successful in their application, they are let out with a parole licence and a set of conditions that they have to keep. Once out of prison the prisoner is on 'conditional release' and has to keep in touch with probation officers. If the conditions of the license are broken, the offender can be recalled to prison.

Probation and parole have helped to relieve pressure on the prison system. At the same time they provide effective support to the offender in helping to adapt successfully to life outside prison.

Community service

Community Service Orders were first introduced in 1972. Under this system offenders were required to do a number of hours of unpaid work for the community. The system was more cost-effective than probation. Although community service was very successful with older offenders, it had little deterrent effect on young offenders.

Since 2003, community service has developed into 'community payback'. Offenders who have committed certain crimes are ordered to do between 40 and 300 hours of community payback. The work is unpaid and demanding and is aimed at giving something back to the local communities by forcing the offenders to pay for the wrong they have done. Local people are able to nominate a project or vote for the project they would like to see benefit from this unpaid work.

The aims of community payback are:

- to punish the offender without serving a prison sentence
- to force the offender to pay the community back for the crimes committed.

Offenders may be seen wearing bright orange jackets, with 'Community Payback' on them. The work in the community has involved graffiti removal, street clean-ups, rubbish removal, gardening, repair and recycling projects. It is intended to be an alternative to method to punish wrongdoers rather than sending them to prison, and it serves to make the public and offenders aware that punishment is being carried out.

THINK ?

'Attempts to reduce prison over-crowding were the real reason for the introduction of alternative methods of punishment.' How far do you agree with this statement? Give reasons to support your answer.

FOCUS TASK REVISITED

As you have worked through this chapter you will have completed an overview grid which has enabled you to see how punishment has changed or remained the same across the centuries.

Use this information, together with any additional knowledge you will have acquired, to help you answer the following questions:

1 What punishment, if any, was common across all historical eras?
2 Which periods saw the introduction of new types of punishment and why?
3 What, in your opinion, has been the greatest change in the method of punishment across the period c.1500 to the present day? Give reasons to support your answer.

TOPIC SUMMARY

- Society has always taken action to punish wrongdoers.
- During the Tudor period rogues and vagabonds were subjected to physical punishment such as whipping, branding and, ultimately, hanging.
- Punishment which involved some form of public humiliation such as the stocks and pillory was in use up to the nineteenth century.
- Public execution was meant to be the ultimate deterrent, and public hangings became popular events attracting large crowds, especially during the eighteenth century.
- During the eighteenth and nineteenth centuries transportation was used to banish criminals overseas, first to North America and later to Australia.
- When transportation to North America ended in 1776 and before transportation to Australia commenced in 1787, hulks (floating prisons) were used to house convicted criminals.
- Between 1788 and 1868, 160,663 criminals were transported to Australia.
- The need to improve conditions in prisons was highlighted through the work of three prison reformers – John Howard, Sir George O. Paul and Elizabeth Fry.

- The Gaols Act of 1823 marked the start of the reform of the prison system.
- The Separate System attempted to reform prisoners through isolation, religious teaching and the undertaking of productive work.
- Pentonville Prison in London is the best example of the use of the Separate System.
- The Silent System attempted to deter prisoners from re-offending by making prison life as unpleasant as possible through harsh treatment and the undertaking of monotonous and pointless tasks.
- Changes in the punishment of young offenders resulted in the introduction of borstals in 1902.
- Open prisons were first set up in 1932 to accommodate non-violent, low-risk offenders.
- Alternative methods of punishment were introduced during the twentieth century, such as probation, parole and community service, all of which aimed to reduce the acute problem of prison overcrowding.

Practice question

1 Complete the sentences below with an accurate term:
   a) A wooden framework which confined petty criminals by the ankles and put them on public show was called the ....
   b) The main place in eighteenth-century London for public execution was ....
   c) Transportation to Australia finally ended in 18...
   d) Pentonville Prison is one of the best examples of the .... System of punishment.
   (For guidance, see page 252.)
2 Look at Source B [whipping, page 217], Source F [public execution, page 219] and Source O [prison, page 230] to identify one similarity and one difference in the types of punishment used over time. (For guidance, see pages 253–4.)
3 Describe the work of Elizabeth Fry in reforming prisons in the early nineteenth century. (For guidance, see page 255.)
4 Describe the key features of the Silent System used in nineteenth-century prisons. (For guidance, see page 255.)
5 Explain why transportation was introduced as a punishment in the early eighteenth century. (For guidance, see page 257.)
6 Explain why alternative methods of punishment to prison sentences were introduced during the early twentieth century. (For guidance, see page 257.)
7 To what extent has the use of prison been the main method of punishment over time? In your answer you should:
   - show how prison has been the main method of punishment over three historical eras
   - discuss the importance of other types of punishment over three historical eras
   - include direct references to the history of Wales.
   (For guidance, see pages 260–1.)

7 The study of a historic site connected with crime and punishment. 'China': The growth of crime in industrial Merthyr Tydfil in the nineteenth century

Key question: To what extent did the growth of crime in Merthyr Tydfil during the nineteenth century impact upon the development of policing within the town?

The rapid growth and development of the iron industry in Merthyr Tydfil in the early nineteenth century caused it to become the first 'industrial town' in Wales, a town which possessed Wales' largest population. The need to accommodate an ever-growing workforce caused the unregulated building of houses, which were cramped together in a disorganised manner. This gave rise to public health problems linked to poor sanitation: frequent outbreaks of disease and high rates of mortality. Slum areas developed and these emerged as pocket areas of crime. The most notorious was called 'China', where incidents of theft, drunkenness and public disorder were common. Such a sharp rise in crime overwhelmed the existing system of law enforcement and it was not until the 1840s that Merthyr developed a police force. However, it still took several decades to break the cycle of crime in areas like China. In this chapter you will explore how law enforcement developed in Merthyr to tackle the high incidence of crime in the town.

FOCUS TASK

As you work through this chapter gather together information to enable you to complete the table below. Once completed you should then be in a position to make an overall judgement as to how increased levels of crime impacted upon the development of policing in Merthyr Tydfil.

	What impact did this factor have on the level and type of crime?	What impact did this factor have upon the methods of law enforcement?
Living conditions in Merthyr		
The growth of urban Merthyr		
Changes in the methods of policing		

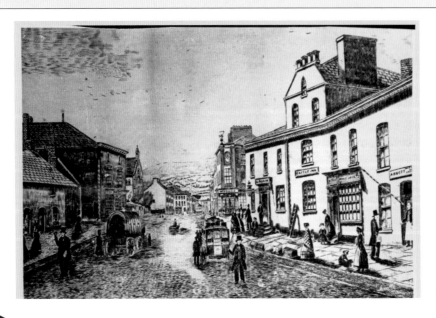

◀ Source A: Merthyr Tydfil picture in 1841

Living conditions in urban Merthyr Tydfil in the nineteenth century

In 1750, Merthyr Tydfil was a small village and most of the 40 or so families who lived there worked the land. One hundred years later that village had grown to become Wales' largest town which, in 1851, had a population of 46,378 inhabitants. The reason for this quite dramatic growth was the development of the iron industry.

The development of the iron industry

The iron industry transformed Merthyr. The town grew around four great ironworks, each of which had its own furnaces, workshops, machine sheds, warehouses and a village of houses for its workers:

- **Dowlais ironworks** – Thomas Lewis of Llanishen was the first to establish an ironworks at Dowlais, a short distance from Merthyr village in 1748. In 1767, he made John Guest, a Staffordshire man, the manager of the works and within a short time he had taken over the ownership and running of the plant.
- **Plymouth ironworks** – Anthony Bacon, a London merchant, started the second ironworks at Plymouth and, at the same time, began to build another furnace at Cyfarthfa. Richard Hill was appointed to manage the Plymouth works.
- **Cyfarthfa ironworks** – Richard Crawshay, a Yorkshireman, was appointed manager of the Cyfarthfa works and under the direction of his leadership and later that of his sons, it grew to become the largest ironworks in the world. By 1806, it had six furnaces and was producing 11,000 tonnes of iron a year.
- **Penydarren ironworks** – this was started in 1784 by two brothers from Staffordshire, Samuel and Jeremiah Homfray.

One reason for this phenomenal growth was that Merthyr was rich in the raw materials needed to make iron. The land around the rapidly expanding town contained plentiful supplies of coal and ironstone (iron ore), the essential ingredients to manufacture iron. The ironmasters were quick to open up their own coalmines in the area and they were employing as many individuals in the coalmines as they were in the ironworks.

Improved transport facilities were also a factor in this growth. In 1794, the Glamorgan canal was opened which provided a direct link between Merthyr and Cardiff. Each barge could carry 24 tonnes of iron ore and needed just one horse, a man and a boy to attend it. Previously such a load would have required 12 wagons, 48 horses, 12 men and 12 boys to take it by road. In 1834, the ironmasters Guest and Hill set up a railway company to build a line connecting Merthyr to the new docks being constructed in Cardiff to export coal and iron. The Taff Vale Railway, as it was called, was opened in 1841.

By the 1840s, Merthyr possessed the essential ingredients to help turn it into an industrial 'boomtown':

- enterprising industrialists, mostly Englishmen, willing to invest in industrial development – the Guests, Crawshays, Homfrays and Hills.
- plentiful supplies of raw materials – coal, ironstone, water.
- good transport links – the Glamorgan canal and the Taff Vale railway.
- a rapidly expanding population to service its labour needs.

What drove all these factors was the ever growing demand for iron fuelled by the development of the Industrial Revolution. In 1806, the ironworks in Merthyr were producing 16,000 tonnes of iron, by 1850, that had increased to 300,000 tonnes. By the 1840s, Dowlais had overtaken Cyfarthfa as the largest ironworks in the world. By 1845, it employed 7,300 men, women and children, and its 18 furnaces were producing 89,000 tonnes of iron annually.

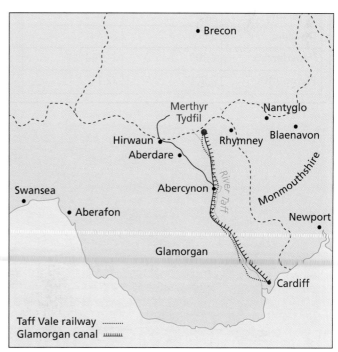

▲ **Figure 7.1:** Merthyr Tydfil and its surrounding area in the middle of the nineteenth century

The decline of Merthyr's iron industry

However, this boom was not to last and the development of the steel industry during the second half of the nineteenth century signalled the decline of Merthyr's industrial development. Merthyr was not suited to the new steel industry. Its supply of ironstone was beginning to run out and, more significantly, it was not of the right quality for the manufacture of steel. Supplies of suitable ironstone had to be imported from abroad which meant it was more convenient to move and build new steelworks on the coast at Port Talbot, Briton Ferry, Aberavon, Neath and Swansea. The Plymouth and Penydarren ironworks were not suited to manufacture steel and by the 1880s they had closed down. By the 1860s Merthyr's great days of iron making were over.

> **Source B: An account of iron making in Merthyr Tydfil described by two tourists, W. and S. Sandby in October 1819**
>
> About five miles from Merthyr, we saw ... a faint glimmering redness ... as we advanced it became more fixed with occasional deeper flashes ... Everything was in utter darkness heightened by a thick, wet fog. The road was miserably bad and dirty ... we could now see men moving among the blazing fires, and hear the noise of huge hammers, clanking of chains, whiz of wheels, blast of bellows, with the deep roaring of the fires ... The effect was almost terrific when contrasted to the pitchy darkness of the night.

> **Source C: The tonnage of iron sent from Merthyr ironworks to Cardiff for export**
>
> | Works | 1796 | 1830 |
> |-----------|-------|--------|
> | Cyfarthfa | 7,204 | 19,892 |
> | Dowlais | 2,800 | 27,647 |
> | Penydarren | 4,100 | 11,744 |
> | Plymouth | 2,200 | 12,117 |

> **Source E: A description of the Cyfarthfa ironworks which appeared in Benjamin Heath Malkin's *The Scenery, Antiquities and Biography of South Wales* (1807)**
>
> The number of smelting furnaces at Merthyr Tydfil is about fifteen, six of them belonging to the Cyfarthfa Works ... which are now by far the largest in the kingdom; probably the largest in Europe; and in that case, as far as we know, the largest in the world ... employing constantly upwards of two thousand men. At present more than two hundred tons of iron is sent down the canal weekly to the port at Cardiff, whence it is shipped off to Bristol, London, Plymouth, Portsmouth, ... America. Around each of the furnaces are erected forges and rolling mills for converting pig into plate and bar iron.

> **THINK** ?
>
> 1 a) Explain how each of the following factors helped Merthyr to develop into Wales' largest industrial manufacturing town:
>   - enterprising individuals
>   - supplies of raw materials
>   - transport links
>   - expanding population
>   b) Which of these factors, in your opinion, played the most important role in expanding the industrial growth of Merthyr? Give reasons to support your answer.
>
> 2 Study Sources B, D and E.
>   a) What do they tell you about the iron industry in Merthyr in the early nineteenth century?
>   b) What are the strengths and weaknesses of such sources to a historian studying the history of Merthyr?
>
> 3 'The Cyfarthfa ironworks are now (1807) the largest in the kingdom.' Use the information in Sources C and D, together with your own knowledge, to investigate the accuracy of this statement between the period 1796 and 1830.

◀ Source D: A print showing Penydarren ironworks in 1813

The growth in the population of Merthyr Tydfil

The growth in the population of Merthyr was staggering. The census returns illustrate a dramatic rise each decade.

Year	Population
1750	400
1801	7,705
1831	22,000
1851	46,378
1861	51,949

This growth was due to the demand for workers in the ironworks, coalmines and ironstone quarries and was met through the constant arrival of immigrants. Most the people who came to Merthyr travelled relatively short distances from the rural parts of Glamorganshire. Although some skilled and unskilled workers came from England and Ireland, the majority of this 'new' population of Merthyr was Welsh. The 1841 census reveals that only nine per cent of the people in the town came from outside Wales.

The ironmasters had to build houses for their workers, as close to the ironworks and coalmines as possible, crammed together in the new villages that developed around each ironworks. Eventually, as more and more people poured into Merthyr, the villages joined up and by 1860 Merthyr was a large industrial town of over 50,000 inhabitants (see Figure 7.2). There were no planning laws or town council to regulate this expansion and, as a consequence, the town quickly became overcrowded, filthy and unhealthy (see Source B).

Source F: A description of the early development of Merthyr contained in Benjamin Heath Malkin's *The Scenery, Antiquities and Biography of South Wales* (1807)

The first houses that were built were only very small and simple cottages for furnace-men, forge-men, miners ... These cottages were most of them built in scattered confusion without any order or plan. As the works increased, more cottages were wanted, and erected in the spaces between these that had been previously built.

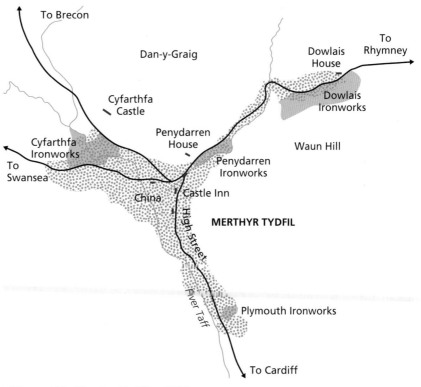

▲ **Figure 7.2:** Merthyr Tydfil, c.1830

The majority of the workers lived in houses owned by the ironmasters. The quality of housing, though generally very poor, varied. Skilled workers, who were paid the highest wages, could afford to rent better quality housing which was usually in a row of terraced houses along a street, with a small yard at the back of each one. These houses normally had two or three rooms but no bathroom; the toilet would be outside in the yard (see Source G).

Unskilled workers were more likely to live in the poorer quality homes found in the 'courts'. This was where the houses were built in a square with a yard in the centre. The building was entered through a narrow alleyway between two of the houses, the yard being a communal area shared by all the inhabitants, including the shared toilet.

The poorest of all housing was to be found in the 'cellar-dwellings'. These were often three-storey-high houses, with the lower floor, being accessed by going down a set of steps to enter the cellar. Such dwellings accommodated the poorest people in dark, often windowless, damp cellars. Here a single room might be the home to an entire family, and possibly even a lodger (see Source I).

> **Source G: A report on the houses rented by skilled artisans which appeared in the *Morning Chronicle* newspaper, c.1850**
>
> [These houses] are of two stories, have four small sash windows (which, by the way, are never opened), two above, and one on each side of the door. On the ground floor there is a room kitchen with a stone floor; adjoining is a small room, just large enough to contain a four-post bed, a chest of drawers, a small corner-cupboard, two chairs and a window table, which usually form its contents. The ceiling is not plastered, and the rafters are used for hanging up the crockery and household utensils. Above stairs are two bed-rooms, one large and the other small; the ceiling here is of lath and plaster. This is all, except, perhaps, a narrow cupboard, cut off from the lower bedroom, and dignified with the name of 'pantry'. There is no strip of garden, no backdoor or outlet, no place of accommodation (toilet), no drain to carry away house refuse, nor any pump or pipe for the supply of water.

> **Source H: A description of the slum housing in Merthyr contained in a health report written by T. W. Rammell (1849)**
>
> Some of the worst description of dwellings are those called 'the cellars', near Pont-y-Storehouse. These are small two-roomed houses, situated in a dip or hollow between a line of road and a vast cinder heap. In these miserable tenements, which are closely packed together, and with nothing in front or between them but stagnant pools of liquid and house refuse, it is said that nearly 1,500 living beings are congregated. The rents of these pest-holes are high, considering 'the accommodation', ranging from 3/- to 5/- a month. Many of the tenants take lodgers, mostly of course, vagrants and trampers who swarm daily into the town.

> **Source I: A description of overcrowded housing in Merthyr written by De La Beche in 1845**
>
> Michael Harrington's is a lodging house. On visiting today I found 45 inmates, but many more come in to sleep at nights ... there are no bed-steads, but all the lodgers lie on the ground or floor. The children were sleeping in old orange boxes, and on shavings: that is, the younger ones, or they would be liable to be crushed in the night by persons rolling over them. Each party had with them all their stock, consisting of heaps of rags, bones, salt-fish, rotten potatoes, and other things ... the stench was sickening ... It is the common practice for these rooms to be occupied by relays of sleepers, some of them being engaged on work during the night, and some during the day.

> **THINK** ?
>
> 1 Study Figure 7.2 and Source F. What do they tell you about living conditions in Merthyr in the early nineteenth century?
>
> 2 If you had been a government health inspector in 1850, what actions would you recommend to improve the quality of accommodation on offer to the industrial workers of Merthyr?

Issues of public health

Merthyr Tydfil's rapid growth, together with a neglect of formalised planning and building regulations, meant that many of the houses lacked any proper sanitation or supply of clean water. During the 1840s and 1850s unhealthy and squalid living conditions resulted in waves of epidemics sweeping through the town, making it one of the unhealthiest of towns in the whole of Wales. By 1849 Merthyr's mortality rate was the highest in Wales and the third highest in Britain.

The average life expectancy of an industrial worker in Merthyr was just 22 years, compared with that of an ironmaster's family which stood at more than double, at the age of 50 years. The highest date rate was amongst children and during the early nineteenth century three-quarters of all deaths in the town were of children under the age of five (see Figure 7.3).

Outbreaks of disease were frequent in the town. Due to the overcrowded, damp and dirty housing, tuberculosis was ever present, as were frequent outbreaks of smallpox, typhoid, scarlet fever and measles. However, the most significant killer was cholera and outbreaks of this disease attacked Merthyr on four occasions between 1832 and 1866 (see Figure 7.4). The worst outbreak occurred in 1849 and resulted in 1,467 deaths. The cause of this killer disease was a contaminated water supply.

Much of the water supply to the town was contaminated with waste from the ironworks, sewage and rubbish (see Source J). Many of the houses had no toilets and the occupants had no choice but to tip the contents of their chamber pots out onto the street or empty them into the river. For those who did have access to toilets they were no more than holes in the ground that had to be emptied regularly (see Source K). There was no refuge collection and the streets were never cleaned, causing them to be covered with filth and rubbish (see Source L).

The supply of fresh water was extremely poor and even though the River Taff ran through the town it had become an open sewer. People obtained their water from a few wells and springs, some of which dried up during the summer months, resulting in long queues in the remaining wells (see Source M). It was not until 1861 that the Merthyr Board of Health began to provide piped water and public taps, but it took another seven years for the building of a sewer system.

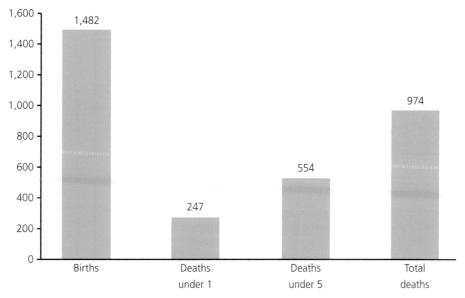

▲ **Figure 7.3:** Child death rates in Merthyr Tydfil, 1841

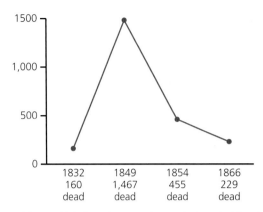

| 1832 | 1849 | 1854 | 1866 |
| 160 dead | 1,467 dead | 455 dead | 229 dead |

▲ **Figure 7.4:** Death rates from cholera in Merthyr

Source J: A comment upon the dirty town of Merthyr made by Dr Holland of the General Board of Health in 1853

The first circumstance that most strikes every visitor at Merthyr is the extreme and universal dirtiness and wetness of the town. I have visited many dirty places, and have generally been taken to see the worst parts of most of the worst towns in England; with the worst parts of London and Manchester I am familiar, that extremely dirty city of Bristol I have recently examined but never did I see anything which could compare with Merthyr.

Source K: A comment made upon the lack of sanitation in Merthyr made in a Report on the State of Education in Wales, 1847

In a sanatory point of view, the state of Merthyr is disgraceful ... The vast majority of houses have no privies; where there is such a thing, it is a mere hole in the ground, with no drainage. ... This is the case nearly all over Wales; but, in a dense population, the consequences of such neglect are more loathsomely and degradingly apparent.

Source L: An account of the rubbish on the streets which appeared in the *Morning Chronicle* newspaper in March 1850

The courts, and often the middle of the streets are obstructed with heaps of ashes, ordure, the refuse of vegetables and the clotted hay of which the Irish and some of the Welsh make their beds. Upon this is thrown all the slops from the houses ... The roadways of the streets, especially in ... Dowlais and Penydarren, are in rainy weather absolutely impassable; they are a mass of festering black mud, into which the wheels of the carts which carry coal to the houses sink deeply.

Source M: An excerpt from *an Enquiry into Merthyr Tydfil*, 1850

During the winter months there are from six to eight spouts, some half a mile, some two miles distant from the houses, but in summer they are often reduced to three, the remainder being dried up. At these water-spouts I have seen 50, 80 and as many as 100 people waiting for their turn ... The women have told me that they have waited six, eight and ten hours at a time for their turn.

THINK

1   What do Figures 7.3 and 7.4 tell you about the state of public health in Merthyr during the mid-nineteenth century?

2   Explain why outbreaks of disease were common in Merthyr during the early nineteenth century.

3   'The dirtiest industrial town in Wales.' What evidence can you find in Sources J–M to support this view of nineteenth-century Merthyr Tydfil?

Poverty caused by the truck system

Wages in the iron industry were dependent upon the sales of manufactured iron. When the price for iron fell the ironmasters responded by reducing wages as they did during the depression of 1815–16 when wages were reduced by up to 40 per cent. Similar reductions in wages of between 30 and 60 per cent occurred in the years 1833, 1842 and 1847–48. This cut in pay only added to the poverty experienced by working-class families. As workers were only paid once a month this meant they often had to go into debt towards the end of the month, a system of payment known as long pay.

Some of the ironmasters paid out part of the wages in special tokens called 'truck' rather than in the official coinage. These tokens could only be exchanged for goods in special 'tommy shops' which were owned by the iron companies. Prices were generally higher than in ordinary shops which was an additional burden for the hard-pressed worker. The truck shop would encourage workers to go into debt by allowing them to 'buy on loan' until the next pay day, thereby ensuring their continued custom. Two of the four Merthyr ironmasters operated the truck system: the Guests set up a truck shop at Dowlais in 1796 and the Homfreys operated one at Penydarren (see Source N). However, neither the Crawshays nor the Hills operated such a system.

▲ **Source N:** A trade token issued to the Penydarren ironworkers as part of their wages. This could only be spent in the company's truck shop

Such frequent debt often resulted in workers having to appear before a special debtors court, the Court of Requests, which had the power to collect debts by ordering bailiffs to confiscate goods to the value of what was owed. The Court of Requests became hated by the people of Merthyr and it was action of the Court in the ordering bailiffs to retrieve goods from an ironworker which triggered a major rising in Merthyr in 1831. Following this disturbance Parliament made it illegal to pay wages in anything but official coinage, an action which marked the end of the truck shops.

THINK

1 Explain how the truck system added to the poverty experienced by the industrial workers of Merthyr.

2 Why do you think the Court of Requests became one of the most hated badges of authority in Merthyr?

Increased opportunities for crime in urban Merthyr Tydfil in the nineteenth century

The main focus of Merthyr was its iron industry and when demand for iron was high and prices were stable, as it was in the 1820s and mid-1840s, law and order was relatively stable. However, during periods of depression when wages were cut, or during periods of high food prices due to bad harvests, there was an increase in lawlessness and disorder.

It is possible to identify periods of high crime rates during the early 1840s, between 1847–48 and during the early 1850s, peaks which mirror times of depression, wages cuts, poor harvests or high food prices.

It is possible to divide the criminal acts into four broad categories:

- Crimes caused by poverty
- Crimes connected to the ironworks
- Crimes associated with leisure time
- Crimes of a sexual nature

Crimes caused by poverty

Crimes associated with poverty mainly concerned theft. Nearly 70 per cent of all reported cases of theft were to do with the stealing of clothing, food, coal, or stealing from the person. Much of this crime was associated with vagrants and beggars who were attracted to Merthyr in large numbers during the 1840s and 1850s (see Source O).

> **Source O: Extract from a report issued by the Chief Constable of Glamorgan, Captain Charles Napier, in June 1842**
>
> There can be no doubt that the present universal distress conduces in a great measure to the committal of crime, many persons having declared to me their intention to work when they could get it, but when that became impossible to steal, but never to starve.

Crimes connected to the ironworks

Theft of company property, especially the stealing of coal, was a common crime. In the years between 1848 and 1854 over 100 people in the Merthyr and Aberdare area were charged with stealing coal from the ironworks. Other crimes connected with this category included the destruction of company property, ill-discipline while at work and illegal strike activity.

Crimes associated with leisure time

The bulk of the crimes in this category relate to incidents of drunkenness and disorderly behaviour. Assault and drunkenness made up a fifth of all recorded incidents of crime in Merthyr. While drunken brawls were largely a male phenomenon, some women, many of whom lived in the tougher slum areas like China, established reputations for their unruly behaviour. One such person was Julia Carroll, 'the heroine of a hundred brawls'. Some of the worst drunks in Merthyr were women such as 'Brecon Jane' Powell, 'Snuffy Nell' Sullivan and 'Savey Stack' Edwards. Extreme cases of drunkenness could also account for lost production in the ironworks.

Drunkenness and its associated violent behaviour was a particular problem among the Irish population of the town (see Source P). Violence was a real problem and common assault accounted for a high proportion of all charges.

> **Source P: A report of a disturbance at Quarry Row in the Irish quarter which appeared in the *Merthyr Guardian* in 1857**
>
> This locality is the Irish quarter of Merthyr, and bears a very bad reputation, being continually disgraced by scenes of a most riotous description; drunkenness and fighting are of perpetual recurrence; the police are frequently assaulted in the execution of their duty, and heavy brickbats and missiles fly about on the slightest provocation.

Crimes of a sexual nature

The most common crime within this category was 'stealing from the person' by the town's prostitutes. Merthyr was very much a 'Wild West' town, which had a high percentage of prostitutes and their minders, gamblers, conmen and thieves. The criminal element tended to be based in the poorest parts of the town, the slum areas of China and Pontstorehouse. The prostitutes in China were notorious for stealing from their clients. Once inside the brothel the prostitutes would encourage the men to drink until they were completely drunk, making the theft of their personal items such as watches, boots and money an easy task to accomplish.

> **THINK** ?
>
> Study Sources O and P. What reasons are given in these sources for the high levels of crime in Merthyr in the 1840s and 50s?

Spotlight on crime – the Celestial Empire of 'China'

'China' was an area of Merthyr which came to be known as 'Little Hell' and which was situated near to the Cyfarthfa ironworks in the district of Georgetown (see Figure 7.5). By the 1840s China had become a den of drunkards, thieves, rogues and, above all, prostitutes and their minders. It was a haven for the criminal element of the town, a region where there was little, if any, formal policing. Entrance into China was under an arch and there were doorkeepers to send messages warning the residents. Few strangers were able to return safely from China with all their possessions.

China's criminal underworld

The criminals ruled themselves and this 'Celestial Empire' was dominated by the most powerful criminals who were given the titles of 'Emperor' and 'Empress' (see Source Q). China became a hiding place for criminals hoping to escape the arm of the law. A wanted person could stay hidden and protected within the criminal underworld that operated within China. Constables entered this district at their peril for its occupants would gang together to resist the arrest of any of its inmates.

The most widespread crime within China was linked to prostitution, namely petty theft. There were said to be up to 60 prostitutes operating in this district in the period 1839–40. They were instructed by their minders or 'Bullies' to steal from their clients, waiting for them to become drunk before they stole items of worth. Due to the commonality of surnames the women acquired working names such as Margaret Llewellyn, better known as 'Peggy Two Constables', Jane Thomas or 'Big Jane' and Margaret Evans 'The Buffalo'. Such women were protected by the 'Bullies' who often assisted them in their robberies. These Bullies also protected their partners in crime, the prostitutes, by making sure that the police did not arrest them and if they did, securing a quick release, and also protecting them from other members of the criminal underworld.

China's close proximity to the High Street and Market Square provided another group of criminals known as the 'Rodnies' with rich pickings. 'Rodnies' were child thieves and pickpockets operating under the supervision of Fagin-like gang masters. They were perpetual criminals who were constantly charged with petty crimes (see Source R).

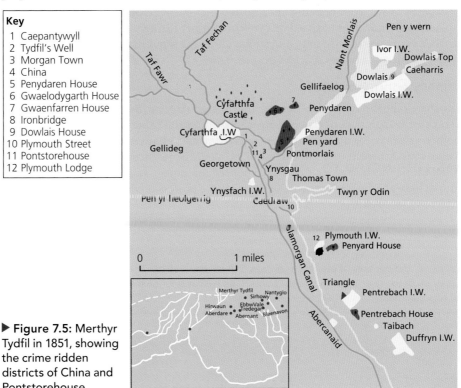

Key
1 Caepantywyll
2 Tydfil's Well
3 Morgan Town
4 China
5 Penydaren House
6 Gwaelodygarth House
7 Gwaenfarren House
8 Ironbridge
9 Dowlais House
10 Plymouth Street
11 Pontstorehouse
12 Plymouth Lodge

▶ **Figure 7.5:** Merthyr Tydfil in 1851, showing the crime ridden districts of China and Pontstorehouse

Source Q: A description of the crime ridden district of China in Merthyr Tydfil, which appeared in the *Morning Chronicle* newspaper in April 1850

... mere huts of stone – low, confined, ill-lighted and unventilated; they are built without pretensions to regularity, and form a maze of courts and tortuous lanes ... Like the unhappy and lawless people who inhabit it, the place has an alias, and is generally known by the name of 'China' ... Here it is that, in a congenial atmosphere, the crime, disease and penury of Merthyr are for the most part located. Thieves, prostitutes, vagrants, the idle, the reckless, and the dissolute, here live in a miserable companionship.

Source R: An account of two thieves working under a master which appeared in the *Merthyr Guardian* newspaper in 1849

John Sweeny and John Williams, two notorious thieves, living at China, were charged on suspicion of stealing a till containing about £3 from the shop of Mr Jones ... Superintendent Wrenn stated the prisoners were seen lurking about the premises at the time the till was stolen; they were notorious thieves; Williams had been in custody 20 times; they lived in China, at the house of Jenkin Rees, alias 'Shenkin Bach', who employed them and took them about the country to steal.

Attempts to police China

During the 1840s efforts were made to clean up China and restore law and order. Between May 1846 and May 1847, over 50 criminals of the 'Empire' were apprehended. The Emperor and Empress, Benjamin Richards and Anne Evans, were arrested, found guilty of various crimes and sentenced to transportation, but as soon as they left other criminals took their place and inherited the imperial titles. When things got too hot in China a previous Emperor, John Jones, alias 'Shoni Sgubor Fawr', a bare-knuckle mountain fighter, thief and minder of prostitutes, moved west along with his friend, Dai'r Cantwr, where they later took a leading part in the Rebecca Riots of 1839–44 (see page 158).

Yet within this criminal underworld there was an element of self-policing and the use of the ceffyl pren or wooden horse (see page 221) was not unknown. In 1834, Anne Harman, who was accused by her peers of being unfaithful to her husband on several occasions, was forcibly placed on a ladder and carried in a violent manner through China to the house of her mother, being pelted with mud and stones along the way. On this occasion public humiliation was deemed to be sufficient punishment.

China finally conquered

Following the establishment of the Glamorgan Constabulary in 1841 efforts were made to tackle the high rates of crime in areas like China and other criminal dens like Pontstorehouse, where the inhabitants were referred to as 'Cellarites' due to the numerous cellars being found there. It took time to establish a police presence and command respect but by 1860 China was in decline. Continued police harassment and sterner sentences were beginning to have an impact. By the 1870s many of the professional criminals had moved to Cardiff for richer pickings.

> **THINK** ?
>
> To what extent did the area of Merthyr known as 'China' deserve its reputation as the 'chief crime district' of the town? Use Sources Q and R, as well as your own knowledge, to help you answer this question.

The impact of the growth of urban Merthyr Tydfil on changes in policing in the nineteenth century

As Merthyr Tydfil developed as an industrial town, its rapidly expanding population forced the need to modify, update and enlarge the system used to maintain law and order. The authorities in Merthyr, namely the ratepayers, were slow to react to the need for change and it took instances of serious rioting, such as the Rising of 1831, and the sharp rise in crimes during periods of economic recession to eventually cause them to change their attitude and release funds to finance the setting up of a police force.

Failings of the inherited system of law and order

Traditionally the responsibility for ensuring that law and order was maintained rested with the community. At the top of the hierarchy of responsibility was the Lord Lieutenant of the County of Glamorgan and below him the Sheriff. However, in practical terms, by the early eighteenth century this responsibility had fallen upon the shoulders of the justices of the peace and their helpers, the parish constable. JPs served as the local magistrates, administering justice through the Quarter Session Courts which met four times a year, but the day-to-day policing duties were performed by the parish constables.

Constables were elected annually from among the better-off tradesmen of the town. Service was compulsory and had to be performed on top of any existing job, helping to make the task generally unpopular. During times of trouble, the constable could be reinforced by the appointment of temporary 'special constables' sworn in for the occasion. When Merthyr was just a hamlet this system had generally worked and had proved effective over the centuries in maintaining law and order. However, the rapid growth of Merthyr during the early nineteenth century quickly overwhelmed the old system which had been designed to be used amongst a sparsely populated agricultural community. By the 1830s, as Merthyr's population had grown to over 20,000, the inherited system was proving to be totally inadequate. There were areas of the town which had fallen outside the rule of law – areas like China and Pontshorehouse, which were controlled by the villains who operated there.

Popular disturbances and the use of the military

In an emergency, as was the case with disturbances and rioting in 1800, 1816 and 1831, the authorities would have to call upon the support of the local militia forces to help restore law and order. In September 1800 a disturbance broke out in Merthyr, caused by high food prices and a scarcity of food (mainly grain) following a poor harvest. Workers expressed their discontent by attacking the company truck shop belonging to the Penydarren ironworks, forcing the shopkeepers to reduce their prices. The protest was only stopped following the arrival of troops, 20 soldiers of the 7th Dragoons, who had marched from Gloucester. They promptly arrested the ringleaders, but it was only the prompt request for military support by one of the town's magistrates that had prevented the rioting from escalating further (see Source S).

> **Source S: Letter written by G. Lyndon requesting that military assistance be sent to Merthyr from the barracks at Brecon**
>
> Monday, 4 o'clock
>
> Sir,
>
> The Riot is now at such a height that it will be impossible to Quell it without the Assistance of the Military. Morgan Lewis' shop is totally demolished, the Goods taken out & carried away, & what will be the end nobody knows. Immediate assistance must be had. I fancy 2000 People are at present doing all the Mischief they can. Morgan Lewis' shop is not the only one destroyed. They have stop'd everything at Cyfarthfa & Penydarren but the furnaces.
>
> I am yours,
>
> G. Lyndon, 22 September.

In 1816 there was a strike by workers across south-east Wales. A depression in the iron trade had resulted in ironmasters reducing the wages of their workers by up to 40 per cent and this took place at a time when the price of food was rising sharply. In Merthyr there were riots and the workers took over the ironworks, halting production (see Source T).

> **Source T: Part of a letter written by William Crawshay the owner of the Cyfarthfa ironworks to John Guest of the Dowlais ironworks informing him of the disturbances. Guest was away in North Africa this time**
>
> 16 October 1816, 9 o'clock by our time … The enemy in too great strength to oppose with any probability of success, have possessed themselves of all our Works and wholly stopped them … My spies tell me they threaten hard your shop, for they are hungry. I have been in the midst of them all and found as usual argument useless. I have just had a messenger from Mr Hill. He says all his works are stopped the same as ours.

As in 1800 it took the arrival of troops, the Glamorgan Militia who had rushed to Merthyr from Cardiff, to bring an end to the strike and restore peace to the town (see Source U). There were no further outbreaks of discontent for over a decade, the 1820s being a time of relative prosperity for the iron industry. However, there was a growth in radicalism which culminated in the Merthyr Rising of 1831.

▲ **Source U:** Soldiers of the Glamorgan Militia under the command of Captain Ray arriving to control the disturbances in Merthyr in 1816

THINK **?**

1 Why had the traditional system of maintaining law and order in Merthyr collapsed by the 1830s?

2 Using Sources S, T and U together with your own knowledge of this topic, complete the following table:

Year	Summary of the disturbance	How was law and order restored?
1800		
1816		
1831		

The Merthyr Rising of 1831 and its impact

A depression in the iron industry which started in 1829 led to wage cuts and rising unemployment. Many workers ran into increasing debt and this resulted in the Court of Requests ordering the widespread confiscation of property which was unpopular. This coincided with a demand by middle-class radicals for an extension of the vote which only added to the growing discontent in the area. The spark which ignited the rioting was the decision by the ironmaster William Crawshay to cut the wages of his ironstone miners and to lay off 84 **puddlers**, some of his highest-paid ironworkers.

On 2 June 1831, a large crowd marched through Merthyr, raiding shops and houses, driving off the magistrates and special constables. Soldiers were summoned from Brecon but their arrival did not stop a large crowd from attacking the Castle Inn in the centre of the town, which was where the magistrates, special constables and soldiers had set up their headquarters. On 3 June, a crowd of upwards of 7,000 gathered outside the Inn, causing the soldiers to open fire. In the resulting skirmish 16 soldiers were wounded and at least two dozen rioters were killed and over 70 wounded (see Source V). The authorities were forced to flee to Penydarren House but it was not until 6 June that law and order was restored to the town.

On 13 July 1831, the trials began in Cardiff Assizes of 28 men and women on charges connected with the rising. Most were sentenced to imprisonment, four to transportation for 14 years or life, and one, Richard Lewis (Dic Penderyn) was sentenced to death for wounding a soldier, Donald Black. The rising caused the ironmasters and ratepayers to question whether Merthyr was in need of some kind of professional police force.

> **Source V: An account of the events outside the Castle Inn on 3 June as described by William Crawshay in his book** *The Late Riots at Merthyr Tydfil* (1831)
>
> The most terrific fight followed ... the soldiers were nearly overcome; the major and many men were wounded and knocked down by bludgeons, and stabbed by the bayonets taken from them ... The soldiers who had been placed in the windows ... fired on the mob in the street. Three were killed dead upon the spot at the first fire ... after most determined and resolute fighting, on both sides, for a quarter of an hour, the few brave Highlanders ... succeeded in putting the rioters to flight ... Major Falls was most severely cut about the head, and was covered with blood; two of the Highlanders were carried in nearly lifeless, with contusion of the brain; and the streets and house were deluged with blood, from the dreadful wounds in the head given by the bludgeons of the mob to the soldiers.

> **THINK**   ?
> To what extent was the rising of 1831 a serious threat to the maintenance of law and order in Merthyr?

Experiments in early policing

The Merthyr Rising of 1831 had highlighted the problem of law enforcement. In an attempt to restore order in the town the magistrates had requested that some of the constables of the Metropolitan Police force be sent down from London. They asked for two sergeants and between four and six experienced constables to help organise their special constables but they only received three retired policemen. One of them, however, Thomas Jamieson, was soon after appointed the Chief Police Officer of Merthyr on a salary of £80. His appointment demonstrates a shift in attitude within a section of the community, namely the magistrates and ironmasters, who had come to realise the value of having a professional police force in the town.

However, the experiment was short lived. The continued presence of the militia in the town together with a feeling that the force was too expensive to operate, resulted in the dismissal of Jamieson. In 1834 the *Merthyr Guardian* newspaper reported that the town was now only patrolled by two constables, a force which was insufficient to handle the depth of crime. To punish the apprehended criminals the constables could make use of the old stocks or a lock-up which was used as a place of confinement to house disorderly persons. Nicknamed the 'black hole' this lock-up had been built in 1809 and consisted of a wooden shack measuring between 3.5 and 4.2 metres. Inside it was dark, damp and unpleasant, and did not prove to be a very secure place of confinement.

Establishment of the Glamorgan County Constabulary, 1841

The rising of 1831 and the growth of Chartism during the 1830s, which culminated in the march on Newport in 1839, worried the middle classes of Merthyr. They became increasingly concerned over the protection of their property and this caused them to release funds to establish a police force. The Glamorgan County Constabulary was formed in October 1841 to police the industrialised region of the county. Its Chief Constable was an ex-Rifle Brigade officer, Captain Charles Napier, who held the post from 1841 to 1867. Out of a total force of 34 men, 12 were assigned to Merthyr Tydfil and Dowlais. They formed the 'A' Division of the county force.

The inappropriateness of the 'black hole' as a place of confinement led Captain Napier to request the building of a police station in Merthyr (see Source W). It was opened in 1844 in Graham Street in the centre of the town, with an additional station being opened at Dowlais in 1862 and at Merthyr Vale in 1898.

> **Source W: A request made by the Chief Constable, Captain Napier, to a meeting of ratepayers in the early 1840s**
>
> I have inspected the cells at present in use at Merthyr and found them totally unfit for the reception of prisoners, indeed so much so that the magistrates find it necessary to place prisoners at public houses in charge of a constable, at considerable expense to the County ... I urge the construction of a station house at Merthyr, not only for placing the men under the eye of the Superintendent, but also for the security of the prisoners. The dampness of the present cells render them totally unfit for the reception of prisoners [and] ... they are so extensively insecure.

In charge of Merthyr 'A' Division was Superintendent Davies, an experienced officer who had served as a constable and later sergeant in the Metropolitan Police and also as a superintendent in the Essex Constabulary. Below him an inspector was placed in charge of each of the three stations, residing there with his family and any unmarried constables. The constables were forced to operate under strict rules, especially relating to their private lives. When not on duty they were required to specify where they would be so that they could be contacted if needed. Money was deducted from their wages to cover accommodation and living costs, and if a constable missed work due to illness, 1s was deducted from his wages for each day's absence.

The effectiveness of Merthyr's first police force

A force of just 13 men hoping to maintain law and order in a town with a population of over 46,000 was always going to be a difficult challenge. The impact and effectiveness of the force in its early days was limited. Two reasons impacted upon this, the first being the problem of recruiting sufficient numbers of suitable men. Constables were expected to display 'honesty, sobriety and a sound constitution' together with knowledge of the Welsh language and the ability to keep accounts, as well as the ability to read and write. The second, more serious problem, was being able to retain good constables who, with such skills, could earn much higher wages in the ironworks.

To begin with Superintendent Davies realised that it would take some time to establish a presence in the lawless areas of China and Pontstorehouse and so these areas were not included in the beats patrolled by the constables. However, two police constables were put on each of the two beats adjoining these areas at night. When it became necessary to enter either China or Pontstorehouse the whole body of the police would enter, led by the Superintendent (see Source X).

During the 1840s, the police continued with their efforts to enforce law and order and by the 1850s the beat had been extended to the whole town, although it was not until the end of the century that it was possible for just one constable to patrol the 'China' district. While there certainly was a police presence in the town it was not until September 1908 that it had its own district force with the establishment of the 'Merthyr Tydfil Borough Police Force' (see Source Y).

> ### Source X: Chief Constable Napier's description of the beat system that operated in Merthyr
>
> One Sergeant and five Constables are set on night duty every night at 9 pm and remain out until 5 am. Before retiring the men who have come off duty clean the station. In addition the two day Sergeants patrol alternatively as Inspectors during the night to see that all duties are performed. The whole of the town is traversed during the night by these two Sergeants. The Sergeant who has the early night patrol goes to bed at one, and is out again at six, while the other patrols from one to six and is expected to be clean and ready for duty at 10am, at which hour two Sergeants and one Constable must be ready for day duty and to attend to magistrates' meetings.

Conclusion

By the end of the nineteenth century the levels of crime in Merthyr had been considerably reduced when compared to what it had been like mid-century. By the 1860s, the iron industry was showing the first signs of decline and workers had begun to leave the town for the new steel plants being built along the coast or for the rapidly expanding coal mines in the Rhondda and Aberdare valleys. By this time a range of organisations had been established to help promote alternative leisure activities as a distraction to crime, such as the Young Men's Improvement Society, a Library Association and Temperance Recreation Associations. The growth in chapel attendance together with the associated fêtes, excursions, musical and sports events, all helped to improve the range of leisure alternatives. By the 1870s the *Merthyr Guardian* could claim that the habits of the people of Merthyr had improved. The establishment of an organised and disciplined police force had also proved of prime importance in helping to keep the criminal underworld in check and reduce crime levels to what they had been much earlier in the century.

▲ **Source Y:** The Glamorgan Constabulary Merthyr Contingent pictured in 1895.

> ### ACTIVITY
>
> Use the internet, together with your knowledge of this topic, to compile a report detailing the growth and development of the 'Merthyr Division' of the Glamorgan County Police Force. You may wish to use the following sub-headings to help structure your report:
>
> - Origins of the Merthyr Division
> - Merthyr's first police station
> - Establishing law and order over the whole of Merthyr
> - Development of the Merthyr Division during the second half of the nineteenth century.

FOCUS TASK REVISITED

Look back at the table you have completed as you have worked through this chapter. Use your findings to help you make a judgement about the development of crime and law enforcement in Merthyr during the nineteenth century by answering the following questions:

1 To what extent did the rapid development of Merthyr Tydfil in the nineteenth century cause a growth in crime?

2 How successful, in your opinion, were the attempts at law enforcement in Merthyr Tydfil at each of the following dates: (a) 1800, (b) 1850 and (c) 1899? Support your answer with evidence.

TOPIC SUMMARY

- The town of Merthyr Tydfil grew rapidly due to the growth of the iron industry.
- There were four large ironworks in Merthyr – Dowlais, Cyfarthfa, Plymouth and Penydarren.
- The demand for workers caused many people to migrate to Merthyr causing the population of the town to grow from 7,705 in 1801 to 51,949 by 1861.
- Ironmasters had to build houses for their workers close to the ironworks and coal mines.
- There were no building regulations and the housing was closely packed, with no piped water or any sewage disposal system.
- Frequent outbreaks of disease such as cholera and typhoid caused serious public health concerns.
- Workers were paid monthly and often in tokens which could only be spent in the company tommy shops where prices were higher.
- Workers frequently went into debt and their poverty was a factor in the rise in crime rates.
- Slum housing developed in areas of the town such as China and Pontstorehouse which became the centres of crime.
- China was the crime-ridden centre of Merthyr and was home to prostitutes, pickpockets, petty thieves and other criminal elements.
- China was ruled over by its own Emperor and Empress, the chief criminals.
- As Merthyr continued to grow the traditional method of maintaining law and order began to fail, causing crime to go undetected and unpunished.
- Popular disturbances in 1800 and 1816, together with the Rising of 1831, caused the authorities to begin to experiment in policing.
- The Glamorgan County Constabulary was formed in 1841 and a force of 13 constables was based in Merthyr.
- A police station was opened in Merthyr in 1844.
- It took several decades before all areas of Merthyr, including China, came under an effective system of policing.
- The new police force did have an impact on reducing levels of crime in Merthyr.
- Merthyr had its own Borough Police Force established in 1908.

Practice questions

1 Describe the development of the police force in Merthyr after 1841.
(*For guidance, see page 255.*)

2 Explain why areas such as 'China' in nineteenth century Merthyr were significant in the development of crime and policing in Wales. (*For guidance, see pages 258–9.*)

WJEC Examination Guidance

This section will give you step-by-step guidance on how best to approach and answer the types of questions that you will face in the exam. Below is model exam paper with a set of exam-style questions (without the sources).

Unit three: thematic study

In Question 1 you have to provide a specific historical term to complete the sentence. It may be a name, date, specific method or crime related term.

In Question 2 you have to compare and contrast what you can see in three sources. You need to pick out features that are the same/similar and also points of difference/contrast.

In Question 3 you have to demonstrate your own knowledge and understanding of a key feature. You should aim to include specific factual detail.

In Question 4 you have to demonstrate your own knowledge and understanding of a key feature, and include specific information relating to Wales and the Welsh context.

In Question 5 you have to identify a number of reasons to explain why a key development/issue was important or significant. You should aim to include specific factual detail.

In Question 6 you have to use your knowledge to explain the importance/significance/effectiveness of a key issue. You need to provide specific information relating to Wales and the Welsh context.

3A Changes in Crime and Punishment, c.1500 to the present day

Time allowed: 1 hour and 15 minutes

1 Complete the sentences below with an accurate term.

    a) Streets in some Tudor towns were patrolled at night by ....

    b) The Bow Street Runners were established by Henry ....

    c) The Metropolitan Police Act was passed in 18 ....

    d) A type of prison for young offenders first opened in 1902 was called ....   **[4 marks]**

2 Look at the three sources which show types of punishment used over time and answer the question that follows.

Use Sources A, B and C to identify one similarity and one difference in the methods of punishing criminals over time.   **[4 marks]**

[Use at least two of the sources to answer the question]

3 Describe the role of a Tudor justice of the peace in combating crime.   **[6 marks]**

4 Describe the work of John Howard in reforming prisons in the late eighteenth century.   **[6 marks]**

[In your answer you are advised to refer to the state of prisons in Wales at this time]

5 Explain why opportunities for crime increased by the end of the eighteenth century.   **[12 marks]**

6 Explain why areas such as 'China' in nineteenth century Merthyr were significant in the development of crime and policing in Wales.   **[12 marks]**

7 To what extent has poverty been the main cause of crime over time?   **[16 marks]**

In your answer you should:

■ show how poverty has been a cause of crime over three historical eras

■ discuss the importance of other causes of crime over three historical eras

■ include direct references to the history of Wales.

Marks for spelling, punctuation and the accurate use of grammar and specialist language are allocated to this question.   **[4 marks]**

Total marks for the paper: 64

In Question 7 you have to develop a two-sided answer which provides specific evidence to support and counter the key issue named in the question. You must cover three historical time periods and you must provide detail on the Welsh context. Remember to check your spelling, punctuation and grammar.

Examination guidance for the WJEC examination

Examination guidance for Question 1

This section provides guidance on how to answer the factual knowledge questions. Look at the following question:

> Complete the sentences below with an accurate term.
> a) An important law officer during Tudor times was the parish ....
> b) A famous eighteenth century highway robber was Dick ....
> c) Protests in south-west Wales which involved the smashing of tollgates were known as the .... Riots
> d) The Metropolitan Police Act was passed in 18 ....

How to answer

- Make sure you revise your notes well – these questions require good factual knowledge.
- In your revision concentrate upon key issues such as:
  - ☐ the different types of crime common in a particular period
  - ☐ the reasons for the growth in crime at certain time periods
  - ☐ the reasons for the development of policing at particular periods
  - ☐ the names of important individuals connected with the development of policing
  - ☐ the different types of punishment common in different time periods
  - ☐ the reasons why the methods of punishment have changed over time
  - ☐ key developments in the history of crime and punishment.
- If in doubt, have a guess – never leave the space blank.

Example

> a) An important law officer during Tudor times was the parish constable.
> b) A famous eighteenth century highway robber was Dick Turpin.
> c) Protests in south-west Wales which involved the smashing of tollgates were known as the Rebecca Riots.
> d) The Metropolitan Police Act was passed in 1829.

> **Now try answering the following question:**
>
> Complete the sentences below with an accurate term.
> a) During Tudor times criminals guilty of petty crime were placed in the ....
> b) The crime-ridden district of nineteenth-century Merthyr Tydfil was known as ....
> c) Floating prisons during the eighteenth century were in old warships known as ....
> d) Capital punishment in England and Wales was finally abolished in 19 ....

Examination guidance for Question 2

This section provides guidance on how to answer the 'similarity and difference' question. You will have to pick out information from three sources to identify both similarities and differences. Look at the following question:

> Look at the three sources below which show different methods of punishment over time. Use Sources A, B and C to identify one similarity and one difference in the methods of punishment over time.

THE PILLORY (16TH CENTURY).

▲ **Source A** Two men placed in the pillory during the sixteenth century

▲ **Source C** A prison in the twenty-first century

▲ **Source B** A public execution during the eighteenth century

How to answer

- Study the three sources – pick out features that are the same or similar.
- Pick out points that contrast – which show things that are different.
- Make sure you refer to both similarity **and** difference in your answer.

Example

The sources show that society has always punished people for committing crime. The punishments shown in Sources A and B were undertaken in public and were intended to both entertain the crowd and deter others from committing such crimes. The two sources show how punishment in public remained the same across several centuries. Sources B and C are more extreme punishments, both aiming to take the criminal away from society.

Step 1: Identify features of similarity – things which are the same across the sources.

The sources also show how punishment has changed over time. In Source C the criminal is punished by being locked away out of sight of society. In Sources A and B the punishment is taking place in full public view. This shows that attitudes to punishment have changed over time, becoming less acceptable of extreme and humiliating methods.

Step 2: Identify features of difference – things which contrast and are not the same across the sources.

Now try answering the following question:

Look at the three sources below, which show different methods of policing. Use Sources A, B and C to identify one similarity and one difference in the methods of policing over time.

▲ Source A A night watchman in the late sixteenth century

▲ Source B A modern police officer

◀ Source C A contemporary print showing the Bow Street Runners in action, capturing two muggers in 1806

Examination guidance for Question 3

This section provides guidance on how to answer a 'describe' question. You will have to demonstrate your own knowledge and understanding of a key feature. Look at the following question:

> Describe the role of the parish constable during Tudor times.

How to answer

- You need to identify and describe at least two key features.
- Only include information that is directly relevant.
- Be specific, avoid generalised comments.

Example

Step 1: Identify and develop a key reason/feature, supporting it with specific detail.

Parish constables were appointed annually from among the tradesmen and farmers of the area. They were expected to undertake their role alongside their existing job. They were answerable to the justice of the peace who monitored their day-to-day duties. The main part of their job concerned general policing duties, dealing with unruly behaviour or petty theft. They had the power to make arrests and were responsible for ensuring accused individuals appeared before the JP and were held securely until their trial.

Step 2: Identify and develop other key reasons/features. Aim to cover two to three reasons/features in some detail.

Parish constables were also expected to carry out a range of other tasks such as the prevention of trespassing and poaching, the impounding of stray animals, and the watching out for vagabonds. A further aspect of their work involved the administering of punishments as ordered by the justice of the peace. This normally involved such things as the public whipping of those accused of being vagabonds, and placing those found guilty of petty crimes in the stocks or pillory. In times of need the parish constable could call upon fellow citizens to help with the hue and cry and the pursuit of criminals across parish lands.

Now try to answer the following question:

Describe the work of Henry Fielding in the setting up of the Bow Street Runners.

Examination guidance for Question 4

This section provides guidance on how to answer a 'describe' question. You will have to demonstrate your own knowledge and understanding of a key feature and make references to the Welsh context, providing specific examples. Look at the following question:

> Describe the use of transportation to Australia as a punishment in the eighteenth and nineteenth centuries.
>
> In your answer you are advised to refer to the Welsh context and provide examples from Wales.

How to answer

- You need to identify and describe at least two key features.
- Only include information that is directly relevant.
- Be specific, avoid generalised comments.
- You must make sure you make reference to the Welsh context and provide specific Welsh examples.

Example

The first convoy of ships carrying convicts to Australia reached Botany Bay on 26 January 1788. It was a nine-month voyage from Britain. Over the next eighty years over 160,000 criminals were transported to Australia, and within this number over 2,200 were sent from Wales. Transportation was seen as a method of getting rid of the criminal element of society and as an alternative to execution. By the 1770s there was increasing opposition to the harshness of the Bloody Code and there were calls for alternative forms of punishment to hanging to be found. Transportation was seen as the answer. It had the advantage of not having to house criminals in prisons in England and Wales and it was hoped that the fear of banishment to the other side of the world would serve as a deterrent and reduce crime levels.

Step 1: Identify and develop a key reason/feature, supporting it with specific detail.

The majority of the criminals sent from Wales to Australia had been convicted of horse or sheep stealing, burglary, house-breaking or theft of items from a person. Francis Williams, who travelled on the first convey ship carrying female convicts to Australia in 1787, had been convicted of house-breaking and the theft of laundry. For these crimes she was given a sentence of seven years' transportation. A few Welsh convicts were convicted of more serious crimes such as taking part in popular disturbances. Lewis was found guilty of being one of the leaders of the Merthyr Rising of 1831 and was sentenced to transportation for life. John Jones was sentenced to transportation for life for his part in the Rebecca Riots of 1839–44, while his accomplice David Davies received a twenty-year sentence. The use of transportation continued until 1868, although it had been stopped in some parts of Australia such as New South Wales as early as 1839.

Step 2: Identify and develop other key reasons/features. Aim to cover two to three reasons/features in some detail, including specific reference to Wales/Welsh examples.

> ## Now try to answer the following question:
>
> Describe the attempts made in industrial towns like Merthyr Tydfil to improve policing during the second half of the nineteenth century.
>
> In your answer you are advised to refer to the Welsh context and provide examples from Wales.

Examination guidance for Question 5

This section provides guidance on how to answer the explanation question. This requires you to identify and discuss a number of reasons to explain why a key development/issue was important or significant. Look at the following question:

> Explain why prison reformers were important in helping to secure improved conditions in prisons during the late eighteenth and early nineteenth centuries.

How to answer

- You should aim to give a variety of explained reasons.
- Try to include specific details such as names, dates, events, developments and consequences.
- Always support your statements with examples.
- Remember that you need to provide a judgement, evaluating the importance or significance of the named individual, development or issue.

Example

Step 1: Provide several reasons to support the view that the factor mentioned in the question was important or significant. Include specific factual detail to support your judgement.

The work of a small number of prison reformers played a very important and significant role in securing improved conditions in prisons during the late eighteenth and early nineteenth centuries. They visited prisons, gathered together evidence of the harsh and squalid conditions they found, reported on the cruel and unfair treatment of prisoners, and came to the conclusion that prisons were badly run and unhealthy institutions. Through the work of three reformers, John Howard, George O. Paul and Elizabeth Fry, pressure was put on the government to investigate prison conditions and this eventually resulted in the passing of the Gaols Act in 1823 which was a major turning point in prison reform.

Step 2: Make sure you provide a reasoned judgement upon the degree of importance or significance. Make links to the longer-term impact.

John Howard visited many prisons and wrote up his findings in a book, 'The State of the Prisons in England and Wales' in 1777. This was an important work because it provided a detailed report on the bad state of prisons. Howard gave evidence to parliament and he called for the building of new prisons which would separate prisoners according to their crimes and sexes, and provide clean and damp-free cells which had means of sanitation. He also called for gaolers to be given a wage so that they would no longer charge prisoners for food and bedding. He wanted prisons to be inspected regularly. Another important reformer was George O. Paul who published his research in a book called 'Thoughts on the Alarming Progress of Gaol Fever' in 1784. He was important because he campaigned for the building of new model prisons based upon three principles – security, health and separation, such as the one he had built in Gloucester. Its design was later copied in the construction of new prisons in other towns. The third important reformer was Elizabeth Fry who did much to improve conditions for female prisoners in Newgate prison in London. In 1817 she formed the 'Association for the Improvement of Women Prisoners in Newgate'. Her campaigning resulted in rules being drawn up to regulate life in prison. Female warders were appointed, regular work such as needlework was introduced and schools set up. As a direct result of the campaigns of such prison reformers as Howard, Paul and Fry the government began to take charge of the running of prisons, the Gaols Act of 1823 starting this process. These reformers therefore played a very important and significant role in securing these changes.

Now try to answer the following question:

Explain why changes in technology were significant in the development of policing in the twentieth century

Examination guidance for Question 6

This section provides guidance on how to answer the question that relates to the study of a historic environment connected with crime and punishment. It is an explanation question which requires you to identify and discuss a number of reasons to explain why a key development/issue was important or significant. Look at the following question:

> Explain why the growth of industrial towns like Merthyr Tydfil were significant in causing a rise in crime during the early nineteenth century.

How to answer

- You should aim to give a variety of explained reasons.
- Try to include specific details such as names, dates, events, developments and consequences.
- Explain how and why the historical environment under study brought about such changes.
- Remember that you need to provide a judgement, evaluating the importance or significance of the named individual, development or issue.
- Remember the Welsh context – give specific examples relating to Wales.

Example

The Industrial Revolution resulted in the development of factories and the growth of towns in which they were sited. In the case of Merthyr its population grew dramatically from just over 7,700 in 1801 to over 46,000 by 1851, making it the largest industrial town in Wales. Urban growth was a primary cause of a rise of crime in many towns. The demand for workers caused the building of large numbers of houses, most of which were built without any planning regulations or concern over public health. They were closely packed and lacked supplies of clean water and any sewage disposal system. Living conditions quickly deteriorated, resulting in frequent outbreaks of disease and the development of slum areas such as those in the China and Pontstorehouse areas of the town. Poor living and housing conditions were therefore significant factors in causing a sharp rise in crime in Merthyr, as poverty caused people to turn to crime in order to survive.

Step 1: Provide several reasons to support the view that the factor mentioned in the question was important/significant. Include specific factual detail to support your judgement.

Another aspect of poverty which had an impact upon crime was wage reduction and regulation. Most of the workers in Merthyr were employed in the ironworks, the ironstone mines or coal mines. They were paid monthly and part of their wages were in tokens. These could only be spent at the company Truck shops which charged higher prices than ordinary shops. By the end of each month many workers had fallen into debt and were forced to borrow money or turn to crime. This situation was made worse during times of depression when the ironmasters laid off workers or cut their wages. This was common in Merthyr during the early nineteenth century and families without a wage coming in had little option but to turn to petty crime to survive. Bad harvests could also have a serious impact as these caused a sharp rise in food prices. As a result protests were common when people took to the streets to complain about high food prices, wage cuts and poor living conditions. Violence was often the result as shops were attacked and looted. The lack of any police force meant that crime went unchecked and many of the culprits went unpunished. This provided opportunities in industrial towns like Merthyr, Swansea and Cardiff to experience an increase in crime.

Step 2: Make sure you provide a reasoned judgement upon the degree of importance/significance. You must make reference to the Welsh context and include specific examples relating to Wales.

As these industrial towns grew so rapidly the inherited system of maintaining law and order using JPs and parish constables failed to cope with the increase in crime levels. The lack of an organised and effective police force explains the sharp rise in crime in towns like Merthyr. Areas like China became the haven for criminals and even when a police force was established in Merthyr in 1841 the new constables only entered China as a group for fear of being attacked. China had its own criminal underworld, ruled over its 'Emperor' and 'Empress', and it was not until much later in the century that the police force was able to gain control over this empire of crime. Industrial development created the environment for crime to develop and provided increased opportunities for criminal activity.

Now try to answer the following question:

Explain why rapid industrialisation in towns like Merthyr Tydfil was significant in the development of policing during the nineteenth century.

Examination guidance for Question 7

This section provides guidance on how to answer the synoptic question which requires you to use your knowledge to analyse and evaluate the importance of a key issue against other issues. Look at the following question:

> To what extent has the use of a police force been the main method of combating crime over time?

How to answer

- You need to develop a two-sided answer which has balance and good support.
- You should start by discussing the key factor mentioned in the question, using your knowledge to explain why this factor was most effective, important or significant.
- You then need to consider a counter-argument, discussing a range of other relevant factors.
- Make sure your answer covers three historical time periods – the medieval, early modern and modern era.
- You must include a number of specific references to the Welsh context, i.e. say what was happening in Wales.
- Conclude your answer with a reasoned and well-supported judgement.

Example

It is only since the early nineteenth century with the development of the Metropolitan Police force that a formal method of policing has been in use and that did not spread across the whole country until the second half of that century. Before this, the methods used to combat crime relied upon the community policing itself through the actions of unpaid law officers.

Step 1: Introduce the topic to be analysed and discussed in the answer.

During the Tudor and Stuart times community policing using such methods as the hue and cry were still in use but the JPs, constables and watchmen had become more important as the principal law enforcers. The Act of Union of 1536 introduced the English legal system upon Wales and many members of the Welsh gentry such as Sir Edward Stradling and Sir John Wynn were quick to occupy the important posts of justice of the peace which gave them added social status. JPs could send people to be flogged, whipped and punished but on top of that they had many other jobs such as licensing alehouses. The JP's job became very burdensome. Constables were part-time and unpaid. They had to do their own job on top of the work of a constable. At the lowest level watchmen were paid to patrol the streets but were often unfit for the job and not very effective. The idea of an organised, paid and professional police force did not exist before the early nineteenth century. It was generally expected and accepted that society would police itself.

Step 2: Discuss the key factor identified in the question – this should relate to one time period. Provide specific factual detail, remembering to make links to what was happening in Wales.

The Industrial Revolution which started in the eighteenth century caused a sharp rise in population and with it the growth of large industrial towns. In these growing towns the JPs, constables and watchmen struggled to deal with rising levels of crime. As a result some private individuals took the issue of policing into their own hands and began to experiment with the introduction of private police forces. In the 1750s in London Henry Fielding set up the Bow Street Runners. They were paid, full-time and later trained and were quite effective. They lowered crime rates but were not that successful as they could only patrol in Bow Street. Other methods of policing included

Step 3: Begin to develop a counter-argument – this should relate to a different time period. Make links to other time periods to show improvement/changes or lack of improvements/changes that have taken place. Make links to Wales.

the Horse Patrol, River Police and the newspaper called 'Hue and Cry', which was set up by John Fielding. This was the start of a paid force that also worked full time. However, it only touched upon a small area of London and had no impact upon other areas such as Wales where community policing continued to the norm.

Step 4: Continue with the argument and counter-argument, selecting other time periods to illustrate change/improvement. Remember to provide links to what was happening in Wales.

The biggest change in policing, however, came in the nineteenth century. In industrial towns like Merthyr centres of crime like China were developing, attracting large numbers of criminals, operating in small highly populated areas. Central London was particularly burdened with crimes such as pickpocketing. Recognising a need for change the then Home Secretary, Robert Peel, set up the Metropolitan Police force in 1829. The new constables, or 'Peelers', were trained, paid and employed full-time. They proved to be very effective in controlling and reducing crime in central London and in 1856 the Rural Police Act made it compulsory for all towns across England and Wales to set up their own police forces. Some regions of Wales had already followed the London example, Denbighshire being the first county to establish a Constabulary in 1840, followed by Glamorgan in 1841. Boroughs quickly followed with forces being set up in Swansea, Cardiff, Neath and Pwllheli by mid-century. Merthyr opened its police station in 1844, operating a force of twelve constables. This was a major change in the methods of combating crime, placing the responsibility for crime detection in the hands of paid professionals.

Step 5: Aim to cover a range of factors, making judgements about the importance/significance of these developments. Make direct links to the question.

By the second half of the nineteenth century the police force had developed into an efficient method of combating crime. Forces had been established across England and Wales and by the twentieth century they had begun to develop specialist units to deal with particular issues of policing and crime detection. This had resulted in the setting up of the Flying Squad, CID, Special Branch and the Murder Squad. In the 1920s women police officers started to appear and today women have risen to the top ranks within the force, becoming Chief Constables. Police specialisation is still increasing. Forensic science has helped to solve many crimes by using scientific methods. DNA and finger printing has also helped police to solve crimes. By the end of the twentieth century Wales had four police forces – the Gwent, South Wales, North Wales and Dyfed-Powys constabularies which offered a more efficient and effective method of policing than the JPs and parish constables of earlier centuries.

Step 6: Write a conclusion which contains a reasoned judgement upon the question. Remember to check through your answer for correct spelling, punctuation and grammar.

The establishment of the Metropolitan Police force in 1829 was the start of a major change in the methods of combating crime. It replaced a system which had relied upon unpaid amateurs and replaced it with a force of paid, professional police officers. By the end of the century this method of policing had been established across the country and today there are 43 constabulary forces operating across England and Wales. The rapid growth in population resulting from the Industrial Revolution had forced the pace of change and resulted in major changes in the methods of combating crime. The use of a police force is now the main method used to maintain law and order.

Now try to answer the following question:

To what extent has the use of prison been the main method of punishing criminals over time?

Glossary

Changes in health and medicine in Britain, c.1340 to the present day

anaesthetics   something used to lessen pain

anticyclone   an area of high atmospheric pressure, in which the air sinks; often winds are light

apothecaries   people who prepare and sell medicines

astrology   study of the planets and the stars to decide what actions to take

barber-surgeons   medieval doctors who performed surgery; they often acted as barbers too!

Board of Guardians   the body responsible for the relief of the poor

Boer War   the (Second) Boer War (1899–1902) between Britain and Boers of South Africa over control of the territories (and their gold and diamond deposits) that would later become South Africa

Bondman   an unfree tenant farmer who worked the land without wages

Cistercian   order of monks founded at Citeau in France in 1098, they wore white robes

cut-purse   a pickpocket or thief. In the medieval period money was often carried in a purse (a small bag or pouch attached to a belt); the thief would cut the purse free and escape

emetic   a medicine designed to make the patient vomit

four humours   Ancient Greek belief that the body was made up of four body fluids, and that people became ill when these humours were out of balance

gangrene   decay of a part of a person's body because blood has stopped flowing there

Great Exhibition   the first of a series of world fairs exhibiting advances in industry. It was housed in the purpose built Crystal Palace, a huge temporary glass and steel structure

gout   form of arthritis when joints, such as feet, ankles or toes, become inflamed. Often thought to be caused by heavy drinking

heredity   inheriting a disease or illness from parents or grandparents

homeopathy   a system of alternative medicine, based on healing people with natural substances rather than chemical medicines

indulgence   if you bought an indulgence from the church, the church would lessen the punishment for your sins, allowing you to get to heaven more quickly when you died

infant mortality   the number of children who die, usually measured per thousand of the population – for example, infant mortality might be 100 per thousand

inoculation   early form of vaccination where the skin is scratched rather than injected

laissez-faire   a belief that some things were not the job of government, but should be 'left alone' or left to individuals to do for themselves

latrines   toilets

life expectancy   how long, on average, people might expect to live

ligature   a cord used to tie something very tightly, in this case in order to stop bleeding

nationalisation   take over something by government, so government runs the service, factory or industry

osteopathy   form of treating disease by manipulating bones and muscles

Ottoman Empire   Based on Turkey, with its capital of Constantinople, the Ottoman Empire controlled much of the Mediterranean area from around 1300 until 1922

pandemic   disease covering a huge area or the whole world

poultice   a soft, moist mass of material, often made from bran, flour, herbs, and so on, applied to the body to relieve soreness and inflammation and kept in place with a cloth

Renaissance   meaning rebirth or renewal, usually refers to the period from the fourteenth to seventeenth centuries when great advances were made in learning, science and art

Royal Society   set up in 1660 by Charles II, this is the national organisation for science and learning. It was designed to promote changes in scientific knowledge

secular   not to do with religion

septicaemia   blood poisoning by infection

sterile   free from bacteria or other living micro-organisms; totally clean

vaccination   injection of a mild form of a disease to stop you getting a more dangerous version of the disease

Welfare State   introduced after the Second World War, this provided a free health service, unemployment support, council housing and free secondary education

World Health Organization   set up by the United Nations in 1948, the WHO aims to improve public health across the whole world

Changes in crime and punishment, c.1500 to the present day

Agricultural Revolution   Changes in farming practices such as the rotation of crops, use of new technology and selective breeding of animals

Alms houses   A house for the poor, paid for by charity

Banishment   To send somebody away from a country and not allow them to return

Beadle   An officer of the law who dealt with small offences in the local area

Borstal   A type of prison set up especially for young offenders in the early twentieth century. Abolished in 1982

Bloody Code   The harsh laws gradually introduced in the late seventeenth and eighteenth centuries that made even minor crimes punishable by death

Capital punishment   The death penalty. Crimes carrying this punishment are known as capital crimes

Chain gang   A group of prisoners chained together to perform a physical task as a form of punishment

Civic responsibility   The responsibility of a person to serve their community

Contraband   Smuggled goods

Corporal punishment   A physical painful punishment such as whipping and flogging

Council in the Marches   The body that ruled Wales in the name of the monarch between the fifteenth and seventeenth centuries; it was based in Ludlow Castle

Criminal Investigation Department (CID)   A department in the police force that employs detectives to investigate crimes

Enlightenment   An intellectual movement which pushed forward the world of ideas in Europe during the eighteenth century

Heresy   Religious opinions or views that contradict the official religion of the country

Hue and cry   Raising the alarm (by means of loud shouts or cries) when a crime has been committed. Everyone within hearing distance was expected to join the hunt for the suspect

Hung, drawn and quartered   A punishment in which the criminal was drawn (dragged) behind a horse to a place of execution. The person was then hung from the gallows, the body was then beheaded and quartered

Industrial Revolution   A time of great change when people began to make goods in factories using machines

Jail fever   A form of typhus disease passed to humans through contact with infected fleas, lice or mites

Justices of the peace (JPs)   Local magistrates appointed to keep the peace, hear minor legal cases and ensure the Poor Laws were being maintained

Metropolitan Police force   The official name for the police force responsible for London. Established in 1829

Napoleonic Wars   A long period of warfare between Britain and France which lasted between 1793 and 1815

Parish constable   A law official who patrolled the streets to ensure law and order was maintained

Pillory   A Wooden or metal frame on a post used to secure people's head and hands

Poor relief   Action taken by the government, the church or private individuals to help the poor

Privy Council   A committee of ministers appointed by the monarch to advise them

Protestant Reformation   Religious upheaval in the sixteenth century following a spilt in the Roman Catholic church and the formation of a protest movement led by Martin Luther King

Puddlers   Men who stirred molten iron while it cooked so that impurities were brought to the surface and burnt off

Recant   To say in public that your past beliefs were wrong

Retribution   To receive punishment for a crime committed

Riot Act   A statement read as a warning to rioters, ordering them to disperse

Rotten borough   An election district which had few people living in it but still had an MP representing it in parliament

Smuggling   Bringing goods into the country illegally or not paying tax on legal goods entering

Stocks   Large hinged wooden boards used to secure people by the ankles

Thief-takers   People who made money from collecting the rewards offered for the return of stolen goods or the capture of criminals

Town watchman   A law official who patrolled the streets at night to keep the peace

Treason   Plotting against the monarch or government

Urbanisation   The growth of large towns and cities

Vagrancy   Wandering from place to place without a settled home or job

Index

Acknowledgements

The Publishers would like to thank the following for permission to reproduce copyright material.

Photo credits

p.6 © Trinity Mirror/Mirrorpix/Alamy Stock Photo; **p.7** *t* © Jochen Sands/DigitalVision/Thinkstock/Getty Images; *c* © Justin Kase zsixz/Alamy Stock Photo; *b* © Martin Siepmann/Stockbyte/Getty Images; **p.10** © Georgios Kollidas/iStock/Getty Images; **p.12** © Okea/iStock/Thinkstock; **p.16** © The British Library Board (Royal 20 C. VII, f.51); **p.20** The Black Death (gouache on paper), Nicolle, Pat (Patrick) (1907-95)/Private Collection/© Look and Learn/Bridgeman Images; **p.23** © gbimages/Alamy Stock Photo; **p.24** © Wellcome Images (available under Creative Commons Attribution only licence CC BY 4.0); **p.25** © INTERFOTO/Alamy Stock Photo; **p.26** © Wellcome Images (available under Creative Commons Attribution only licence CC BY 4.0); **p.27** *l* © Mary Evans Picture Library/Alamy Stock Photo; *r* © Maidstone Museum & Bentlif Art Gallery; **p.29** © Liquid Light/Alamy Stock Photo **p.30** © Jean Williamson/Alamy Stock Photo; **p.31** © The National Library of Medicine; **p.34** © Niday Picture Library/Alamy Stock Photo; **p.35** © Heritage Image Partnership Ltd/Alamy Stock Photo; **p.36** © classicpaintings/Alamy Stock Photo; **p.37** © Mary Evans Picture Library/Alamy Stock Photo; **p.38** © Wellcome Images (available under Creative Commons Attribution only licence CC BY 4.0); **p.39** © The Granger Collection/TopFoto; **p.41** © Wellcome Images (available under Creative Commons Attribution only licence CC BY 4.0); **p.44** *l* © Wellcome Images (available under Creative Commons Attribution only licence CC BY 4.0); *r* © Wellcome Images (available under Creative Commons Attribution only licence CC BY 4.0); **p.47** *t* © Robana/Rex/Shutterstock; *c* © Wellcome Images (available under Creative Commons Attribution only licence CC BY 4.0); *b* © Wellcome Images (available under Creative Commons Attribution only licence CC BY 4.0); **p.48** *r* © The Art Archive/Alamy Stock Photo; *l* © age fotostock/Alamy Stock Photo; **p.50** © R. Paul Evans; **p.52** *l* © Wellcome Images (available under Creative Commons Attribution only licence CC BY 4.0); *r* © Wellcome Images (available under Creative Commons Attribution only licence CC BY 4.0); **p.53** © Wellcome Images (available under Creative Commons Attribution only licence CC BY 4.0); **p.55** © World History Archive/Alamy Stock Photo; **p.56** © Science and Society/Superstock; **p.62** © Wellcome Images (available under Creative Commons Attribution only licence CC BY 4.0); **p.64** © Wellcome Images (available under Creative Commons Attribution only licence CC BY 4.0); **p.68** *t* © Universal History Archive/Getty Images; *b* © Old Visuals/Alamy Stock Photo; **p.69** © Westend61 GmbH/Alamy Stock Photo; **p.70** © Science Photo Library/Alamy Stock Photo; **p.77** © Heritage Image Partnership Ltd/Alamy Stock Photo; **p.79** © DI002916 HMS HAMADRYAD © National Museum of Wales; **p.81** *l* ©Wellcome Images (available under Creative Commons Attribution only licence CC BY 4.0); *r* © Wellcome Images (available under Creative Commons Attribution only licence CC BY 4.0); **p.82** © Wellcome Images (available under Creative Commons Attribution only licence CC BY 4.0); **p.83** *l* © Amoret Tanner/Alamy Stock Photo; *r* Supplied by Llyfrgell Genedlaethol Cymru/National Library of Wales; **p.84** © Mary Evans/The National Archives, London. England; **p.85** © Trades Union Congress Library Collections, London Metropolitan University; **p.87** © © Joseph McKeown/Getty Images; **p.86** © Pictorial Press Ltd/Alamy Stock Photo; **p.89** © Mirrorpix; **p.91** courtesy of John D Clare; **p.92** © North Wind Picture Archives/Alamy Stock Photo; **p.93** © London Metropolitan Archives; **p.94** © The Granger Collection/TopFoto; **p.96** © SSPL/Getty Images; **p.97** © The National Archives; **p.98** © Mary Evans Picture Library/Alamy Stock Photo; **p.99** © Pictorial Press Ltd/Alamy Stock Photo; **p.100** © Hulton Archive/Getty Images; **p.101** © Darren Grove - stock.adobe.com; **p.103** © RDImages/Epics/Getty Images; **p.105** © Public Health England; **p.109** © Cardiff Libraries; **p.113** © Cardiff Libraries; **p.116** © Realimage/Alamy Stock Photo; **p.120** *tl* © Bettmann/Contributor/Getty Images; *b* © Davies/Getty Images; *tr* © Media Minds/Alamy Stock Photo; *tl* © courtesy of John D Clare; *b* © RDImages/Epics/Getty Images; *tr* © The National Archives. **p.129** © Topfoto; **p.133** © World History Archive/Alamy; **p.140** © highwaystarz - stock.adobe.com; **p.141** © Eddie Mulholland/REX/Shutterstock; **p.145** © Pictorial Press Ltd/Alamy Stock Photo; **p.146** © Paul Fearn/Alamy Stock Photo; **p.148** *t* © Clive Sawyer; *b* © Paul Fearn/Alamy Stock Photo; **p.152** © Chronicle/Alamy Stock Photo; **p.154** © Granger Historical Picture Archive/Alamy Stock Photo; **p.155** © Granger Historical Picture Archive/Alamy Stock Photo; **p.156** © Lebrecht Music and Arts Photo Library/Alamy Stock Photo; **p.157** © World History Archive/Alamy Stock Photo; **p.158** © Hulton Archive/Rischgitz/Getty Images; **p.159** © Hulton Archive/Topical Press Agency/Getty Images; **p.161** *l* © Brian Jackson - stock.adobe.com; *r* © Shutterstock/Shaun Wilkinson; **p.164** © Daily Post Wales/Mirrorpix; **p.168** © British Library Board. All Rights Reserved/Bridgeman Images; **p.169** © Heritage Image Partnership Ltd/Alamy Stock Photo; **p.170** © Chronicle/Alamy Stock Photo; **p.174** © British Library, London, UK/Bridgeman Images; **p.181** © Crown copyright: Royal Commission on the Ancient and Historical Monuments of Wales; **p.182** © Chronicle/Alamy Stock Photo; **p.183** © World History Archive/Alamy Stock Photo; **p.185** © Peter Horree/Alamy Stock Photo; **p.186** © Chronicle/Alamy Stock Photo; **p.187** © Georgios Kollidas - stock.adobe.com; **p.188** © Mary Evans Picture Library; **p.189** © Gwasg Carreg Gwalch; **p.192** © Trinity Mirror/Mirrorpix/Alamy Stock Photo; **p.193** *t* © Gwasg Carreg Gwalch; *b* © Copyright Mick Lobb/https://creativecommons.org/licenses/by-sa/2.0/; **p.194** © INTERFOTO/Alamy Stock Photo; **p.197** *t* © Sung Kuk Kim/123RF.COM; *b* © macfromlondon/123RF.COM; **p.203** © Mary Evans Picture Library; **p.210** © Kurt Hutton/Picture Post/Getty Images; **p.212** 3 © Popperfoto/Getty Images, **p.214** © Roger Bamber/Alamy Stock Photo; **p.217** © Fotosearch/Getty Images; **p.218** l © Classic Image/Alamy Stock Photo; r © Chronicle/Alamy Stock Photo; **p.219** © Metropolitan Museum of Art/Harris Brisbane Dick Fund, 1932/https://creativecommons.org/publicdomain/zero/1.0/; **p.220** © Pictorial Press Ltd/Alamy Stock Photo; **p.223** © Chronicle/Alamy Stock Photo; **p.226** © Georgios Kollidas - stock.adobe.com; **p.228** *tl* © Mary Evans/Peter Higginbotham Collection; *tr, bl, br* © Mary Evans Picture Library; **p.229** *tl* © Mary Evans/The National Archives, London. England; *tr, bl* © Mary Evans Picture Library; **p.229** *br* © Library and Archives Canada, Quebec. Shot Drill